The Growth of Islamic Finance and Banking

This book covers the recent literature concerning Islamic banking and finance (IBF), focuses on the history of IBF since its inception and introduces the latest innovative concepts and practices in the field.

The authors cover important topics such as the role of ownership, *Shari'ah* compliance and governance structures in raising debt capital using IBF practices, including Fatwa issues and the use of benchmarking practices. The book also addresses topics like archival data, the influence of leverage on ownership structure and *sukuk* structures, as well as misconceptions, threats, challenges and opportunities in IBF. Finally, the book deals with prominent issues such as business score-carding, Takāful (Islamic Insurance), IBF implications for block-chain-based fintech and finance hub concepts in Islamic microfinance models.

This edited volume is an important contribution to the IBF literature as it provides a much-needed in-depth look into industry practices through the perspective of corporate finance and governance. With its interdisciplinary approach covering legal and financial issues along with a wide variety of notable contributors, this book will be a valuable reference guide to both teachers and students of Islamic banking and economics.

Hussain Mohi-ud-Din Qadri is an Associate Professor at the School of Economics and Finance, Minhaj University, Lahore, Pakistan.

M. Ishaq Bhatti is an Associate Professor and the Founding Director of the Islamic Banking and Finance Programme at Latrobe University, Australia.

Islamic Business and Finance Series

Series Editor: M. Ishaq Bhatti

There is an increasing need for western politicians, financiers, bankers, and indeed the western business community in general to have access to high quality and authoritative texts on Islamic financial and business practices. Drawing on expertise from across the Islamic world, this new series will provide carefully chosen and focused monographs and collections, each authored/edited by an expert in their respective field all over the world.

The series will be pitched at a level to appeal to middle and senior management in both the western and the Islamic business communities. For the manager with a western background the series will provide detailed and up-to-date briefings on important topics; for the academics, postgraduates, business communities, manager with western and an Islamic background the series will provide a guide to best practice in business in Islamic communities around the world, including Muslim minorities in the west and majorities in the rest of the world.

Islamic Social Finance
Entrepreneurship, Cooperation and the Sharing Economy
Edited by Valentino Cattelan

Rethinking Islamic Finance
Markets, Regulations and Islamic Law
Ayesha Bhatti and Saad Azmat

Social Justice and Islamic Economics
Theory, Issues and Practice
Edited by Toseef Azid and Lutfi Sunar

The Growth of Islamic Finance and Banking
Innovation, Governance and Risk Mitigation
Edited by Hussain Mohi-ud-Din Qadri and M. Ishaq Bhatti

For more information about this series, please visit www.routledge.com/Islamic-Business-and-Finance-Series/book-series/ISLAMICFINANCE

The Growth of Islamic Finance and Banking

Innovation, Governance and Risk Mitigation

Edited by
Hussain Mohi-ud-Din Qadri and M. Ishaq Bhatti

Routledge
Taylor & Francis Group
LONDON AND NEW YORK

First published 2020
by Routledge
2 Park Square, Milton Park, Abingdon, Oxon OX14 4RN

and by Routledge
52 Vanderbilt Avenue, New York, NY 10017

Routledge is an imprint of the Taylor & Francis Group, an informa business

British Library Cataloguing-in-Publication Data
A catalogue record for this book is available from the British Library

Library of Congress Cataloging-in-Publication Data
A catalog record has been requested for this book

ISBN: 978-0-367-20588-1 (hbk)
ISBN: 978-0-429-26243-2 (ebk)

Typeset in Times New Roman
by codeMantra

MIX
Paper from responsible sources
FSC www.fsc.org FSC® C013056

Printed and bound in Great Britain by
TJ International Ltd, Padstow, Cornwall

Contents

List of figures

List of tables

List of contributors

Dr Najam Abbas
East West Institute, Brussels, Belgium
nabbas@eastwest.ngo

Dr Tariq Ali
CS. Department (CUI) Sahiwal, Pakistan
tariqali@ciitsahiwal.edu.pk

Professor Dr Mohamed Ariff
Sunway Business School, Sunway University Selangor, Malaysia
ariff13@gmail.com

Professor Dr Toseef Azid
Department of Finance and Economics, College of Business and Economics, Qassim University Qassim, Saudi Arabia
toseefazid@hotmail.com

Associate Professor M. Ishaq Bhatti
La Trobe University, Melbourne, Australia
i.bhatti@latrobe.edu.au

Associate Professor Darren Henry
La Trobe University, Melbourne, Australia
d.henrry@latrobe.edu.au

Dr Maria Bhatti
Western Sydney University, Penrith, Australia
M.Bhatti@westernsydney.edu.au

Associate Professor Dr Muhammad Omer Chaudhry
Department of Economics, Bahauddin Zakariya University, Multan, Pakistan
chaudhryomer@hotmail.com

Professor Dr Masudul Alam Choudhury
Faculty of Economics, Trisakti University, Jakarta, Indonesia
masudc60@yahoo.ca

Umar Draz
CS. Department (CUI) Sahiwal, Pakistan
Sheikhumar520@gmail.com

Ummara Fatima
School of Commerce & Accounting, Minhaj University, Lahore, Pakistan
ummarafatima@ymail.com

Professor Dr Abdul Ghafar Ismail
School of Commerce and Accountancy of Malaysia, Selangor, Malaysia
agibab62@gmail.com

Dr Mohd Adib Ismail
School of Economics, National University of Malaysia, Selangor, Malaysia
mohadis@ukm.edu.my

Dr Shair Ali Khan
International Islamic University Islamabad, Pakistan
shair.ali@iiu.edu.pk

Mohsin Khawaja
La Trobe Business School, Latrobe University, Bundoora, Australia
m.khawaja@latrobe.edu.au

Professor Dr Musferah Mehfooz
Humanities, COMSATS, Lahore, Pakistan
musferahmehfooz@ciitlahore.edu.pk

Dr Hazik Mohamed
Stellar Consulting Group, Singapore
stellar.xic@gmail.com

Dr Hussain Mohi-ud-Din Qadri
School of Economics and Finance, Minhaj University, Lahore, Pakistan
hmqadri@hotmail.com

Dr Naseem Al Rahahleh
King Abdulaziz University, Jeddah, Saudi Arabia
nalrahahleh@kau.edu.sa

Associate Professor Dr Osamah Al Rawashdeh
College of Business and Economics, Qassim University, Saudi Arabia
osamahr@yahoo.com

Awais ur Rehman
University of Brunei Darussalm, Bandar Seri Begawan, Brunei
ever.awais@gmail.com

Muhammad Shujat Saleem
Institute of Business Management, Karachi, Pakistan
saleemmshujaat@gmail.com

Malik Shahzad Shabbir
University of Brunei Darussalm, Bandar Seri Begawan, Brunei
mshahzad786.pk11@gmail.com

Ahmad Shaf
CS. Department (CUI) Sahiwal, Pakistan
Ahmadshaf22@gmail.com

Dr Muhammad Hakimi Mohd. Shafiai
School of Economics, National University of Malaysia, Selangor, Malaysia
hakimi@ukm.edu.my

Dr Shahida Shahimi
School of Economics, National University of Malaysia, Selangor, Malaysia
shahida@ukm.edu.my

Dr Masoumeh Shahsavari
Iran Fara Bourse, Iran
ifb.shahsavari@gmail.com

Dr Salman Ahmed Shaikh
School of Economics, National University of Malaysia, Selangor, Malaysia
salman@siswa.ukm.edu.my

Professor Nasim Shah Shirazi
College of Islamic Studies - Hamad Bin Khalifa University, Doha, Qatar
nshirazi@hbku.edu.qa

Sundas Sohail
School of Commerce & Accounting, Minhaj University, Lahore, Pakistan
sundasnaeem15@gmail.com

Professor Dr Muhammad Tahir-ul-Qadri
Chairman, MQI and the Board of Governor, Minhaj University Lahore, Pakistan
Farooqrana@gmail.com

Raiha Tallat
CS. Department (CUI) Sahiwal, Pakistan
raiha.tallat@live.com

Dr Imam Uddin
Institute of Business Management, Karachi, Pakistan
imamuddin@iobm.edu.pk

Sana Yasin
CS. Department (CUI) Sahiwal, Pakistan
sanayaseen42@gmail.com

Dr Alireza Zarei
Sunway Business School, Sunway University Selangor, Malaysia
alirezaz@sunway.edu.my

Preface

Rodney Wilson

EMERITUS PROFESSOR, DURHAM UNIVERSITY, UNITED KINGDOM

This edited volume represents a valuable contribution to the growing literature on Islamic banking and finance. It covers a wide range of topics which have been debated and written about already, but the studies included here take the discussions further and provide fresh insights. The work is interdisciplinary, as it covers legal, financial and developmental issues. Notable contributions include the debates over the standardisation of Islamic financial contracts and the evolution of *fatawa* rulings by Islamic scholars. There is a fascinating contribution which critiques the different approaches to the translation of the verses dealing with economic matters in the Quran. Another chapter provides a history of opinions concerning *riba* in an inter-faith context.

Although many of the studies are focused on Islamic banking there is also coverage of *sukuk* securities, *takaful* Islamic insurance and *zakat*. One of the chapters on *sukuk* examines the significance of ownership and governance structure when raising funds. The second chapter on *sukuk* uses Iranian data to examine the relationship between stock and *sukuk* prices. A third chapter on *sukuk* pricing uses Malaysian data, as Kuala Lumpur has become the leading international centre for *sukuk* issuance and trading. The chapter on *takaful* is particularly innovative as the author examines the benefits of using a block-chain approach, which has been applied to conventional financial products, but not hitherto to Islamic insurance.

In another highly innovative chapter, the researcher considers the merits of applying Information Technology to *zakat* collection and administration. This could facilitate the devolution of collection and local accountability, increasing the confidence of *zakat* payers through increased transparency. The development of a common platform for financial reporting purposes could enable meaningful comparisons to be made between regions, highlighting success and best practices. Similar issues arise in the case of Islamic philanthropy, which is the subject of a separate chapter on the relationships between the public, private and voluntary sectors. The authors support the case for tax relief for charitable giving, although unfortunately in many Muslim countries tax collection remains inefficient.

As the book contains the papers presented at an Islamic banking and finance conference in Lahore, it is appropriate that the experience of Pakistan is covered in depth, with lessons for other countries. Pakistan's large population and favourable demographic trends make it one of the leading markets in the world for Islamic banking and finance. The two chapters on the country's experience are complementary, with one focusing on social finance and the other on *Shari'ah* compliance in financing in Pakistan.

Overall the work expands the boundaries of research in Islamic banking and finance. The conference organisers and editors are to be congratulated in bringing such an excellent group of researchers together, many of whom are young scholars at the start of promising academic careers.

Acknowledgements

We are grateful to all the referees who helped with the reviewing process in both conference papers and chapters of the book. Our special thanks are due to Rodney Wilson, Nasim Shirazi, Maria Bhatti and Toseef Azid, who supported us to finalise this book in a timely manner. We are also thankful to all the authors for their great contribution in the cross-reviewing process of all chapters. We appreciate the publisher team, especially Kristina Abbotts and Christiana Mandizha, for all their helpful assistance. We acknowledge the partial financial support from Minhaj University and La Trobe Business School. Our thanks are due to Umair Abbas, Khurram Shahzad (Minhaj University) and Quoc Cuong Phan (La Trobe Business School) in their assistantship in this project. However, we take all responsibilities of any potential errors.

Thanks and kind regards,

Dr Hussain Mohi-ud-Din Qadri[1] and Dr M. Ishaq Bhatti[2]
[1]Minhaj University, Lahore, Pakistan
Email: hmqadri@minhaj.org
[2]La Trobe Business School, Melbourne, Australia.
E-mail: i.bhatti@latrobe.edu.au
December, 2019.

The growth of the Islamic finance and banking industry

An introductory note

Hussain Mohi-ud-Din Qadri and M. Ishaq Bhatti

This edited volume comprises of the best papers chosen from those presented at the First World Islamic Economics and Finance Conference (WIEFC 2018), held on 3 and 4 January, 2018. The conference was organized by the Minhaj University Lahore (MUL) in collaboration with the Islamic Development Bank's Jeddah-based Research Institute (IRTI) and La Trobe University, Melbourne, Australia. The theme of the conference was developing Muslim economies through Islamic finance. This edited volume contains 19 chapters based on selected articles, each reviewed by two referees and the editorial committee. The volume begins with a preface by Rodney Wilson, an Emeritus Professor at Durham University, and an introductory note by the editors, H. M. Qadri and M. I. Bhatti, summarizing the contents. The book covers the following important topics;

- Standardization of Islamic banking and finance (IBF) products under inclusion (*Taqlid al-Madh'hab)*
- Islamic bonds (*sukuk*)
- Islamic insurance (*takāful)*
- An information technology-based *zakat* distribution model
- *Fatawa* on the IBF industry
- The Islamic Interbank Offer Rate (IBOR)
- The pricing volatility of Islamic stocks and *sukuk*
- Provision on interest *(riba)*
- Misconceptions concerning IBF
- Islamic commercial and social finance
- Tale of two similar credit-rated bonds (*sukuk)*
- Islamic finance disputes and arbitration

The book begins with **Chapter 1** by Shaykh-ul-Islam Professor Dr Muhammad Tahir-ul-Qadri, Chairman of MQI, BOG and MUL. He argues the case for the standardization of the IBF products across various schools of Islamic thought. Tahir-ul-Qadri proposes the adoption of a uniform model of IBF products using *Taqlid al-Madh'hab* – an inclusive research methodology which is acceptable to the adherents of the major schools of Islamic economic thought.

In **Chapter 2** M. Ishaq Bhatti, Naseem Al Rahahleh and Hussain Mohi-ud-Din Qadri discuss recent developments in Islamic finance and the financial products currently offered. The authors briefly review the historical development of IBF products from the early days of Islam to the 21st century. They address the issue of risk management in the IBF industry. The ability of IBF institutions to safeguard the global finance industry during periods of financial crises is also explored, particularly how the performance of IBF institutions is anti-cyclical, providing a hedge for international finance.

Chapter 3 deals with the issuance of Islamic bonds (*sukuk*), focusing on the role of ownership and governance structure in raising capital. A *sukuk* case study undertaken by Mohsin Khawaja and M. Ishaq Bhatti addresses the issue of whether the ownership and the governance structure of firms influence the decision to raise funds. They also address the question of how to select financial instruments to ensure *Shari'ah* compliance.

In **Chapter 4**, Hafiz Mohamed of the Stellar Consulting Group of Singapore addresses the topic of Islamic insurance – *takāful*, using an innovative block-chain approach. The *takāful* Islamic insurance industry is evolving processes to safeguard the assets of its clients from losses and reduce uncertainty. It may be described as a social device to reduce or even eliminate the risks of loss to life and property. In this chapter, the author provides a strategic discourse on how the adoption of a block-chain methodology can provide additional value to the insurance and *takāful* industries. Hafiz Mohamed demonstrates his detailed understanding of the industry by identifying the issues which need urgent attention, in order to achieve the projected cost savings through careful risk management.

In **Chapter 5** the merits of the application of information technology to *zakat* collection are discussed. The five co-authors, Umar Draz, Tariq Ali, Sana Yasin, Ahmad Shaf and Raiha Tallat, propose the establishment of an information technology-based finance hub at a local Union Consul (UC) level rather than the collection of *zakat* being centralized at national level, as is currently the policy in Pakistan and several other countries. The authors believe a UC level hub collection could improve the current *zakat* collection and distribution system, which would result in greater confidence among *zakat* donors by ensuring local accountability.

In **Chapter 6**, Professor Masudul Alam Choudhury proposes a method for standardizing Islamic economic, financial and banking practices through the adoption of consensual, comprehensive *fatawa.* The author critically examines current practices of ensuring *Shari'ah* compliance, in particular the increasing diversity of *fatawa* concerning matters of *muamalat*, finance, banking and the real economy. To overcome the inevitable confusion Masudul Alam Choudhury proposes a unified system for the issuance of *fatawa.*

Chapter 7 contains an examination of the fallacy of using conventional benchmarks in IBF. Imam Uddin and M. Shujat Saleem use archival data to demonstrate why it is inappropriate to use conventional indices, especially as *Shari'ah* compliant indices have been developed in recent years, which are already widely used. Researchers and professional financial analysts who use *Shari'ah* compliant indices have found them to be useful benchmarks when measuring the performance of Islamic securities. The two authors of the chapter advocate the use of the IBOR instead of conventional benchmarks, as this minimizes misconceptions and misunderstandings among end users.

Chapter 8 is an empirical study authored by Ummara Fatima of MUL. The focus of the study is on the influence of leverage on the ownership structure-performance relationship. Through the use of panel data, it provides interesting insights into the ownership structure-performance relationship of Islamic and conventional banks on parallel lines. The findings provide a better understanding of the management challenges facing both Islamic and conventional banks. Ummara Fatima explores how both Islamic and conventional banks can improve their systems of ownership structure to improve their financial performance.

In **Chapter 9** Masoumeh Shahsavari from Iran's Fara Bourse considers the dynamic correlation and volatility linkages between stocks and *sukuk*. He explores the issue of how volatility influences investment behavior and the statistical co-variance between returns on *sukuk* and Iran's Islamic stock indexes. The author explains the main reasons for the importance of institutional investors and asset managers. Especially crucial are their timing and expertise in selecting securities in order to maintain a diversified *sukuk* portfolio, a challenge which demands specialist skills.

In **Chapter 10** the acceptability or rejection of *riba* in various religious faiths is examined. A key disputed issue is whether *riba*, an addition to a principal sum, equates with interest or usury or both. Excessive interest payments on debt are often argued as being exploitative, with excessive power in the hands of the lending institutions, which may offer unfair contracts given their monopolistic or oligopolistic positions in the absence of meaningful competition. The critique in this chapter adopts a comparative analysis starting from ancient scriptures regarding *riba* and examining how attitudes have evolved over the centuries until the present day. In some respects the treatment is evidence based, with the examination of *riba* based on its social impact as a matter of historical fact.

In **Chapter 11** Malik Shahzad Shabbir and Awais ur Rehman of the University of Brunei Darussalam examine the misconceptions surrounding IBF. The authors focus on the threats, challenges and opportunities which confront Islamic banks and the implications for portfolio management by investors. The misconceptions about Islamic banking by depositors, clients who have obtained finance and potential, but skeptical, customers are addressed.

Pakistan is one of the most important markets for IBF, and the conference upon which this book is based was held in Lahore. Hence, the volume would not have been complete without a country study of IBF in Pakistan.

In **Chapter 12** Salman Ahmed Shaikh of Greenwich University undertakes a review of Islamic commercial and social finance in Pakistan. There is an objective evaluation of the growth of the IBF industry in Pakistan focusing on its achievements and ongoing challenges. The chapter covers the financial performance of *Shari'ah* compliant equities and *sukuk*. In addition, the author also provides a brief account of the Islamic asset management sector and the footprint of the Islamic microfinance sector in Pakistan.

In **Chapter 13** Shair Ali Khan of the International Islamic University of Islamabad provides a translation of the verses in the Quran dealing with economic issues. The author draws on earlier translations, notably that by Shaykh-al-Islam Professor Dr Tahir-ul-Qadri. The main aim of the chapter is to elaborate on the translational strategies used by Tahir-ul-Qadri in comparison with the translations of three other renowned translators of the Quran: Mohammad Asad, Pickthal and Abdullah Yousaf Ali. Shair Ali Khan also analyses the structural level of both the source language and target language. He also examines the level equivalence in terms of terminologies, specifically those of an economic nature.

In **Chapter 14**, Najam Abbas of the East West Research Centre in London highlights the contribution of IBF to socio-economic development, a largely neglected topic in the field. The focus is on the teaching of Ali ibn Talib on socio-economic development, notably his advocacy of collective responsibility toward the destitute in a multi-ethical society, and how the destitute can be employed in modern economies.

The findings from an empirical study of *sukuk* pricing by M. Ariff, A. Zarei and M. I. Bhatti are presented in **Chapter 15**. The investigation is of two similar credit-rated *sukuk* and conventional bonds with different yields. The theory of *sukuk* and conventional bond pricing is the same for both types of security as yields are determined by market expectations and ratings by independent agencies, the latter reflecting risk perceptions. The empirical data is drawn from Malaysia where both the government and corporations raise funds by issuing *sukuk*. The *sukuk* market in Malaysia is the most developed in the world in terms of both issuance and trading. Nevertheless, the lessons from this study have relevance for other countries, even though their markets are less active.

In **Chapter 16** Maria Bhatti addresses the issue of resolving IBF disputes through arbitration with special references to the Middle East. This region has experienced rapid growth in IBF while becoming a significant player in international commercial and financial markets. A crucial issue is whether disputes involving Islamic financial institutions can be dealt with by national secular courts or arbitration bodies. As Islamic financial contracts are subject to *Shari'ah* law, it can be argued that disputes would be best dealt with by *Shari'ah* courts, where scholars specialized in *fiqh* can adjudicate. Maria Bhatti finds that Islamic traditions influence arbitration in the Middle East, and therefore Islamic jurisprudence plays a crucial role when trying to understand and analyze the function of international commercial arbitration in resolving IBF disputes. Nevertheless, she argues that it is vital for countries in the Islamic Middle East to consistently recognize and enforce arbitral awards under the New York Convention, and ensure *Shari'ah* laws are in harmony to avoid legal conflict and uncertainty.

In **Chapter 17** Toseef Azid, Osamah Al Rawashdeh and Muhammad Omer examine the formation of tangible and intangible capital through venture philanthropy from an Islamic finance perspective. The authors argue that philanthropy can be significant in strengthening social solidarity and community bonds. There is a two-way causality of happiness and satisfaction between givers and receivers. Moreover, there is a gap in the provision of goods and services which cannot be filled by either the public or private sectors. This gap can instead be filled through philanthropy involving the voluntary sector. In the western society, this sector is well organized, as governments provide tax deductions which encourage charitable donations, whereas in Islamic societies the voluntary sector is often unorganized. The chapter concludes by suggesting that Islamic financial intuitions can play a significant role in strengthening the relationship in between the market and philanthropy with a resultant positive impact on social well-being. An active voluntary sector comprising of Islamic charities can facilitate economic inclusion and help ensure the poor become stakeholders in wider society.

Hussain Qadri, the author of **Chapter 18**, discusses the development of the IBF industry in Pakistan from an ideological, practical and legal perspective. He reviews the workings of various socio-economic systems, notably those based on capitalism and socialism, and then presents an alternative Islamic economic system based on *Shari'ah* compliant finance. Hussain Qadri focuses on Pakistan as a case study that demonstrates the shortcomings of capitalism and socialism, both of which are incompatible with religious values as is apparent from discourses by academics, students, religious scholars and government agencies. In contrast, the adoption of *Shari'ah* compliant finance as a way forward for economic development appears to have widespread support.

In the last chapter, **Chapter 19**, Shirazi analyses poverty in the context of Pakistan. Although the government introduced multiple measures to tackle this challenge in the last six decades, there was no sign of this problem being significantly slowed down. This article overviews the incidence of poverty, social safety nets including Islamic social finance programs of the country and discusses why these programs did not bring results as expected. From his analysis, Shirazi also highlights some recommendations to efficiently mitigate poverty in Pakistan.

Concluding remarks are provided by the editors in the **Conclusion**, which evaluates the contribution of this volume to wider literature on Islamic economics and finance.

1 Standardization in the Islamic banking & financial system

The methodology of inclusion (*Taqlid al-Madh'hab*)

Shaykh-ul-Islam Muhammad Tahir-ul-Qadri

1.1 Introduction

Islamic banking and finance (IBF) industry is making enormous contribution in terms of its products development, delivery and services around the globe. It is estimated that *Shari'ah* compliant assets are reached to more than US$2.431 trillion with a double digital over the world. Its growth is much above global average when it comes to Islamic countries; for example Pakistan is considered to be one of the fastest growing IBF industries in the world followed by Saudi Arabia, Iran and Malaysia. Main objective of this chapter is to contribute towards standardization of the IBF; hence, building bridges among various schools of thoughts to suggest a uniform model based on the *Taqlid al-Madh'hab* philosophy of Islamic *Shari'ah.* This new research methodology is to avoid exclusion of various schools of thoughts within Muslim majority or Muslim minority's countries. It presents historical context of the problem, Qur'anic Injunctions on the Principle of Facilitation (*al-Tashil*) and Flexibility (*al-Tawassu'*). This chapter also explains about the principle of distinction and option of choice between different juristic verdicts, including al-Hanafi, al-Maliki, al-Shafi'i and al-Hanbali's. This chapter also highlights on three main jurist's intra-school position based on the guiding principles for the methodology of inclusion and flexibility:

- i *Ashab al-Takhrij* (Jurists: Who are competent to conduct inference)
- ii *Ashab al-Tarjih* (Jurists: Who are competent to conduct preference)
- iii *Ashab al-Tamyiz* (Jurists: Who are competent to conduct distinction)

This chapter also reviews some of the work of the earlier jurists and their laws of making Ijtihad based on some juristic principles, agreed upon and practiced by all great scholars of the earlier day's pre-formation of various schools of law. One of these principles relates to interactions. According to this principle, wherever flexibility and facilitation is necessarily required, anyone of the four schools or anyone of the *Shari'ah* evidences will be adopted on the basis of compatibility between the spirit of Islamic teachings and the need and demands of the time.

The rest of the chapter is organized as follows. In the subsequent sections research problem is presented followed by historical context of the problem and its suggested solution in light of the two main sources of *Shari'ah*. In Section 5, research methodology of juristic inclusion is discussed, while Section 6 concentrates on the principle of distinction and option of choice between different juristic verdicts. The issue of juristic strategy for resolving contemporary issues through the principle of inclusion and expansion is presented in Section 7. Section 8 contains guiding principles for the methodology of inclusion, fairness and flexibility, whereas Section 9 presents categories of conformist jurists and their ways of framing the opinions on the application of intra-school position based on four main school of thoughts. The final section contains some concluding remarks.

1.2 Research problem

One of the major challenges the IBF industry is facing is the lack of harmonized rules and regulations, and the non-uniformity in Islamic banking products and services being offered in various parts of the world. For example, different standards are applied for financial reporting, accounting, disclosure and transparency,[1] different countries follow different standards, i.e., the Gulf Cooperation Council (GCC) and Malaysia.[2] Moreover, the lack of standardization of Islamic principles[3] in a Muslim majority country is different from Muslim minority countries. In literature, a number of studies are conducted to discuss the advantages of unified standardization of IBF product, e.g. reducing the time and cost, increasing the efficiency and decreasing the confusion among the stakeholders.[4]

Some researchers have pointed out this issue without due regard being given to the solution. Some indicated the validity or invalidity of certain products offered by the Islamic banks across the world which is due to divergence of opinion among Muslim jurists on the basis of the schools of *fiqh* (Hanafi, Maliki, Shafi'i and Hanbali) they follow. Regional differences in interpretation and derivation of rulings, in accordance with the popular school of law of that region, stand as the main reason for not having a standardized, harmonized, uniform and universal Islamic banking system across the world. For example, as mentioned by Smolo and Habibovic (2012), "The practice of BBA in Malaysia is allowed by the Shafi'i school. On the other hand, this practice in not allowed in the Middle East because of bay' al-'inah structure embedded in BBA" (p. 18).

The resultant multiple interpretations by various schools of law and different jurists belonging to different *madhahib al-fiqh* regarding Islamic financial products result in minor and major disparities and became hurdle in launching the different products.[5] In view of this fact, it is logical that, without a universally unified and uniform *Shari'ah* Code, the acceptability of products introduced in Islamic financial industry will remain fragmented.[6]

Prompt attention and action by Muslim scholars and Islamic finance experts is essential. A failure would damage the growth of the IBF industry in the years ahead.

If global harmony and universal standardization of Islamic banking products and services cannot be achieved within the Muslim world, how can the Islamic economic and banking system be proposed as a viable alternative to the conventional economic and banking system to the world at large?

Considering the necessity and importance of the issue of standardization of products, we have made this particular point the subject of our research.

1.3 Historical context of the problem

Countries differ in their approach to *Shari'ah* governance. For instance, Bahrain has both a *Shari'ah* governance committee at the institutional level and the National *Shari'ah* Advisory Board at the national level, i.e., in the Central Bank of Bahrain. However, its role is limited to advise the central bank on *Shari'ah* matters. Malaysia and Indonesia have a higher *Shari'ah* authority at the national level to standardize fatwa and *Shari'ah* practices in IFIs (Islamic financial institutions). In the case of other GCC countries such as Kuwait, UAE and Qatar, they have their own *Shari'ah* committees at the institutional level and another independent body, i.e., the Ministry of *Awqaf* and Religious Affairs or the Ministry of Justice and Islamic Affairs, which are given the authority to oversee *Shari'ah* governance practices. The higher *Shari'ah* authorities in UAE, Qatar and Kuwait only act when there are conflicts of opinion among *Shari'ah* scholars regarding *Shari'ah* rulings. In the case of Saudi Arabia, it prefers leaving the *Shari'ah* governance practices at the voluntary choice of IFIs and at the influence of the market. They further state that the higher *Shari'ah* authority is not effective in controlling the *Shari'ah* compliance for IFIs resulting in negative impacts on the stability of the Islamic finance industry.[7]

The different interpretations of *Shari'ah* rules amongst *Shari'ah* scholars create confusion in the general public as well as in banking communities. This difference of opinion applies not only to some of the products, but also to some of the operations of the Islamic banks.

For example, there is no uniformity in opinion pertaining to the principle of the trust financing contract (*al-mudaraba*) in business transactions. The Maliki and Shafi'i schools of jurisprudence are of the view that *al-mudaraba* should be confined to trade and trade-related activities alone, and should not include the activities of manufacturing. According to them, the contract for manufacturing should be excluded from *al-mudaraba*, which is a profit-loss sharing contract but formed under a specific long-term contract whereby a party undertakes to manufacture, i.e., *al-istisna'*. However, the Hanafi school of law does not object to the application of *al-mudaraba* for manufacturing activities, while the Hanbali school of law allows two separate agreements using *al-mudaraba* and *al-istisna'* principles as long as the two agreements do not impose conditions upon each other.[8]

Such non-uniformity of opinion amongst the Islamic scholars from different schools of law generates confusion amongst the bankers, the customers as well as the public. Customers will not really understand what are the 'dos and don'ts' of the Islamic banking industry, and will make their own personal interpretations. This situation is unhealthy for banker-customer relations, as both parties may have different interpretations.[9]

1.4 Suggested solution

The reason behind this issue lies in strict conformity with one school of law (*Taqlid al-Madh'hab*) in a particular region and with some other school of law in another region. A third school of law may be strictly followed by people of a third locality, while a fourth may be adhered to in yet another community. This principle of *Taqlid al-Madh'hab*—strict conformity with one school of law—seems to be the sole reason behind the whole confusion in the matter of standardization. The solution to this problem lies in adopting a "neo-juristic approach of inclusive accommodation and flexibility." This approach is based on the *Qur'anic* principle of facilitation and juristic principle of expansion. This approach will be known as conformity with all schools of law (*Taqlid al-Madh'hab*).

1.4.1 Qur'anic injunctions on the principle of facilitation (al-Tashil) and flexibility (al-Tawassu')

Islam as a religion was revealed to the Prophet (blessings and peace be upon him) in order to facilitate human kind and remove burdens, difficulties and hardships from their lives.

i The *Qur'an* states:
Allah desires ease for you and does not desire hardship for you.[10]

ii The entire religion of Islam is structured upon the provision of ease and the removal of difficulty. Almighty Allah says:
He has chosen you, and has not laid upon you any hardship or constriction in the matter of Din.[11]

iii He also said:
Allah does not want to make things hard for you.[12]
Since Allah knows the weakness of human beings, He has lightened for them the legal responsibilities and lessened from them the obligations that they would not be able to fulfil.

iv Allah said:
Allah intends to lighten your burden. And man has been created weak (and infirm).[13]

v He also said:
Allah has, at present, lightened the burden (of His commandment) on you. He knows that there is (some degree of) weakness in you.[14]

1.4.2 Evidence from the Hadith

i Jabir (may Allah be well pleased with him) reported that Holy Prophet (blessings and peace be upon him) said:

"Indeed, Allah did not send me to be harsh or cause harm; He sent me to teach and make things easy."[15]

ii 'A'isha (may Allah be well pleased with her) said:

"Never was Allah's Messenger (blessings and peace be upon him) presented with two options except that he would choose the easier of the two, so long as it was not a sin."[16]

Agreed upon.

iii According to Anas b. Malik (may Allah be well pleased with him), the Prophet (blessings and peace be upon him) said:

"Make things easy and do not make things difficult. Give glad tidings and do not make people feel averse."[17]

Agreed upon.

iv Abu Hurayra (may Allah be well pleased with him) reports that Allah's Messenger (blessings and peace be upon him) said:

"You were sent to make things easy and not to make things difficult."[18]

Agreed upon.

v Imam Ahmad b. Hanbal narrated in *al-Musnad* that the Holy Prophet (blessings and peace be upon him) said:

"Verily, the best of your *Din* is the easier part. Verily, the best of your *Din* is the easier part. Verily, the best of your *Din* is the easier part."[19]

That's why 'Allama Ibn Qudama—a great jurist of *al-Fiqh al-Hanbali*—writes in his book "*Rawda al-Nazir fi Usul al-Fiqh*": "If a jurist is approached for an edict and his edict remains devoid of openness and flexibility because of his rigidity the edict-seeker should be guided towards some other jurist who is open-minded and flexible."[20]

Furthermore, 'Allama Ibn Qudama reports that al-Husayn b. Bashshar inquired from Imam Ahmad b. Hanbal about an issue. He said, "If he does it, he will become a perjurer." al-Husayn b. Bashshar said, "If someone issues me the edict that he will not be a perjurer then (what will be the case)? Imam Ahmad replied, "Do you know of the Medinans' session (at Rasafa)?" He asked, "If they issue the edict, would that be permissible?" Imam Ahmad replied in affirmative.[21]

Here, Imam Ahmad himself is guiding the inquirer to go to *Rasafa* and get the answer from the Medinan scholars because their opinion was based on openness, inclusion, flexibility and facilitation. These juristic principles are always closer to the basic spirit of Islamic teachings.

1.5 Research methodology of juristic inclusion

Someone may question where the idea of *Taqlid al-Madh'hab*—benefitting from all schools of law instead of one particular school—has sprung from?

1 Addressing this question, I would quote Imam Hasan b. 'Ammar al-Shurunbulali al-Hanafi, the author of *Nur al-Idah* and *Maraqi al-Falah*. He has promulgated this concept of *Taqlid al-Madh'hab* in his treatise—*al-'Iqd al-Farid li-Bayan al-Rajih mina'l-Khilaf fi Jawaz al-Taqlid*. He has quoted Imam Abu al-Mahasin al-Ruyani al-Shafi'i (415–502 ah), one of the great ancient jurists, who says:

Conforming to different schools of law or departing from one and shifting towards others is permissible on three conditions.

Firstly, a person should not accumulate or assimilate them in a way that contravenes the consensus of Umma (*ijma'*).

Secondly, He should believe that Prophetic traditions on the subject in question have reached the one he wants to conform with, which were possibly not available to the *madh'hab* he is conforming with currently.

"Thirdly, he should not follow the objective of the licenses and freedoms provided by different schools of law in order to avoid the commandments of *Shari'ah* (i.e. adopting and following only all lenient instructions and exemptions offered by every school and abandoning the strict ones)."[22]

2 'Allama al-Shinqiti al-Maliki (1152–1233 ah) supports the same viewpoint in his book *Nashr al-Bunud 'ala Maraqi al-Sa'ud*.[23]

3 A similar viewpoint has been promoted by Imam Abu al-'Abbas Ahmad b. Idris al-Qarafi al-Maliki (d. 684 ah) in his book *Sharh Tanqih al-Fusul ila Ikhtisar al-Mahsul fi'l-Usul*. He states quoting Imam Yahya al-Zanati:

Conformity with schools of law and shifting from one school to the other in peripheral matters is permissible under three conditions:

First, one should not accumulate or assimilate two schools in a way that contravenes the consensus of the Umma (*ijma'*).

Second, he should believe that hadiths on the subject in question have reached the one he wants to conform with.

"Third, he must not be looking for the licenses provided by different schools of law. Indeed, all the schools of law are paths that lead to piety and Paradise. The one who treads anyone of these paths, will certainly reach the ultimate goal.

"Admonition: (Apart from al-Zanati) other Jurists have said, "Conformity with and turning towards schools of law is permissible in every matter wherein the Lawgiver's decree is not infringed. Remember that the Lawgiver's decree is breached in four ways: violation of the consensus of the Umma (*ijma'*), basic principles of *Shari'ah*, Divine text or manifest analogy."[24]

4 Imam al-Qarafi al-Maliki further describes a rule with these words:

"There is consensus on it that a person who embraces Islam has the choice to adopt conformity with any of the Imams without any restriction. Similarly, there was a common consensus between the Companions (may Allah be well pleased with them) about a person who sought an edict from Abu Bakr al-Siddiq and ʻUmar b. al-Khattab (may Allah be well pleased with both of them), or conformed to them, had the right to seek an edict from Abu Hurayra, Muʻadh b. Jabal (may Allah be well pleased with both of them) and others and could also abide by their verdict without any constraint."[25]

5 Imam al-Qarafi al-Maliki further quotes Imam ʻIzz al-Din b. ʻAbd al-Salam al-Shafiʻi (577–660 ah) with the following words:

"We believe in permissibility of conformity as well as in shifting from one school of law to the other. However, we maintain it only in issues where the ruling of the judge is not breached."[26]

6 He elaborates the idea by saying:

"This is the adopted view of ʻIzz al-Din b. ʻAbd al-Salam, Sayf al-Din al-Amidi and a group of other scholars as already described, it is governed by the condition that one should not assimilate all schools of law in a way that goes against the consensus of the Umma."

7 al-Qarafi commenting on the issue, further says:

"The Prophet (blessings and peace be upon him) has said: 'I have been raised with the *Din* that provides facilitation.'[27] This Prophetic statement demands its permissibility at large because this is a type of ease and lenience. The Islamic law does not want to put people in trouble, rather it declares mandatory the acquisition of special and better expediencies, if they are burdened heavily."[28]

8 Imam Sayf al-Din Abu al-Hasan al-Amidi al-Shafiʻi (551–631 ah) writes in *al-Ihkam fi Usul al-Ahkam*:

"When a conformist, following his Imam, acts upon his verdict about a matter pertaining to ritual prayer (*al-sala al-maktuba*), the Imams agree that, in regard to this matter, he does not have the right to turn towards some other Imam. However, in matters other than acts of worship, the Imams disagree about turning towards other Imams and following them. It has been prohibited as well as permitted by different jurists. The consensus amongst the Companions (may Allah be well pleased with them) makes it evident that a conformist has the right to seek a verdict from any scholar regarding any disputation. Nothing has been reported about any Imam from the pious predecessors, prohibiting common people from it. Had it been prohibited, it would not have been permissible for the Companions (may Allah be well pleased with them) to be negligent of this prohibition or observe silence on this forbiddance."

"In view of that, if a person determines to fix for himself a school of law for adherence, like Shafiʻi or Hanafi or any other school, and declares to stick to it, a large group of Imams have accorded permissibility to following another Imam or school of law in a given matter."[29]

9 Imam Kamal al-Din b. al-Humam al-Hanafi (790–861 ah) writes in *al-Tahrir fi Usul al-Fiqh, al-Jamiʻ bayn Istilahay al-Hanafiyya wa'l-Shafiʻiyya*, which is his masterpiece on the amalgamation and combination of terminologies of the Hanafi and Shafiʻi schools of law:

"The conformist should not turn towards any other imam about an issue for which he abides by a specific school. This idea raises the question whether or not the conformist should pursue, for a disputation, an imam other than the one whom he adheres to in other matters. According to the adopted school (*al-madh'hab al-mukhtar*), he can certainly do it because people have been seeking edicts the first time from one scholar and the second time from another, without conforming to only one jurist for all the matters. It is said that if one adopts a specific school of law such as Hanafi or Shafi'i, then one must hold it fast. However, at the same time, it has also been said that he should not adhere to one school alone for all the issues in consideration. It is also viewed that such a person would be perceived as if he was not originally bound to any school. So, he adheres to one jurist in one matter and to the other in another. He further states: This also establishes the conformist's justification of following the permissions provided by different schools of law. There is no legal prohibition to stop him from this option, because one has the lawful right to adopt the easier option, while the mode to utilize it is also available. This is so because he has not adopted the verdict of other Imam in this regard. The Prophet (blessings and peace be upon him) too would like ease and comfort for his followers."[30]

10 Ibn Amir al-Hajj al-Halabi al-Hanafi (d. 879 ah) wrote the explanation of the above-mentioned book of Ibn al-Humam. He says:

"The Prophet (blessings and peace be upon him) would like ease and comfort for his followers. As has been described in the preceding section about preference, Imam al-Bukhari has narrated a hadith reported by 'A'isha (may Allah be well pleased with her) with the word *'an-hum* (for them), while another narration has reported *ma yukhaffif-u 'an-hum*. The Prophet (blessings and peace be upon him) would like anything that causes ease and relaxation for his Umma. Therefore, we have mentioned several hadith reports that prove the principles (of ease and relaxation)."

He further elaborates the concept, saying:

"It connotes that, apart from the Imam one has conformed with in one issue, he can also conform with another Imam (in another disputation), like the conformist who would abide by Imam Abu Hanifa in a problem and followed some other Imam in some other issue. (This is the adopted view) as has been described by al-Amidi and Ibn al-Hajib. (Yes, most certainly) he can do it on the basis of ample and accomplished proofs (*al-istiqra' al-tam*). (Indeed) in the Companions' times, the edict seekers of every era and their Successors (used to get a verdict now from this and then from that *mujtahid*, without tenaciously adhering to any mufti). This has been a general and repeated practice, and, this has not been denied. ... Moreover, it is stated by Imam al-Rafi'i and others that determining according to a particular school of law in every matter is not mandatory. Nothing is imperative for a man other than what Allah and His Messenger (blessings and peace be upon him) have declared obligatory. Allah and His Messenger (blessings and peace be upon him) have not made it imperative for a person to adopt the way of anyone of the Umma and only conform with what he says and give up everything else."[31]

11 'Allama 'Abd al-Hayy al-Faqih al-Hanafi al-Laknawi has also supported the same idea answering a particular question in his *Majmua' al-Fatawa*:

"The Hanafi school does not imply hiding the truth so that the searcher of that truth should exit from the Hanafi school of law. Many of the eminent Hanafi authorities have endorsed this permission in their books. One of the eminent scholars Mufti al-Hanafiyya of Mecca (d. 1061 AH) Muhammad b. 'Abd al-'Azim al-Makki has written in his booklet *al-Qawl al-Sadid fi Ba'd Masa'il al-Ijtihad wa'l-Taqlid*:

'It is not binding on us that we should not accept the opinion or the evidence from what appears right against our own opinion, because Almighty Allah has plentifully blessed us with the wealth of contemplation through which it is possible to find what is right or appropriate in a given situation. Despite this openness, thank God, we do not exit from the conformity with Imam Abu Hanifa'."[32, 33]

1.6 The principle of distinction and option of choice between different juristic verdicts

The intent of the wholesome of *Shari'ah* is to create ease and facilitation for humankind. Keeping in view this principle, the jurists have promoted ease, expansion and facilitation for humans in making inferences from the sources. While describing various disputations, they have reported different verdicts and opinions that contain greater flexibility and facilitation. Mentioning these verdicts, the Imams have frequently referred to statements, using descriptions like:

- *Hadha asahh* (This is the most correct.)
- *Hadha awsa'* (This is the vastest.)
- *Hadha ahwat* (This is the safest.)
- *Hadha aqyas* (This is the best analogy.)
- *Hadha awla* (That is better.)
- *Hadha awdah* (This is more evident.)
- *Hadha awfaq li'l-qiyas* (This is more compatible to analogy.)
- *Hadha arfaq li'n-nas* (This is more lenient and easier for the people.)

The jurists who have used such epithets do not represent any specific period, nor do they belong to any single school of law; rather they belong to all the eras and all the schools of law. They include Imam Abu Hanifa, Imam Malik, Imam al-Shafi'i, Imam Ahmad b. Hanbal, Imam Muhammad, Imam

Abu Yusuf, al-Samarqandi, al-Sarakhsi, al-Kasani, al-Zayla'i, al-Subki, al-Nawawi, al-Shurbini, al-Ramli, Ibn Hazm, Ibn Muflih, Ibn Qudama, Ibn Taymiyya, Ibn Nujaym, al-Haskafi, Ibn 'Abidin al-Shami, etc. Here are some examples of their inclusive accommodation and flexible approach:

1.6.1 al-Hanafi authorities

1 Ibn Nujaym states in *al-Bahr al-Ra'iq*:

"He [Qasim b. Qutlubugha] says at the end: It is proven that the position (*qawl*) of Imam Abu Hanifa is the most correct view (*asahh*). And by this it is apparent that no legal ruling (*fatwa*) is to be passed or acted upon unless it is the verdict (*qawl*) of al-Imam al-A'zam [Abu Hanifa]. His position will not be abandoned for the position of [Imam Abu Yusuf and Imam Muhammad], or either of them, or anyone else besides them, except in the case of necessity due to weakness of evidence or in the case where popular practice and conventions are against his verdict, such as sharecropping (*al-muzara'a*) [for example].

"If the scholars declare that the legal ruling (*fatwa*) is on the verdict of [Imam Abu Yusuf and Imam Muhammad], as in this example and quoted in *al-Siraj al-Wahhaj*, then their position is [to be viewed as] the more accommodating (*awsa'*) position, whereas the Imam's position is the more precautionary (*ahwat*)."[34]

2 Ibn Nujaym says at another occasion:

"Something more accommodating (*awsa'*) than that has been stated by our teachers/colleagues, and that is: if an upright jurist (*faqih*) is asked for a legal ruling (fatwa) and he passes judgement on the nullification of an oath (*al-yamin*), it is permitted for him to act upon his legal ruling (fatwa) or to withhold it. Even something more accommodating (*awsa'*) than this has also been reported, and that is: if a legal expert (*mufti*) passes a legal ruling (fatwa) for permissibility and then another [legal expert (*mufti*)] passes a legal ruling (fatwa) for impermissibility after the first legal ruling (fatwa) has been passed, then the second legal ruling (fatwa) can be implemented with regards to another woman, but not the first. Both legal rulings can be implemented in two (separate) incidents."[35]

3 In a matter of theft, al-Haskafi quotes two verdicts, The Hanafite and the Shafi'ite. Regarding the first he says: It is the most correct view (*asahh*). And about the second verdict he says: It is the more accommodating (*awsa'*) position, thus it would be adopted for practice in times of necessity.[36]

4 al-Haskafi discussing the time of the *Maghrib* ritual prayer quotes two positions on determining the meanings of twilight. He says:

In *al-Mabsut*, it is related that Imam Abu Hanifa's position is the safest (*ahwat*), whereas their (Imam Abu Yusuf, Imam Muhammad and Imam al-Shafi'i) position is the more accommodating (*awsa'*), i.e., more lenient for people.[37]

5 Imam al-Sarakhsi relates two positions regarding the size of the water basin in order to explain the apparent standpoint of the *madh'hab* in interpreting what constitutes ritual ablution; first the position of Imam Abu Hanifa and the second of Imam Abu Yusuf. Finally he says, the report of Imam Abu Hanifa, however, is more accommodating (*awsa'*).[38]

6 Imam al-Sarakhsi writes in *al-Mabsut*:

"If two people entrusted a person with gold coins (*dinar*), silver coins (*dirham*), clothes, riding beasts and servants, and then one of them went back to reclaim his possessions from him, according to Imam Abu Hanifa it would not be permitted for him to do so unless both are present. Whereas according to Imam Abu Yusuf and Imam Muhammad, he will be ordered to divide the property and pay him his rightful share.

"Imam Muhammad states in *al-Amali*: The verdict of Imam Abu Hanifa is closer to juristic reasoning (*aqyas*), while the verdict of Imam Abu Yusuf is more accommodating (*awsa'*)."[39]

7 It is stated in *Bada'i' al-Sana'i'*:

"As for the case of a well—where it [first] becomes impure, then its water sinks into the earth with its bottom part becoming dry, and then it is replenished with water again—in the opinion of Nusayr b. Yahya, it is pure, whereas according to Muhammad b. Salama it is impure. The same is said to be the opinion of Imam Abu Yusuf."

Imam al-Kasani commenting on both opinions, says:

"The second position is more precautionary (*ahwat*), whereas the former is the more accommodating (*awsa'*)."[40]

8 At another occasion, Imam al-Kasani reports:

"Nusayr b. Yahya and Abu Bakr al-Iskaf said: 'There is no good in it.' Ibn al-Mubarak was asked about it and he said, 'There is no harm in it.' It is also the verdict of Shaykh Abu Hafs al-Kabir, and this is the more accommodating (*awsa'*) position, but the first is the more precautionary (*ahwat*)."[41]

9 At another place, al-Kasani, after quoting two different opinions, says:

"What is stated by Imam Muhammad is closer to juristic reasoning (*aqyas*), but the position of Imam Abu Yusuf is more accommodating (*awsa'*)."[42]

10 Imam al-Kasani states in the section of ritual seclusion (*al-i'tikaf*):

"If he leaves the mosque without an excuse, then his ritual seclusion (*al-i'tikaf*) in the mosque is nullified according to Imam Abu Hanifa, even if it is momentarily. Whereas according to Imam Abu Yusuf and Imam Muhammad, it is not nullified unless he leaves for more than half a day.

"Imam Muhammad said, 'The verdict of Imam Abu Hanifa is closer to juristic reasoning (*aqyas*), while the verdict of Imam Abu Yusuf is more accommodating (*awsa'*).'"[43]

11 The same approach has been endorsed by al-Zayla'i in these words:

"His position is closer to juristic reasoning (*aqyas*), whereas their position is based on juristic preference (*al-istihsan*), and it is the more accommodating (*awsa'*) position.[44]

12 Abu al-Layth al-Samarqandi also reports the same comments in *Tuhfa al-Fuqaha'*.

13 Ibn 'Abidin al-Shami, discussing a situation related to the question of purity, says:

"The former opinion is closer to juristic reasoning (*aqyas*), whereas the latter is more accommodating (*awsa'*). And this is the position adopted in *al-Durar* as the legal ruling (fatwa)."[45]

14 Ibn 'Abidin al-Shami discussing about the purification of honey and oil, mentions two positions, and states:

"This is according to Imam Abu Yusuf, whose position is in contrast to Imam Muhammad. His position is the more accommodating (*awsa'*), and it is upon this position the legal ruling (fatwa) is based. This is what has been stated in the commentary of Shaykh Isma'il from *Jami' al-Fatawa*."[46]

15 Ibn 'Abidin al-Shami says:

"It is stated in *al-Hilya*: 'Yes, there is a difference of opinion between the scholars concerning the beginning of dawn, the scattering of light or its spread over the horizon as mentioned in *Sharh al-Zahidi* from *al-Muhit*.'"

"It is mentioned in *Khizana al-Fatawa* from *Sharh al-Sarakhsi 'ala al-Kafi* that the first position is more precautionary (*ahwat*), while the second is more accommodating (*awsa'*). He says in *al-Bahr*: 'The apparent position (of the *madh'hab*) is the last opinion.'"[47]

16 The Hanafi jurists have decreed on several issues pertaining to the protection of people's rights on the basis of the rules of other schools. For example, a person owes money to someone but does not pay him. Then it so happens that some belonging of the debtor, somehow, gets into the hands of the creditor. In the Hanafi original view, it is not permissible for the creditor to sell it for the compensation of his right. However, the later Hanafi jurists declared it permissible, following the Shafi'i verdict.

'Allama Ibn 'Abidin al-Shami reports from al-Hamawi:

"Non-permissibility of recovering one's right from the opposite gender in the olden times of jurists was owing to the common practice of observance of the rights of the people. However, in modern times, by having power and possession of other's property or wealth, an edict exists on the permissibility of recovering from that, especially in case of our countries, because people are persistently practising disobedience."[48]

17 The original text of *al-Durr al-Mukhtar* reads as under:

"It is not lawful for a (legally) rightful person to recover his right from other than the gender of his own right. However Imam al-Shafi'i, has declared it permissible, and this is the more capacious view. (This provides facility to the people, so this should be adopted.)"[49]

18 In the case of a sale before time or its advance payment, the Hanafis make it a pre-requisite that the material sold must remain in the market until the stipulated time expires. However, Shafi'is find it sufficient if it is present on the time of actual sale. As found in *al-Hidaya*, there is no harm if this verdict is followed in the time of need; this is allowed.[50]

19 The Hanafi school does not hold silent or sleeping partnership lawful, but Imam Malik regards it permissible.[51] Some modern Hanafi jurists have held that the partners setting up a company shall not have only an investing partnership (*al-shirka bi'l-nafaqa*), rather their partnership can also be operational and material in business (*al-shirka bi'l-'urud*).[52] It is stated:

"According to a report narrated by Imam Ahmad b. Hanbal, partnership in operation and investment in material (for sale) is permissible. As described in *al-Mughni*, this is the verdict of Imam Malik and Ibn Abi Layla as well."[53]

1.6.2 al-Maliki view

20 It is stated in *al-Mudawwana al-Kubra*, Ibn al-Qasim said that this is what reached him from Imam Malik as he adopted the accommodating (*awsa'*) position in respect to performing the *tayammum* over something frozen.[54]

1.6.3 al-Shafi'i view

21 Imam al-Shafi'i says, explaining a verse of the Holy Qur'an:

"Some of my companions said to me: it applies only to the distribution of inheritance. And others said: it includes the distribution of inheritance and other similar matters, such as the spoil of war. This is the more accommodating (*awsa'*) position and it is dearer to me."[55]

22 The same approach is found in the words of Sulayman al-Jamal al-Shafi'i. But the statement of al-Zarkashi is more accommodating (*awsa'*) than it.[56]

23 Shams al-Din al-Ramli also uses the same legal expression in the words:

"'The first is the more accommodating (*awsa'*) [and hence permissible].'"[57]

24 al-Mawardi elucidates the rationale of this approach in these words:

"This command relates to the common good and this principle can also be extended to other transactions and agreements."[58]

1.6.4 al-Hanbali view

25 Ibn Hazm states expressing the same principle:

"Rabi'a said: 'I do not think there is anything more accommodating (*awsa'*) on the issue of the animal's foetus than the *ijtihad* adopted by the Imam.'"[59]

26 Ibn Muflih al-Hanbali also expresses the same juristic rule in the words:

"This comes under public interest (*al-masalih al-mursala*). But al-Qadi has adopted a position more accommodating (*awsa'*) than this in *al-Ahkam al-Sultaniyya*."[60]

27 Imam Ibn Muflih further says at another occasion:

"However, the absolute nature of cash is more accommodating (*awsa'*), and for this reason it is validated in kinds of transactions."[61]

28 Imam Ibn Qudama states:

"This is because letting out (*al-ijara*) for the same purpose is permissible but borrowing (*al-i'ara*) is the more accommodating situation (*awsa'*).[62]

29 'Allama Ibn Taymiyya states:

"The position of Imam Ahmad (on this issue) is more accommodating (*awsa'*) than others."[63]

1.7 Juristic strategy for resolving contemporary issues through the principle of inclusion and expansion

In this regard, a reasoned strategy needs to be developed, which will enable us to benefit from the juristic reservoir of all the four schools in order to sort out the complexities of life without any deferment and hindrance.

1 Pursuing this principle, Imam Shah Wali Allah al-Muhaddith al-Dihlawi states:

- i In most of the juristic reasoning characterized by difference of opinions, the truth spreads through all of these opinions.
- ii There is no narrowness in *Din*; rather it offers ease, expansion and accommodation.
- iii Sticking only to one way and believing firmly that the opponent's viewpoint is definitely wrong is baseless.[64]

2 Imam 'Izz al-Din b. 'Abd al-Salam, expressing the same strategy, states:

"Successful is the person who acted upon things the scholars agreed upon and refrained from things that the scholars declared unlawful without any disagreement, and believed in the permissibility of matters, which the scholars and jurists decreed unanimously, also performed the acts, which the scholars unanimously regarded commendable; and abstained from the acts that the scholars unanimously agreed to disapprove.

"However, the things where the scholars disagreed and could not concur on one opinion can be divided into two forms.

- i The matter wherein they have had difference of opinion on the disputations about which the command of the Lawgiver can be repealed. In this case, no chance of following that opinion remains permissible, because such a ruling will be considered a mistake in totality. It will be rejected because the mistake lies in its original legality, and this mistake has detached the ruling from the basic will of the Lawgiver and spirit of the textual law.

ii The second form is related to the matter where difference of opinion does not pertain to the issues about which the command of the Lawgiver can be repealed. There is no harm in obeying or disobeying such a ruling, with the condition that one should follow some authentic juristic opinion and not an unauthentic one. The practice in the early centuries of Muslim Umma, when the traditional schools of law were not formulated and enforced, was not to follow any specific jurisprudence; but people used to follow any legal opinion of a competent scholar, which at least enjoyed the consensus of some jurists."[65]

3 Imam 'Izz al-Din b. 'Abd al-Salam further asserted on a question:
"If the school that he is abandoning and the one that he is adopting are without much distance closer to one another in their sources and origins, then it is permissible to leave one and join the other. It is because from the period of the Companions until the formation of four juristic schools, the Muslims have been following all the schools of jurisprudence instead of one of them. Whoever, one would consider a better scholar, superior in God-consciousness, he would approach him for an edict and follow him. Nobody used to dislike this way, nor was considered disliking by anyone worth any notice. Had it been the wrong way, the scholars would have rejected it and stopped others to follow it."[66]

1.7.1 Categories of juristic opinions

Imam Shah Wali Allah al-Dihlawi further writes that the difference of opinion is of four kinds:

1 Determined Opinion: The difference of opinion is not justified in matters wherein the truth is absolutely and certainly determined. Its compliance is mandatory and differing from this position is definitely void.
2 Preferred Opinion: The problem where the truth is determined by majority vote of the schools and the jurists, and it weighs in predominant scale. Differing from this position is probably voidable.
3 Un-preferred Opinion: This is a problem where both aspects are under equal authority and none of the aspects is preferred to the other. In this matter, an open choice between the two opinions is granted definitely.
4 Compatible Opinion: This is an issue where similar choice is given on both sides with a dominant opinion. Therefore, in this case also, a jurist is free to adopt either of the two authorities or opinions, based on the compatibility of the evidence and the given circumstances.[67]

Therefore, the scholars and jurists, leaving the first kind aside, can use their juristic discretion in adopting any viewpoint in the last three situations, following the above-mentioned principles of jurisprudence.

1.7.2 The occasions to differ

Imam Shah Wali Allah al-Dihlawi describes the occasions to differ at another place in his book *'Iqd al-Jid*:

It is an established fact that the difference amongst the jurists and *mujtahidun* arose due to four reasons:

1 A *mujtahid* found a hadith about an incident, while the other missed it. In this case, the one who found the truth is called *mujtahid mu'ayyan*.
2 Every *mujtahid* has hadiths of the Prophet (blessings and peace be upon him) and the reports of the Companions. Every one of them exercised *ijtihad* (deductive reasoning) in preferring or finding compatibility among hadiths and Companions' reports regarding any given legal situation. Their *ijtihad* (deductive reasoning) took it to the status of a determined command, due to which the difference of opinion transpired to the scope of adopting any of the opinions.
3 The *mujtahids* differed in the following matters:

   i The connotations and interpretation of words and idioms in use and determining their meanings and implications.
   ii Pinpointing and determining the confines of usages.
   iii The true recognition of conditions and constituent elements of a legal act or its effects. Thus, *ijtihad* (deductive reasoning) of every *mujtahid* took him to a separate and permanent opinion in framing the legal position of that act.
   iv A different approach in formulating the juristic principles. Since the framed juristic principles or conditions were different from one another, resultantly, difference of legal opinion occurred also in peripheral issues.

That is why the Prophet (blessings and peace be upon him) said: "Difference of opinion amongst my Umma is a blessing."[68]

This difference of opinion has been declared to be a blessing of Almighty Allah, because none of them is negating the command of God. All of them are trying to determine the meanings and specify the implications of a particular verse, hadith or word in question in different ways. Therefore, these juristic differences have expanded the scope of legal options for the Umma.

"Therefore, all of the *mujtahids* are on straight path in all the above-mentioned forms when their sources are akin to and compatible with the indicated methodology. That is why, one can easily accept anyone of them without any confusion."[69]

1.7.3 Qur'anic verdict on shifting from one school to another

It can be asserted in the light of legal arguments that, apart from the Prophets, it is not legally prohibited to differ with any person of any exalted position in any issue under any circumstances. This station is only exclusive for

Allah and His exalted Messenger (blessings and peace be upon him). The four Imams too have expanded upon this matter. The Qur'an states:

> *Ya ayyuha'l-ladhin-a amanu ati'ul-Lah-a wa ati'ur-Rasula wa uli'l-amr-i min-kum* [O believers! Obey Allah and obey the Messenger (blessings and peace be upon him) and those who hold the authority amongst you.][70]

The Qur'an and Sunna come under the article of:

> *Ati'ul-Lah-a wa ati'ur-Rasula* [Obey Allah and obey the Messenger (blessings and peace be upon him).][71]

The schools of law and their Imams fall under the article of:

> *Uli'l-amr-i min-kum* [Those who hold the authority amongst you.][72]

As mentioned in this verse, the commandment of "*ati'u*" [obey] has been repeated for *Rasul* in the same way as for Allah, to declare the absolute and unconditional authority vested with the commandment of the Holy Prophet (blessings and peace be upon him). However, in the case of "*uli'l-amr*", the command of obeying "*ati'u*" has not been verbally repeated. This style of linguistic composition signifies that the obedience rendered to "*uli'l-amr*" is qualified, conditional and challengeable. That is why, Almighty Allah has further commanded:

> *Fa-in tanaza'tum fi shay'in fa-rudduhu ilal-Lah-i wa'r-Rasul-i in kuntum tu'minun-a bilLah-i wa'l-yawm-il akhir* [Then if you disagree amongst yourselves over any issue, refer it to Allah and the Messenger ([blessings and peace be upon him] for final judgment), if you believe in Allah and the Last Day.][73]

This Qur'anic article promulgates three basic principles:

- i The principle of the supreme and absolute juristic authority of the Qur'an and Sunna.
- ii The principle of subordinate and conditional authority of the juristic opinions.
- iii The principle of permissibility of differing from one opinion and adopting the other, due to the reason of stronger supporting evidence of the Qur'an and Sunna.

1 Imam Shah Wali Allah al-Dihlawi states:

"The overwhelming majority of scholars belonging to the four schools have followed the middle course between two extremes of excess and paucity we have mentioned. All the four Imams instructed their followers of the same path of moderation. Shaykh 'Abd al-Wahhab al-Sha'rani has reported from Imam Abu Hanifa in *al-Yawaqit wa al-Jawahir*, saying, 'It is unjust for a person who is not acquainted with the proof contained in my words to issue an edict just on the basis of my words.' When he decreed his edict he would point towards himself and say, 'As far as I know, this is the opinion of al-Nu'man b. Thabit [Abu Hanifa], and, this is more acceptable to me. If there is a better opinion, that is more authentic and would be closer to the truth.' Similarly, Imam Malik used to say, 'Except for the Messenger of Allah (blessings and peace be upon him), everyone can be seized for his words and his words can be rejected.' al-Hakim and al-Bayhaqi have reported from Imam al-Shafi'i, saying, 'When the authenticity of hadith is proved, that is my school.'"[74]

2 al-Zarkashi states:

"The Companions had a common agreement on this point that there was a difference in their level of knowledge and understanding but, despite that, there was consensus among them on the permissibility of following a path of a person of lower rank in the presence of a person enjoying a higher rank in knowledge and wisdom."[75]

This principle reveals that, under peculiar circumstances, it is permissible to prefer another Imam's verdict due to legal expediency, evidential strength or circumstantial necessity. The majority of jurists maintain the same standpoint. However, the juristic conditions and limits have to be observed compulsorily.

3 Ibn Taymiyya states:

"Sometimes, Allah Most High bestows upon a scholar the wisdom and insight which the other lacks."[76]

4 Ibn 'Abidin al-Shami al-Hanafi has stated with reference to *al-'Iqd al-Farid* authored by 'Allama al-Shurunbulali al-Hanafi:

"It is not imperative for a person to follow a particular school of law in all cases, without any exception."

He further states:

"In certain issues, it is permissible for a person to follow another Imam's school against the school of his own Imam, provided he cares for all the terms and conditions fixed by the other Imam."[77]

We learn from these proofs and statements that, about a given disputation, shifting from one juristic school to the other is permissible. However, this permissibility is dependent upon the fulfilment of certain conditions described by the jurists.

1.8 Categories of conformist jurists and their ways of framing the opinions

According to the juristic classification, after the three levels of *Mujtahidin* (*al-Mujtahid fi'l-Shar'*, *al-Mujtahid fi'l-Madh'hab* and *al-Mujtahid fi'l-Masa'il*), there are three categories of conformist jurists:

1.8.1 Ashab al-Takhrij *(Jurists: Who are competent to conduct inference)*

They get to the origin of the proof and apply it to new circumstances according to the similarity or compatibility of the origin (*asl*) and the branch (*far'*). In this way, they conduct juristic research with analogies and examples and continue extending and applying the rules on newly emerging situations.

1.8.2 Ashab al-Tarjih *(Jurists: Who are competent to conduct preference)*

They give priority or preference to rulings and verdicts available within their own school on the basis of analogies and strength of other evidences in order to prove them more capacious, facilitating and beneficial for the people.

1.8.3 Ashab al-Tamyiz *(Jurists: Who are competent to conduct distinction)*

They are equipped with the capability of making distinctions, as to which verdict or evidence is stronger, strong or weak, or which opinion is the most correct, correct or incorrect.

On the basis of the principles of *takhrij* (inference) and *tarjih* preference and *tamyiz* (distinction), the jurists continue expanding the juristic vision and its content, to make it all-inclusive and accommodating based on the inherent vastness of the legal evidence.[78]

1.9 Application of intra-school position to inter-school position

In like manner, the above-mentioned intra-school principles should be applied to inter-school matters, in order to infer, extend, prefer or adopt a verdict of any of the schools of law as per requirements. This is how the truthfulness and veracity of all the four schools of law would be practically applied and enforced. Otherwise, it will negate Islam's global immensity and vastness.

One of the main Divine objectives, and why various schools of law earned acceptance and popularity amongst the Umma, was that all the commands and teachings of the Prophet Muhammad (blessings and peace be upon him) should be protected, practiced and transmitted in their real manifestation. In this way every single Sunna of the Holy Prophet (blessings and peace be upon him) would always remain alive. None of the Prophets' practices, teachings and commands may be abandoned at any given time. Almighty Allah has practically protected all aspects of the holy life of the Prophet (blessings and peace be upon him) in the form of different schools of law.

Nevertheless, the protection of the whole of the Sunna of Holy Prophet (blessings and peace be upon him) would not have been possible through one school of law only, because some variations and alterations gradually took place in the Sunna from time to time, in accordance with occasional needs and circumstantial requirements. Therefore, the real purpose of the existence of different *madhahib* is to create a total comprehension of the Prophetic practices, and not to create a narrow and rigid vision of Islamic commands.

1.10 Guiding principles for the methodology of inclusion and flexibility

The following are the guiding principles for finding juristic solutions for modern issues, through the methodology of inclusive accommodation and flexibility (*al-tawassu'*).

1 As far as possible and whatever way it works, we should normally try to draw inferences from the rulings of the great Imams and must not exit from all of the four schools of jurisprudence. There is no harm in deserting one school of law and taking up the other in solving a specific complicated issue.
2 Of the followed schools, whichever offers any key or solution to any modern-day complication or complex development, should be adopted to solve the problem. Therefore, conducting a modern *ijtihad* does not become the only solution, nor do we open the door of *ijtihad* to every Tom, Dick and Harry.
3 This is so because the demand of necessity or compulsive intervention of time neither does open the door of *ijtihad* wide apart nor shuts it absolutely. The right and moderate path lies between these two extremes, so that juristic reasoning is practiced under real necessity. And this juristic reasoning does not transgress or go independent of the principles and juristic procedures laid down by the schools of law. In brief, if the desired solution is found in the master books of any of the four schools, the edict can be issued from there, and so new juristic reasoning remains beyond any need.
4 The change of school of law should not be due to personal desire; it should rather be owing to religious necessity or general expediency as stated by 'Allama Ibn 'Abidin al-Shami:

   "A person's change from one juristic school to the other due to worldly desires and pursuits without a solid reason will be an extremely condemnable act, because he has followed the prohibitions of *Din* and degraded his School of law."[79]
5 Leaving one's own Imam's verdict and following the other's should be based on the strength of proof, legal expediency or circumstantial necessity. It should not be for the sake of avoiding the Divine commandments.
6 Only such a person is allowed to shift from one school to another who is sufficiently competent to distinguish between weak and strong reasons and equipped with knowledge of legal expediencies.

7 If a solution is not explicitly found, even in any of these sources, there is no harm in exercising analogical deduction [*al-ijtihad al-qiyasi*] for unsolved matters provided the analogy is not absolutely differential [*al-qiyas ma' al-fariq*].
8 However, if all the four schools do not offer any analogical solution to a modern-day problem, then we should go for exegetical deduction (*al-ijtihad al-bayani*). This is reinterpretation of the text, following the exegetical and juristic principles and general legal provisions of the Qur'an and Sunna.
9 Last but not the least, if we do not find any clear text of the Divine command that can be used as juristic basis for the above-mentioned deductions, then we should go for deductive reasoning based on public interest. This can be conducted in the forms of juristic preference (*al-istihsan*), presumption of continuity (*al-istis'hab*), public good (*al-istislah*), common benefit (*al-masalih al-mursala*)', 'usage (*al-'urf*) and convention (*al-'ada*)', 'legal necessity (*al-darura*)', 'change of law by change of time (*taghayyur al-ahkam bi taghayyur al-zaman*)', etc.
10 Finale

In view of the current national and international complexities and changing ground realities, the jurists have followed the path of openness, flexibility and liberality (*al-tawassu'*) instead of tenacious adherence to a single school of law or the path of narrowness and rigidity. As the basis of the problems grows wider and expands in span and novelty, the rules to resolve the problems also demand adoption of an open-minded and a holistic approach. If the issue is related to personal matters, adherence to a particular school of law will be preferred. However, if the problem happens to be wide-spectrum and involves a broader span of activity and extensive international repercussions, the methodology to deal with it would also be all-inclusive, liberal and wide-ranging.

Keeping the above in view, the IFIs in the current complex situation of international financial market should follow the way of flexibility and should be more open towards the formulation of their policies, launching the new products and dealing with the customers but they have to follow the lines of *Qur'an* and Sunna.

Notes

1 Robinson, K. (2007) "Islamic Finance Is Seeing Spectacular Growth," *NY Times* (5 November). www.nytimes.com/2007/11/05/business/worldbusiness/05iht-bankco 106.3.8193171.html (accessed 15 June 2009). And Ahmed, (2006) *Islamic Banking Finance and Insurance: A Global Overview* (Kuala Lumpur: A.S. Noordeen).

2 Smolo, E. and Habibovic, E. (2012) Barriers to Growth of Islamic Finance: Issue of Standardisations, in Trakic, A. and Tajuddin, H. H. A. Islamic Banking and Finance: Principles, Instruments, Operations, CLJ Publications, Malaysia.

3 Shanmugam, B. and Zahari, Z. R. (2009) *A Primer on Islamic Finance* (Charlottesville, VA: Research Foundation of CFA Institute).
4 Ainley, M. (1997) "Under a Veil of Regulation," The Banker, October 01; KPMG International; Seera Investment Bank; Shanmugam and Zahari.
Jassar Al-Jassar (2002) "Islamic Finance: Successes, Prospects, and Neglected Areas," in Islamic Finance: The Task Ahead – Proceedings of the Fourth Harvard University Forum on Islamic Finance (Cambridge, MA: Center for Middle Eastern Studies, Harvard University); Ijlal Alvi (2009) "Standardization of Documentation in Islamic Finance & Role of the International Islamic Financial Market (Iifm)," in Islamic Financial Sector Development (IFSD) Forum 2009 (Ashgabat, Turkmenistan, May);
Shanmugam and Zahari; Smolo, "Sustainable Growth of Islamic Financial Industry (Ifi): Some Unresolved Issues."; Smolo, "Sustaining the Growth of Islamic Financial Industry: What Needs to Be Done?."
5 "There are many examples where this industry suffers due to the lack of standardisation. An example of problem in this industry due to the standardisation problem is Japan Bank for International Cooperation's ('JBIC') plan to issue *sukuk*. Initially, JBIC was about to issue its first *sukuk* in May 2008. Two respective banks were selected to arrange the deal, namely Citibank of Dubai and CIMB Malaysia. However, due to the disagreement that existed between the *Shari'ah* boards of the two banks on whether *sukuk* are *Shari'ah*-compliant or not, the issuing of *sukuk* was delayed. As a result, the deal had to be restructured from the original *murabahah* structure to *musharakah*. All of this created additional problems in terms of time, cost and frustration for the issuer"(Smolo and Habibovic 2012, p. 17).
6 Rafay, Abdul, Ramla Sadiq and Mobeen Ajmal. "Fragmentation of Islamic Financial Products: An Exploratory Study of Islamic Schools of Thought." *Abasyn Journal of Social Sciences—Special Issue: Towards Financial Inclusion*: 48.
7 Kasim, Nawal, Sheila Nu Nu Htay and Syed Ahmed Salman. "Empowering the *Shari'ah* Committee towards Strengthening *Shari'ah* Governance Practices in Islamic Financial Institutions." *Review of European Studies* 8 (March 2016): 144.
8 Ahmad Shaharudin Bin Abdul Latiff (2013) "The Need for an Information System for the Dissemination of Knowledge on Islamic Banking."
9 Ibid.
10 Qur'an 2:185.
11 Ibid., 22:78.
12 Ibid., 5:6.
13 Ibid., 4:28.
14 Ibid., 8:66.
15 Set forth by •Muslim in *al-Sahih:* Bk.: *al-Talaq* [The Divorce], Ch.: "Merely Giving a Woman the Option of Divorce Does not Make the Divorce Effective, But Only When it is Actually Intended," 2:1104 §1478.
16 Set forth by •al-Bukhari in *al-Sahih:* Bk.: *al-Manaqib* [The Exemplary Virtues], Ch.: "The Qualities of the Prophet (blessings and peace be upon him)," 3:1306 §3367; •Muslim in *al-Sahih:* Bk.: *al-Fada'il* [Virtues], Ch.: "The Prophet's Distance Away from Sins," 4:1813 §2327.
17 Set forth by •al-Bukhari in *al-Sahih:* Bk.: *al-'Ilm* [Knowledge], Ch.: "On the Prophet (blessings and peace be upon him) Being Careful about Giving People Admonition and Knowledge Lest They Feel Aversion to It," 1:38 §69; •Muslim in al-*Sahih*: Bk.: *al-Jihad wa al-siyar* [The Striving and Military Expeditions], Ch.: "The Command to Make Things Easy and Not Making Others Feel Aversion," 3:1359 §1734.
18 Set forth by •al-Bukhari in *al-Sahih:* Bk.: *al-Wudu'* [The Ablution], Ch.: "Pouring Water Over Urine in the Mosque," 1:89 §217; •Muslim in *al-Sahih:* Bk.: *al-Tahara*

[The Purification], Ch.: "The Obligation to Wash Away Urine and Other Impurities," 1:236 §§284–285.
19 Imam Ahmad b. Hanbal, *al-Musnad*, 3:479; 4:338; 5:32.
20 Ibn Qudama, *Rawda al-Nazir*, 1:386.
21 Ibid.
22 al-Shurunbulali, *al-'Iqd al-Farid li-Bayan al-Rajih mina'l-Khilaf fi Jawaz al-Taqlid*, University of King Sa 'ud, Saudi Arabia.
23 al-Shinqiti, *Nashr al-Bunud 'ala Maraqi al-Sa'ud*, p. 349.
24 al-Qarafi, *Sharh Tanqih al-Fusul ila Ikhtisar al-Mahsul fi'l-Usul*, p. 339.
25 Ibid.
26 Ibid., *Nafa'is al-Usul fi Sharh al-Mahsul*, 9:3964.
27 Set forth by •Ahmad b. Hanbal on the authority of Abu Umama in *al-Musnad*, 5:266 §22345. •al-Ruyani in *al-Musnad*, 2:317 §1279. •al-Tabarani in *al-Mu'jam al-Kabir*, 8:170, 216, 222 §§§7715, 7868, 7883.
28 al-Qarafi, *Nafa'is al-Usul fi Sharh al-Mahsul*, 9:3965.
29 al-Amidi, *al-Ihkam fi Usul al-Ahkam*, 4:244–245. al-Qarafi, *Nafa'is al-Usul fi Sharh al-Mahsul*, 9:3962–3963.
30 Ibn al-Humam, *al-Tahrir fi Usul al-Fiqh, al-Jami' bayn Istilahay al-Hanafiyya wa'l-Shafi'iyya*, pp. 551–552.
31 Ibn Amir al-Hajj, *al-Taqrir wa al-Tahbir 'ala al-Tahrir fi Usul al-Fiqh, al-Jami' bayn Istilahay al-Hanafiyya wa'l-Shafi'iyya*, 3:446.
32 Ibn Mulla Farrukh, *al-Qawl al-Sadid fi Ba'd Masa'il al-Ijtihad wa'l-Taqlid*, p. 129.
33 'Abd al-Hayy al-Hanafi al-Laknawi, *Majmu'a Fatawa*, pp. 319–320.
34 Ibn Nujaym, *al-Bahr al-Ra'iq*, 1:259.
35 Ibid., 4:7.
36 al-Haskafi, *al-Durr al-Mukhtar*, p. 323.
37 Ibid., *Majma' al-Anhur fi Sharh Multaqa al-Abhur*, 1:106.
38 al-Sarakhasi, *al-Mabsut*, 1:71.
39 Ibid., 11:123.
40 al-Kasani, *Bada'i' al-Sana'i'*, 1:73.
41 Ibid., 1:74.
42 Ibid., 1:89.
43 Ibid., 2:115.
44 al-Zayla 'i, *Tabyin al-Haqa'iq*, 1:351.
45 Ibn 'Abidin al-Shami, *Radd al-Muhtar*, 1:332.
46 Ibid., 1:334.
47 Ibid., 1:357.
48 Ibid., 6:151.
49 al-Haskafi, *al-Durr al-Mukhtar*, p. 688.
50 al-Marghinani, *al-Hidaya*, 3:71.
51 al-Sarakhsi, *al-Mabsut*, 11:160. al-Marghinani, *al-Hidaya*, 3:6.
52 al-Kasani, *Bada'i' al-Sana'i'*, 6:62.
53 Ibn Qudama, *al-Mughni*, 5:11.
54 Malik b. Anas, *al-Mudawwana al-Kubra*, 1:46.
55 al-Shafi 'i, *Kitab al-Umm*, 5:102.
56 Sulayman al-Jamal, *Hashiya al-Jamal 'ala Sharh al-Manhaj*, 2:514.
57 Ibid., 2:459.
58 al-Mawardi, *al-Ahkam al-Sultaniyya*, p. 48.
59 Ibn Hazm, *al-Muhalla*, 11:38.
60 Ibn Muflih, *al-Furu'*, 6:116.
61 Ibid., *al-Nukat wa al-Saniyya 'ala Mukhskil al-Muharrar*, 1:303.
62 Ibn Qudama, *al-Mughni*, 5:135.
63 Ibn Taymiyya, *Majmu' al-Fatawa*, 21:139.

64 Shah Wali Allah al-Muhaddith al-Dihlawi, *'Iqd al-Jid fi Ahkam al-Ijtihad wa al-Taqlid*, p. 178.
65 Ibid., pp. 178–179.
66 'Izz al-Din 'Abd al- 'Aziz b. 'Abd al-Salam, *Qawa'id al-Ahkam fi Masalih al-Anam*, 2:158.
67 Shah Wali Allah al-Muhaddith al-Dihlawi, *'Iqd al-Jid fi Ahkam al-Ijtihad wa al-Taqlid*, p. 172.
68 Set forth by •al-Jassas in *Ahkam al-Qur'an*, 2:314; •al-Ghazali in *Ihya' 'Ulum al-Din*, 1:27; •al-Nawawi in *Sharh Sahih Muslim*, 11:91–92; •Mulla 'Ali al-Qari in *Mirqat al-Mafatih*, 1:59; •al-Hindi in *Kanz al-'Ummal*, 10:59.
69 Wali Allah al-Dihlawi, *'Iqd al-Jid fi Ahkam al-Ijtihad wa al-Taqlid*, pp. 173–174.
70 Qur'an 4:59.
71 Ibid.
72 Ibid.
73 Ibid.
74 al-Sha'rani, *al-Yawaqit wa al-Jawahir*, 2:478. Shah Wali Allah al-Dihlawi, *'Iqd al-Jid fi Ahkam al-Ijtihad wa al-Taqlid*, p. 216.
75 al-Zarkashi, *al-Bahr al-Muhit fi Usul al-Fiqh*, 4:577.
76 Ibn Taymiyya, *Majmu' al-Fatawa*, 20:19.
77 Ibn 'Abidin al-Shami, *Radd al-Muhtar 'ala al-Durr al-Mukhtar*, 1:87.
78 Ibid., *Sharh 'Uqud Rasm al-Mutfi*, pp. 6–8.
79 Ibid., *Radd al-Muhtar 'ala al-Durr al-Mukhtar*, 4:80.

Bibliography

The Holy Qur'an.

'Abd al-Hayy al-Hanafi al-Laknawi, *Majmu'a Fatawa*. India, Lucknow: Matba' Yusufi, 1321 ah.

———. *Tabaqat al-Fuqaha'*, Peshawar, Pakistan: Amin Allah b. Muhammad Islam b. Nur al-Islam.

Ibn 'Abidin al-Shami, Muhammad (d. 1252 ah). *Radd al-Muhtar 'ala Durr al-Mukhtar 'ala Tanwir al-Absar*. Beirut: Dar al-Fikr, 1386 AH | 1421/2000. + Quetta, Pakistan: al-Maktaba al-Majidiyya, 1399 ah.

———. *Sharh 'Uqud Rasm al-Mutfi*. Lahore, Pakistan: Suhayl Academy, 1396/1976.

AHmad b. Hanbal, Abu 'Abd Allah b. Muhammad (164–241/780–855), *al-Musnad*. Beirut, Lebanon: al-Maktab al-Islami, 1398/1978.

Ahmad Shaharudin Bin Abdul Latiff. 2013. "The Need for an Information System for the Dissemination of Knowledge on Islamic Banking."

al-Amidi, Sayf al-Din Abu al-Hasan 'Ali b. 'Ali b. Muhammad (551–631/1156–1233), *al-IHkam fi Usul al-AHkam,* Riyadh, Saudi Arabia: Dar al-Sami'i, 1424/2003. + Beirut, Lebanon: Dar al-Kutub al-'Ilmiyya, 1400/1980.

Ibn Amir al-Hajj, Abu 'Abd Allah, Shams al-Din Muhammad b. Muhammad (d. 879 ah), *al-Taqrir wa al-Tahbir 'ala al-Tahrir fi Usul al-Fiqh, al-Jami' bayn Istilahay al-Hanafiyya wa'l-Shafi'iyya*. Beirut, Lebanon: Dar al-Kutub al-'Ilmiyya, 1419/1999.

al-Baghawi, Abu Muhammad al-Husayn b. Mas'ud b. Muhammad (436–516/1044–1122), *SharH al-Sunna, Beirut, Lebanon: al-Maktab al-Islami, 1403/1983.*

Abu Bakr al-Jassas, Ahmad b. 'Ali al-Razi (305–370 ah), *Ahkam al-Qur'an*, Beirut, Lebanon: Dar al-Ihya' al-Turath, 1405 ah.

al-Bukhari, Abu 'Abd Allah Muhammad b. Isma'il b. Ibrahim b. Mughira (194–256/810–870), *al-Sahih*, Beirut, Lebanon, Damascus, Syria: Dar al-Qalam, 1401/1981.

al-Ghazali, Abu Hamid Muhammad b. Muhammad al-Ghazali (450–505 ah), *Ihya' al-*'Ulum al-Din, Beirut, Lebanon: Dar al-Ma'rifa.
al-Haskafi, Muhammad b. 'Ali b. Muhammad al-Hisni al-Hanafi (d. 1088 AH), *al-Durr al-Mukhta sharh Tanwir al-Absar,* Beirut, Lebanon: Dar al-Kutub al-'Ilmiyya, 1423/2002.
al-Hindi, 'Ala' al-Din 'Ali b. Hussam al-Din al-Muttaqi (d. 975 AH), *Kanz al-*'Ummal fi Sunan al-Afal wa al-Aqwal, Beirut, Lebanon: Mu'assisa al-Risala, 1399/1979.
Ibn al-Humam, Kamal al-Din Muhammad b. 'Abd al-Wahid (d. 861 ah), *al-Tahrir fi Usul al-Fiqh, al-Jami' bayn Istilahay al-Hanafiyya wa'l-Shafi'iyya.* Egypt: Matba'a Mustafa al-Babi al-Halabi wa Awladuhu, 1351 ah.
'Izz al-Din 'Abd al-'Aziz b. 'Abd al-Salam (557–660/1181–1262), *Qawa'id al-Ahkam fi Masalih al-Anam.* Beirut, Lebanon: Dar al-Kutub al-'Ilmiyya.
al-Kasani, Abu Bakr b. Mas'ud b. Ahmad al-Hanafi (d. 587 ah), *Bada'i' al-Sana'i',* Beirut, Lebanon: Dar al-Kitab al-'Arabi, 1982.
Kasim, Nawal, Sheila Nu Nu Htay and Syed Ahmed Salman. "Empowering the Shari'ah Committee towards Strengthening Shari'ah Governance Practices in Islamic Financial Institutions." *Review of European Studies* 8 (March 2016): 144.
al-Marghaynani, Abu al-Hasan 'Ali b. Abi Bakr (511–593 ah), *al-Hidaya.* al-Maktaba al-Islaamiyya.
al-Mawardi, 'Ali b. Muhammad b. Habib (370–450 ah), *al-Ahkam al-Sultaniyya.* Beirut, Lebanon: Dar al-Kitab al-'Arabi, 1420/1999.
Mulla 'Ali al-Qari (d. 1014/1606), *Mirqat al-Mafatih sharh Mishkat al-Masabih.* Multan: Maktaba Imdadiyya, n.d.
———. *Mirqat al-Mafatih sharh Mishkat al-Masabih.* Beirut, Lebanon: Dar al-Fikr, 1422/2002.
Ibn Mulla Farrukh, Muhammad b. 'Abd al-'Azim (996–1061 ah), *al-Qawl al-Sadid fi Ba'd Masa'il al-Ijtihad wa'l-Taqlid,* Kuwait: Dar al-Da'wa, 1988 ad.
Muslim, Ibn al-Hajjaj Abu al-Husayn al-Qushayri al-Naysaburi (206–261/821–875), *al-Sahih,* Beirut, Lebanon: Dar al-Ihya' al-Turath al-'Arabi.
al-Nawawi, Abu Zakariyya Yahya b. Sharaf b. Murri b. al-Hasan b. al-Husayn b. Muhammad b. Jumu'a b. Hizam (631–677/1233–1278), *Sharh Sahih Muslim,* Karachi, Pakistan: Qadimi Kutub Khana, 1375/1956.
al-Qarafi, Abu al-'Abbas Shihab al-Din b. Idris b. 'Abd al-Rahman al-Maliki al-Shahir (d. 684/1285), *Sharh Tanqih al-Fusul ila Ikhtisar al-Mahsul fi'l-Usul.* Beirut, Lebanon: Dar al-Fikr, 1424/2004.
———. *Nafa'is al-Usul fi Sharh al-Mahsul.* Mecca, Saudi Arabia: Maktaba Nazar Mustafa al-Baz.
Ibn Qudama, Abu Muhammad 'Abd Allah b. Ahmad al-Maqdasi (541–620 AH), *al-Mughni fi Fiqh al-Imam Ahmad b. Hanbal al-Shaybani, Beirut, Lebanon: Dar al-Fikr, 1405* AH.
———. *Rawda al-Nazir.* Riyadh, Saudi Arabia, 1399. + Mu'assisa al-Rayyan, 1423/2002.
Rafay, Abdul, Ramla Sadiq and Mobeen Ajmal. "Fragmentation of Islamic Financial Products—An Exploratory Study of Islamic Schools of Thought." *Abasyn Journal of Social Sciences—Special Issue: Towards Financial Inclusion.*
al-Ruyani, Abu Bakr Muhammad b. Harun (d. 307 AH), *al-Musnad,* Cairo, Egypt: Mu'assisa Cordoba, 1416 AH.
al-Sarakhsi, Muhammad b. Ahmad b. Abi Sahl (d. 483 ah), *al-Mabsut.* Beirut, Lebanon: Dar al-Ma'rifa.

Shah Wali Allah al-Muhaddith al-Dihlawi, Ahmad b. 'Abd al-Rahim b. al-Shahid Wajih al-Din b. Mu'azzam b. Mansur (1114–1176 ah), *'Iqd al-Jid fi Ahkam al-Ijtihad wa al-Taqlid*. Kuwait: Dar al-Diya', 1435/2014.

al-Sha'rani, 'Abd al-Wahhab b. Ahmad b. 'Ali al-Misri al-Hanafi (d. 973 ah), *al-Yawaqit wa al-Jawahir fi Bayan 'Aqa'id al-Akabir*. Beirut, Lebanon: Dar Ihya' al-Turath al-'Arabi.

al-Shinqiti, Abu Muhammad, 'Abd Allah b. Ibrahim (d. 1235/1820), *Nashr al-Bunud 'ala Maraqi al-Sa'ud*. Saudi Arabia.

al-Shurunbulali, Hasan b. 'Ammar b. 'Ali al-Misri al-Hanafi (994–1069/1585–1659), *al-'Iqd al-Farid li-Bayan al-Rajih mina'l-Khilaf fi Jawaz al-Taqlid*, University of King Sa'ud, Saudi Arabia.

al-Tabarani, Abu al-Qasim Sulayman b. AHmad b. Ayyub b. Matir al-Lakhmi (260–360/873–971), *al-Mu'jam al-Kabir*, Cairo, Egypt: Maktaba Ibn Taymiyya.

Ibn Taymiyya, AHmad b. 'Abd al-Halim b. 'Abd al-Salam al-Harani (661–728/1263–1328), *Majmu' al-Fatawa*. Maktaba Ibn Taymiyya.

al-Zarkashi, Shams al-Din Muhammad b. 'Abd Allah (d. 772 ah), *al-Bahr al-Muhit fi Usul al-Fiqh*. Beirut, Lebanon: Dar al-Kitab al-'Ilmiyya, 1421/2000. + Dar al-Kutubi, 1414/1994.

al-Zayla'i, 'Uthman b. 'Ali al-Hanafi (d. 743 ah), *Tabyin al-Haqa'iq*. Cairo, Egypt: Dar al-Kutub al-Islami, 1313 ah.

2 Recent development in Islamic finance and financial products

M. Ishaq Bhatti, Naseem Al Rahahleh and Hussain Mohi-ud-Din Qadri

2.1 Introduction

In general, banks and financial institutions[1] operate as service providers to connect between borrowers and lenders. Their main function is to receive money from individuals (depositors) and channel it to clients who need the money (entrepreneurs) for joint venture and/or infrastructure investment projects. Most of these transactions and services are based on interest (Ribah) in conventional banking industry. However, practicing Muslim clients are not using interest-based banking because under Islamic *Shari'ah* jurisdiction Ribah-based transactions are strictly prohibited. Islam encourage trade but paying and/or charging interest (Ribah) is not allowed. To overcome on this issue Muslim jurists proposed interest-free (without usury) financial transactions which is an ethical approach to banking services called Islamic Banking and Finance (IBF). The demand for an IBF industry is expanding to cater the need of more than 1.4 billion Muslims around the world. The general consensus amongst orthodox interpretations recognize clear regulations in the "Quran",[2] which states that all business transactions should be free from 'Ribah'.[3] The demand for IBF around the world creates this niche market, so banking industry is rushing to tap-up their services to attract Muslim clients. IBF is an interest-free banking system based on the strict adherence of *Shari'ah* norms, which are stated in the Quran as below.

> Those who consume interest cannot stand [on the Day of Resurrection] except as one stands who is being beaten by Satan into insanity. That is because they say, 'Trade is (just) like interest'. But Allah has permitted trade and has forbidden interest. So whoever has received an admonition from his Lord and desists may have what is past, and his affair rests with Allah. But whoever returns to (dealing in interest or usury) – those are the companions of the Fire; they will abide eternally therein.
>
> Quran 2:275

> O you who have believed, do not consume usury, doubled and multiplied, but fear Allah that you may be successful.
>
> Quran 3:130

The IBF model can be derived from the two verses of the Quran above, which prohibit Ribah in any business transaction. Therefore, the IBF industry is regulated under five pillars of *Shari'ah* principles (Islamic law)[4]: (i) interest-free, (ii) ethical financial activities – halal or permissible, (iii) asset-based and asset-backed, (iv) partnership investment based on PLS between financer and entrepreneur, and (v) sharing the risk.[5]

In recent years, IBF has proven to be the fastest growing (12%–15%) sector. Its popularity is increasing globally, particularly in regions with a large Islamic population, such as the Gulf Cooperation Council (GCC), Bangladesh, Brunei, India, Indonesia, Iran, Malaysia, and Pakistan. This growth in IBF can be seen largely as a result of the technology boom, as well as record high oil and commodity prices. The Islamic banking system enjoys higher positive returns compared to its conventional counterparts. Additionally, returns in the IBF sector have been relatively stable during recent financial crises, such as the global financial crisis (GFC) in 2007 and the Asian financial crisis (AFC) in 1997.

Moreover, IBF has the potential to play a crucial role in supporting the implementation of the Sustainable Development Goals (SDGs). In the face of significant financing needs for the SDGs, Islamic finance has untapped potential as a substantial and non-traditional source of financing for the SDGs. The growth of Islamic finance has been rapid over the past two decades, including GFC and AFC periods.[6] This can be seen as a result of religiously based investment made by a large number of Muslims. The main motivating factor may be the risk-sharing characteristics, which can play a key role in mobilizing funds to long-term investments. This is a pertinent example of how IBF can be utilized to release the potential of long-term financing that advances social, environmental, and economic goals (see Islamic Development Bank Group 2018).[7]

The aim of this chapter is to review recent literature on the IBF industry. Divided into four sections, the chapter follows the development of Islamic finance from its historical background to its modern advancement. It begins with a brief introduction of the history associated with the IBF industry in the time of the Prophet Muhammad (PBUH). The proceeding sections present the major products of IBF and discuss the complexity of risk associated with the industry. The final section contains some concluding remarks.

2.2 History of Islamic banking and its recent development

The establishment of Islamic banking, in its wider sense, dates back to the early days of Islam and the rise of the Islamic Empire in the 6th century. Various consequential Islamic governments thrived in internal and external trades, and thus formed Islamic financial tools such as deposits, money transfers, checks and bills of exchange to cope with these commercial developments. IBF history is a new phenomenon based on old financial instrument. Its historical development can be divided into three parts: (i) the

Era of the Prophet and the orthodox caliphs, (ii) the Umayyad and Abbasid Eras, and (iii) the modern day. In the following section, we will briefly elaborate on the development of IBF in various eras.

2.2.1 The Era of the Prophet and the orthodox caliphs

The concept of IBF started in 595 CE, when Prophet Muhammad (PBUH) entered into a profit-and-loss sharing (PLS) contract with Khadijah, a wealthy business woman who later became his wife. Throughout his lifetime, Prophet Muhammad (PBUH) was involved in various modes of financial transaction. Some of these include *Shirkah* (partnership based on PLS), *Al qard Al hassan* (benevolent loan), *Salam* (Forward contract), *Sarf* (exchange), and *Ijarah* (leasing). These fundamental modes of IBF were developed further by the four rightly guided caliphs, following the death of the Prophet. The first caliph, Abu Bakr Assidique (632–634 CE) established an institution of *zakat* to be paid by capable individuals to the state's central bank, as a compulsory alms (or charity) and one of the five pillars of Islam – all Muslim must pay 2.5% *zakat* out of their annual savings if the total is more than the Nisab for an entire year at any given month.

The second caliph, Umar ibn Al-Khattab (634–644 CE), made dramatic reforms in the economic policy of the Islamic state. Namely, the introduction of a centralized and permanent *Bait al-mal* (the Treasury House) in which all the state's earnings, including *Zakat* and tax, should be deposited for appropriate use by the government. The third caliph, Uthman ibn Affan (644–656 CE) was the first Muslim ruler who adopted precious metal coins as the state money. He introduced gold and silver coins into an Islamic financial system to run Islamic state business with rest of the world. The last caliph, Ali ibn Abi Talib (656–661 CE) established equidistributional of wealth and financial justices based on Islamic financial products which were established by earlier caliphs. He instructed governors of various regions under Islamic state to adopt simple lifestyle and establish strict financial management system to encourage savings and investment in infrastructure development. The post-661 CE era is called the *Period of the Noble Companions and the Succeeding Generations,* who further advanced as a result of the tremendous increase in commercial interaction between merchants in the Islamic state and the rest of the world. During this period, academic scholars concentrated on the development of *fiqh* (Islamic jurisprudence) and furthered economic reforms which were based on self-exerted judgment *(Ijtihad)* to cater for the rising demand of IBF.

2.2.2 The Umayyad and Abbasid Eras

The Umayyad Caliphate (661–750 and 1031 CE) became one of the largest unitary states in history and one of the few states to ever extend direct rule over three continents. When the Abbasid's took over from the Umayyad, one of the Umayyad family members, Abd al-Rahman ibn Mu'awiya, migrated to modern Spain, resulting in an Umayyad Caliphate in Al-Andalus (or the Caliphate of Córdoba), which lasted until 1031 CE. The period was characterized by an expansion of trade and culture, where the IBF industry thrived and advanced. As the financial hub of Europe, the state of Córdoba saw the innovation and successful practice of IBF products such as PLS, Musharkah, Mudarbah and Murabaha, deposits, money transfers, checks and bills of exchange. As the capital of the Umayyad Caliphate shifted to Damascus, the Treasury House was formed as a separate building designated as *Bait al-mal*, which was still significant during the Abbasid and Mamluk periods that followed. The Abbasid's used Gold dinar and silver dirham as mediums of exchange. On the other hand, the Ottoman empire had minimal contribution to IBF, as they focused on socio-economic development. The historical details are summarized in Table 2.1.

2.2.3 Modern-days experiments of Islamic banking and finance

Islamic financial practices gradually withered as a result of the demise of Islamic empires such as the Umayyad, Mughal, and Ottoman empires. The rise of western colonial powers in the 16th century resulted in the replacement of IBF practices by interest bearing western financial models.

Table 2.1 Islamic Banking at an Historical Glance

Islamic Banking Brief History		
During Prophet Era 570–632 CE	*Period of the Caliphs: (632–661 CE)*	*The Umayyad and Abbasid Eras (661–1258 CE)*
1 *Musharkah* or *Shirkah* (partnership) based on PLS. 2 *Al-Qard al-Hassan* (No interest – benevolent loan). 3 *Salam* (Forward) contract. 4 *Sarf* (exchange of money), i.e. gold for gold and silver for silver at the same sitting. 5 *Ijarah* (leasing). 6 Trans-regional trade involved trade caravans from Makkah to greater Syria and back. 7 *Zakat* (2.5% the obligatory giving of alms to the poor and needy)	1 Abu Bakr Siddiq – Established obligatory *Zakat* Institution. 2 Umar ibn Al-Khattab – Established *Bait al-mal* (the Federal Treasury House). 3 Uthman ibn Affan – The introduction of the first Muslim Gold/Silver coins. 4 Ali ibn Abi Talib – Strengthened the Prophet and former caliphs' established sustainable economic and financial policies.	1 Issuance of Islamic dirham and dinar coins. 2 Treasury House extension as central *Bait al-mal*. 3 The Central Bank/ Treasury House became significant during the Abbasid era and the dinar (Gold) and dirham (Silver) were still being used as mediums of exchange 4 Establishment of House of Wisdom. (To innovate new business, promote science, engineering, and finance.) 5 Establishment of the Institution of *Ijtihad*.

However, the demise of these powers after the Second World War led to the revival of IBF in Muslim countries – an event widely known as the beginning of the era of Islamic resurgence. The emergence of several Islamic scholars and movements became the impetus for Muslims to apply Islamic teachings in all areas of human endeavors, including economics and finance, as part of *mumalat*. As a result, the elimination of *Ribah* from the economic and banking system became an increasingly common focus amongst contemporary Islamic scholars. The historical date-wise events in this new era of IBF industry are given in Table 2.2.

Table 2.2 Modern History IBF from 1962 to 2016

Time line	*Country*	*IBF Activities*
1940	Malaysia	The objective of the first institution in Malaysia was to invest prospective pilgrim savings in the real estate and plantations in accordance with *Shari'ah* but it was unsuccessful.
1947–1962	Pakistan	In 1947, Pakistan establishment a local Islamic Bank in the rural area in which land owners deposited their money to the bank, which was later loaned to other land owners for the purpose of agriculture development. In 1962 when the State Bank of Pakistan (SBP) was asked to explore the possibilities of implementing IBF in the country. The IBF products included PLS, Mudarbah, Musharkah, and Islamic deposits – held by fully-fledged Islamic banks and Islamic windows of conventional banks. These banks attract 9.7% of total bank deposits and offer Islamic Financial Services with a value of 9% of banking assets in the country. Pakistan becomes the first nation to "Islamize" banking practices at the state level, and this process continues until 1985. Currently, there are eight IBFs in Pakistan.
1963–1967	Egypt	Mit Ghamr Local Savings Bank in Egypt started the first modern-day trial of Islamic banking by Ahmad El Najjar but there is no reference to Islam due to the secular dictatorial regime of Gamal Abdel Nasser.
1963–1969	Malaysia	The Malaysian Pilgrims Savings Corporation was incorporated in 1962 but not launched until 30 September 1963. It became the Board of Tabung Haji in 1969, facilitating Islamic believers' savings for their pilgrimage to Makkah by investing in *Shari'ah*-compliant investment.
1975	Saudi Arabia	In October 1975, the umbrella Islamic financing institution, the Islamic Development Bank (www.isdb.org) opens in Jeddah, Saudi Arabia. It gave the Islamic finance industry an international presence, recruited member countries, and then offered them financial products to promote economic and community development. Between 1975 and 2005 it funded more than $50 billion worth of projects in Organisation of Islamic Cooperation (OIC) member countries.

Time line	*Country*	*IBF Activities*
1975	UAE	Dubai Islamic Bank (DIB) was the first fully-fledged Islamic world commercial bank to start operating in 1975. The DIB model was based on five main business operations: retail banking, corporate banking, real estate, investment banking, and proprietary trading investments.
1976		The Islamic Economics Institute (IEI) is an academic institution that promotes the 'Just economic system' as a way to achieve human happiness. IEI believes in concerted efforts to make this aim possible. It was established in 1976 as a research center, and evolved into an "Institute" in 2011, to provide educational graduate programs, and to serve the private sector by conferring diplomas and implementing training courses.
1977	Egypt and Sudan	Faisal Islamic Bank was established with major branches in Egypt and in Sudan.
1977	Kuwait	Kuwait Finance House was established in 1977, and it is the largest IBF in the world with branches in the UK, Australia, and Malaysia.
1978	Jordan	Jordan Islamic Bank established in Amman in 1978.
1979	Sudan	In 1979, the first Islamic insurance (or *Takāful*) company – the Islamic Insurance Company of Sudan – was established. (Muslims cannot purchase conventional insurance products because those products involve interest-based transactions, uncertainty, and gambling, which are all prohibited by Islamic law.)
1979	Iran	Soon after the Islamic revolution in 1979 (lead by Ayatollah Khomeini) the Islamic Republic of Iran's national banking system was transformed to 100% IBF. In 1983, the Law of Usury-Free Banking was passed, and on March 21, 1984, it was implemented to all sorts of public and private banks and financial institutions.
1983	Malaysia	July 1983: Malaysia opens its first official *Shari'ah*-compliant bank, known as Bank Islam Malaysia. Other banks also offer Islamic products and are supervised by the central bank, which is advised by a board of *Shari'ah* scholars.
1983	Sudan	Sudan reforms its banking system on Islamic principles after President Gaafar Al-Nimeiry establishes *Shari'ah* law. Dual banking system develops, wherein it is Islamic in the north and conventional in the south.
1984	Iran	Iran switches to interest-free banking at the national level after passing a 1983 Islamic banking law that was promised in the 1979 Islamic revolution. The second country to fully Islamisize it's banking services.
1986	USA	The Amana Income Fund, the world's first Islamic mutual fund (which invests only in *Shari'ah*-compliant equities), was created in Indiana.
1987	Saudi Arabia	Al Rajhi Bank was established, and it is now one of the largest banks in the Muslim world. Its branches are now operating in the KSA, UAE, Malaysia, Indonesia, and Turkey.
1990	Bahrain	The international Islamic accounting standards organization known as Accounting and Auditing Organization for Islamic Financial Institutions (www.aaoifi.com) was established in Bahrain by the IDB.

(*Continued*)

Time line	*Country*	*IBF Activities*
1991	Indonesia	Indonesia's first officially sponsored Islamic bank, Bank *Muamalat*, established.
1993	Malaysia	Negara Malaysia (BNM) began offering *Shari'ah*-approved products and services through the Islamic window which is also known as the Interest-free Banking Scheme (IFBS) in 1993.
1996	Bahrain	Citibank began offering Islamic banking services when it established the Citi Islamic Investment Bank in Bahrain.
1999	USA, Malaysia, UAE	The Dow Jones Islamic Market Index (DJIMI) was established, becoming the first successful benchmark for the performance of Islamic investment funds.
2002	Malaysia	The international standard setting organization known as the Islamic Financial Services Board (IFSB, see www.ifsb.org) was established in Kuala Lumpur to set the standards for Islamic financial institutions.
2004	UK	Islamic Bank of Britain – the country's first *Shari'ah*-compliant high street bank – opens in London.
2006	UAE	Dubai's main stock exchange, the Dubai Financial Market, announces it is restructuring itself to become the world's first Islamic bourse.
2009	Singapore	Singapore launches the first Islamic bond program in its competition with Malaysia for market share.
2009	Indonesia	Indonesia, the world's most populous Muslim country, sells its first retail *Shari'ah*-compliant bonds, known as *sukuk*.
2009–2010	Australia	Launches the first ever IBF program and organizes the world's largest IF conference in the Australasian region. At the 2010 IFN conference in Malaysia, Federal Minister Nick Sherry announces government's commitment to IBF with new IBF regulations.
2014	UAE	The UAE Islamic banking sector was valued at US$127 billion at the beginning of 2014 and is expected to reach to US$265 billion by the end of 2019.
2016	North America	Thomson and Reuters in its 2016 report estimate that in Canada alone, 8–10 billion IF activities will be required in the near future. It states that Canada's Islamic finance aspirations are strong in several areas: across asset management, Islamic investment fund, *Shari'ah* mortgages, *sukuk*, retail and wholesale banking, and as a source of foreign capital. These will benefit the country's companies and its government operations, given that Canada has large infrastructure investment needs to carry on future projects.

However, the inability of IBF to successfully integrate within the economy in the early 20th century can be seen as a result of various factors, the most prominent of which was excess demand in credit – where the number of borrowers exceeded the amount of money being leant. This rising dynamic between available capital and credit demand, as well as a lack of autonomy for employees in the banking system, can be seen as major setbacks in the integration of IBF in the early 20th century.

2.3 IBF products and its recent development

The process of *Ijtihad* allows innovation within the IBF industry to meet the increasing demand of both Muslims and non-Muslims. In general, the modes of Islamic finance are divided in four major types: (i) participatory mode, (ii) sale mode, (iii) rent-based mode, and (iv) Islamic capital market (ICM) based modes of financing capital.

Participatory Mode	Sale Mode	Rent-Based Mode	ICM
Mudarba	Murabaha	Ijarah	*Sukuk*
Musharkah	Istisna	Tawarruq	Takāful
Diminishing Partnership	Salam		Re-takāful

The most popular and practiced products in the Islamic Financial Industry are *Murabaha, Bai Bithaman Ajil (BBA)*, and *Tawarruq*. The second most frequently used is *Ijarah*, and the least practiced modes of finance in the world are *Musharkah and Mudarbah*. For financing capital, the most popular products among Muslims and non-Muslims are *sukuk* and *Takāful*. For the sake of continuity in our understanding, these products are defined below:

2.3.1 Brief explanation of historical IBF products

The IBF products can broadly be divided into two major classes: equity-based and debt-based. Among equity-based products the most common are *Mudarbah* and *Musharkah* (partnership financing). Equity financing are the joint ventures between the banks and individuals. Debt-based financing, which tends to involve lending and providing credit, is the more popular group of products, and is provided by Islamic banks. In terms of debt-based products, there is a very broad range, and can be divided into leasing and forward sale financing.[8]

i BBA: It is a sale in which the payment is at a deferred time and price, with the bank purchasing goods on a deferred payment basis (Shanmugam and Zaharina, 2009). The sale is on a cost-plus basis, in which there is a guarantee on the deferred payment price of goods, regardless of the costs which amount to the price (such as markups). In such sales, both parties involved must agree and know the costs, profits, and markup of the transaction in question. In most occasions, such sales involve a third party (Obaidullah, 2005). BBA is however a predominantly Malaysian practice but is now being practiced in other countries.

ii *Murabahah*: A debt-based product whereby the bank, on a customers' request, purchases goods and then sells it to the customer at a marked-up price. This form of financing tends to be used on the short term and currently is the backbone of Islamic financing (Shanmugam and Zaharina, 2009).

iii *Ijarah* (leasing): It is the hiring of a physical object or asset, in which payments are made on predetermined rentals. The bank is never the actual user of the asset, as they have purchased the asset on the request of the customer. However, the bank legally owns the asset, regardless of whether the full payment has been received for the asset. Based on the pre-agreed rentals of the item, the bank is able to receive substantial returns on the asset over time. The bank essentially is the vendor of the asset for the period of the leasing. At the end of the period of leasing, the asset still remains owned by the bank. This differs from *Murabahah*, where the assest's ownership is then transferred to the customer.

iv *Salam* (Deferred Delivery Sale): It is when there is a forward agreement established for goods, where delivery is deferred. Under such an agreement the trader can sell the goods and attain short-term funds immediately, and then would receive the full payment once the delivery has taken place. Bai Salam is a form of deferred delivery whereby the bank purchases goods from sellers as a forward sale and then sells the goods upon attainment in the market.

v *Istisna* (Manufacturer Sale): It is a form of forward sale which is specific to manufactured goods. Both the buyer and the seller form a contract for a sale on goods which will be manufactured in the future, with the price set beforehand. The buyer must however be fully aware of the specifications of the sale. The sale takes place with the bank as the mediator between the buyer and seller.

vi *Istijrar*: It is the delivery of a commodity in installment, over a period of time. The payment is made for total commodity over a period of time. The time and payment price of the commodity is fixed when the contract is made.

vii Qard or Qard Hassan (no interest loans): This is when an amount of capital is borrowed by a customer and then returned on maturity without any additional charges of interest. Essentially, it is an interest-free loan, with the borrower only charged a small sum to cover the administrative expenses. Recent development in the application of Qard Hassan can be seen in Australia.[9]

viii Partnerships financing: There are two main asset-based and assets-backed products provided by Islamic banks (*Mudarbah* and *Musharkah*) in the form of financial partnerships between the bank and the investor/entrepreneur.

a *Mudarbah*: It is more entrepreneurial in financing than Musharkah. Both forms of financial involve the bank providing capital finance for a certain or specific venture identified by the customer. Although the bank is the owner of the capital, management and success lies with the entrepreneur. When setting up such a partnership, the bank and the entrepreneur first establish a business plan which indicates the venture and the purpose and flow of capital. After this the entrepreneur establishes the business and operation and generates (after a period of time) either a profit or loss. The profit is shared on a predetermined ration between the bank and the entrepreneur with any loss being absorbed by the bank, which would reduce the overall value of the assets and investment.

b *Musharkah*: This is more so a joint venture, in which both the customer and the bank equally contribute to the investment. Both the bank and the customer pool capital together which is then invested into a venture, with the profit-sharing ratio being predetermined. The losses are also shared in relation to the amount of capital invested by each party. After both the customer and the client have established a business plan for the venture, they jointly contribute capital and share responsibilities of managing the business and its operations on pre-agreed terms.

Adeinat, Al Rahahleh, and Bhatti (2019) stated that IBF in the current banking environment concentrates on debt-based financing and is hesitant to offer equity-based financing contracts. The main reason is the higher credit risk associated with equity financing as compared with debt-based financing, as a result of greater risk in equity financing for banks if the lessee does not provide collateral (Ariffin, Kassim, and Abdul Razak, 2015). Samad, Gardner, and Cook (2005) have shown that in the IBF context, mark-up products, such as *Murabahah* and *Ijarah*, are easily the most popular such that they dominate Islamic banking.

2.3.2 New financial products (new innovations)

i Cryptocurrency-Bitcoin

Meera (2018) stated that "cryptocurrency is a digital money that is made highly secure using some leading edge cryptography technology. It secures the issuance of the digital money, its transfers and its historical chronological transactions record" (p. 477). Currently, Bitcoin is the most popular form of cryptocurrency.

Bitcoin has long been subject to debate on its compliance with the Islamic world of finance. Meera (2018) concludes that cryptocurrencies that are not backed with real assets are not *Shari'ah*-compliant. However, the majority of *Shari'ah* scholars are leaning towards approving Bitcoin on a basis of maslahah. Meera (2018) also concludes that gold-backed cryptocurrencies are argued to be desirable and consistent with the *maqasid al Shari'ah*. Asif (2018) concludes that although the technology of cryptocurrencies in itself is Halal, the cryptocurrency ecosystem consists of both Halal and Haram elements. Evans (2015) analyses the blockchain technology along with Bitcoin, he concludes that both conform to the requirements laid out by Islamic law. Adam (2017) argues that although Bitcoin possesses the traits of wealth and legal value, it fails to stand as a currency, yet any return attained would be lawful according to Islam.

ii Islamic Derivatives Products

In this subsection, we will examine IBF contracts that have derivative-like features that can be used for the same purpose of hedging as forwards, futures, options, and swaps. Kunhibava (2010) states that there are two main schools of thought regarding the status of derivatives in Islamic finance. The first one, with the majority of scholars opposed to the conventional derivatives (i.e., forwards, futures, and options) are impermissible in Islamic finance. However, there is a need to find Islamic alternatives that comply with the *Shari'ah* or develop derivative-like instruments (e.g., *salam, istisna, arbun, wa'd,* and *Jialah*). Uddin (2015) pointed out that majority of the scholars argue that conventional futures are not permissible under Islamic law because of specific features, such as delay in both counter values, sale of one debt for another, excessive uncertainty, and speculation. The second school of thought,[10] which is the minority view, believes that conventional derivatives are a greatly needed tool to enable Islamic finance to proceed to further heights.

Research on Islamic derivatives from the perspective of Islamic law is still in its early stages. Uddin (2015) pointed out that futures contracts are being urged to be reconsidered by the ulama' for hedging purposes and still unresolved. He further states that "although the issue has been addressed by a number of institutions, such as Makkah-based *Fiqh* Academy, ... the outcome of these discussions has been to urge the prohibition of derivatives"(pp. 4).

Kunhibava (2010) and Uddin (2015) pointed out that Malaysia resolved that commodity futures, as well as several others, are permissible and in accord with *Shari'ah* law. In 1997, the *Shari'ah* Advisory Council (SAC) of the Securities Commission in Malaysia concluded that commodity futures on Crude Palm Oil contracts are permissible and in accordance with *Shari'ah* principles. In 1998, SAC resolved that trading stock-index futures contracts are allowed, which is accomplished by ensuring that the index component is made up of *Shari'ah*-compliant securities. In November 2006, Malaysia witnessed the signing of the derivative master agreement to document Islamic derivative transactions between Bank Islam Malaysia Bhd. and Bank Muamalat Malaysia Bhd.

Nevertheless, these developments have been primarily based in Malaysia; there has yet to be a similar movement to adopt derivatives in other parts of the Islamic financial world. Perhaps this is due to the overwhelming objections to these instruments.

2.4 Risk associated with IBF industry[11]

The concept of risk in financial institutions consists of two unique attributes that can be applied to both IBF and conventional banks (CB) (Hazli Zakaria and Ghafar Ismail, 2008). Risk in financial institutions can be grouped into systematic and unsystematic risks. Both types of risks will have a negative consequence for financial institutions' performance if they fail to manage operations well. Excessive risk exposure can affect not only the profitability of the banks but also the safety and soundness of banks in the future. The GFC in 2008–2009 witnessed a few established commercial banks collapsing due to their excessive risk-taking activities. Abedifar et al. (2015) find there has been an increased interest in risk in banking in general as well as in the Islamic world following the GFC. Saunders and Cornett (2006) explain in more detail about the types of risks in financial institutions. According to them risk can be categorized into five types: (i) credit risk, (ii) interest rate, (iii) liquidity risk, (iv) underwriting risk, and (v) operating risk. A few scholars claim that in the case of commercial banks these five categories can be further narrowed down to three major risks: credit risk, market risk, and operational risk (Apostolik, Donohue, and Wnet, 2009; Basel, 2003a; Carey and Stulz, 2005). They argued that these further classifications will help banks' management be more focused and develop better risk management frameworks. These three risk types are explained in more detail below.

Credit risk is defined as risk where the value of a portfolio may change due to unexpected changes in the credit quality of the issuer or trading partner (McNeil, Frey, and Embrechts, 2005). Changes in credit quality such as downgrading of borrowers in an internal or external rating system can cause losses to financial institutions. Marrison (2002), Hull (2007) and Arunkumar and Kotreshwar (2005) define credit risk as the possibility of the borrower, bond issuers, or counter-parties defaulting or being unable to meet the contractual obligation and repay back the promised amount. Financing is the main source of income for commercial banks, and therefore credit risk cannot be avoided.

Market risk arises due to uncertainty about cash flows emanating from changes in the value of financial instruments caused by the adverse movement of market indicators. These include, for example, interest rates, market prices, and exchange rates. Bangia et al. (2002) claim that market risk is a risk related to portfolio value changes driven by trading returns. Trading return can be calculated by estimating the difference between bids and asking price of financial instruments. Therefore, the more volatile the prices, the greater the market risk.

Operating risk is a potential risk where the technology or support system may malfunction or break down. A failure in back-office systems is one example of operational risk. However, according to Saunders and Cornett (2006) operational risk is not only limited to technology or system failure, but at least five sources of operational risk: technology, employees, customer relationships, capital assets, and external events. Basel (2003b) defines operational risk as the risk of losses resulting either from inadequate or failed internal processes, people, and systems, or from external events. Operational risk has become an important part of financial institutions' risk management partly because it was highlighted by the Basel Committee on Banking Supervision (BCBS), and partly because of disruptions associated with the September 11, 2001, attacks. Since then financial institutions have increasingly allocated capital to operational risk (Carey and Stulz, 2005). A survey done by Vasseux (2009) on ten large international banks reveals that banks allocated 53% of their economic capital to credit risk, 26% to operational risk and other risks, and 21% to market risk and asset-liability rate risks.[12] A higher proportion of operational risk compared to market risk shows that banks start to realize the impact of operational risk on their functions and therefore are making more effort to allocate more capital.

Iqbal and Mirakhor (2007) discuss risks in IBFs. They classified risk in IBFs into four major categories: financial risk, business risk, treasury risk, and governance risk. In the discussion of categories of risk by Iqbal and Mirakhor (2007), they do not explain which one belongs to systematic and unsystematic risk. Al Rahahleh, Bhatti, and Misman (2018) proposed a framework for the grouping of risk for IBFs by making some changes to the previous discussions. Figure 2.1 illustrates the risk profile of IBFs by considering systematic and unsystematic risk classification. This framework divides risk into three main groups: systematic, unsystematic, and a

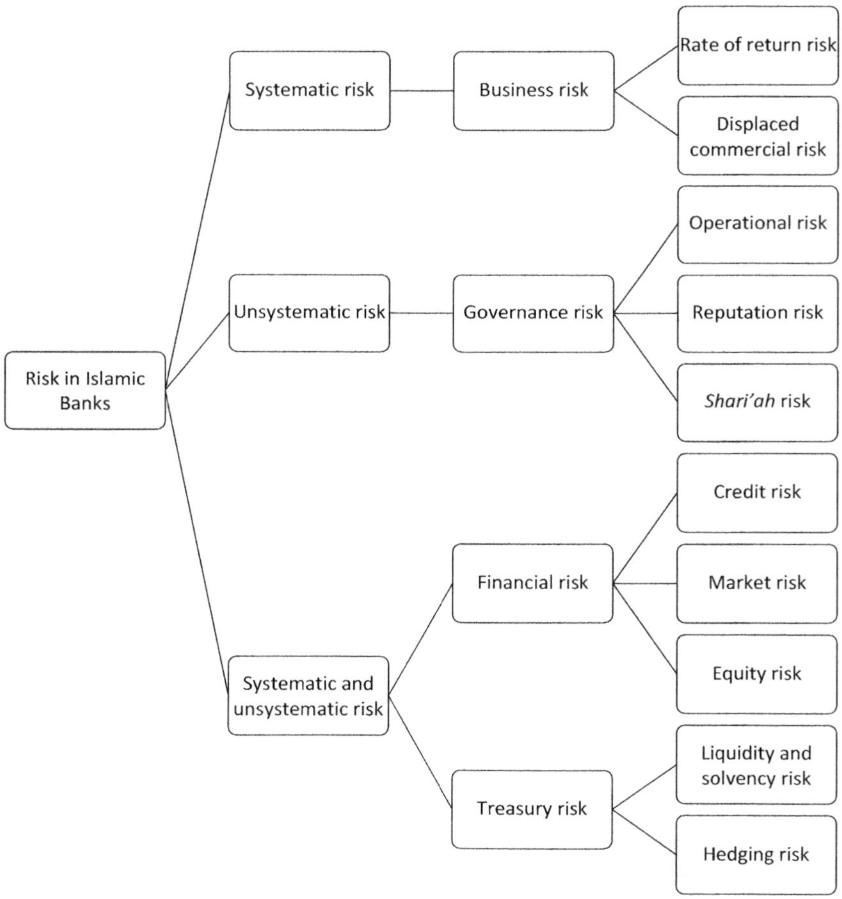

Figure 2.1 Classification of risks in IBFs.

combination of the two called SUR. Under this new framework, only business risk belongs to systematic risk. Governance risk that consists of operational, reputation, and *Shari'ah* risk is classified under unsystematic risk. The other two groups of risks are financial risk and treasury risk, and they are classified under SUR and not under the traditional types of risk. This is because systematic and unsystematic risks are due to their very nature.

Financial risk consists of credit, market, and equity risk and cannot only be classified under systematic or unsystematic risk because the risk involved comes from both external and internal sources. For example, credit risk is of a default payment by the borrower, but in the case of IBFs, banks operating as an entrepreneur or buyer, in that IBFs provide financing rather than just a normal loan. Therefore, credit risk in IBFs may result from changes in economic or market conditions or from internal weaknesses of the banks. In *Shari'ah* an Islamic bank is either an investor or seller when it provides financing to its customers. In this way, it will be able to control risk exposure when making decisions about providing any finance. The failure to making the right decision will contribute to the possibility of credit risk in the future. Risk becomes a big challenge in IBFs particularly in an age of globalization. In order to ensure the survival of IBFs in the finance market, any issues concerning risk and its management must be handled properly and not jeopardize *Shari'ah* prohibitions.

2.5 Development in ICM

Recent trends in global capital markets have been driven by a gradual pickup in economic conditions, global policy uncertainties, and emerging and developed markets' causality forward and backward relations in terms of risk vis-à-vis return balance. The year 2016/2017 witnesses an increase in investors' risk appetite, strengthening of the stock market in many jurisdictions, and a moderation in financial volatility amid a generally optimistic global financial and liquidity environment. In this section, we attempt to show the ICM expansion and current situation effecting the future IBF industry.

2.5.1 Sukuk industry

Global *sukuk* issuances in 2017 saw a growth of 22.8%, with the total volume of annual issuances reaching US$91.9 billion as at the end of 2017, compared to US$74.8 billion in 2016. This continues the gradual recovery of *sukuk* markets over the past two years following the sharp contraction observed in 2015. At the end of 2017, the total volume of *sukuk* outstanding stood at US$399.92 billion, which represents a 10% growth in volume of *sukuk* outstanding from 2016. However, total issuances for 2017 still remain below the US$131 billion mark – the highest annual volume of *sukuk* issuances to date – although the recent growth trajectory indicates a gradual closing of this gap (IFSB 2018).

2.5.2 *Takāful industry*

The global takāful industry has sustained double-digit growth in recent years although growth has moderated in key markets, owing to challenging economic conditions, complex regulations, and compliance and operational challenges in the takāful industry. In 2016, the global insurance market reported steady growth rates, supported mainly by emerging markets. Non-life premiums in emerging Asia expanded at a rate of 7.3% in 2016, after a strong 9% growth in 2015. Another notable trend in emerging Asia was the slowdown in motor insurance uptake following lower car sales. The expansion of general takāful business outpaced that of family product line, aided mainly by mandatory covers in the medical and motor businesses.

2.5.3 *Future of Islamic finance industry*

The global IBF industry has grown rapidly over the past two decades, reaching total assets of US$2.2 trillion as of the end of December 2016 – an increase of 7% over 2015. In keeping with this growth, *Shari'ah*-compliant financial products and services have increased their reach to more than 50 Muslim and non-Muslim countries. Asian countries such as Japan, South Korea, Hong Kong, and China are tapping up with the industry. In predominantly Muslim countries, governments have enacted laws such as the Islamic Financial Services Act 2013 in Malaysia and Act No. 21 of 2008 in Indonesia to provide *Shari'ah*-compliant legal frameworks for the regulation of Islamic banks and their business operations. There is also growing demand for IBF in non-Muslim countries, fueled by individuals and corporations seeking safe and ethical banking solutions. This broader popularity is evident in the change of Australian regulation can now cater the need of IBF regulations. Similarly, UK Financial Services Authority's policy of fairness and justice is in line with the guidelines set out by the IFSB 2018. The sector is expected to continue to expand in 2018 with the same rate as previous years.

2.6 Concluding remarks

This is a comprehensive review chapter covering all the aspects of IBF industry. It begins with the first ever IBF contract between Prophet Muhammad (PBUH) in 595 CE with Khadija, the richest business women of Arabia at that time. Since then the practice of various IBF contracts continued during his life time and soon after. The IBF contract practices strictly follow *Shari'ah* laws which were implemented by all caliphs in all over Islamic empire, called Caliphate from 632 CE. The IBF institutional structure was observed by Umayyad, Abbasid, Al-Andalus (Spain – 1031 CE), and Ottomans and the Moghuls empires (1530 CE).

IBF's recent operation started from Pakistan in 1947, followed by Malaysia and Egypt in 1963 from a small town of Mit Ghamr's (MG). The chapter discuss historical development of IBF products from the very beginning until the 21st century. It reviews various products in a summarized tabular format and analyses issues of risk associated with the IBF industry. The chapter concludes with a summary of many new contracts and products based on derivatives, cryptocurrencies, blockchain, and an innovative approach to IBF industry.

Notes

1 Banking functions operated, as deposit-taking institutions (ADIs), facilitate intermediation between savers and investors; transfer funds from surplus units to deficit units; and manage payments and clearing systems (EFTPOS, cards, BPAY, cheques, etc.). IBF is based on three main rules: They (i) are not involved in business activities where there is *Ribah* (interest, usury), *gharar* (excessive uncertainty), and *haram* (impermissible) activities; (ii) operate on PLS principle; and (iii) emphasize productivity and real economic activity rather than credit worthiness.

2 The *Quran* is the holy book for all Muslims and their main source of guidance when conducting their daily lives and activities, to seek pleasure of God – Almighty Allah $(\Omega)^{\infty}$ through two major kinds of actions: first, doing *Ibadah* (Ωi: man-to-God relationship to enhance spirituality); and second, *Muamalat* (Ωm: man-to-man relationship) which covers socio-economic, geopolitical, business, social, and education activities. Thus, the objective is to maximize $\Omega = \Omega i \cup \Omega m$. If Ωm is not achieved up to the required level then life after death will be one of miseries spent in hell. So, there exists a positive unidirectional causality between Ωm and paradise.

3 *Ribah* is divided into two major categories: (i) *Ribah An-Nasee'ah* relates to *Ribah* in debt and (ii) *Ribah Al-Fadl* which refers to *Ribah* in exchange.

4 For Choudhury's epistemological Tauhidi Model, see details in Choudhury and Bhatti (2016). Islamic finance assets are expected to reach US$3.2 trillion by the end of 2020 (refer to www.arabianbusiness.com).

5 Basov and Bhatti (2016).

6 https://blogs.worldbank.org/category/tags/islamic-finance.

7 www.irti.org/English/News/Documents/GRIF-2018-Overview.pdf.

8 Some of these definitions are taken from Basov and Bhatti (2016), Shanmugam and Zaharina (2009) and Obaidullah (2005).

9 Islamic council of victoria Qard Hassan product building bridges between Muslims and non-Muslims: www.icv.org.au/icv-stories-nils.

10 For more information on these differing views, please refer to Kunhibava (2010) and Uddin (2015).

11 Some of the material in this section is taken from our joint paper entitled "Developments in Risk Management in Islamic Finance: A Review". Working paper 1440–1, Dept of Finance, King Abdulaziz University, Jeddah, KSA.

12 See Kuritzkes, Schuermann and Weiner (2002).

References

Abedifar, P., Ebrahim, M.S., Molyneux, P., and Tarazi, A. (2015). Islamic Banking and Finance: Recent Empirical Literature and Directions for Future Research. *Journal of Economic Surveys*, 29(4), pp. 637–670.

Adam, M. (2017). Shariah Interpretations of Bitcoin. Retrieved from https://afinance.org/2017/12/30/shariah-interpretations-of-cryptocurrencies.

Adeinat, I., Al Rahahleh, N., and Bhatti, M.I. (2019). Customer Satisfaction with Ijarah Financing: The Mediating Role of Clarity and Accuracy for Services Offered. Qualitative Research in Financial Markets, forthcoming.

Al Rahahleh, N., Bhatti, M. I., and Misman, F. (2018). Developments in Risk Management in Islamic Finance: A Review". Working paper 1440–1, Dept. of Finance, King Abdulaziz University, Jeddah, KSA.

Apostolik, R., Donohue, C., and Wnet, P. (2009). *Foundations of Banking Risk: An Overview of Banking, Banking Risks and Risk-Based Banking Regulation*. Hoboken, NJ: John Wiley and Sons Inc.

Ariffin, N. M., Kassim, S. H., and Abdul Razak, D. (2015). Exploring Application of Equity-Based Financing through Musharkah Mutanaqisah in Islamic Banks in Malaysia: Perspective from the Industry Players. *International Journal of Economics, Management and Accounting*, 23(2), pp. 241–261.

Arunkumar, R., and Kotreshwar, G. (2005). Risk Management in Commercial Banks (A Case Study of Public and Private Sector Banks). SSRN eLibrary.

Asif, S. (2018). The Halal and Haram Aspect of Cryptocurrencies in Islam. *Journal of Islamic Banking and Finance*, 35(2), pp. 91–101.

Bangia, A., Diebold, F. X., Schuermann, T., and Stroughair, J. D. (2002). *Modeling Liquidity Risk, with Implications for Traditional Market Risk Measurement and Management*. US: Springer.

Basel Committee on Banking Supervision. (2003a). Overview of the New Basel Capital Accord: Issued for comment by 31 July 2003. 3rd Consultative Document. April 2003. Bank for International Settlements.

Basel Committee on Banking Supervision. (2003b). The New Basel Capital Accord: Issued for comment by 31 July 2003. 3rd Consultative Document. April 2003. Bank for International Settlements.

Basov, S., and Bhatti, M. I. (2016). *Islamic Finance in the Light of Modern Economic Theory*. London: Pagrave-MacMillan.

Carey, M., and Stulz, R. M. (2005). *The Risks of Financial Institutions*. SSRN eLibrary.

Choudhury, M. A., and Bhatti, M. I. 2016. *Heterodox Islamic Economics: The Emergence of an Ethico-economic Theory*. London: Routledge.

Evans, C. W. (2015). Bitcoin in Islamic Banking and Finance. *Journal of Islamic Banking and Finance*, 3(1). doi:10.15640/jibf.v3n1a1

Hazli Zakaria, R., and Ghafar Ismail, A. (2008). Does Islamic Banks' Securitization Involvement Restrain their Financing Activity? *Humanomics*, 24(2), pp. 95–109.

Hull, J. C. (2007). *Risk Management and Financial Institutions*. Hoboken, NJ: Pearson.

Iqbal, Z., and Mirakhor, A. (2007). *An Introduction to Islamic Finance: Theory and Practice*. Singapore: John Wiley and Son (Asia).

Islamic Development Bank Group. (2018). Global Report on Islamic Finance 2018. Retrieved from www.irti.org/English/News/Documents/GRIF-2018-Overview.pdf.

Islamic Financial Services Board. (2018). Islamic Financial Services Stability Report 2018. Retrieved from www.ifsb.org/sec03.php.

Kunhibava, Sherin, 2010. Derivatives in Islamic Finance. International Shari'ah Research Academy for Islamic Finance (ISRA). Research Paper, No. 7.

Marrison, C. (2002). *The Fundamentals of Risk Measurement*. New York: McGraw-Hill.

McNeil, A. J., Frey, R., and Embrechts, P. (2005). *Quantitative Risk Management: Concepts, Techniques and Tools*. Princeton, NJ: Princeton University Press.

Meera, A. K. M. (2018). Cryptocurrencies from Islamic Perspectives: The Case of Bitcoin. *Bulletin of Monetary Economics and Banking*, 20(4), pp. 475–492.

Obaidullah, M. (2005). *Islamic Finance Services*, Islamic Economics Research Centre: King Abdulaziz University, Jeddah, KSA.

Saunders, A., and Cornett, M. M. (2006). *Financial Institutions Management: A Risk Management Approach* (5th ed.). New York: McGraw-Hill Irwin.

Samad, A., Gardner, N. D., and Cook, B. J. (2005), Islamic Banking and Finance in Theory and Practice: The Experience of Malaysia and Bahrain. *The American Journal of Islamic Social Sciences*, 22(2), pp. 69–86.

Shanmugam, B., and Zahari, Z. R. (2009). A Primer on Islamic Finance, Research Foundation of CFA Institute.

Uddin, M. A. (2015). Conventional Futures: Derivatives from Islamic Law of Contract Perspective, University of Creative Technology, Chittagong, Working Paper, November 2015.

Vasseux, M. (2009). The Next Chapter in Islamic Finance: Higher Rewards but Higher Risks. Oliver Wayman Financial Services.

3 On the role of ownership and governance structure in raising capital

A *sukuk* example

Mohsin Khawaja, M. Ishaq Bhatti and Darren Henry

3.1 Introduction

The decision of a firm to raise capital comes with a number of difficult choices, one of which is the type of security to choose from a range of securities with different features. While raising funds externally the firm faces the trade-off of either choosing equity, which dilutes the ownership stake (Admati et al., 2018; Ellul, 2008; Harris and Raviv, 1998; Israel, 1991; Lu et al., 2012; Stulz, 1988), or issuing debt and facing potential bankruptcy costs (Fama, 1980; Fama and Jensen, 1983; Masulis, 1988). The trade-off eventually leads to the formulation of the firm's capital structure. In other words, the choice of security reflects the shareholders' view through the board of directors on relative risk aversion and their desire for the control of firm. This paper attempts to examine the role of ownership and governance structure of a firm in determining the choice of security to raise capital related to *Shari'ah* compliance product, '*sukuk*'.

In most of the corporate finance literature, the decision to choose between debt and equity is evaluated based on debt as a set of homogenous instruments (Dong et al., 2012; Jung et al., 1996; Loughran, 2008; MacKie-Mason, 1990; Walsh and Ryan, 1997). In other studies the focus remained solely on hybrid securities such as non-core assets (Edmans and Mann, forthcoming 2018), convertible debt, warrants, or preferred shares (Balachandran et al., 2017; Gatchev et al., 2009; Lewis et al., 2003; Suchard and Singh, 2006). However, there are other instruments that firms may use to raise long-term funds with varying degrees of impact on their ownership and governance mechanisms. Our choice of securities for this study includes equity, bonds, syndicated loans, and a recent innovation called *sukuk* – usually referred to as Islamic bonds. *Sukuk*, although branded as debt shares, is categorized as equity due to its risk-sharing nature. Furthermore, *sukuks* are certificates of shares and rights in assets which could be tangible assets, services, or equity of a given project (Yatim, 2009). Hence, from a risk-sharing perspective they lie between equity and debt. Figure 3.1 highlights each of these instruments in a graph based on their relative risk aversion and the shareholders' desire for control.

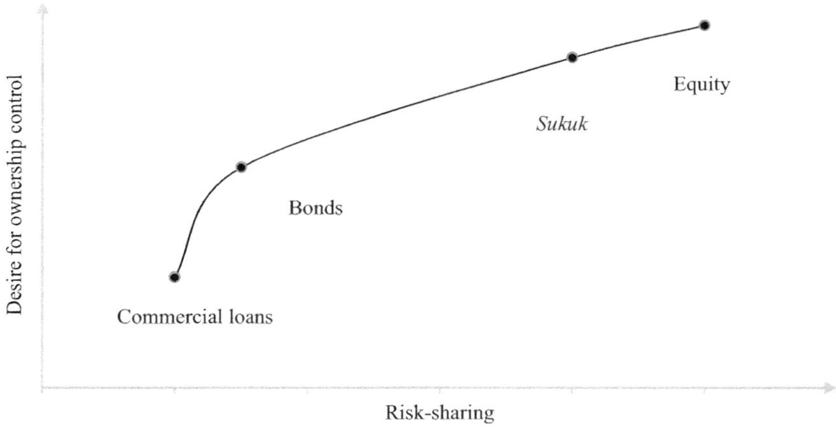

Figure 3.1 A visual display of the trade-off between the desire of ownership control and risk aversion, namely equity, bonds, loans, and *sukuk*. Equity is the least risky security for an issuer but dilutes ownership control while loans are the most risky but do not lead to ownership dilution.

The major capital structure theories addressing firm behaviour related to the choice of funding instruments are static trade-off theory, pecking order theory, market timing theory, and agency theory. Trade-off theory suggests that the choice of new capital instrument, whether equity or debt, is a trade-off of tax shields and bankruptcy costs.[1] Pecking order theory suggests firms prefer debt issuance over equity.[2] Market timing theory, on the other hand, indicates that firms benefit from their high valuation by issuing equity.[3] Agency theory highlights the conflict of interest between shareholders and management in a firm that could lead to circumstances whereby management does not act in the interest of the shareholders.[4] One of the shortcomings of these major capital structure theories, with the exception of agency theory, is that they do not incorporate the influence of ownership structure. Instead, they largely consider the benefit of tax shields or firm's financial strength as the major determinant of security issuance. Findings by Ellul (2008), Liu et al. (2011), Santos et al. (2014), and Mak and Kusnadi (2005) suggest that a firm's ownership structure, and the independence and structure of their board of directors, affects capital issuance (for details refer to Modigliani and Miller 1958). This study extends the corporate finance literature by exploring whether ownership structure and governance mechanisms play any role in the choice of instruments to raise long-term funds subject to the decision of raising funds externally.

Both decisions to raise funds and the selection of a specific financing instrument suggest the presence of a sample selection bias. This is because issuance decisions can be observed over a non-random subsample of firms raising funds. To avoid sample selection bias we use a simultaneous equation model to determine the factors affecting the decision to raise funds and, conditional on the decision to raise funds, the choice of financing instrument based on control and risk aversion motives. We assume that shareholders do not play an active role in the first decision to raise capital, but their role in the second decision of the choice of security is much more pronounced. Management and the board of directors initiate the decision to choose the appropriate security. However, since the board is a proxy for the shareholders, we believe that they reflect the shareholders' desires when they make the second decision. Since the first decision is primarily a binary decision, which does not involve shareholders' views, the board does not have to incorporate shareholders' interests, i.e. they can decide independently if raising capital would be beneficial for the firm or not.

By using a sample of 1,565 firms with 67,734 firm-quarter observations from Malaysia, Indonesia, Singapore, and Pakistan from 2000 to 2015, we find that firms with concentrated ownership are less likely to issue equities to avoid ownership dilution. Similarly, firms with a concentration of power (CEO also acting as the chairperson of the board of directors) prefer debt instruments if such firms are to raise funds externally. Furthermore, the size of boards of directors and the proportion of female members on the board also lead to a higher probability of raising funds externally. However, the higher probability does not reflect any particular preference towards a specific type of financing instrument. Among firm-specific variables, we find that leverage and firm size affects the choice of instruments. Firms that are highly leveraged and larger in size prefer to raise capital using debt-based instruments. However, firms with high future growth potential prefer to raise funds externally using equity financing.

This paper contributes to the literature in several ways. Currently, there is limited research identifying the factors of security issuance based on the nexus of relative risk aversion and firm control. One of the key distinguishing features of this paper is the use of a two-staged model which treats the two decisions on security issuance and risk choice separately, whilst dealing with endogeneity bias. Furthermore, this study extends the literature by testing whether ownership and governance structures affect the choice of security for raising funds. In this study we use a unique data set of firms from countries where corporations have access to a variety of financing instruments when seeking to raise funds (including *sukuk*), allowing us to observe a wider range of securities, each carrying unique risk characteristics.

Findings of this study provide an insight into understanding the nexus of shareholders' desire to control their firms and their relative risk aversion in raising funds, and the choice of financing instrument. These findings could be of interest to investors in better understanding the financing preferences of firms where higher ownership concentration and CEO duality is associated with higher degrees of control and lower risk aversion. Furthermore, such firms have a greater tendency to be highly leveraged, which could potentially drive down firm valuation.

The remainder of the chapter is structured as follows. Paper is motivated by description of the past literature reviews which is presented in Section 2. In Section 3, we describe the model and research methodology used in the chapter. Section 4 is devoted to the summary of the interesting variables used in this study along with research question and hypothesis development. The data details and the measures of important statistics are reported in Section 5. In Section 6, we provide details of multivariate analysis including section reports the estimation results for the empirical model. The model incorporates an equation for the issuance decision for the choice of instrument to raise capital based on the trade-off between control and risk motives. The final section contains some interesting concluding remarks.

3.2 Literature review

One of the major decisions when deciding to raise funds is the choice between debt and equity. This choice reflects the trade-off between control and risk-reduction. Firms may resist equity issuance to avoid dilution of ownership, or they may oppose excessive debt issuance, particularly loans, as they might lead to covenants that reduce their shareholders' potential dividend earnings (Jensen and Meckling, 1976).

Most of the empirical literature investigates the debt-equity trade-off in the context of capital structure and focuses on the change in the proportion of debt and equity in the capital structure. For example, profitable firms adjust their capital structure more rapidly than less profitable firms (Lemma and Negash, 2014). Furthermore, it is well known in the literature that a change in capital structure is a function of the size of operating cash flows which include dividend-paying firms and those with higher credit ratings benefit from having better access to the capital market. Consequently, this leads to the raise of debt more often (Faulkender et al., 2012). However, Lemmon et al. (2008) illustrate empirically through a 38-year study on US firms beginning from 1965 to 2003 that the capital structure of firms is usually stable and does not change more frequently.

On the issue of the choice among debt and/or equity financing, the empirical literature provides mixed findings. On the one hand, proponents of pecking order theory assert that firms use equity financing as a last resort due to information asymmetries, whereas advocates of market timing theory suggest firms would use time equity issuance when they are overvalued or profitable. Furthermore, Dong et al. (2012) suggest that pecking order theory is applicable only when firms are financially constrained. However, Suchard and Singh (2006) find that firms under high financial risk tend to issue warrants as opposed to convertible debt. In another study, Jung et al. (1996), while comparing the role of the agency theory, pecking order theory, and market timing theory in equity issuance, conclude that it is, in fact, agency theory that best explains the equity issuance decision by firms. One of their major findings was that equity financing enhances management's discretion as opposed to that of shareholders. This may suggest that the choice of instrument can be influenced by a conflict of interest between the firm's ownership and its management.

A key element of pecking order theory is the presence of a tax shield which tempts firms to choose debt over equity. MacKie-Mason (1990) found strong evidence of a relationship between tax shields and marginal tax rates, implying that marginal tax rates affect financing decisions. However, Walsh and Ryan (1997) disagree finding that while both tax and agency considerations are important in explaining corporate financing decisions, it is the agency effect that appears to dominate financing decisions. Balachandran et al. (2017) also contend that agency costs are among the prime drivers of equity issuance. The presence of agency conflicts highlights the importance of observing how the governance structure influences financing decisions.

Findings are inconclusive as to how ownership structure can affect the security selection decision when raising funds. Rajan and Zingales (1995) theorize that the presence of a large shareholder lowers agency costs and encourages more equity issuances, whilst raising aversion to debt. Santos et al. (2014) found a negative relationship between ownership concentration and leverage among European firms. Farooq (2015) found similar results while analysing firms from the Middle East and North Africa (MENA) region. He argues that lower levels of leverage is due to information asymmetry associated with ownership concentration. Autore and Kovacs (2010) also contend that higher information asymmetry leads to fewer equity issuances.

The trade-off between control motive and risk-taking (risk aversion) may not be relevant for those firms with higher government ownership, as higher government ownership may encourage more debt issuance due to implied guarantees by the government. Liu et al. (2011) found higher leverage ratios associated with Chinese state-owned enterprises. However, Borisova et al. (2015) found that firms with higher government ownership face higher costs of debt. Evidence regarding institutional ownership suggests that higher institutional ownership has little influence on capital structure (Gillian and Starks, 2000; Karpoff, 2001; Wahal, 1996). However, Boubaker et al. (forthcoming 2017) suggest that long-term institutional ownership not only prefers debt to equity but also makes slower adjustments to capital structure, implying fewer issuance of securities.

Berkovitch and Israel (1996) argue that corporate governance structure also plays a vital role in defining a firm's capital structure. However, Daily et al. (1998) and Vafeas and Theodorou (1998) assert that the duality of CEO and Chairman role (CEO duality) appears to have an insignificant influence on capital structure. CEO duality may also increase agency costs, and lower cost efficiency and profitability (Pi and Timme, 1993). However, Brickley et al. (1997) found empirical evidence which implied that separating the roles of the CEO and the Chairman of the board results in greater agency costs than having dual roles.

The composition of the board of directors may have an influence on the capital structure of the firm. Heng et al. (2012) found evidence of a positive relationship between independent non-executive directors with leverage and an inverse relation between the board size and leverage ratio. However, Pearce and Zahra (1992) suggest that firms with a larger board size have greater reliance on debt financing. On a different note, Eisenberg et al. (1998) found that small boards would have fewer communication and coordination problems, helping to achieve consistent and timely decisions on capital structure. One of the important limitation of this strand of the literature is the limited focus on leverage of firms without any consideration to the efficiency of the financing process and especially the choice of instrument to raise funds.

In terms of board diversity, Adams and Funk (2012) suggest that financing preferences of directors can be different based on gender. More precisely, female board members have a higher tolerance of risk in relation to capital structure. Sila et al. (2016) and Matsa and Miller (2013), on the other hand, assert that risk-seeking or risk aversion is not a significant part of women's approach towards corporate decision-making.

Autore and Kovacs (2010) and Bayless and Chaplinsky (1996) suggest that the presence of information asymmetry plays a vital role in deciding whether a firm uses equity financing. In the presence of information asymmetry, potential investors would be less likely to invest in the equity of firms. They suggest that large firms and those with a greater number of analysts providing recommendations to invest bridge the information asymmetry gap leading to lower information asymmetry, consequently encouraging equity issuance. However, Gatchev et al. (2009) found no evidence of information asymmetry having a significant impact over equity issuance. Instead, their findings suggest that small firms and those with low profitability are more inclined to issue equity. Empirical studies by Titman and Wessels (1988), Rajan and Zingales (1995), Booth et al. (2001), Frank and Goyal (2009), De Jong et al. (2011), Alam et al. (2018), Al Rahahleh et al. (2017), and Al Rahahleh and Bhatti (2017) help to explain that the firm size, asset tangibility, and profitability lean towards raising capital through debt financing while firms with higher growth opportunities may prefer equity issuance. Hovakimian (2006) found that the market-to-book (MBV) ratio has a significant impact on a firm's financing decisions. Similarly, Graham and Harvey (2001), while using multiyear survey data of chief financial officers (CFO) from US corporations, suggest that profitability and stock price overvaluation influence equity issuance, while credit rating, interest rates, and financial flexibility determine bond issuance.

In terms of security choice for raising funds, the empirical literature usually analyses two classes of capital, namely bonds and equities (Hovakimian et al., 2004). However, firms often raise long-term funds using syndicated finance, and, in some jurisdictions, now use *sukuk*. *Sukuk* has largely been the missing link in the corporate finance literature as an instrument of choice for raising capital. *Sukuk* has emerged globally as an Islamic finance product to raise external funds with over $97 billion worth of *sukuk* issued in 2017.[5] Research on *sukuk* has recently gained momentum, with *sukuk* having been analysed in the context of economic determinants of *sukuk* market development (Smaoui and Khawaja, 2016), motivation for issuing *sukuk* (Abdul Halim et al., 2017; Alam et al., 2018; Nagano, 2017), issuer's choice of the type of *sukuk* (Azmat et al., 2014), application of bond ratings on *sukuk* (Azmat et al., 2015), market reactions upon issuance of *sukuk* (Godlewski et al., 2013, 2016; Klein et al., 2018), and corporate determinants of *sukuk* issues (Klein and Weill, 2016; Mohamed et al., 2015; Nagano, 2016).

Most of the studies on the determinants of raising capital analyse the decision of fund raising in a single decision framework although clearly the decision to raise funds and the choice of instruments are two simultaneous decisions. This study attempts to fill this gap by analysing four major sources of capital for long-term funding, namely loans, bonds, *sukuk*, and equity financing in a simultaneous equation framework by focusing on the interaction of ownership control motives and relative riskiness associated with the source of funding. The next section develops a methodology for empirical analysis.

3.3 The model and methodology

The empirical methodology used in this paper is based on the model which premise that a firm decides to raise capital in a two-step sequential process. Once a firm makes the decision to raise capital, in the basic financing model each firm chooses instrument I among J alternatives based on decreasing levels of desired control and higher risk levels. We can only observe the actual choice I_j, where j ∊ {1, …, j}, not the desired instrument I_j^*, a latent continuous variable reflecting the desired level of control and relative riskiness.

Each firm chooses the instrument that maximizes the expected utility of alternative instruments $I_{j,}$ given some observable characteristics x:

$$\text{MAX}_{j \in \{1,\dots,j\}} r(I_j \mid x) - c(I_j \mid x) \tag{1}$$

Each firm maximizes the expected utility by maximizing control c and minimizing relative risk r, associated with raising fund using instrument I_j. The utility maximizing function $\varphi_c(\varphi_r)$ is affected by a set of observable variables x and other random unobservable factors $\varepsilon_c(\varepsilon_r)$. The optimal instrument I_j^* maximizes the utility given certain assumptions (see Lauer, 2002, 2003) that:

$$\Pr(I_j \mid x) = \Pr\left[\mu_{j-1}\frac{1}{\varphi(x)} < \ln\varepsilon \leq h_j\frac{1}{\varphi(x)}\right] \tag{2}$$

where in Equation (2), $\varphi(x)$ is expressed as,

$$\varphi(x) = \frac{\varphi_c}{\varphi_r}, \varepsilon = -\frac{\varepsilon_c}{\varepsilon_r} \text{ and } \mu_j = \ln\left(\frac{r(I_{j+1}) - r(I_j)}{c(I_{j+1}) - c(I_j)}\right)$$

The odds that a firm chooses the desired instrument I_j with expected control and risk are given by the probability that the error term falls between two thresholds. This implies that firms may choose increasing levels of control and riskiness for raising capital given their respective constraints x. The levels of control and riskiness can be expressed in thresholds whereby firms may opt for instrument I_{j+1} if it increases the marginal utility for higher levels of control and lower level of riskiness, and vice versa. $\varphi(x)$ and ε measure the net impact of observable characteristics and unobservable individual heterogeneity on the thresholds h_j, respectively. From Equation (2), one cannot assess the actual control benefits and cost of financial risk related to the behavioural choice of firms for each alternative instrument. However, it is enough to determine how observed variables x influence the perceived marginal benefit of control to the financial risk ratio and, therefore, the choice of instrument.

Assuming that $\varphi(x) = \exp[\beta x]$ and that $\ln \varepsilon$ is normally distributed with mean zero and variance one, we can rewrite Equation (2) as:

$$\Pr(I_j \mid x) = \Phi(h_j - \beta x) - \Phi(h_{j-1} - \beta x) \tag{3}$$

where Φ is the cumulative standard normal distribution function. This expression corresponds to an ordered probit model for behavioural choice.

The behaviour of firms towards risk and control in terms of choice of instruments can be observed only over a non-random sample of those firms who have raised capital. To examine the behaviour of firms in raising capital using a single equation model like ordered probit model as proposed in Equation (3) assuming homogeneity is unrealistic due to the unobserved heterogeneity of non-issuing firms (Heckman et al., 2006). Essentially, the estimation model is similar to Cameron and Heckman (1998) where there is a need to account for two decisions: a binary choice selection decision and a discrete choice of observed ordered behavioural decision.

To account for the two decisions a firm makes, i.e. raise capital and choose security, De Luca and Perotti (2011) suggest an ordered probit model with sample selection through the following bivariate threshold crossing models:

$$I_{it}^{*} = \alpha_0 + \alpha' w_{it} \quad i = 1, \ldots, I \tag{4}$$

$$I_{jt}^{*} = \beta_0 + \beta_1 x_{it} + \varepsilon_{it} \quad \textit{if } I_{it} = 1 \tag{5}$$

where I_{it}^{*} is a latent variable related to the first decision and indicates the likelihood of firm i to raise capital in year t, if $I_{it}^{*} + u_{it} > 0$. w_{it} is a vector of covariates with coefficients α to be estimated. Equation (4) is observed over all sample firms. I_{jt}^{*} is continuous latent variables choice of instrument and is observable through $I_{jt} = \sum_{j=0}^{J} h\, I(\lambda_h < I_{jt}^{*} \leq \lambda_{h+1})$, where $\lambda = 1, \ldots\ldots, \lambda_h$ that partition I_{jt}^{*} into $(h+1)$ exhaustive and mutually exclusive thresholds. Equation (5) is observable only for those firms that issue any instrument, i.e. where $I_{it} = 1$. In Equations (4) and (5), the error terms are assumed to be jointly normally distributed (bivariate normal) with a (unknown) coefficient of correlation between the latent errors u_{it} and ε_{it}. For empirical estimation, the dependent variable, in the case of Equation (5), is a categorical variable based on control-risk motives.

3.4 The variables and hypothesis

Appendix A provides a summary list of variable definitions and their expected signs. We classify our independent variables largely as those related to ownership structure, corporate governance, information asymmetry, macroeconomic factors, and firm-specific control variables.

3.4.1 Ownership structure

Control motive theory suggests that share dilution is a concern for those firms with concentrated ownership. Studies in the literature have found that ownership structure significantly determines a firm's risk-taking behaviour (Borisova et al., 2015; Santos et al., 2014; Su, 2010). Furthermore, studies by Farooq (2015), Santos et al. (2014), and Mitton (2002) suggest that ownership concentration affects firms' decisions on capital structure and performance.

We believe that shareholders do not actively participate in the initial decision on whether or not to raise capital, but they do participate in the second decision of the choice of instrument since this potentially affects their ability to exert influence over the firm. Based on this premise our ownership variables are included in Equation (2) on the choice of risk, but not in Equation (1) on raising funds. We estimate how ownership concentration leads to the choice of a certain level of risk by the firm. The *concentration* variable is incorporated in our model as this indicates share ownership by the highest shareholder in the firm. We expect highly concentrated ownership may prefer to raise funds from debt financing in order to avoid ownership dilution.

Type of ownership may also affect the choice of instrument for raising funds. To reflect the impact of types of ownership, we included three distinct categories of shareholders. *Govt*, which is the percentage of share ownership by government, is included to control for state-ownership in the firm. An aggregate variable named *Financials* is included to control for the effect of institutional ownership including banks, hedge funds, venture capital, mutual funds, private equities, and insurance firms. We further control the effects of ownership by individual/family shareholding with variable, *Individual* representing the proportion of ownership by a person or family in the overall ownership structure.

3.4.2 Corporate governance

The governance structure of a firm directly affects the decisions of issuance as well as the choice of instrument due to the direct involvement of the board of directors in such decision-making. We account for the board's structure through several variables.

Sundaramurthy and Lewis (2003), Daily et al. (1998), Brickley et al. (1997), and Boyd (1994) have argued how the dual role of CEO and Chairman affects a firm's decision-making process. To control for the unitary leadership structure with shared incumbency of the Chairman and CEO positions, a dummy variable *CEO duality* equals 1 if the CEO and Chairman positions are held by the same individual and 0 otherwise.

Studies by Heng et al. (2012) and Falaye et al. (2011) discuss the effects on capital structure as the independence of the board changes. We include the variable *Board independence,* which takes on numeric values corresponding to the BvD independence indicator by Orbis,[6] which assigns independence indicators of A+, A, A−, B+, B, B−. We choose discrete numbers with higher values indicating a greater degree of board independence.

Board size and its diversity are important indicators of corporate governance. Several studies including Heng et al. (2012), Mak and Kusnadi (2005), Yermack (1996), Eisenberg et al. (1998), and Pearce and Zahra (1992) have mixed findings on the effect of board size on firm's leverage choice. *Board size*, the number of directors on the board, is included as a control variable for this purpose.

Adams and Funk (2012) found female board members exhibit a higher tolerance towards risk in regard to capital structure. To account for the effect of gender diversity, we include the proportion of female members on the board of directors through the variable *Female ratio.*

3.4.3 Information asymmetry

In the presence of higher information asymmetry, investors are less keen to invest in firms as equity. Large firms and those with a greater number of analysts' coverage may face lower information asymmetry and consequently be able to raise more capital using equity. Based on the existing literature, we use several proxies that can be considered as important in mitigating information asymmetry. *Firm size,* indicated by the logarithm of total assets, is often considered to reduce information asymmetry (Autore and Kovacs, 2010; Frank and Goyal, 2003). Furthermore, large firms are also found to have easier access to debt financing (Sakai et al., 2010; Zeghal, 1984).

We use the number of analysts covering each firm through the variable *Analyst coverage* (Gomes and Phillips, 2012; Krishnaswami and Subramaniam, 1999). *Analyst variance,* which is the standard deviation among the analyst recommendations, is another variable to address information asymmetry. It helps us determine whether analysts arrive at a wider scale of recommendations for the firm that indicates high information asymmetry.

Autore and Kovacs (2010) have utilized asset tangibility to represent information asymmetry. They claim that firms with higher growth opportunities would resort to debt in the presence of high information asymmetry.

Hence, we have control variables *Tangibility* and *ROA*, representing the ratio of tangible assets to total assets and the return on assets, respectively, to control for information asymmetry.

3.4.4 Macroeconomic variables

Korajczyk and Levy (2003) highlight the significance of macroeconomic variables in the choice of security. Tawatnuntachai and Yaman (2007) found that GDP growth has a negative effect on bond issuance. In another study, Choe et al. (1993) observe the effect of certain macroeconomic factors on equity issuance, asserting that equity issues rise during business cycle expansions. Therefore, *GDP*, measured as the gross domestic product in millions of US dollars, is included as a control variable for economic growth.

Graham and Harvey (2001) suggest that financial flexibility, credit rating, and interest rates influence the decision to issue bonds. This is consistent with the earlier findings of Flannery (1986) that firms issue short-term debt securities when their credit ratings improve. We control for interest rates through our variable *Interbank rate*, which is the three-month interbank rate prevalent in the respective country where the firm is based.

3.4.5 Other control variables

Adjustment in capital structure has conventionally been evaluated by observing leverage ratios, as evident from studies by Öztekin and Flannery (2012), Kayo and Kimura (2011), Korajczyk and Levy (2003), Kayhan and Titman (2007), Leary and Roberts (2005), and Welch (2004). *Leverage*, which is the ratio of total debt to equity, is included to measure the effect of leverage on issuance and risk choices.

Empirical studies endorsing static trade-off theory by Titman and Wessels (1988), Rajan and Zingales (1995), Booth et al. (2001), Frank and Goyal (2009), and De Jong et al. (2011) help explain that firm size, asset tangibility, and profitability indicators of firms' decision to raise debt. We can assume that high tangibility offers opportunities to issue bond and *sukuk* by acting as collateral. Our variables *Firm size*, *Tangibility*, and *ROA* incorporate these three factors.

Market timing theory regards the market-to-book ratio (MBV) as a significant determinant of equity issuance (Hovakimian, 2006; Kayo and Kimura, 2011). *MBV*, which reflects the ratio of market capitalization to the book value of equity, is also added as a control variable. It is meant to describe price overvaluation, which offers market timing opportunities to the firm issuing equity (Baker and Wurgler, 2002). Rajan and Zingales (1995) suggest that asset tangibility is another important control variable. We expect growth firms to issue debt according to pecking order theory and so generate growth measures by taking the ratio of capital expenditures with total assets, and name it *Capex*. We also expect firms with relatively large amounts of cash on their balance sheets to raise capital less frequently. *Cash*, ratio of cash to total assets, serves to control for this.

3.5 The data sources and statistics

The data set includes non-financial firms from those countries where a variety of instruments are available to raise funds, namely equity, *sukuk*, bonds, and loans. The sample consists of all non-financial firms listed on the stock exchanges of Malaysia, Indonesia, Singapore, and Pakistan. Financial statement data is extracted from Thomson Reuters Worldscope Global, issuance data from Bloomberg, and the data related to ownership and board of directors is acquired from Orbis. We also use Institutional Broker's Estimate System (IBES) for data on analyst's recommendations on firms.

Due to multiple sources of data, we use the firm name up to 92% matching as the common identifier. All observations with missing data on assets, debt, equity, board of directors, or ownership information are dropped. We further winsorize data at the 1st and 99th percentile to account for the outliers. The final data set consists of 1,565 firms with 67,734 firm-quarter observations over the years 2000–2015. A graphical representation of the number of security issues made by the sample firms is shown in Figure 3.2. Clearly, the majority either did not issue or only made a small number of security issues during the sample period.

Table 3.1 presents the summary descriptive statistics of the non-dummy variables used in this study. The statistics are divided into three

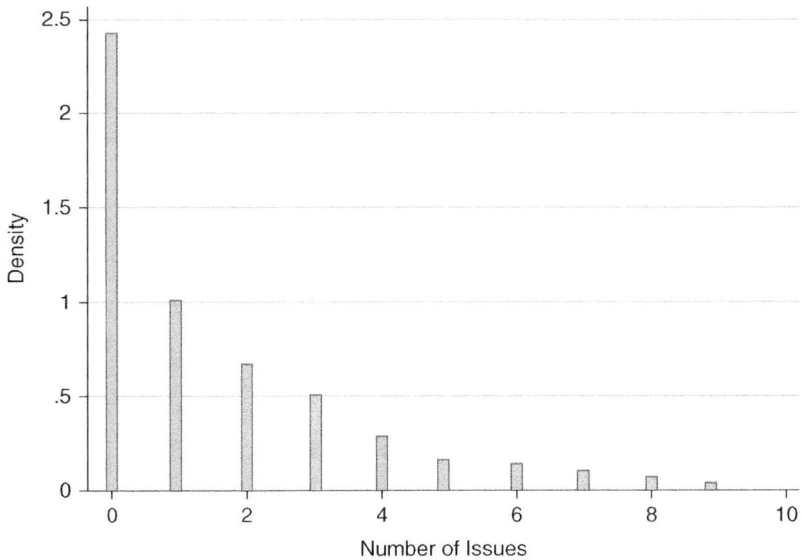

Figure 3.2 The histogram shows on the *x*-axis the number of issues made by the sample firms and on the *y*-axis the frequency density of the number of firms that issued a security in any quarter during 2000–2015. The highest density is for zero issues implying that the majority of firms did not raise capital during the sample period. The number of firms that made a single issue during the sample period is second to highest after non-issuers.

Table 3.1 Descriptive Statistics of Control, Ownership, Governance, and Information Asymmetry Variables. The Quarterly Data Ranges from Year 2000 to 2015 for Our Sample Firms from Countries of Dual Issuers of Bonds and *Sukuk*. These Countries Are Malaysia, Indonesia, Singapore, and Pakistan. Definitions of the Variables Are Given in Appendix A

Variable	*Panel A: All Firms*			*Panel B: Issuing Firms*			*Panel C: Non-Issuing Firms*			*K-Wallis*
	Obs.	*Mean*	*SD*	*Obs.*	*Mean*	*SD*	*Obs.*	*Mean*	*SD*	
Firm size	67,734	18.447	1.6	38,786	18.686	1.647	28,948	18.127	1.474	2,044***
Leverage	67,700	0.617	1.207	38,776	0.627	1.102	28,924	0.605	1.334	676***
MBV	64,865	1.445	1.723	37,218	1.482	1.693	27,647	1.397	1.76	184***
Capex	67,734	0.003	0.008	38,786	0.003	0.008	28,948	0.003	0.008	205***
Tangibility	67,549	0.364	0.225	38,729	0.365	0.224	28,820	0.363	0.227	3.524*
ROA	59,634	0.048	0.095	34,536	0.047	0.093	25,098	0.051	0.097	21.679***
Cash	67,658	0.13	0.131	38,738	0.127	0.124	28,920	0.133	0.14	28.902***
Analyst coverage	67,734	1.7	4.332	38,786	2.19	4.927	28,948	1.044	3.261	1,626***
Analyst variance	67,734	0.18	0.418	38,786	0.226	0.457	28,948	0.119	0.351	1,221***
Concentration	66,478	37.903	21.377	38,300	37.754	20.429	28,178	38.105	22.601	0.052
Govt	67,734	0.996	7.447	38,786	1.328	8.45	28,948	0.552	5.809	209***
Individual	67,734	12.328	17.948	38,786	11.702	16.779	28,948	13.167	19.374	18.327***
Financials	67,734	14.521	22.325	38,786	14.671	21.91	28,948	14.319	22.87	43.174***
CEO duality	67,680	0.029	0.167	38,786	0.025	0.155	28,894	0.034	0.182	54.050***
Board size	67,680	7.097	2.465	38,786	7.17	2.345	28,894	7.000	2.614	43.158***
Board independence	67,562	3.739	1.201	38,687	3.759	1.178	28,875	3.712	1.231	8.124***
Female ratio	67,427	0.116	0.138	38,766	0.121	0.138	28,661	0.111	0.138	130***

Notes: where *** $p < 0.01$; ** $p < 0.05$; * $p < 0.1$.

panels: Panel A reports the summary statistics of the overall sample, whereas Panels B and C report the summary statistics of subsample issuers and non-issuer firms, respectively. Issuer firms include all those firms that have raised funds externally during the sample period. The last column of Table 3.1 reports the Kruskal-Wallis test statistics for differences in means to understand if issuing firms are significantly different in their ownership and governance structures, information asymmetry, and financial attributes as compared to those of non-issuing firms.

The variables on ownership structure show significant differences in terms of the type of ownership, albeit the variable on ownership concentration does not vary significantly across the two types of firms. Issuing firms, on average, have a significantly higher ownership stake held by the government as compared with non-issuing firms. Interestingly, higher ownership concentration associated with individual or family shareholding is found to be significantly less frequent among issuing firms, which may highlight the conservative nature of such shareholders. Firms with high financial institution ownership appear to be frequent issuers.

In terms of the difference in governance variables of issuer and non-issuer firms, Table 3.1 shows a statistically significant difference among the two groups. For example, board size, female ratio, and proportion of board of directors with dual management roles are significantly higher in issuing firms, accompanied with lower standard deviation except for the female ratio. CEO duality, on the other hand, is lower in the case of issuing firms. This further supports the argument that separation of the two roles can be an influential determinant of the decision to raise capital externally.

Table 3.1 also indicates that issuing firms, on average, are larger in size, highly leveraged, and growth oriented as compared to firms that did not issue any security during the sample period. Variables on tangibility and market-to-book ratio show the same trend. However, non-issuing firms have significantly higher profitability and cash holdings. Intuitively, we would expect firms with high cash holdings to be averse to raising capital. Finally, variables on information asymmetry, including analyst coverage and variance, are on the higher end in the case of issuing firms and have a higher standard deviation.

To further understand the dynamics of the sample, Table 3.2 provides descriptive statistics based on a breakdown of instruments that firms used to raise capital in our sample. Firms that issued multiple securities during the same quarters are placed in the respective risk panel depending on the size of issue, i.e. amount of capital raised would determine the level of risk assumed by the firm. The Kruskal-Wallis test for differences in means is shown in the last column.

One of the interesting findings from Table 3.2 is that the average size of issuing firms decreases in the order of loans, bonds, *sukuk*, and then equity that is the exact order observed in Figure 3.1. A similar pattern can be observed in the case of leverage whereby firms issuing equities are the least

Table 3.2 Descriptive Statistics of Firms Segregated by Their Issuance Trend. Issuers of More than One Security during a Quarter Are Placed in the High Risk Issuer Category. The Quarterly Data Ranges from Year 2000 to 2015 for Our Sample Countries: Malaysia, Indonesia, Singapore, and Pakistan with Issuers of Equity, Bonds, *Sukuk*, and Loans. The Definitions of Variables Are Given in Appendix A

Variable	*Loans*			*Bonds*			*Sukuk*			*Equity*			*K-Wallis*
	Obs	*Mean*	*SD*	*Obs*	*Mean*	*SD*	*Obs*	*Mean*	*SD*	*Obs*	*Mean*	*SD*	
Firm size	521	20.419	1.518	692	19.951	1.537	593	19.849	1.453	764	18.320	1.880	1,606***
Leverage	521	1.063	1.133	692	1.210	1.148	593	0.874	0.531	764	0.570	0.860	1,155***
MBV	504	2.128	2.050	671	1.492	1.470	586	1.273	1.022	585	2.400	2.270	428***
Capex	521	0.004	0.010	692	0.003	0.009	593	0.002	0.007	764	0.000	0.010	35.540***
Tangibility	521	0.421	0.252	692	0.385	0.203	592	0.390	0.201	764	0.330	0.240	72.840***
ROA	465	0.072	0.076	632	0.047	0.059	578	0.049	0.051	448	0.060	0.120	56.297***
Cash	521	0.106	0.087	692	0.113	0.095	593	0.087	0.065	760	0.160	0.130	76.444***
Analyst coverage	521	6.392	7.800	692	4.608	6.698	593	5.137	7.527	764	2.414	5.429	1,168***
Analyst variance	521	0.502	0.543	692	0.423	0.526	593	0.503	0.587	764	0.197	0.395	1,078***
Concentration	501	51.589	20.818	691	39.406	19.314	567	39.670	20.372	760	33.482	19.530	242***
Govt	521	4.556	15.627	692	2.200	11.112	593	0.688	4.599	764	1.034	7.129	148***
Individual	521	2.489	8.758	692	8.662	14.038	593	7.907	12.636	764	13.631	16.547	338***
Financials	521	22.882	27.816	692	20.185	25.722	593	21.673	28.060	764	15.722	22.789	126***
CEO duality	521	0.021	0.144	692	0.027	0.164	593	0.002	0.041	764	0.020	0.139	19.460***
Board size	521	7.455	2.753	692	8.042	2.254	593	8.233	2.272	764	7.215	2.441	280***
Board independence	519	3.175	1.223	691	3.592	1.145	593	3.629	1.264	763	4.010	1.106	162***
Female ratio	521	0.131	0.142	691	0.128	0.113	593	0.152	0.151	764	0.114	0.139	64.187***

Notes: where *** $p < 0.01$; ** $p < 0.05$; * $p < 0.1$.

leveraged as compared to firms who prefer borrowing from banks. Financing using loans may be associated with the sophisticated evaluation and monitoring functions of banks (Rajan, 1992; Zeghal, 1984). Furthermore, firms issuing equities reflect higher future growth potential as reflected by the market-to-book ratio. In line with Rajan and Zingales (1995), we find that tangible assets are higher in firms that prefer to issue debt including loan and *sukuk* issuers. This is intuitive as well since *sukuk* is largely an asset-backed security and banks often require collateral for financing.

Both variables on ownership concentration and CEO duality are significantly different in each of the four categories of issuing firms. The independence of the board of directors is also associated with higher equity financing as compared with loan financing where boards of directors are least independent. Other variables on ownership and governance structure also differ significantly across different types of issuers but do not reflect any specific patterns.

Table 3.3 shows the correlation matrix of the variables related to ownership, governance, and the type of issuance by firms in the sample. The negative correlation sign between individual ownership and type of issuances indicates that firms with a higher percentage of ownership with individual or families exhibit a lower tendency towards raising capital. A similar trend can be seen in the case of firms with CEO duality. For all other variables the sign and level of association are in line with our expectations and warrant multivariate analysis to shed light on the significance of how ownership and governance affect a firm's tendency to raise capital and the desired level of risk.

3.6 Multivariate analysis

This section reports the estimation results for the empirical model. The model incorporates an equation for the issuance decision and, conditional on this decision, an equation for the choice of instrument to raise capital based on the trade-off between control and risk motives. In the issuance equation, the dependent variable is binary indicating whether the firm issued any security or not by assuming a value of 1 in the case of issuance and 0 otherwise. To incorporate the second decision regarding choice of instrument, we use a categorical variable that takes the value of 1, 2, 3, and 4 if a firm has raised funds using loans, bonds, *sukuk*, or equity, respectively. The categorical variable reflects an order based on the ownership control (see Zhang et al., 2012) and relative risk aversion as shown in Figure 3.1. For empirical estimation, we use the Heckman ordered probit (HOP) model.

During the sample period, 867 of the 1,565 firms issued one of the four securities at some point reflecting the selection effects that have to be taken into consideration while performing a multivariate analysis. Although the data set indicates the application of the HOP model as appropriate due to observed sample selection bias, to further confirm the existence of sample

Table 3.3 Matrix of Correlation Coefficients

	Concentration	*Individual*	*Govt*	*Financials*	*CEO duality*	*Board independence*	*Board size*	*Female ratio*	*Loan*	*Bond*	*Sukuk*	*Equity*
Concentration	1											
Individual	−0.2609	1										
Govt	0.1373	−0.09	1									
Financials	0.1669	−0.1697	−0.0502	1								
CEO duality	−0.0016	0.0548	−0.0231	0.0523	1							
Board independence	−0.8293	0.2508	−0.1549	−0.1838	−0.0144	1						
Board size	−0.0973	−0.0379	0.0818	0.1039	0.0313	0.0073	1					
Female ratio	0.0747	−0.0078	−0.0163	0.0203	−0.0313	−0.0581	−0.0207	1				
Loan	0.0148	−0.018	0.0166	0.027	−0.0038	−0.0147	0.0153	0.0025	1			
Bond	0.0091	−0.0103	0.0106	0.0347	0.0014	−0.015	0.0238	0.0053	0.0204	1		
Sukuk	0.0167	−0.0243	−0.0047	0.0577	−0.0078	−0.0132	0.0345	0.0393	0.0064	0.0008	1	
Equity	0.0155	−0.0163	0.0188	0.0216	−0.0035	−0.0123	0.0197	0.0096	0.0085	0.0025	0.0113	1

Notes: where *** $p < 0.01$; ** $p < 0.05$; * $p < 0.1$.

selection bias, we perform a z-test of the null hypothesis, in which the disturbance terms in the issuance and choice equations are uncorrelated ($H_0: \rho = 0$), that produces $z = 612.99$ (p-value $=0.000$). A Wald test of the same null hypothesis produces $\chi^2(1) = 15.349$ (p-value $= 0.000$). Both results support the use of the HOP model.

Table 3.4 reports the empirical results using the HOP model. The selection of independent variables in both equations are on the premise that the decision to raise capital largely rests on the governance structure, the needs of the firm, and economic environment. However, the choice decision

Table 3.4 HOP Model. Equations (1) and (4) Describe How the Variables in Column 1 Determine the Firm's Decision to Raise Capital in Column 2 and Choice of Security in Column 3. The Dependent Variable CHOICE is an Ordered Variable Ranging from 1 to 4 to Indicate the Level of Risk-Sharing Based on the Chosen Security. Quarterly Data Ranges from 2000 to 2015. Standard Errors in Parentheses

	Ordered Probit Model	
Variables	*Issued*	*Choice*
Concentration		-0.0062^{***}
		(0.0023)
Individual		0.0041^{*}
		(0.0023)
Govt		−0.0012
		(0.0028)
Financials		−0.0004
		(0.0011)
CEO duality	-0.3517^{***}	-0.9157^{***}
	(0.0762)	(0.3247)
Board independence	-0.0175^{**}	0.0360
	(0.0087)	(0.0403)
Board size	0.0297^{***}	0.0140
	(0.0043)	(0.0226)
Female ratio	0.3575^{***}	0.4588
	(0.0755)	(0.3032)
Firm size		-0.2139^{***}
		(0.0277)
Analyst coverage		0.0017
		(0.0060)
Analyst variance	0.4327^{***}	0.0658
	(0.0204)	(0.2800)
Tangibility	0.0042	−0.1480
	(0.0495)	(0.1219)
Capex	0.6667	-7.3552^{**}
	(1.2641)	(2.9127)
Leverage	0.1008^{***}	-0.1612^{**}
	(0.0084)	(0.0636)
MBV	0.0140^{**}	0.1212^{***}
	(0.0062)	(0.0228)
ROA	0.0133	−0.0603
	(0.1308)	(0.3768)

(*Continued*)

	Ordered Probit Model	
Variables	*Issued*	*Choice*
Cash	−0.7482***	1.1209**
	(0.1042)	(0.5147)
Interbank rate	−3.7289***	−14.5156***
	(0.3718)	(3.3206)
GDP		−0.0559
		(0.0567)
Constant		−1.9698***
		(0.0581)
Chi^2 (20)		561.80***
Hausman		15,349.11***
Observations		57,163

Notes: where *** $p < 0.01$; ** $p < 0.05$; * $p < 0.1$.

depends not only on firm-specific and economic factors but also depends on the ownership structure of the firm. Accordingly, the independent variables representing the percentage of ownership by government, institutional investors, individual/family, and concentration of ownership by the highest shareholder are considered in the choice equation only. Firm-specific factors, whether related to governance, financial, or economic variables, are considered in both equations.

One of the important findings from Table 3.4 is that ownership concentration is associated with low risk aversion. The negative and significant coefficient of ownership concentration with the issue decision suggests that firms with a higher concentration of ownership irrespective of the category of shareholdings, on average, prefer to raise capital via debt-based instruments. This suggests shareholders prefer to avoid ownership dilution over risk-reduction. This result complements the findings of Friend and Lang (1988) regarding the positive relationship between ownership concentration and debt ratios.

The empirical evidence suggests that governance structure significantly influences a firm's decision to raise capital. The coefficient of the CEO duality is negative and significant in both ISSUE and CHOICE equations, namely Equations (4) and (5), suggesting that firms with a concentration of power at the top level prefer not to raise capital externally. Subsequently, if those firms are to raise capital externally, they would prefer bank loans. This is in line with stewardship theory (Donaldson and Davis, 1991). Evasion of external capital may be due to the fact that external financiers, especially those from capital markets, may challenge power concentration and require better governance mechanisms with separate management and board structures. On the other hand, Rajan (1992) and Zeghal (1984) suggest that banks usually lend to those firms with whom they have established a strong relationship and prefer to deal with a unitary leadership structure.

Among other governance-related covariates, board independence is negative and significant in the ISSUE decision. However, it is insignificant in the CHOICE Equation (5). The significant negative coefficient in the ISSUE decision suggests that firms with more independent boards prefer not to raise capital externally. However, once the decision to raise capital is made, higher board independence is not associated with any specific form of capital financing.

Board size and the proportion of female members on the board are positive and significant in the ISSUE decision suggesting that firms with a larger board and a higher proportion of female board members prefer to raise capital externally. However, depending on the decision to raise capital, both factors do not affect the choice of any specific mode of financing. This supports the findings of Sila et al. (2016) that female board members do not necessarily tend to be risk averse or risk-seekers, contradicting the findings of Adams and Funk (2012) whose research suggests women have a higher tolerance of risk.

The variables on information asymmetry include the number of analysts covering a firm, standard deviation of the analysts' recommendations, firm size, and tangibility. We assume the observed variance in opinion and tangibility of assets can affect both decisions; however, firm size and the number of analysts providing coverage may affect the choice of instrument decision only. Interestingly, we find that the higher variance in analysts' opinions positively influences the decision to raise capital. However, once the decision to raise capital is reached the variance of analysts' opinions is insignificant. The association of tangibility of assets and firm's profitability are insignificant in both decisions.

We find that firms that are larger in size or are highly leveraged exhibit lower risk aversion and prefer to raise capital through debt-like securities. The inclination towards debt financing associated with leverage and firm size in the CHOICE decision is consistent with the view that larger and highly leveraged firms are more likely to borrow from banks (Rajan, 1992; Zeghal, 1984), or through bonds (Tawatnuntachai and Yaman, 2007).

Among other firm-specific variables we find that firms with higher future potential as reflected by the market-to-book ratio (MBV) are associated with a higher likelihood for raising funds externally and, depending on the ISSUE decision, are more likely to raise funds through equity financing. These findings are in line with the common belief that firms with higher future potential are more likely to raise funds through equity (Baker and Wurgler, 2002; Viswanath, 1993). We also find that firms with a higher proportion of liquid assets prefer not to raise capital as reflected by the negative and significant coefficient of the *Cash* variable in the ISSUE decision. However, if such firms raise capital externally there is evidence, albeit weak, that they will raise capital through equity financing.

Regarding the macroeconomic variables, we find evidence that firms do not raise capital in a higher interest rate environment. However, if the decision to raise funds is reached in such an environment, the preferred mode of financing is debt. The GDP does not appear to be a statistically significant factor in the choice of instruments.

In summary, the empirical results in Table 3.4 highlight that ownership concentration and CEO duality are important determinants in the choice of security for raising funds. Firms with high ownership concentration and CEO duality, on average, prefer to raise capital using debt instruments. However, firms with higher future growth potential are more inclined to raise capital using equity financing.

3.7 Concluding remarks

Based on the control and risk-reduction hypotheses, we investigated how firm ownership and governance structure affects decisions on raising capital and the choice of security. We find evidence that firm ownership and governance structure play a significant role in external financing decisions in firms from Malaysia, Indonesia, Singapore, and Pakistan. Our sample consisting of multiple issuers of *sukuk*, bonds, equity, and bank loans helps us determine how firms adjust their choice of risk while raising capital.

One of the important contributions of this study is the application of better estimation methodology where the decision to raise capital and the choice of instrument for capital financing are treated separately. By incorporating the HOP model, this study demonstrated that capital financing decisions can be better understood by taking each of these two decisions sequentially.

We find support for control theory suggesting that firms with higher ownership concentration prefer to raise capital through debt instruments such as loans and bonds. The empirical findings further suggest that companies prefer to adopt debt financing in the case of CEO duality. Larger board size and the proportion of females on the board of directors have the opposite influence in the decision to raise capital, although the choice of instruments stays unaffected.

The results of this study imply that firm ownership and governance structure play a significant role in a firm's decision to raise capital and, subsequently, to choose the relative riskiness of the security. Further research can investigate how similar sets of factors explain the volume of issuance by firms.

One of the possible limitations of this study is that it incorporates four different types of instruments which are commonly observed for raising capital, namely equity, bonds, bank loans, and *sukuk*. However, this list is not exhaustive, and instruments such as convertible bonds, global bonds, warrants, and preferred shares have been the subject of study by Balachandran et al. (2017), Lewis et al. (2003), Tawatnuntachai and Yaman (2007), and Suchard and Singh (2006). A broader list of securities could expand the data and open future research opportunities, but the scope of the study in terms of risk and control would still be the same.

Acknowledgement

We would like to thank Dawood Ashraf for his constructive comments to improve the presentation of this chapter.

Appendix A

List of variables with their descriptions, accompanied by their expected impact on a firm's decision to raise capital and their choice of product in terms of riskiness

Variable	*Description*	*Expected Sign*	
		Issuance	*Selection*
CEO duality	Dummy variable indicating CEO and Chairman are the same person	–	+
Concentration	Percentage ownership of highest shareholder		–
Board independence	BvD indicator value for board independence	–	+
Board size	Number of directors on the board	–	+
Female ratio	Percentage of females on the board of directors		+/–
Individual	Percentage ownership by individuals/families		–
Govt	Percentage ownership by government		+/–
Financials	Percentage ownership by financial institutions		+/–
Firm size	Logarithm function applied to total assets	+	+/–
Leverage	Total debt-to-equity ratio	+	–
ROA	Return on assets	+	+
Cash	Cash-to-asset ratio	–	+/–
MBV	Market-to-book value of equity	+	+/–
Capex	Ratio of capital expenditure to total assets		+/–
Tangibility	Ratio of plant, property, and equipment to assets	+	–
Analyst coverage	Number of analysts that gave a forecast on firm performance	+	+
Analyst variance	Standard deviation among analyst recommendations		
GDP	Logarithm function applied to the GDP of the firm's country in millions of US dollars		+/–
Interbank rate	Three-month interbank rate of the country where the firm is based where the company is based	+/–	–

Notes

1 Tradeoff theory (Kraus and Litzenberger, 1973; Myers, 2001; Zou and Xiao, 2006).
2 Pecking order theory (Myers, 1984; Myers and Majluf, 1984).
3 Market timing theory (Baker and Wurgler, 2002).
4 Agency theory (Jensen and Meckling, 1976).

5 Global *Sukuk* Market Outlook: Another Strong Performance in 2018: available at www.spratings.com/.
6 BvD independence indicator is issued by Bureau van Dijk. It shows each company's degree of independence with regard to its shareholders. Available at: www.bvdinfo.com/en-us/our-products/our-expertise/find-out-how-we-add-value-to-company-information/corporate-ownership-structures.

References

Abdul Halim, Z., How, J., and Verhoeven, P. (2017). Agency costs and corporate sukuk issuance. *Pacific-Basin Finance Journal, 42*, 83–95.
Adams, R. B., and Funk, P. (2012). Beyond the glass ceiling: Does gender matter? *Management Science, 58*(2), 219–235.
Admati, A. R., Demarzo, P. M., Hellwig, M. F. and Pfleiderer, P. (2018). The leverage ratchet effect. *The Journal of Finance, 73*, 145–198.
Alam, N., Bhatti, M. I. and Wong, J. (2018). Assessing Sukuk defaults using value-at-risk techniques. *Managerial Finance, 44*(6), 665–687.
Al Rahahleh, N., and Bhatti, M. I. (2017). Co-movement measure of information transmission on international equity markets. *Physica A: Statistical Mechanics and its Applications, 470*, 119–131. ABDC 2013- A.
Al Rahahleh, N., Bhatti, M. I., and Adeinat, I. (2017). Tail dependence and information flow: Evidence from international equity markets. *Physica A: Statistical Mechanics and its Applications, 474*, 319–329. A.
Autore D. M., and Kovacs, T. (2010). Equity issues and temporal variation in information asymmetry. *Journal of Banking and Finance, 34*(1), 12–23.
Azmat, S., Skully, M., and Brown, K. (2014). Issuer's choice of Islamic bond type. *Pacific-Basin Finance Journal, 28*, 122–135.
Azmat, S., Skully, M., and Brown, K. (2015). The (little) difference that makes all the difference between Islamic and conventional bonds. *Pacific-Basin Finance Journal, 42*, 46–59.
Baker, M., and Wurgler, J. (2002). Market timing and capital structure. *Journal of Finance, 57*, 1–32.
Balachandran, B., Kanapathippillai, S., Krishnamurti, C., Theobald, M., and Velayutham, E. (2017). The issuance of warrants in rights offerings: Agency costs and signaling effects. *Australian Journal of Management, 42*(4), 608–636.
Bayless, M., and Chaplinsky, S. (1996). Is there a window of opportunity for seasoned equity issuance? *The Journal of Finance, 51*(1), 253.
Berkovitch, E., and Israel, R. (1996). The design of internal control and capital structure. The *Review of Financial Studies, 9*(1), 209–240.
Booth, L., Aivazian, V., Demirguc-Kunt, A., and Maksimovic, V. (2001). Capital structure in developing countries. *Journal of Finance, 56*, 87–130.
Borisova, G., Fotak, V., Holland, K., and Megginson, W. L. (2015). Government ownership and the cost of debt: Evidence from government investments in publicly traded firms. *Journal of Financial Economics, 118*(1), 168–191.
Boubaker, S., Chourou, L., Saadi, S., and Zhong, L. (Forthcoming 2017). Does institutional investor horizon influence US corporate financing decisions? *International Review of Financial Analysis*. Available at SSRN: https://ssrn.com/abstract=3077367.
Boyd, B. K. (1994). Board control and CEO compensation. *Strategic Management Journal, 15*(5), 335–344.

Brickley, J. A., Coles, J. L., and Jarrell, G. (1997). Leadership structure: Separating the CEO and chairman of the board. *Journal of Corporate Finance, 3*(3), 189–220.

Cameron, S. V., and Heckman, J. J. (1998). Life cycle schooling and dynamic selection bias: Models and evidence for five cohorts of American males. *Journal of Political Economy, 106*(2), 262–333.

Choe, H., Masulis, R. W., and Nanda, V. (1993). Common stock offerings across the business cycle: Theory and evidence. *Journal of Empirical Finance, 1*(1), 3–31.

Daily, C., Johnson, J., Ellstrand, A., and Dalton, D. (1998). Compensation committee composition as a determinant of CEO compensation. *Academy Of Management Journal, 41*(2), 209–220.

De Jong, A., Verbeek, M., and Verwijmern, P. (2011). Firms' debt–equity decisions when the static tradeoff theory and the pecking order theory disagree. *Journal of Banking & Finance, 35*, 1303–1314.

De Luca, G., and Perotti, V. (2011). Estimation of ordered response models with sample selection. *Stata Journal, 11*(2), 213–239.

Donaldson, L., and Davis, J. (1991). Stewardship theory or agency theory: CEO governance and shareholder returns. *Australian Journal of Management, 16*(1), 49–64.

Dong, M., Loncarski, I., Horst, J., and Veld, C. (2012). What drives security issuance decisions: Market timing, pecking order, or both? *Financial Management, 41*(3), 637–663.

Edmans, A., and Mann, W. (Forthcoming 2018). *Financing Through Asset Sales. Management Science*. Available at doi:10.2139/ssrn.2024513.

Eisenberg, T., Sundgren, S., and Wells, M. (1998). Larger board size and decreasing firm value in small firms. *Journal of Financial Economics, 48*(1), 35–54.

Ellul, A. (2008). *Control Motivations and Capital Structure Decision*. Available at SSRN: https://ssrn.com/abstract=1094997.

Falaye, O., Hoitash, R., and Hoitash, U. (2011). The cost of intense monitoring. *Journal of Financial Economics, 101*(1), 160–181.

Faulkender, M., Flannery, M. J., Hankins, K. W., and Smith, J. M. (2012). Cash flows and leverage adjustments. *Journal of Financial Economics, 103*(3), 632–646.

Fama, E. (1980). Agency problems and the theory of the firm. *The Journal of Political Economy, 88*(2), 288.

Fama, E., and Jensen, M. (1983). Separation of ownership and control. *The Journal of Law and Economics, 26*(2), 301–325.

Farooq, O. (2015). Effect of ownership concentration on capital structure: Evidence from the MENA region. *International Journal of Islamic and Middle Eastern Finance and Management, 8*(1), 99–113.

Flannery, M. (1986). Asymmetric information and risky debt maturity choice. *The Journal of Finance, 41*(1), 19–37.

Frank, M. Z., and Goyal, V. K. (2003). Testing the pecking order theory of capital structure. *Journal of Financial Economics, 67*(2), 217–248.

Frank, M. Z., and Goyal, V. K. (2009). Capital structure decisions: Which factors are reliably important? *Financial Management, 38*(1), 1.

Friend, I., and Lang, L. (1988). An empirical test of the impact of managerial self-interest on corporate capital structure. *Journal of Finance, 43*(2), 271–281.

Gatchev, V. A., Spindt, P. A., and Tarhan, V. (2009). How do firms finance their investments? The relative importance of equity issuance and debt contracting costs. *Journal of Corporate Finance, 15*(2), 179–195.

Gillan, S. L., and Starks, L. T. (2000). Corporate governance proposals and shareholder activism: The role of institutional investors. *Journal of Financial Economics, 57*(2), 275–305.

Godlewski, C. J., Turk-Ariss, R., and Weill, L. (2013). Sukuk vs. conventional bonds: A stock market perspective. *Journal of Comparative Economics, 41*(3), 745–761.

Godlewski, C. J., Turk-Ariss, R., and Weill, L. (2016). Do the type of Sukuk and choice of Shari'a scholar matter? *Journal of Economic Behavior & Organization.* Available at: doi:10.1016/j.jebo.2016.04.020.

Gomes, A., and Phillips, G. (2012). Why do public firms issue private and public securities? *Journal of Financial Intermediation, 21*(4), 619–658.

Graham, J. R., and Harvey, C. R. (2001). The theory and practice of corporate finance: Evidence from the field. *Journal of Financial Economics, 60*, 187–243.

Harris, M., and Raviv, A. (1998). Capital budgeting and delegation. *Journal of Financial Economics, 50*(3), 259–289.

Heckman, J. J., Urzua, S., and Vytlacil, E. (2006). Understanding instrumental variables in models with essential heterogeneity. *The Review of Economics and Statistics, 88*(3), 389–432.

Heng, T., Azrbaijani, S., and San, O. (2012). Board of directors and capital structure: Evidence from leading Malaysian companies. *Asian Social Science, 8*(3), 123–136.

Hovakimian, A. (2006). Are observed capital structures determined by equity market timing? *The Journal of Financial and Quantitative Analysis, 41*(1), 221–243.

Hovakimian, A., Hovakimian, G., and Tehranian, H. (2004). Determinants of target capital structure: The case of dual debt and equity issues. *Journal of Financial Economics, 71*(3), 517.

Israel, R. (1991). Capital structure and the market for corporate control: The defensive role of debt financing. *Journal of Finance, 46*, 1391–1409.

Jensen, M. C., and Meckling, W. H. (1976). Theory of the firm: Managerial behaviour, agency costs and ownership structure. *Journal of Financial Economics, 3*(4), 305–360.

Jung, K., Kim, Y., and Stulz, R. M. (1996). Timing, investment opportunities, managerial discretion, and the security issue decision. *Journal of Financial Economics, 42*(2), 159–185.

Karpoff, J. M. (2001). *The Impact of Shareholder Activism on Target Companies: A Survey of Empirical Findings.* Available at SSRN: https://ssrn.com/abstract=885365.

Kayhan, A., and Titman, S. (2007). Firms' histories and their capital structures. *Journal of Financial Economics, 83*(1), 1–32.

Kayo, E., and Kimura, H. (2011). Hierarchical determinants of capital structure. *Journal of Banking and Finance, 35*(2), 358–371.

Klein, P. O., and Weill, L. (2016). Why do companies issue sukuk? *Review of Financial Economics, 31*, 26–33.

Klein, P., Weill, L., and Godlewski, C. (2018). How sukuk shapes firm performance. *World Economy, 41*(3), 699–722.

Korajczyk, R. A., and Levy, A. (2003). Capital structure choice: Macroeconomic conditions and financial constraints. *Journal of Financial Economics, 68*(1), 75–109.

Kraus, A. H., and Litzenberger, R. (1973). A state-preference model of optimal financial leverage. *The Journal of Finance, 28*(4), 911–922.

Krishnaswami, S., and Subramaniam, V. (1999). Information asymmetry, valuation, and the corporate spin-off decision. *Journal of Financial Economics, 53*, 73–112.

Lauer, C. (2002). A model of educational attainment application to the German case. *ZEW Discussion Paper No. 02–06.* Available at SSRN: https://ssrn.com/abstract=327382.

Lauer, C. (2003). Education and unemployment: A French-German comparison. *ZEW Discussion Paper No. 03–34*. Available at SSRN: https://ssrn.com/abstract=439742.

Leary, M., and Roberts, M. (2005). Do firms rebalance their capital structures? *Journal of Finance, 60*(6), 2575–2619.

Lemma, T. T., and Negash, M. (2014). Determinants of the adjustment speed of capital structure: Evidence from developing economies. *Journal of Applied Accounting Research, 15*(1), 64–99.

Lemmon, M. L., Roberts, M. R., and Zender, J. F. (2008). Back to the beginning: Persistence and the cross-section of corporate capital structure. *Journal of Finance, 63*(4), 1575–1608.

Lewis, C. M., Rogalski, R. J., and Seward, J. K. (2003). Industry conditions, growth opportunities and market reactions to convertible debt financing decisions. *Journal of Banking and Finance, 27*(1), 153–181.

Liu, Q., Tian, G., and Wang, X. (2011). The effect of ownership structure on leverage decision: New evidence from Chinese listed firms. *Journal of the Asia Pacific Economy, 16*(2), 254.

Loughran, T. (2008). The impact of firm location on equity issuance. *Financial Management, 37*(1), 1–21.

Lu, Z. F., Zhu, J. G., and Zhang, W. N. (2012). Bank discrimination, holding bank ownership, and economic consequences: Evidence from China. *Journal of Banking and Finance, 36*(2), 341–354.

MacKie-Mason, J. (1990). Do taxes affect corporate financing decisions? *Journal of Finance, 45*(5), 1471.

Mak, Y. T., and Kusnadi, Y. (2005). Size really matters: Further evidence on the negative relationship between board size and firm value. *Pacific-Basin Finance Journal, 13*(3), 301–318.

Masulis, R. W. (1988). *The Debt/Equity Choice*. Cambridge, MA: Ballinger.

Matsa, D., and Miller, A. (2013). A female style in corporate leadership? Evidence from quotas. *American Economic Journal: Applied Economics, 5*(3), 136–169.

Mitton, T. (2002). A cross-firm analysis of the impact of corporate governance on the East Asian financial crisis. *Journal of Financial Economics, 64*(2), 215–244.

Modigliani, F., and Miller, M. (1958). The cost of capital, corporation finance and the theory of investment. *The American Economic Review, 48*(3), 261–297.

Mohamed, H. H., Masih, M., and Bacha, O. I. (2015). Why do issuers issue Sukuk or conventional bond? Evidence from Malaysian listed firms using partial adjustment models. *Pacific-Basin Finance Journal, 34*, 233–252.

Myers, S. C. (1984). The capital structure puzzle. *Journal of Finance, 39*(3), 575–592.

Myers, S. (2001). Capital structure. *Journal of Economic Perspectives, 15*(2), 81–102.

Myers, S., and Majluf, N. (1984). Corporate financing and investment decisions when firms have information that investors do not have. *Journal of Financial Economics, 13*(2), 187–221.

Nagano, M. (2016). Who issues Sukuk and when? An analysis of the determinants of Islamic bond issuance. *Review of Financial Economics, 31*, 45–55.

Nagano, M. (2017). Sukuk issuance and information asymmetry: Why do firms issue sukuk? *Pacific-Basin Finance Journal, 42*, 142–157.

Öztekin, O., and Flannery, M. (2012). Institutional determinants of capital structure adjustment speeds. *Journal of Financial Economics, 103*, 88–112.

Pearce, J. A., and Zahra, S. A. (1992). Board composition from a strategic contingency perspective. *Journal of Management Studies, 29*(4), 411.

Pi, L., and Timme, S. G. (1993). Corporate control and bank efficiency. *Journal of Banking and Finance, 17*(2), 515–530.
Rajan, R. G. (1992). Insiders and outsiders: The choice between informed and arm's length debt. *Journal of Finance, 47*, 1367–1406.
Rajan, R. G., and Zingales, L. (1995). What do we know about capital structure? Some evidence from international data. *Journal of Finance, 50*, 1421–1460.
Sakai, K., Uesugi, I., and Watanabe, T. (2010). Firm age and the evolution of borrowing costs: Evidence from Japanese small firms. *Journal of Banking and Finance, 34*(8), 1970–1981.
Santos, M., Moreira, A. C., and Vieira, E. S. (2014). Ownership concentration, contestability, family firms, and capital structure. *Journal of Management & Governance, 18*(4), 1063–1107.
Sila, V., Gonzalez, A., and Hagendorff, J. (2016). Women on board: Does boardroom gender diversity affect firm risk? *Journal of Corporate Finance, 36*, 26–53.
Smaoui, H., and Khawaja, M. (2016). The determinants of Sukuk market development. *Emerging Markets Finance and Trade, 7*, 1501–1518.
Stulz, R. (1988). Managerial control of voting rights: Financing policies and the market for managerial control. *Journal of Financial Economics, 20*, 25–54.
Su, L. (2010). Ownership structure, corporate diversification and capital structure. *Management Decision, 48*(2), 314–339.
Suchard, J. A., and Singh, M. (2006). The determinants of the hybrid security issuance decision for Australian firms. *Pacific-Basin Finance Journal, 14*(3), 269–290.
Sundaramurthy, C., and Lewis, M. (2003). Control and collaboration: Paradoxes of governance. *Academy of Management Review, 28*(3), 397–415.
Tawatnuntachai, O., and Yaman, D. (2007). Why do firms issue global bonds? *Managerial Finance, 34*(1), 23–40.
Titman, S., and Wessels, R. (1988). The determinants of capital structure choice. *Journal of Finance, 43*, 1–19.
Vafeas, N., and Theodorou, E. (1998). The relationship between board structure and firm performance in the UK. *The British Accounting Review, 30(*4), 383–407.
Viswanath, P. V. (1993). Strategic considerations, the pecking order hypothesis, and market reactions to equity financing. *Journal of Financial and Quantitative Analysis, 28*, 213–234.
Wahal, S. (1996). Pension fund activism and firm performance. *Journal of Financial and Quantitative Analysis, 31*(1), 1–23.
Walsh, E. J., and Ryan, J. (1997). Agency and tax explanations of security issuance decisions. *Journal of Business Finance and Accounting, 24*(7–8), 943–961.
Welch, I. (2004). Capital structure and stock returns. *Journal of Political Economy, 112*(1), 106–131.
Yatim, M. (2009). Sukuk (Islamic Bond): A crucial financial instrument for securitisation of debt for the debt-holders in Shari'ah-compliant capital market. *International Journal of Business and Management, 4*(10), 166–172.
Yermack, D. (1996). Higher market valuation of companies with a small board of directors. *Journal of Financial Economics, 40*(2), 185–211.
Zeghal, D. (1984). Firm size and the information content of financial statements. *Journal of Financial and Quantitative Analysis, 19*, 299–310.
Zhang, M., Liu, Z., and Zhang, W. (2012). Related loans and compensation contracts of commercial banks. *Journal of Financial Research, 5*, 108–122.

4 Takāful (Islamic insurance) on the blockchain

Hazik Mohamed

4.1 Introduction

The takāful and insurance is an evolving process of preserving individuals and businesses from loss and uncertainty. It can be described as a financial product to decrease or eradicate risk of loss and protection, be it life or property. Insurance offers financial protection to both individuals and business, in the risk of loss hence playing a vital function in reducing risks through risk-sharing in the face of uncertain but likely losses or damages. Insurance and takāful companies take on risk dangers of individuals and businesses so that they can survive such events to develop in a sustainable way. The risk landscape is continually evolving, and in order to keep up, the insurance industry needs to trace and provide customized insurance policies that can serve specific indemnity needs of the new economy. The insurers have to possess full understanding of every risk covered in their policies, and when disaster hits, compensation and claims will be done in a sensible and timely manner.

Latest developments in fintech promise more efficiency and reduced costs causing significant shifts in the financial landscape, and the impending disruption in the insurance industry is inevitable. Blockchain today is something like where the internet was in 1990s – on the strategic interest of forward-looking companies, but still a while from extensive implementation. For that reason, the question is not whether should one accept the blockchain revolution, but instead when and what to start with.

In this paper, we provide a strategic discussion of how blockchain can provide additional value to the insurance and takāful industries, how to understand the change in processes, issues that need to be overcome, and efficiency benefits, projected cost-saving, and risk management.

4.1.1 Blockchain-based takāful (Islamic insurance)

As a niche section of the insurance sector, the takāful segment is significantly interrelated with disruptions occurring in the insurance sector. The global insurance market had a reasonable growth rate, with global real premium growth rates of 2.9% in the advanced economies and 7.4% in the emerging and developing countries in 2014, an improvement over the 2012 and 2013 rates (IFSB, 2016). Likewise, the growth rate of gross contributions in the takāful sector demonstrated a recovery in 2014 from 2013, when the growth rate of premiums was by far the lowest historically.

In its Islamic Financial Services Industry (IFSI) Stability 2016 report, Islamic Financial Services Board (IFSB) observed that the reinvigorated gross contributions of the takāful sector reached US$22.1 billion in 2014, up from only around US$5 billion in 2006. The biggest share of the takāful sector belonged to the Gulf Cooperation Council (GCC) countries, followed by Iran and the East Asia and Pacific region. The other three regions (Africa, South Asia, and Levant) had a very much lesser share in total. As takāful's share of the insurance sector is only 1%, there is a long way to go for the takāful sector. Indeed, the low penetration rates in certain countries in which the takāful industry operates indicate an available market for the takāful sector. Since many of the target markets like Turkey, Saudi Arabia, Pakistan, Qatar, and Egypt have a growing middle-class and young populations with solid growth prospects, there is promise for the takāful sector to grow further.

Three jurisdictions account for 84% of the global takāful contributions: Saudi Arabia (37%), Iran (34%), and Malaysia (14%). However, the types of takāful provision are different for different jurisdictions; for example, in Malaysia nearly two-thirds of the takāful contributions are for family takāful (which features a strong savings/investment component). In Saudi Arabia and Iran, insurance such as medical/health or motor takāful is prevailing. The current low diffusion of takāful services indicate there is ample opportunity for further growth of the insurance/takāful industry, combined with high population growth and a growing middle class.

Also, the IFSI report revealed that the business profiles of takāful operators differ among the countries to a great extent. They found that in Malaysia, family takāful is 68.1% of the total business line, which is the highest number in the sample. The combination of a relatively young population, a high percentage of working population, a vibrant social security system, and saving incentives for retirement plays a part in the high proportion of life insurance in its society, including family takāful. Behind Malaysia is Pakistan and the UAE which comprise a reasonable share of family takāful – around 30%. This is not so in Saudi Arabia, where health coverage is compulsory and a tradition of long-term saving using insurance/takāful products is non-existent. Other countries with low shares of family takāful are Kuwait (at 8.6%) and Bangladesh and Qatar (both at 0%). From the rising trends of births and the middle class, policies geared towards increasing public awareness on such services as well as those encouraging long-term savings such as unit-linked instruments could grow the family takāful business.

Motor takāful is the second-most important business line in the sample countries of the IFSI report, with an average of 27.7% over the entire sample of countries. Kuwait has the highest share of motor takāful, followed by Sri Lanka, Pakistan, and Qatar.

The third-most important business line for takāful was fire, property and accidents, with the highest levels of domestic markets in Qatar and Bangladesh. Other business lines in the takāful sector include workmen's compensation and energy takāful, which has a considerable traction in the UAE and Sri Lanka.

4.2 Blockchain-based takāful

Smart contracts deployed through the blockchain will provide customers and takāful (insurance) companies a system to manage claims in a transparent, quick, and indisputable manner. Takāful policies, along with its terms and conditions, and potential claims can be recorded onto the blockchain and validated by the network, ensuring valid claims are dispensed and rejecting false claims.[1] For example, the blockchain will reject multiple claims for one accident because the network would know that a claim has already been made. Smart contracts would also process claims efficiently, by triggering payments automatically when certain conditions are met and validated. To more effectively detect identity fraud, falsified injury, or damage reports, blockchain can be used as a cross-industry, distributed registry with external and customer data to

- Confirm authenticity, ownership, and origin of goods as well as legitimacy of documents (e.g., medical reports).
- Check for police reports indicating theft, claims history as well as a person's verified identity and expose patterns of deception related to a particular person or identity.
- Proof of date and time stamps of policy issuance or purchase of a product/asset.
- Validate ownership and site changes.

Still, to attain full blockchain-specific benefits from these applications above what is achievable with traditional solutions and other current types of cooperation, e.g. via industry associations, broad cooperation between insurers, customers, manufacturers, and other stakeholders, is needed. This is an example of an ecosystem growing beyond the traditional industry practice in the sharing economy of the digital era. Emerging blockchain applications and four key areas where we see the most potential for evolution and transformation are as follows:

- **Fraud Detection and Risk Mitigation**
  The blockchain has the potential to eradicate mistakes and detect deceptive activity because of its ability to be a public ledger across multiple unknown parties. A distributed digital depot can autonomously confirm the legitimacy of customers, policies, and transactions (such as claims) by presenting a comprehensive historical record. As such,

insurers would be able to spot fake or counterfeit transactions involving doubtful people and suspect entities.

First-movers insurers are already evaluating the use of blockchain to mitigate scams and risks related to cross-border payments and transactions linking multiple currencies. In forte insurance and reinsurance segments, where insurers are often disconnected from the clients, blockchain may be used to tackle the significant inefficiencies, disparities, and errors caused by bad data quality from the front and back offices. In the US, health insurers and regulators view blockchain as a powerful tool for fighting Medicare deceit. Validation and verification form the nucleus of the blockchain business case, which can improve many insurance processes.

Blockchain will lessen administrative and operational costs through automated verification of policyholder identity and contract validity, auditable record of claims and information from third parties (e.g. encrypted patient data between doctor and injured party manageable by insurer to authenticate payment), and disbursement for claims through a blockchain-based payments infrastructure or smart contracts-linked escrow account. Providing reinsurers controlled access to claims and claims histories recorded on the blockchain increases transparency for the reinsurer in an automated yet auditable manner.

- **Claims Processing and Management**

  Besides mobile and digital technologies, blockchain is essential to establishing an efficient, transparent, and customer-focused claims model based on higher degrees of trust through transparency. Within claims management, new data streams can enhance the risk selection process by combining location, external risk, and data analytics. A distributed ledger integrated to existing systems can enable the insurer and various third parties to easily and instantly access and update relevant information (e.g., claim forms, photo evidence, police reports, and eyewitness or third-party accounts).

  The application of data from a mobile phone can simplify claims submission, reduce loss adjustment costs, and increase client satisfaction, with blockchain systems connecting communications to all parties.

  Correspondingly, the use of mobile technologies, satellite imagery, sensor data, and blockchain could facilitate claims payments and rescue services when natural disasters occur in remote areas. Information collected from weather stations could establish claims sum based on actual climate readings, with blockchain facilitating more efficient data sharing and stronger protection against fraud.

  In addition, advanced technology will be able to work effortlessly through the concept of Internet of Things (IoT) where massive devices are linked via the internet. For example, accident claims can be made through an app provided by the insurer by taking pictures or sending videos of accidents which are time-stamped. Together with blockchain solutions for know-your-client (KYC) data, a client can send the verified identity data to other companies for confirmation with the same app, avoiding the need to repeat the verification process, thus expediting efficiency in the onboarding of new users.

- **New Distribution and Payment Models**

  Some international insurers are already developing partnerships and exploring new payment systems and business models (cryptocurrencies and digital wallets) to achieve capital efficiencies through a truly public global ledger system. Increased computerization to acquire risk information in contracts also suggests new opportunities to build market intelligence, simplify payments, and build financing risk. At the very least, global insurers can use the blockchain to remove asset management costs or hedging fees required for mitigating currency fluctuations in cross-border and international transactions.

  In the new business model, the focus of the insurers would be on matching supply and demand to risk calculation research, instead of asset management. The insurer could create a marketplace-like platform where customers can post their insurance demand, which could be either a standardized product or even a specific demand. The insurer then would use its risk models along with 'risk assessment intelligence', based on available historical information, to perform a premium calculation for the expected return. With this expected return, interested investors can bid or subscribe to the demanded insurance.

  With the use of smart contracts and records on a decentralized ledger, the payment from the investor to the customer in the event of an insurance claim become cheaper, transparent, and more efficient than long-established ways. In addition, the investors know their maximum exposure as the amount defined in the smart contracts.

  The insurer can also now play the role of assessor of the damage to validate the authenticity of the insurance claim. But this could as easily be outsourced to a third party and by connecting the blockchain to other ledgers where verification can be done automatically.

- **Reinsurance**

  Property and casualty insurers seeking clearer visibility into their reinsurance contracts and risk exposures may gain it through blockchain. Consider the case of an insurer seeking to offload an equal amount of risk to two separate reinsurers. A blockchain ledger could provide insight and notification if one of those reinsurers then tried to offload some of its portion to a subsidiary of the other reinsurer. It also would help insurers gain confidence that, as they pay out claims, they are appropriately rebalancing their capital exposures against specific risks.

  Within reinsurance, the benefits of blockchain include more accurate reserve calculations based on actual participating contracts and automatic calculation updates once the primary information and data are updated. On top of that, insurers obtain more room to move capital and improve transparency into known risks, capital productivity, and compliance. Operationally, the process of audit trails becomes simpler to chart, modelling requirements are significantly reduced, and there is less coordination required between the finance and IT functions.

4.3 Enablers to blockchain-based insurance

In order to help develop takāful services offered by takāful insurers to their customers, the required enablers to systematize these services are smart contracts and instant payment infrastructures. These enablers will amplify the benefits for takāful insurers, banks, financial institutions, and businesses using digitally dispersed ledgers in fraud detection, claims management, and reinsurance.

4.3.1 Blockchain-based smart contracts

The idea of automating the insurance policy once it is written into a smart contract is appealing. The transparency of events along the supply chain via the blockchain is itself a major enabler of faster payment and improved financing, increased efficiency, reduced risk of fraud, and lower costs. Smart contracts are self-executing computer codes that automatically carry out functions once a triggering event has taken place. It is a linear contract that can include multiple parties (buyer, seller, banks, insurance companies, etc.) and that cannot be altered.

For example, if a smart contract is written between a buyer and a seller to say that once goods have been cleared by customs, 25% of the funds will be released to the seller, a smart contract would automatically pay out once authentication is made via a distributed ledger that the customs office has cleared the goods. The clearance by customs does not trigger any action by a bank but the confirmation entered into the system triggers the payment. With a smart contract, legal terms and conditions are set in the computer program, which facilitates the preset execution of functions determined by a contractual agreement.

4.3.2 What is a smart contract, and how does it work?[2]

Smart contracts are a multifarious set of software codes with parts created to computerize the execution and completion of contractual agreements. In other words, they are programmable agreements which self-execute the terms and conditions of an agreement when preset conditions are set off. Once counterparties assent to all of the terms within the contract, they cryptographically sign the smart contract and release it to a dispersed ledger. When a stipulation specified in the program is satisfied, the code automatically prompts a consequent action. By removing the need for direct human involvement, a deployed smart contract on a distributed ledger could make legal agreements more efficient and cost-effective with fewer errors, delays, or disputes.

Smart contracts on the blockchain

Smart contracts on the blockchain can be referred to Figure 6.1, page 140 in DOI:10.1515/9781547400966-202, by the same authors (see for details: Mohamed and Ali 2018) in which author explains the critical characteristics of smart contracts are

i programmability,
ii multi-signature (or multisig) authentication escrow capability, and
iii predictive inputs.

- A smart contract automatically performs according to programmed logic.
- Multisig allows two or more parties to the contract to consent the execution of an operation independently – an essential requisite for multiparty contracts.
- The escrow facility guarantees the securing of funds with a mediator (e.g. a bank or an online market) which can be released under provisions satisfactory to contracting parties. Sometimes, external data such as prices, performance, or other real-world inputs may be required to carry out an operation, and predictive services help smart contracts with inputs such as these.

There are several types of smart contracts being developed currently but the principal blockchain-based technology uses public key encryption infrastructure (PKI) to program the stipulations of a contract. PKI is a system of cryptography that uses of two types of keys: a public key apparent to all parties and a private key only to its recipient. In a smart contract transaction initiated on a blockchain, the sending recipient encrypts their message into an unreadable 'cipher text' using mathematical algorithms to protect and mask the data. Only the use of a private key can decode the 'cipher text' back into a readable 'plain text'. The vital advantage of PKI is in its security, as it is extremely difficult, to reconfigure a public key to a private one, making it very resilient to failures or hacks.

Smart contracts can be seen as the future of legal agreements, as they enable more efficiencies in commercial contracts through a decrease in manual processing, initiation of contract terms, and risk reduction through the elimination of manual errors and duplicate invoice financing. However, legal and regulatory challenges surround smart contracts in many jurisdictions, and many companies exploring the use of smart contracts are still in the proof of concept stage. To accelerate maturity of this technology, smart contract terms need to be standardized, small-scale B2B smart contract applications need to succeed and grow, and adoption for use in trade finance will pave the way to the actualization of the theoretical benefits.

How the blockchain cryptography works for smart contracts

The detail structure of the blockchain cryptography work can be referred to Figure 6.2, page 141 in DOI 10.1515/9781547400966-202, by the same authors (see for details: Mohamed and Ali, 2018).

4.3.3 Instant payment structures

The development of instant payment infrastructures is another key enabler that will add speed and efficiency to trade transactions. Over 20 countries around the world have already implemented instant payment infrastructures, and major markets such as Australia, the US, the Eurozone, and Asia are in the process of developing and testing instant payment systems. With the ability to send and receive domestic payments within seconds, the movement of money triggered by events along the supply chain can proceed more rapidly, which means that shipping companies, customs offices, and sellers have quicker access to funds. Instant payments can also enable both buyers and sellers to obtain funding from their banks faster than they do today, which can lead to a further optimization of working capital and unlock liquidity from supply chains.

4.4 Moving forward

Blockchain functions as a distributed system, and thus, its value will mostly depend on collaboration with all actors in the value chain like customers, service providers, payment systems, and regulators. Blockchain is an IT investment with a perspective of presumably five years until full realization of benefits. In application areas that do not strongly rely on blockchain's distributed mechanisms, alternative solutions can provide similar benefits much sooner. For the industry as a whole, this means starting to work with consortia, technology experts and start-ups, regulators, and other market participants to identify the challenges around and leverage upon blockchain's open and decentralized nature. Among these challenges are technology limitations as well as market, legal/regulatory (who regulates in the absence of an intermediary or in cross-border transactions), and operational requirements regarding, for example, data protection and standardization.

Individual takāful companies should start with a holistic understanding of customer engagement needs and their own pain points to assess where the most promising blockchain use cases exist. As an innovative technology, blockchain presents a threat for incumbents in the form of innovative business models and/or cost advantages. But there is a range of options to counteract this threat by adopting the way of working of start-ups, partnering with, or acquiring them. Key to shaping the future of the blockchain takāful ecosystem is getting involved in partnerships and industry activities early on.

4.5 Conclusion

The use of distributed ledgers to exchange data related to transfer of goods and information could also enable more granular payments along the supply chain. Enabling all actors in the supply chain to directly input information into a distributed ledger means that there is more visibility of each step along the supply chain. These events could facilitate smaller portions of financing to be released, thereby unlocking liquidity and reducing the risk of non-payment.

In an era of 'point innovations' such as mobile apps and robo-advisory models, blockchain stands out as a more foundational or architectural development. In that sense, blockchain may support, and subsequently drive, increased use and broader adoption of the many other digital innovations that have helped reshape the insurance landscape.

Takāful operations management should recognize how the blockchain can increase trust and transparency, which speaks to the heart of the insurance business. After all, the industry's inherent bond of trust and 'promise to pay' are based on disclosure of accurate personal data describing the insurable interests of the client, the agreement to a contract between two parties, and timely exchange of payment. Blockchain can help remove friction, errors, and risks from all of these essential steps. There is substance behind the hype, but the insurance industry must make investments now to be in a position to take advantage of efficiencies and opportunities blockchain technology can deliver long term.

It is vital that the Islamic economic actors surmount current and future challenges related to insurance by manifesting the objectives of the *Shari'ah*. One of the most fundamental functions of takāful is to provide the efficient compliance to settlements of claims according to agreed contractual stipulations and timely payouts of those genuine claims. The development of a blockchain-based insurance system would help to propel the Islamic takāful industry into a competitive one through cost-efficient processes, faster verifications, and better fraud detection capabilities. This way the takāful operators show nimbleness by adjusting to changing trends and landscapes, and after all, mitigating risks through takāful insurance is perceived as protecting one's lifestyle and livelihood.

Notes

1 An estimated 5%–10% of all claims are fraudulent. According to the estimated global size of the takāful industry, this costs takāful operators more than US$2 billion per year.

2 Taken from an article I wrote for https://journal.wahedinvest.com/smart-contracts-in-islamic-economic-transactions with similar section.

References

Islamic Financial Services Board (IFSB), Islamic Financial Services Industry Stability Report 2016, www.ifsb.org/docs/IFSI%20Stability%20Report%202016%20(final).pdf.

Mohamed, H., and Ali, H. (2018). "Blockchain, Fintech and Islamic Finance", De|G Press, Walter de Gruyter Inc., Boston/Berlin. DOI 10.1515/9781547400966-202.

5 IT-based Finance Hub

A new horizon towards transparent Zakat distribution model

Umar Draz, Tariq Ali, Sana Yasin, Ahmad Shaf and Raiha Tallat

5.1 Introduction

More than 70% of the population of this world live in a very poor miserable condition. The total wealth of this world is circulating among some millionaire families. The unbalance of wealth may cause several conflicts in society. In the 21st century, the ratio of poverty is increased day-by-day. According to Oxfam [1, 2], the 64 richest billionaires have enough wealth that is nearly equal to the half poorer population of the world. Due to this biggest fact, all small countries that have no enough resources do not meet the normal living standards. Due to lack of food and agriculture resources, famine becomes the dominant attack on these types of small countries. But there is a very interesting fact about all these small countries where the famine comes two to three times in last two decades concluded that the lack of food and resources does not cause the occurrence of famine. The unbalance of wealth is the major cause that famine occurs in these areas. In these types of countries where rich become richer and poor become poorer, the house of poverty come into exists for a long time [3]. Due to all these fundamental reasons, Islam teaches us a very efficient concept of Zakat. Being the fifth pillar of Islam, Zakat is very important for the humanity to make it balance. Salah and Zakat simultaneously discussed in Quran at 70 different places. The importance of Zakat in Islam can never be underestimated. Zakat is basically the name of purification of wealth through some Islamic manners. There are many selective parameters that cover the Zakat donor as well as acceptor. The most influential parameters that are more deserving of Zakat are disabled persons. These persons do not perform any single duty due to their disability [5].

Pakistan, being a Muslim country, has established several laws for the collection of Zakat as there are various banks who deduct Zakat amount automatically from the account if account holder meets the requirement of Zakat [6, 7]. Many banking systems are present that performed the mechanism of Zakat at charity month. In charity month they deduct the Zakat amount automatically without the willingness of account holder. The account holder is also not sure about whether its deducted wealth is being given to deserving people or not. Due to these several reasons, it forces the account holder to withdraw their amount at the beginning of charity month and to resubmit at the end of charity month [8]. This chapter presents a new idea: an Information Technology (IT)-based Finance Hub that will be established at Union Council (UC) level under the control of Government of Pakistan. The graphical model of proposed IT-based Finance Hub is shown in Figure 5.1 for a semiformal representation.

Initially, this Finance Hub will support the disabled people in respective areas. This Finance Hub will be responsible to collect Zakat from the wealthy people of their areas and distribute Zakat equally among the registered disabled people for their whole life. The elected heads of the centers will morally counsel the wealthy people in their respective areas towards a donation of Zakat, and they will also be responsible for investigation and registration of deserving disabled people to maintain the transparency of Zakat distribution. The donors will pay Zakat to the financial hub, and the Finance Hub will be linked to the banking systems to ensure that their Zakat will not be deducted again by the banks. All the above process gives the additional confidence to the donor such that they will willingly give the charity to proposed Finance Hub. To make the system clear in a well-disciplined manner the proposed Finance Hub

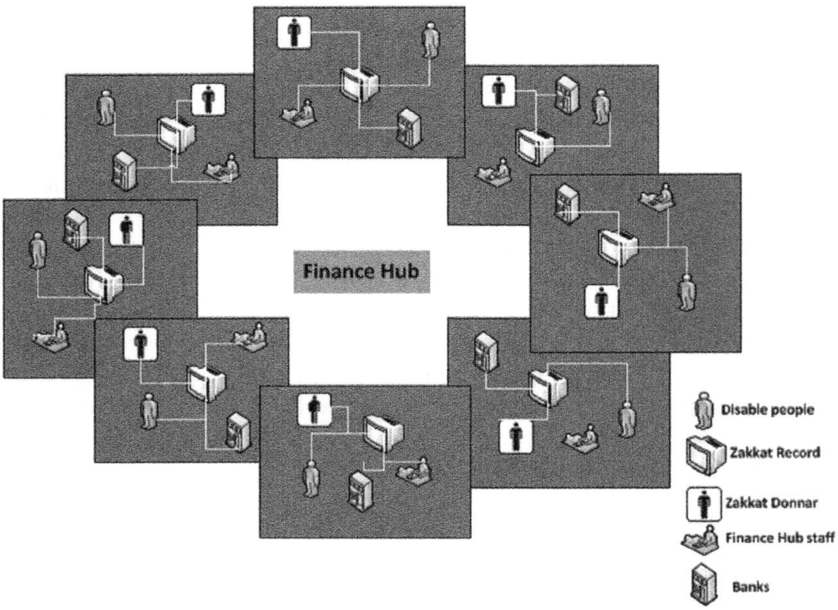

Figure 5.1 IT-based Finance Hub.

is attached to all types of banks that are under the radius of UC. Most of the work on Zakat distribution is already be done in the form of survey or some comparative studies, which have a lot of drawbacks [2, 9–12]. For example, all the proposed model and comparative Zakat system do not provide the correctness of the model. Formal specifications that are applied to formal methods are more effective and efficient to provide the correctness proof of the model.

The Vienna Development Methods-Specification Language (VDM-SL) is used in this research work. The VDM-SL toolbox is used to provide a formal specification of IT-based Finance Hub. To the best of our knowledge, this is the first work that used formal methods in this domain. Previously there are not any formal specifications present that formalize the Zakat system.

Rest of this chapter covers the related work in this area described in Section 2. The proposed high-level algorithm is discussed in Section 3. Section 4 is used to describe the formal section and its invariants of IT-based Finance Hub. At the end, Section 5 concludes the chapter.

5.2 Related work

Many models are present based on Zakat distribution, as Islamic banking is also an example of this domain. A lot of systems and strategies are proposed that manage and control the Zakat transparency and its collection. According to the survey of Organization of Islamic Countries (OIC) that consists of 17 member countries, we found that the ratio of Zakat to GDP exceeds the poverty gap [1, 13, 14]. Pakistan is also the member of this organization so that the poverty ratio is rapidly increased in last five years. In order to evaluate the growth of the economy, there is a need to refine the Zakat system. To mitigate the gap between poor and rich the alternative approach with the Zakat system is used in [15]. '*Zakat*' and '*user*' are two fundamental programs of Pakistan with three main objectives discussed in [16] which adopted some different types of the banking system. The detailed survey that covers the aspect of poverty index, welfare index, wealth index, material poverty index, absolute poverty index, and spiritual poverty index is used a tool of analysis [3, 17]. The objective of this analysis is used to gather information about all relative indexes that directly or indirectly affect the performance of Zakat distribution model. All the welfare potential institutions of Pakistan that have the literature of livestock, tradable inventory, currency in circulation, foreign exchange reserves, and financial assets like national saving scheme are presented in [13]. Nowadays most of the research communities have focused the semiformal specifications; for example, simulation and testing of the proposed model have been done in VDM-SL for this research work.

Recently the researchers used VDM-SL to verify the algorithm and models to overcome the cons of non-formal techniques [18–20]. Z-notation is also used for the verification and validation purposes. Recently the earthquake management system and the forest fire detection system are formalized under the VDM-SL platform. Formal methods are also used for safety-critical systems like to rescue the victim alive or not in disaster management, air traffic control system, railway interlocking system, and intelligent buildings system [21–26]. This work is done with the help of formal specification due to its descriptive power for formal modeling and verification.

5.3 Working mechanism for IT-based Finance Hub

The basic working diagram of this proposed IT-based Finance Hub is starting with creating the hub under the umbrella of government. The collection of Zakat from wealthy people is performed by a transparent method that encourages disabled people under three defined categories. The VDM-SL toolbox is used to verify and validate each credential of this model. The basic flow chart of this hub is discussed in Figure 5.2.

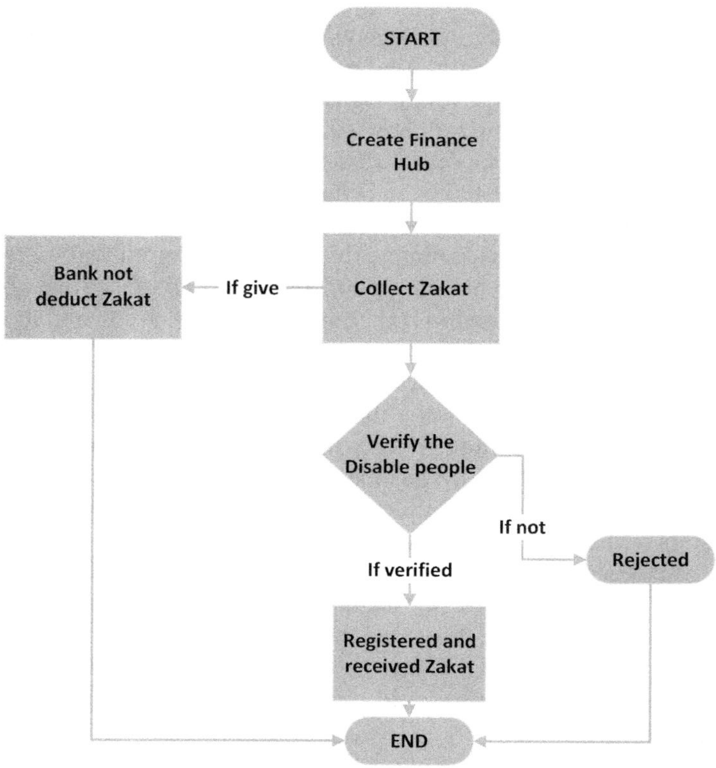

Figure 5.2 Flowchart of Finance Hub.

5.4 High-level pseudocode of IT-based Finance Hub algorithm

We proposed the IT-based Finance Hub algorithm (ITB-FHA), which proactively defines the finance hub centers at union council level. This Finance Hub further links all types of the banking system that is under the radius of UC. The main purpose of linking the banking system with the Finance Hub is to ensure that the Zakat amount paid by the donor to the financial hub is not again deducted by banks. The dedicated staff of the Finance Hub will pursue and guide the wealthy people of the UC level to give the Zakat donation to this worthy and transparent Finance Hub. In the next step, the ITB-FHA makes the criteria for disability. The disability is either in major state or in minor state or in between these two states. To find out the disability and condition the Finance Hub staff makes the policy of giving the total amount of Zakat [27–29]. The entire Zakat amount is distributed according to the disability ratio (DR). The registration of disabled persons is set with its name and its credentials. The DR is also attached to the record of delivering the Zakat amount as per criteria. Collection of Zakat is sent to their homes monthly after ensuring all process. So in this process, the ITB-FHA is transparently not only distributing the Zakat but also achieving the satisfaction of donor people. All the donor and acceptor people will be confidential in the record of the Finance Hub. The high-level pseudocode of the Finance Hub model is described in Table 5.1.

Table 5.1 High-Level Pseudocode of the System

1	The new proposed Finance Hub will be established at the UC level, and it will be controlled by the government.
2	Finance Hub will be linked to the banking systems to ensure that Zakat amount paid by donor to the financial hub will not be deducted by the banks.
3	First, Finance Hub staff will pursue the wealthy people of the UC to give the Zakat donation to the financial hub.
4	Finance Hub center will have eligibility criteria to give the Zakat amount to the disabled people.
5	It divides the disabled people into three categories: major, average, and minor.
6	The people that have no background and their DR is 80% then it will fall under the 'major' category.
7	If people have 60% DR and have some background support then it will fall under the 'average' category.
8	The strong financial background with 40% DR people will fall under the 'minor' category.
9	Zakat amount will be given according to the DR of the people.
10	Each Finance Hub will be able to purely register the disabled person with their name, age, and DR.
11	Total Zakat amount will be equally distributed in the 12th month. Disabled person will be received Zakat amount on monthly basis not annually.
12	In case of any emergency Finance Hub staff will have authority to register, remove, or update the record of disabled people.
13	This center will provide a transparent process that gives the confidence to the wealthy people, and they will willingly give charity to proposed centers.
14	The following process will be continued to provide the transparent way of Zakat distribution.

5.5 IT-based Finance Hub algorithm

The form of inputs examined all the drawbacks of the existing model of Zakat and proposed the first IT-based model that uses the formal specification and verification. Under the umbrella of government, the IT-based Finance Hub model is developing at UC level (line 1). In every UC, development of the Finance Hub is responsible to connect all types of banks. Each bank is linked to the Finance Hub server that makes the records of donor people and informs to bank system (line 2–3). If the donor account already exists in the bank, the Finance Hub informs the bank authority not to deduct the money again in the charity month. Distribution criteria are set and applied to all the disabled persons (line 4–5). Records of all disabled persons are managed in line 6. The distribution criteria and its ratio according to the category of disability are discussed in line 7. If the disabled people find out as per the criteria then distribution of the Zakat ratio as deal in line 8–10 of ITB-FHA. The high-level pseudocode algorithm is shown in Table 5.2.

5.6 Formal specification of ITB-FHA using VDM-SL

In this section formal specifications are to be applied with the help of formal methods using VDM-SL. A lot of terms and constructs are used to identify each formal specification, for example, composite objects, sets, invariants, types, union, and pre/postconditions. Pre- and postconditions play part and parcel role to develop the formal specification of any constructs, and these

Table 5.2 Algorithm of ITB-FH

INPUT: Existing traditional Zakat distribution system
OUTPUT: A new IT-based transparent model for the collection and distribution of Zakat
1 Finance Hub establishment at union council level under government
2 $\forall$ *Finance Hub* F_k *for* $K = 1,2,......n$
3 Bank relation (Finance Hub) // Link each Finance Hub with banking system
4 $\forall$ *Finance Hub* F_k *for* $K = 1,2,......n$
5 ***Set distribution criteria*** (disabled people)
6 If disability ratio<= 40%
7 Then low=disabled people
8 If disability ratio<= 60%
9 Then average=disabled people
10 If disability ratio<= 80%
11 Then major=disabled people;
12 $\forall$ *Disable people* P_k *for* $K = 1,2,......n$
13 While $\boldsymbol{d_0}$< d Do where do=Disability ratio, d=Distribution criteria
14 ***Find disabled people*** ($\boldsymbol{P_k}$).
15 ***If*** found the disable people ***go to line 16***
16 ***Distribute*** ($\boldsymbol{D_i, P_i}$)
D_i = *Distribution criteria*, P_i = *Disable people*
17 This process continues to provide transparent Zakat distribution
18 ***End While***
19 ***End if***
20 ***End For***

strategies usually lead towards the verification and validation of the proposed system. With the help of the dynamic and static nature of the formal specifications that is already defined in the proposed model. The static model deals with all the definition of data types and its related values, whereas the dynamic model deals with the corresponding state and its operations.

The Finance Hub consists of finance staff, disabled people, and its category. All these attributes are generally described as a composite object with the type of Token. The Finance Hub consists of basic rules like types of disabled people with its category, major, minor, and average. Initially, at each UC level, 500 disable people will be selected for Zakat. The decision of distribution money will be taken while observing the category of disability. From the total decided amount of Zakat, the 30% is given to those with minor disabilities. Similarly, for average and major disabilities, the 60% and 80% is given. Registration field deals with the set of all disabled people, and registration of staff field registered the set of all staff members. The total possible category of disability is also registered separately. The formal specification of central hub represents *hub_reg* as the composite object type. The formal condition of staff registration is less than the proposed *limit* value.

```
types
staff=token;
FinanceHub=token;
people=token;

Type:: Disable_people:people
Minor_disable:people
Average_disable:people
Major_disble:people
values
LIMIT:nat=500
MINOR:nat=40
AVERAGE:nat=60
MAJOR:nat=80
```

Invariants: (1) The main state called Finance Hub in which the registration of each module is separately defined. The staff registration consists of staff people that are worked for the Finance Hub. Minor, major, and average disabilities are separately defined to take the specification clear in a scene of Zakat distribution. The specific amount of Zakat is equally distributed according to this three defined categories. The possible invariants and initialization are defined in which the total number of disabled people does not exceed the proposed limit.

```
state FinanceHub  of
reg: set of disable people
staf_reg: set of people
banking_system:banks
finance_hub:hub
Major: set of people
Average: set of people
Low: set of people
Amount_reg: set of amount
Minor_disable_reg: set of disable people
Average_disable_reg: set of disable people
Major_disble_reg: set of disable people
staff: set of staff
hub_reg: set of centers
inv mk_FinanceHub(staf_reg)== card staf_reg <=LIMIT
init p==p=mk_FinanceHub({})
--init mk_FinanceHub(satf_reg)==staf_reg={}
end
```

In our proposed algorithm the first operation that needs to be investigated is the creation of the Finance Hub. The type of Finance Hub is set because the Finance Hub further deals with the collection of items. The external class deals with the registration of all hubs that are further linked with all types of banks in the area of union council. The possible precondition of registration is to include finance center if it is not the part of hub. The formal postcondition is that the existing registration hub is taking the union of all new registration.

```
operations
Create_Sub_Finance_Hub(HubIn:Hub)
ext wr hub_ reg: set of Hubs
pre HubIn not in set reg and card hub_reg <LIMIT
post hub_reg= hub_reg~ union {HubIn};
```

Before adding the disabled persons in a system there is a need to set the eligibility criteria for disabled people in the Finance Hub. The formal specification of these statements is composite type because the set of all categories becomes the part of eligibility criteria.

Invariants: The eligibility criteria deals with three classes like minor, average, and major that cover the disable registration. The main invariants in this regard are that the cardinality of this entire category does not exceed the proposed existing value. In this way, this condition becomes the precondition that is to be executed before postcondition. The post condition deals three possibilities like if the Zakat acceptor fails in minor, major, and average disability then the registered.

```
Eligibal_criteria(peopleIn:people)
ext wr Minor_disable_reg: set of disable people
ext wr Average_disable_reg: set of disable people
ext wr Major_disble_reg: set of disable people
pre
invmk_Eligibal_criteria(Minor_disable_reg,Average_disable_reg,Major_disable_r
eg)==
card Minor_disable_reg <=MINOR, card Average_disable_reg <=AVERAGE, card
Major_disable_reg <=MAJOR;
post Minor_disable_reg= Minor_disable_reg~ union {peopleIn}OR
Average_disable_reg= Average_disable_reg~ union {peopleIn}OR
Major_disable_reg= Major_disable_reg~ union {peopleIn}
```

Invariant Add disabled people: In the formal specification of "add disabled people" in the system, the state is a collection of sets by default data types. If the new people are already the part of the system then do not add them and vice versa.

```
Add_Disable_people(peopleIn:people)
ext wr reg: set of people
pre peopleIn not in set disable_people
post reg=reg~ union {peopleIn};
```

Invariant Remove disabled people: In the formal specification, the remove and add option is frequently used. To remove the already-registered people, the precondition is to ensure if the people are already registered or not. If yes, then they are removed from the system.

```
Remove_Disable_people(peopleIn:people)
ext wr reg: set of People
pre peopleIn in set reg
post reg = reg~ \ {peopleIn};
```

Get Record of disabled people: To take record of the people, the formal specification takes the input as people and the output is also a set of people. There is no such precondition involved here, but formally the '*true*' is written in front of precondition. The postcondition is that set of all registered people belong to any category. **Is Registered:** To make sure that particular people are registered or not, there are two invariants present with formally defined pre- and postconditions. The possible input is the set of people, and the output is the Boolean type. The Boolean-type function is used in this scenario because only true or false output will come that ensures the specification of registration.

```
Get Record()output: set of People
ext rd reg: set of People
pre true
post output=reg;
Is Registered(peopleIn:people)query:bool
ext rd reg: set of people
pre true
post query <=> peopleIn in set reg;
```

Is Eligible: The eligibility criteria of the disabled person is already mentioned. All the pre- and post-conditions that decide the eligibility in any category is formally defined in the particular state of the system. The output of this system is also Boolean type. If the people are satisfied with the criteria mentioned in algorithm, then precondition is true. **Total disabled people:** To find out the cardinality of disabled people that are registered with this system the formal specification is set of all people. The external class is only in reading because there is no need of any operation. If pre condition is true by default then the post condition shows the total number of people that already part of the system.

```
Is Eligible(peopleIn:people,reg:people)query:bool
ext rd reg: set of people
pre true
post query <=> mk_peopleIn in set reg;
Total_Disable_people()total:nat
ext rd reg: set of People
pre true
post  total= card reg;
```

Criteria for disability person: For the distribution of Zakat there are different disability categories like major, minor, and average. (1) In case of major disability, about 80% of the total amount of Zakat is distributed. (2) In case of minor and average disability about 60%–40% of the whole amount is distributed.

```
Major Disability criteria(peopleIn:people,disablityratio:N)
ext wr Major: set of people
pre disablity-ratio<=80% and peopleIn not in set Major_category
post Major=Major~ union {peopleIn};

Average Disability criteria(peopleIn:people, disablityratio:N)
ext wr Average: set of people
pre disablity-ratio<=60% and peopleIn not in set Average_category
post Average=Average~ union {peopleIn};

Low Disability criteria(peopleIn:people, disablityratio:N)
ext wr Low: set of people
pre disablity-ratio<=40% and peopleIn not in set Low_category
post Low=Low~ union {peopleIn};
```

Distribution of Zakat: The formal specification of the distribution of Zakat among different categories is mentioned in below coding section. To make the transparent and fair distribution there is a need to apply the formal methods if the individuals do not fall into more than one category at the same time. The possible specification of this is divided into two formal conditions. (1) First of all, check whether the disabled people are eligible for the Zakat amount; if yes, then it is sure the assigned category in which the person falls is best suited under the proposed criteria, then register them for the best-suited categories like major, minor, and average.

```
Zakat_Distribution for Major(peopleIn:people)
ext wr major_amount_reg: set of amount
pre peopleIn in set disable_people and peopleIn in set Major;
post major_amount_reg=major_amount_reg~ union {peopleIn};

Zakat_Distribution for Average(peopleIn:people)
ext wr average_amount_reg: set of amount
pre peopleIn in set disable_people and peopleIn in set Average;
post average_amount_reg=average_amount_reg~ union {peopleIn};

Zakat_Distribution for Low(peopleIn:people)
ext wr low_amount_reg: set of amount
pre peopleIn in set disable_people and peopleIn in set Low;
post low_amount_reg=low_amount_reg~ union {peopleIn};
```

Bank Verification: For the verification purposes, the Boolean-type data set is used which have two possible values: either yes or no. If the Zakat of individual is deducted by the Finance Hub then the hub administration informs the linked banks to stop deduction the Zakat at the charity month of the same person. If all the stakeholders are the part of the Finance Hub management then their amount will not be deducted from any bank inside the area.

```
Bank  Verification(peopleIn:people)query:bool
ext wr banking_system:banks
Pre  peopleIn  in set finance_hub;
post banks = banks ~ \ {peopleIn};
```

5.7 Model analysis

The proposed formal specification for the IT-based Finance Hub through the technique is available in the VDM-SL toolbox. For the verification and validation purposes, the formal specification is analyzed through a different syntax checker, type checker, C++ code generator, and pretty printer. The main objective of verification through syntax and type checker is to check whether the formal specification is according to the syntax of VDM-SL. Through a type checker, it verifies the correct usage of different data types. Through the code generator of C++, the proposed formal specification is converted into object-oriented language. To avoid the inconsistency the pretty printer is used. The runtime error and the dynamic behavior of the formal specification of the IT-based Finance Hub deal with the pretty printer. It also validates all related properties of type and data checking of some invariants like pre- and postconditions. The model analysis through VDM-SL is shown in Table 5.2. And the formal summary of the proposed result is shown in Table 5.3 (Figure 5.3).

Table 5.3 Analysis of State, Functions, and Operations

Composite object, State, Function, and Operations	*Syntax Check*	*Type Check*	*Pretty Check*	*Integrity Check*
Banks	Y	Y	Y	Y
Finance Hub	Y	Y	Y	Y
Disable people	Y	Y	Y	-
Staff/administration	Y	Y	Y	Y
Eligibility criteria	Y	Y	Y	Y
Model/pseudocode	Y	Y	Y	Y
Algorithm/mechanism	Y	Y	Y	Y
Zakat donor	Y	Y	Y	-
Zakat acceptor	Y	Y	Y	-
Zakat record	Y	Y	Y	-
Distribution	Y	Y	Y	-
Attribute operations	Y	Y	Y	-
Values	Y	Y	Y	Y
Bank verification	Y	Y	Y	Y
Area of UC	Y	Y	Y	Y
People of UC	Y	Y	Y	Y
Collection	Y	Y	Y	Y
Registration	Y	Y	Y	Y
Verification and validation	Y	Y	Y	Y

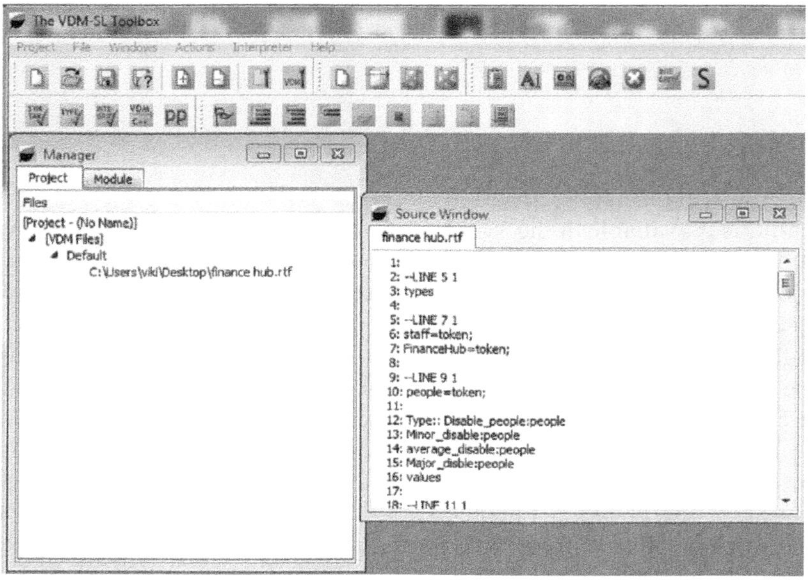

Figure 5.3 Proof of correctness through VDM-SL toolbox.

5.8 Conclusion

Pakistan, being a Muslim country, has established several laws to collect the Zakat as there are various banks who deduct Zakat amount automatically from the account if account holder meets the requirement of Zakat. This system has many problems like account holder willingness is not involved and they are not sure whether their amount is being given to deserving people or not. This chapter presents a new idea: a IT-based Finance Hub that will be established at Union Consul (UC) level under the control of Government of Pakistan. This Finance Hub will be responsible to collect Zakat from the wealthy people in their areas and distribute Zakat equally among the registered disabled people for their whole lives. The elected heads of the centers will morally counsel the wealthy people in their respective areas towards a donation of Zakat, and they will also be responsible for investigation and registration of eligible disabled people to maintain the transparency of Zakat distribution. Up to our best knowledge, through formal specification first time, this work is done on this domain to propose the IT-based Finance Hub. With the help of verification and validation, this work not only achieves the transparent distribution model but also takes the happy willingness of Zakat donor. These centers can also play a vital role to discourage the increasing mendicant's system in the society.

References

1. Shehu Usman Rano, A., *A Treatise on Socioeconomic Roles of Zakah*. 2017.
2. Shahed, A., A. Mamun, and S. Lubaba, Islamic microfinance for youth employment: A tentative model. *Journal of Islamic Philanthropy & Social Finance*, 2017. **1**(1): pp. 14–30.
3. Ahmad, M., et al., Zakat as a Social Safety Net: Assessing its Perception in a Less-Developed Rural District in Pakistan. *Journal of Social Service Research*, 2017. **43**(3): pp. 369–380.
4. Ali, K.M., *Integrating Zakah, Awqaf and Islamic Microfinance for Poverty Alleviation: Three Models Of Islamic Micro Finance*. 2014, IRTI Working Paper Series for Islamic Research and Training Institute.
5. Ahmed, E.R., et al., Zakat and Accounting Valuation Model. *Journal of Reviews on Global Economics*, 2016. **5**: pp. 16–24.
6. Bremer, J., *Zakat and Economic Justice: Emerging International Models and their Relevance for Egypt*. 2015.
7. Bhatti, A., et al., *Availability of an Adequate Compensation for Poor through a Model of Institutionalized Charity System in Pakistan*. Int. J. of Multidisciplinary and Current research, 2017. **5**.
8. M Akram, M. and M. Afzal, *Dynamic Role of Zakat in Alleviating Poverty: A Case Study of Pakistan*. 2014.
9. Mobin, M.A. and A.U.F. Ahmad, *Achieving Sustainable Economic Development through Islamic Microfinance and the Potential of a Proposed Two-Tier Mudarabah Waqf Business Model*. 2017, Edward Elgar Publishing.
10. Pepinsky, T.B. and B.C. Welborne, Piety and Redistributive Preferences in the Muslim World. *Political Research Quarterly*, 2011. **64**(3): pp. 491–505.
11. Rashid, M., et al., *Reporting of Zakat and Charitable Activities in Islamic Banks: Theory and Practice in a Multi-cultural Setting*. 2017, Edward Elgar Publishing.
12. Htay, S.N.N., et al., Integrating Zakat, Waqf and Sadaqah: Myint Myat Phu Zin Clinic Model in Myanmar. *Tazkia Islamic Finance and Business Review*, 2014. **8**(2): pp. 106–111.
13. Suhaib, A.Q., Contribution of Zakat in the Social Development of Pakistan. *Pakistan Journal of Social Sciences (PJSS)*, 2009. **29**(2): pp. 298–306.
14. Suprayitno, E., M. Aslam, and A. Harun, Zakat and SDGs: Impact Zakat on Human Development in the Five States of Malaysia. *International Journal of Zakat*, 2017. **2**(1): pp. 61–69.
15. Suprayitno, E., R.A. Kader, and A. Harun, The Impact of Zakat on Aggregate Consumption in Malaysia. *Journal of Islamic Economics, Banking and Finance*, 2013. **9**(1): pp. 39–62.
16. Turker, D., *Islamic Roots of Corporate Social Responsibility*, in *Cultural Roots of Sustainable Management*. 2016, Springer, Cham, Switzerland. pp. 133–144.
17. ul Mustafa, A.R. and M. Nishat, Role of Social Protection in Poverty Reduction In Pakistan: A Quantitative Approach. *Pakistan Journal of Applied Economics*, 2017. **27**(1): pp. 67–88.
18. Alnuem, M., et al., Formal Specification and Validation of a Localized Algorithm for Segregation of Critical/Noncritical Nodes in MAHSNs. *International Journal of Distributed Sensor Networks*, 2014. **10**(6): pp. 140–973.
19. Riaz, S., et al., Formalizing Mobile Ad Hoc and Sensor Networks Using VDM-SL. *Procedia Computer Science*, 2015. **63**: pp. 148–153.

20. Afzaal, H., M. Imran, and N.A. Zafar. Implementing Partitioning Detection and Connectivity Restoration in WSAN Using VDM-SL. in *Frontiers of Information Technology (FIT), 2015 13th International Conference on*. 2015. IEEE.
21. Afzaal, H., et al. Battlefield Surveillance Formalism Using WSANs. in *Electrical Engineering (ICEE), 2017 International Conference on*. 2017. IEEE.
22. Afzaal, H., et al. Animal Protection Algorithm and Formal Modeling Using WSANs. in *Communication Technologies (ComTech), 2017 International Conference on*. 2017. IEEE.
23. Zafar, N.A. and H. Afzaal, Formal Model of Earthquake Disaster Mitigation and Management System. *Complex Adaptive Systems Modeling*, 2017. **5**(1): p. 10.
24. Zafar, N.A., Formal Specification and Analysis of Take-off Procedure Using VDM-SL. *Complex Adaptive Systems Modeling*, 2016. **4**(1): p. 4.
25. Zafar, N.A., Formal Specification and Verification of Few Combined Fragments of UML Sequence Diagram. *Arabian Journal for Science and Engineering*, 2016. **41**(8): pp. 2975–2986.
26. Afzaal, H. and N.A. Zafar. Formal Localized Reactive Subnet-Based Failure Recovery Model for Sparsely Connected Wireless Sensor and Actor Networks. in *Open Source Systems & Technologies (ICOSST), 2015 International Conference on*. 2015. IEEE.
27. Owolabi Yusuf, M.-B. and A. Mat Derus, Measurement Model of Corporate Zakat Collection in Malaysia: A Test of Diffusion of Innovation Theory. *Humanomics*, 2013. **29**(1): pp. 61–74.
28. Beik, I.S. and L.D. Arsyianti, Measuring Zakat Impact on Poverty and Welfare Using CIBEST Model. *Journal of Islamic Monetary Economics and Finance*, 2016. **1**(2): pp. 141–160.
29. Beik, I.S. and C. Pratama, Zakat Impact on Poverty and Welfare of Mustahik: A CIBEST Model Approach. *AFEBI Islamic Finance and Economic Review*, 2017. **1**(01): pp. 12–21.

6 The way towards standardizing Islamic economic, financial, and banking fatawa

Masudul Alam Choudhury

6.1 Introduction

This is a short chapter focusing on the problems encountered by '*Shari'ah*-compliance' idea and practices of Islamic banking on the issues of standardization of rules and opinions concerning unification of financial fatawa. The chapter presents the authentic alternative means that could be adopted by Islamic banks to universally harmonize '*Shari'ah*-compliance' fatawa and practices in Islamic banking. These areas are now riddled with problems such as the following one: prevalence of the problem of interpretation of jurisprudence (fiqh) by diversity of views of Islamic schools. This is particularly noted for the Shafei school (madhab) in Malaysia, and oppositely by Hanbali and Hanafi madhabs in the Arab region and elsewhere. A concern of this chapter is on the topic of standardizing of fiqh interpretations and practices of Islamic banks. Along with this is the question: How can Islamic banks adjust their financial fatawa within the international monetary and financial system? How can fatawa be applied to matters of financial loans, deposits, and commercial matters including market exchange issues? How can multiplicity of fatawa, sometime by the same mujtahid (e.g. Shafei, Shatibi), and their contending juristic consequences on '*Shari'ah*-compliance' and product development be treated for unification under a standardized shar'iah rule? In answer to all of these questions, this chapter seeks for alternative views on financial pricing:

6.2 Objective

This chapter is simply a critique of the approach to standardization of fatawa around madhabi diversity and the alternative recommendation regarding practices of muamalat in its broad sense of finance, banking, and market exchange. The criticism here points out that the idea of '*Shari'ah*-compliance' cannot be upheld in light of the epistemic worldview of what truly is Islam when unequivocally understood and furthered upon her most indelible law that applies to 'everything'. This is the law of tawhid, oneness of Allah as the episteme of unity of knowledge as methodology leading to applications and inferences.

By tawhid as law, this chapter means the primal ontology of monotheistic unity of knowledge, and its induction and inquiry of all details of the world-system. Such world-systems are muamalat, money, finance, and Islamic banking. We will examine how tawhid as law can be uniquely and uniformly studied in and for standardization. Tawhid as law has a distinctive methodology that applies to formalism, interpretation, application, and sustainability of unity of knowledge in the framework of evolutionary learning on monotheistic unity of knowledge. While the vast details of the field of tawhidi methodological development as primal ontological law and applications are not covered in this chapter, the topic concerning these can be found in the works of Choudhury. Some of these are Choudhury (2006, 2014, 2016a, 2016b, 2017).

This chapter only picks up a few points of contention on the way towards financial standardization of juristic interpretations. By tawhid as law of unification and its methodological worldview this chapter points out how it can be universally acceptable. This is true not only for Muslims, but can also fit in with analytical and practical soundness of monetary, financial, banking, and market exchange matters in the global scene. Tawhid as law provides the gateway to all of these and more issues with an endless breadth of intellection and legal command.

6.3 Towards inevitability of tawhidi methodological worldview: problem with '*Shari'ah*-compliance'

'*Shari'ah*-compliance' is a human-concocted variant for legitimating product development. Yet it has no legitimate and established groundwork for attaining this goal, except by an institutional juristic imposition (e.g. AAOIFI, OIC, IDB, Bank Negare Malaysia, Bank Indonesia). Consider the case of almost all Islamic financial instruments, which altogether are debt instruments. The fatwa of permitting 1/3 of financial resources to be held in debt is sheer clergy pronouncement that has now permeated into *shari'ah* ruling. Then there is the entire pricing mechanism of delayed payments (e.g. ijara, murabaha, takaful, *sukuk*, asset valuation). These are all deeply embroiled in subjectivity of rate-setting, there being no rigorous knowledge and model in '*Shari'ah*-compliance'. The result is a form of riba-setting in asset valuation. The tawhidi alternative of valuation based on the episteme of unity of knowledge remains unknown.

The tawhidi methodological worldview formalizes the model of immersing all pricing matters of muamalat, finance, and banking into their complementary interrelationship by inter-causality between these functions and with their inner defining variables. In the absence of understanding the formalism of tawhidi law of monotheistic unity of knowledge (qurànic pairing), all forms of interest rates have remained inextricably embedded in Islamic asset valuation, in financial instruments, and thereby in Islamic product development.

'*Shari'ah*-compliance' is now overloading muamalat matters with fatawa, not recognizing the precision of mathematical and analytical scientific methodology that arises from the tawhidi law of the Qur'an. The tawhidi law of epistemic unity of knowledge is transmitted by sunnah, and intelligently discoursed by the learned and devoted Islamic scholars. Contrarily, *shari'ah* regulations have now embarrassed lock, stock, and barrel the entire body of Islamic economics, finance, and banking. This has caused a state of impossibility with the complications and confusions of 'shar'iah compliance' idea that have befogged the true Islamic worldview.

6.4 Generalizing the methodology and application of tawhidi law contra '*Shari'ah*-compliance'

The universality and uniqueness of tawhidi law, though not including in this the hidden attributes (sifat), can resolve the standardization problem of muamalat and Islamic banking caused by '*Shari'ah*-compliance' fatawa. The positive complementary interrelationship we refer to here is between money, finance, banking, and real economy. We now raise the question: How the debt problem of Islamic financing instruments, Islamic product development, and absence of formalism and applicative methods can be resolved? '*Shari'ah*-compliance' has not resolved this problem.

Thereby, the inherent pricing mechanisms and product developments have remained mired. For example, '*Shari'ah*-compliance' continues to commit the dire mistake of focusing on shareholder model of asset valuation as opposed to a stakeholder model along with its extensions beyond the mere five elements of maqasid as-shari'ah. Thereby, '*Shari'ah*-compliance' overly focuses on property rights in its narrow financial sense. The goal of maximization of shareholder's wealth with exogenous ethical excitement as opposed to conscious endogeneity is proffered. Thereby, no analytical substantiation is offered regarding valuation with the conscious nature of endogenous inter-variable relations in the well-being function (maslaha) as according to tawhidi law. This is a substantive issue of mathematical formalism and applications.

6.5 Well-being criterion

The well-being criterion (maslaha) would otherwise comprise the abstraction and applied way of asset valuation, product development, and the associated learned ways of quantitatively evaluating the well-being objective criterion. The cardinal, universal, and unique precepts of tawhid as the primal ontological law of monotheistic unity of knowledge could not be embodied in the generality and details of muamalat. This would otherwise comprise the financial world-system of good choices (maqasid), while avoiding the false and questionable ones, even as the evolutionary learning proceeds on discursively (shura).

'*Shari'ah*-compliance' has fallen deeply into confusion. The non-standardization of fatawa by the various fatawa and fiqh interpretations has gone into quagmire of juristic proliferation. A scientific study of muamalat, finance, banking, and real economy, which tawhidi methodology offers, is absent in '*Shari'ah*-compliance' approach.

Consequently, as the global order of intellection is today boldly marching forward with great alacrity into reexamining the epistemological foundations that overarch transdisciplinary areas, so also Islamic economics, finance, banking, real economy, and the archaic practice of fiqh and fatawa must give way to the great tawhidi epistemic questioning. Today's Islamic intellection is confined to innovated ideas of '*Shari'ah*-compliance'. The abstraction and applications by the Qur'anic monotheistic primal ontology of tawhid as law and its world-system embedding for the common good must be evaluated by the well-being criterion (maslaha). Tawhid as law with its epistemic abstraction and methodological worldview with applications in the Islamic economic, finance, banking, and real economy issues remain forgotten in '*Shari'ah*-compliance'.

6.6 Islamic product development by tawhidi law of unity of knowledge

As another example of contrast between the tawhidi methodological worldview and the '*Shari'ah*-compliance' way, we briefly examine the nature of property rights concerning any and everything in Islamic economics, finance, banking, and real economy. The old maqasid as-shari'ah, despite being the blessed gateway towards tawhidi law of unity of knowledge, has been marginalized due to lack of intellection. What has resulted is a narrow understanding of the five elements of maqasid as-shari'ah as permissible independent states of maslaha (Masud, 1984). Thereby, all such untenable goals as maximization of shareholder's wealth replaced by the maslaha function remain absent. Similarly, all the five elements of maqasid as-shari'ah remain static concepts. No conceptualization is done regarding the vista of extensions for well-being (maslaha). This would include Muslims, non-Muslims, and the international monetary system in the case of muamalat, finance, and banking. Contrarily, '*Shari'ah*-compliance' has remained distanced by its approach of methodological individualism and archaic postulates of rational choice. Thereby, much of the analytical methodology, as otherwise established by the study of tawhid as law, has remained distanced, forgotten, and unintelligible to latter-day Muslims. Such Muslims are today working in borrowed mainstream and concocted ideas regarding Islamic everything. Tawhid as law in socio-scientific inquiry presents the unified inquiry of inter-causal relations, and construction of endogenous regulations, policies, inferences, and development of learning institutions. Endogenous intellection in such cases is contrary to Central Bank's exogenously formed regulatory policies and rules.

6.7 Riba problem in muamalat explained by tawhidi law contra '*Shari'ah*-compliance'

According to tawhid as law, product development is secured from riba-like interventions in muamalat, financing, and banking contrarily by the participatory principle of unity between these areas. According to tawhid as law even as inter-causality increases between the functions, so also the debt-ridden instruments of '*Shari'ah*-compliance' are phased out. Conversely, the episteme of unity of knowledge by complementary pairing increases as evolutionary learning proceeds. The result is a true Islamicization (tawhidization) of muamalat, finance, banking, and real economy along with their endogenous complementary internal variables.

The problem of riba and riba-like pricing of debt-ridden Islamic financing instruments as '*Shari'ah*-compliance' ruling on this matter is resolved by taking recourse to the tawhidi organic relational worldview intra-systems and inter-systems with the selected variables. For instance, riba-like pricing is not discounting of futuristic probabilistic expectations according to tawhidi law of unity of knowledge. Rather, such pricing is done at the 'nearest' point of occurrence of contingencies characterizing various resource flows at these points. At such points the tawhidi unity of knowledge by systems works in unifying the monetary, financial, banking, and real economy systems. For sustainability, these systems remain interactive, integrative, and evolutionary by learning processes over knowledge and time. A debt problem is thereby avoided when every event point of temporal valuation with contingencies is evaluated by equivalence between money, finance, and real value of assets. Islamic banks ought to do this kind of participatory financing and carry out the underlying knowledge dissemination. The Central Bank ought to take stock of this kind of learning and valuation. The tawhidi methodological worldview of participative organic pairing (Quràn 36:36) is now active.

6.8 Tawhidi methodology contra '*Shari'ah*-compliance' and Kantian rationalism

Figure 6.1 briefly outlines the contrasting opposites, between tawhid as the primal ontological law of monotheistic unity of knowledge and the human-concocted notion of '*Shari'ah*-compliance'. Figure 6.1 explains that reasoning in '*Shari'ah*-compliance' is discontinuous, as in the case of the Kantian philosophy rationalism (Friedrich, 1977). Although Kant was a thinker along lines of moral imperative (a priori reasoning), yet his methodology relegated the moral origin of reasoning to the human world-system (a posteriori reasoning). By rationalist reasoning, even though a priori reasoning carries the primacy of moral imperative, yet it remains distanced from the origin of monotheism. Thereby, a priori normative reasoning remains separated from a posteriori positivistic reasoning (this nullity is symbolized

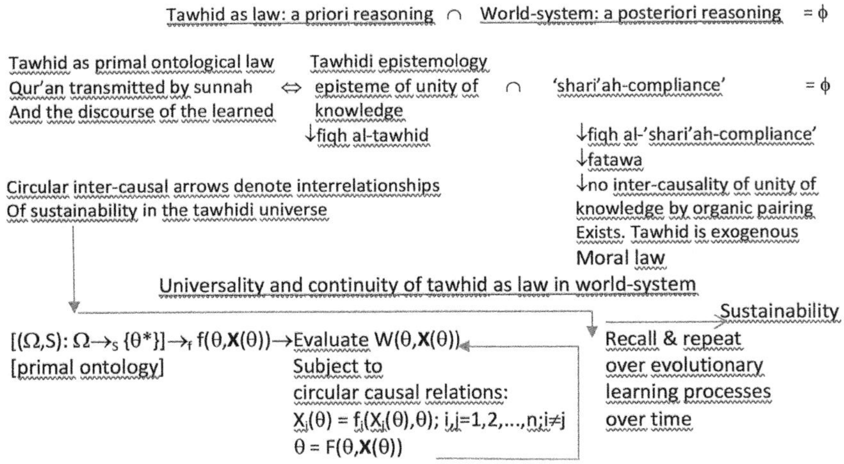

Figure 6.1 Methodological independence between tawhid as law and '*Shari'ah*-compliance'.

by ϕ). Any attempt to unify a priori and a posteriori reasoning in the monotheistic sense failed in Occidentalism. This Kantian way of treating the moral imperative within the dichotomy between God and the unified world-system is repeated in '*Shari'ah*-compliance'. Thereby, the existing approach to the study of Islamic economics, finance, banking, and the needed transdisciplinary inquiry of socio-scientific world-systems with diverse details reflects Kantian rationalism. Morality remained an embellishment of moral philosophy and fails in critical realism (Bhaskar, 1994). Therefore, anything that remains independent of and not substantively embedded by tawhidi law such as monotheistic episteme of unity of knowledge is of human innovation. This is how Ibn al-Arabi explained reality entrenched in tawhid (Chittick, 1989).

Symbols: ∩ denotes integration commonly between domains. ϕ denotes null and void interaction between the domains. ⇔ denotes inter-causality of pairing relations (Quràn 36:36). Ω denotes supercardinal knowledge completed in the Qur'an. S denotes transmission of Qur'an by reference to sunnah. $\{\theta^*\}$ denotes learned discursive interpretation of Qur'anic verses (ayaths) transmitted by S; thus, $\{\theta^*\} \in (\Omega,S)$. $f(\theta,\mathbf{X}(\theta))$ are multiple 'functional ontologies', 'f' (Gruber, 1993) derived from the tawhidi epistemology. Epistemology as knowledge derivation is denoted by $\{\theta\}$. $\{\theta\}$ induces the multivariate vector of systems with their inner variables, such as money, financial instruments, real economy as systems defined by their variables in the vector, $\mathbf{X}(\theta) = \{X_1,X_2,..,X_n\}[\theta]$ in given interactive, integrative, evolutionary learning processes (i.e. ijtihad = shura-consensus, evolutionary learning in unity of knowledge intra-system and inter-system), i.e. within monetary, finance, banking and economic intra-systems, and across these inter-systems. W (.) is the conceptual form of well-being criterion (maslaha) that establishes the most critical overall unifying effect of tawhidi law on standardization of rules and methodical applications derived from the primal ontology and its methodology as shown above. The resulting complementarities evaluated and reconstructed (simulated) in terms of the tawhidi knowledge-induced variables of the well-being functional n-dimensional vector are done by the circular causation equations in accordance with the parameterized values of knowledge, $\{\theta\}$. The circular causation equations are denoted by $X_i(\theta) = f_i(X_j(\theta),\theta)$; $i,j=1,2,\ldots,n$; $i \neq j$. $\theta = F(\theta,\mathbf{X}(\theta))$ denotes the quantitatively evaluated form of the well-being function (maslaha) in the conceptual form, $W(\theta,\mathbf{X}(\theta))$. The primal ontology is continuously recalled intra-systems and inter-systems over continuums of evolutionary learning processes across the historical consciousness of knowledge, knowledge-induced space and time (Qur'an, 76:1). This is the meaning of sustainability of the standardized rules according to tawhidi law of unity of knowledge (inter-causal pairing, complementarities, and participation). The universality, uniformity, and positivistic applications are recursively interrelated with the normative methodology of tawhid as law.

6.9 Summarizing

In conclusion it is noted that, although there is a claimed derivation of injunctions by '*Shari'ah*-compliance' towards tawhid, this does not form a methodological groundwork, except for the use of fiqh and fatawa that support human-concocted implications of '*Shari'ah*-compliance'. The result, thereby, has throughout been its failure to derive the universal and unique foundation as of the tawhidi ontological, epistemological, and phenomenological worldview of a truly meta-scientific nature in unity of knowledge and the unified world-system. No standardization of fiqh and fatawa is possible in the existing framework of '*Shari'ah*-compliance'.

How will the tawhidi law be used to gain and sustain standardization of fiqh and fatawa and *Shari'ah* rulings for Islamic banking on appropriateness of instruments, mainly of the secondary financing type, around which product development is carried out? Tawhid as law represents itself in unity of knowledge and the specific issues under discussion in Islamic banks that arise by means of the principle of pervasive organic pairing as complementarities and participations. This feature of tawhidi rule extends into general-system understanding of the Qur'anic idea of pairing in widening domains of moral-material oneness. Evaluation of the effectiveness of such participatory or complementary processes of adopted rules, instruments, and endogenously derived policies and regulations by discourse is to be done by the estimation and simulation results of the well-being function in terms of the inner variables of the objective criterion.

An example is of organic unity of being between money, finance, banking, and real economy, in terms of the functional defining variables and their extensive inter-causal relations signifying the Qur'anic meaning of pairing the universe and its specific details, as in muamalat, finance, and banking. The result is a substantive simulation of the multivariate well-being function in the maqasid choices while avoiding the false and unrecommended ones. The resulting fiqh and fatawa in all such universal and unique determination of tawhidi unity of knowledge by extensive participation as organic pairing signifies inter-system and inter-variable endogenous complementarities in transdisciplinary phenomenology. This approach does not accept differentiation by systemic disjointness except for unrecommended variables.

Figure 6.1 depicts the human-concocted fiqh and fatawa independently of and not substantively related with tawhidi law that arises from the learning multiverse (a'lameen) by complementary pairing. The pairing indicator of standardization of issues of Islamic economics, finance, banking, and society is derived from the Qur'an (azwaja kullaha) via sunnah and learned discourse on specific issues. These all reflect the Signs of Allah (ayath Allah).

References

Bhaskar, R. (1994). *Critical Realism*. Verso, London, Eng.

Chittick, W.C. (1989). *Sufi Path of Knowledge*, State University of New York Press, Albany, NY.

Choudhury, M.A. (2006). *Koran and Science* (with Generic Titles). 5 volumes. Edwin Mellen Press, Lewiston, NY.

Choudhury, M.A. (2014). *Tawhidi Epistemology and Its Applications (Economics, Finance, Science, and Society)*. Cambridge Scholars Publishing, Cambridge, UK.

Choudhury, M.A. (2016a). *Heterodox Islamic Economics: The Emergence of an Ethico-Economic Theory*. Routledge, London, Eng.

Choudhury, M.A. (2016b). *The Absolute Reality in the Qur'an*. New Palgrave Macmillan, London, Eng.

Choudhury, M.A. (2017). *A Phenomenological Theory of Islamic Economics*. University of Malaya Press, Kuala Lumpur, Malaysia.

Friedrich, C.J., (transl.) (1977). *The Philosophy of Kant: Immanuel Kant's Moral and Political Writings*. The Modern Library, New York, NY.

Gruber, T.R. (1993). "A translation approach to portable ontologies". *Knowledge Acquisition*, 5:2.

Masud, M.K. (1984). *Islamic Legal Philosophy: A Study of Abu Ishaq al-Shatibi's Life and Work*, Islamic Research Institute, Islamabad, Pakistan.

7 The fallacy of conventional benchmarks in Islamic banking and finance

Defining, defending and discussing with evidence from archival data

Imam Uddin Muhammad Shujat Saleem and Abdur Rahman Aleemi

7.1 Introduction

Traditionally, Gulf Cooperation Council (GCC) countries along with Southeast Asian countries were considered to be the only regions for Islamic financial markets; however, at present, Islamic financial markets have surpassed to non-traditional markets including Africa, East Asia and Canada which is considered to be the North American hub for Islamic finance. The total worth of global Islamic financial assets including banks, capital markets and Takaful companies is USD 2 trillion which was expected to reach USD 3 trillion by 2018 (IFDNTM 2016).[1] Despite tremendous worldwide growth of Islamic Banking and Finance (IBF) along with its strong resilience to economic shocks compared to its conventional counterparts, Islamic banks still face some impediments that hinder its growth. Among these are the masses that misinterpret the true essence of IBF due to lack of knowledge about the same. Factually, there is no difference in the business models of both conventional and Islamic banks (Beck 2010). It is argued that Islamic banks are a replica to the interest-based conventional banks as both systems use the same benchmark for pricing their products which makes the de jure distinction but not the de facto difference (Maclean 2007; Pervaiz 2015; Samdhani 2013; Shaikh 2013; Zaharuddin 2013; Zubair & Chaudhry 2014). To counter this argument, many IBF advocates have already done voluminous works in which they inscribed that using conventional benchmark in pricing IBF products does not make it impermissible in the eye of *Shari'ah* (Usmani 2002; Jalil & Rehman 2010). So, who's right: opponents or the proponents of the IBF in this sense? Therefore, a valid question to ask: what is the status of conventional benchmark in *Shari'ah* viewpoint if the same is used for pricing IBF's products? This critical review attempts to investigate the permissibility or impermissibility of the use of conventional benchmark in IBF products by taking Murabaha financing as a proxy for the same. Hence, this research paper aims to answer the following question: does the use of conventional benchmark in pricing Murabaha products render it impermissible in the eye of *Shari'ah*?

7.2 Literature review

Irrespective of the fact that both Murabaha financing and interest-based loan products fulfill similar financing needs of customers, Murabaha is not a loan extended on interest; rather, it is simply a sale with profit in which the seller is obliged to disclose the cost as well as profit to the buyer (Usmani 2002). Jalil and Rehman (2010) complement Usmani by stating that Murabaha transactions are distinct from loan by conventional banks due to the fact that in Murabaha, Islamic bank purchases the products of real nature on the request of customer and sells the same on profit. Contrarily, Abbas et al. (2014) inscribed that theoretical and philosophical differences exist between Murabaha and loan transaction but when it comes to practice, there is no implicit difference between the two. *The Dawn*[2] reports that Murabaha transaction of Islamic banks is similar to that of the loan transaction of conventional banks because Islamic banks charge the same rate of interest in the name of profit which is charged by the conventional banks in loan transaction. In the support of Abbas et al. (2014), Saeed (2010) in his work *Is Islamic banking really Islamic?* raised an objection that contemporary Islamic banks use the same 'term Sheets of KIBOR' that are being used by conventional banks in pricing their loan products.

Similarly, Zubair and Chaudry (2014) argue that in the Murabaha transactions, Islamic banks charge interest rates rather than market rates of the products, which makes no de facto difference between the loan transaction of conventional banks and the Murabaha transaction. Similarly, Holden (2007) puts that, most of the classical jurists do not allow the Murabaha transaction as it follows markup similar to interest rates. To reinforce his findings, Holden quotes an article published in the *Fortune* magazine according to which a customer buys an automobile from an Islamic bank and paid exactly the pre-agreed same markup to the bank as he would have paid to conventional bank, had the financing been acquired from the conventional bank. However, on the other hand, Wahab et al. (2014) support the findings of Jalil and Rehman (2010) and contrast with Holden (2007) as he argues that the Murabaha is useful for both short- and medium-term financing because of its asset-backed provision. Similarly, Maclean (2007) holds that, when someone approaches a bank for financing, the conventional bank after thorough examinations and procedures grants a loan on which the bank charges interest. Similarly, the same is true for an Islamic bank. Islamic bank after thorough examination purchases the required item from a supplier and sells it to the customer on profit similar to the interest rates charged by the conventional bank; hence, the Murabaha transaction is similar to loan transaction. In contrast, Kuran (2004), in his voluminous work, argued that there is no prescribed time in *Shari'ah* which limits the bank to take risk of the product after acquiring from the supplier. Only a millisecond would be sufficient to make the Islamic bank entitled for the profit which in his point of view makes no difference between the Murabaha transaction of Islamic bank and loan transaction of conventional bank.

To sum up, it can be easily concluded that people who argue that the Murabaha financing is nothing but a replica to a loan by conventional banks generally takes into account only one factor i.e. *'Financial burden'* shouldered on the customer. They argue that if, for instance, Mr. A goes to conventional bank to get loanable funds of Rs. 2 million for a year and pays back Rs. 2.2 million (principal plus interest) at maturity, in the same way, an Islamic bank charges almost the same amount from the customer in the Murabaha transaction by merely changing its name. As a result, financial burden on Mr. A remains the same regardless of the bank he chooses to get the financing from. This study in particular intends to extend this discussion in light of archival evidence.

7.3 Research methodology

This critical review uses archival research strategy to answer the research questions by following Bryman (1989). Archival research uses the archival documents as the main source of data. The sources of these documents include: The Holy Quran, Ahadiths, Verdicts of *Shari'ah*' Scholars from various forums including Accounting and Auditing organization for Islamic Financial Institutions (AAOIFI), and verdicts issued by the Counsel of Islamic Ideology of Pakistan. Moreover, the chapter follows the inductive approach to determine the main intent of the study.

7.4 Data analysis and discussion

By using archival data from the aforementioned sources, this section analyzes the main intent of the study; the structure of which is as follows: Section 4.1 introduces the Murabaha financing being undertaken by the contemporary Islamic banks in Pakistan along with *Shari'ah* references. Section 4.1.1 details the *Shari'ah* conditions which should be taken into account by the Islamic banks while undertaking the Murabaha transaction. Section 4.2 discusses the simplistic version of the Murabaha financing. Section 4.3 provides the practical implementation or step-by-step procedures followed by the Islamic banks in order to undertake the Murabaha transaction. Section 4.4 explains *Shari'ah* conditions for profit determination along with what percentage of profit is permissible in *Shari'ah* viewpoint. Section 4.5 deals with benchmarking with KIBOR in determining the selling price of the subject matter of the Murabaha financing along with *Shari'ah* conditions for the same. Section 4.6 presents the difference between both conventional and Islamic banks pertaining to the use of KIBOR. Section 4.7 discusses the rationale for benchmarking with KIBOR. Section 4.8 provides the references for the permissibility of the use of KIBOR as benchmark, and Section 5 concludes.

7.4.1 Murabaha financing

Murabaha is a sale on profit in which the seller is obliged to disclose the cost as well as profit to the buyer. It has nothing to do with financing in its original sense, however, in order to escape from interest, and when Musharaka and Mudaraba cannot be undertaken, Murabaha contract on deferred payment basis may be used as a financing instrument after taking into account the following conditions of *Shari'ah* (Usmani 2002).

7.4.1.1 Shari'ah' conditions for sale: the seller cannot sell an article unless following conditions are met

- a Existence: One cannot sell a commodity unless it has come into existence; hence, non-existent[3] thing cannot be sold out.
- b Ownership: The seller should own the commodity at the time of contract of sale.
- c Possession: The commodity should either be in physical possession or in constructive possession[4] of the seller at the time of contract of sale.[5]
- d Instant and Absolute: The contract of sale[6] must be instant and absolute, thus, forward and future sales are impermissible.
- e Impermissible Use: A seller cannot sell something which can be used only for impermissible purposes[7].
- f Specification: It is a set rule that the item being bought and sold should be specifically known and pinpointed to both the buyer and seller, failing of which makes the transaction invalid because of Gharar-e-Kaseer.[8]
- g Certainty of Price: It is a necessary condition for the validity of contract of sale that the price should be determined and fixed at the time of contract of sale, again, failure of which makes the transaction invalid due to Gharar-e-Kaseer.
- h Certainty of Delivery of the Subject Matter: For the validity of the sale contract, it is necessary for the seller to be able to deliver[9] the subject matter to the buyer. If the seller is not in a position to deliver the subject matter to the buyer, the sale is void in *Shari'ah* viewpoint.
- i Unconditional Contract: Contracts that are contingent to an uncertain future event are void. Moreover, contracts that are conditional[10] on some other contracts are also void in *Shari'ah* viewpoint.

7.4.2 Simplistic version of the Murabaha financing

To understand the very basics of the Murabaha financing, we discuss a hypothetical case as follows: Mr. A is a sugar mill owner and wants short-term financing from Meezan Bank of PKR 10 million for 6 months. In this respect, Mr. A requests the bank to purchase sugarcane with the promise to repurchase the same. Meezan Bank purchases the required sugarcane from open market and sells it to Mr. A for PKR 12 Million on deferred payment basis of 6 months on Murabaha basis.[11]

7.4.3 Practical implementation of the Murabaha financing[12]

This section unveils detailed steps followed by Islamic banks for proper implementation of the Murabaha financing. It is noteworthy that while implementing the Murabaha financing, Islamic banks face business as well as *Shari'ah* risks,[13] unlike conventional banks which counter with only business risks. The following are some steps in implementation of the simplistic the Murabaha contract as mentioned in previous section.

a Promise

When Mr. A approaches Meezan Bank and requests to purchase sugarcane from the supplier,[14] then the bank, after considering standard normal procedures, asks the customer to sign a document of unilateral promise in which the customer promises to repurchase sugarcane from the bank. In this way, Islamic banks try to mitigate the risk of loss[15] in the case of refusal by the customer.

If the customer breaks the promise with reasons[16] acceptable in *Shari'ah*, then Islamic banks have no remedy to recover the actual loss; however, if the customer does not fulfill his promise without any good reason acceptable in *Shari'ah*, then Islamic banks can recover the actual loss from the customer by taking necessary legal actions. It is noteworthy that Islamic banks cannot recover opportunity loss as the same is impermissible in *Shari'ah*.

According the Accounting and Auditing Organization for Islamic Financial Institutions (AAOIFI), Islamic banks are advised not to take promise especially in those Murabaha transactions in which according to the bank's discretion bank faces no credit risk.[17]

b Agency

Islamic bank receives numerous requests from different customers to purchase multiple items, and due to lack of purchase expertise, there is possibility that the required specification may not be met which may expose the bank to a huge risk of loss. To mitigate such risk and to facilitate the customer, Islamic banks enter into a contract of agency with the customer,[18] whereby Islamic bank becomes the principal and the customer becomes the purchase agent who purchases the items from the supplier on behalf of the bank.[19]

c Purchase

Once the promise and agency documents are singed, the customer on behalf of the bank purchases the items from suppliers. According to

AAOIFI, it is preferable for the bank to purchase the item directly from the supplier or appoint third party as an agent. However, in case of dire need, it is also permissible for the bank to appoint customer as its agent.

d Offer

After purchasing the item from the supplier as an agent of the bank, customer makes an offer to purchase the item.

e Acceptance

Bank accepts the offer made by the customer which concludes the Murabaha contract with the customer, whereby Islamic bank becomes the seller of the item and customer becomes the buyer.

As this Murabaha transaction is done on deferred payment basis, buyer's and seller's relationship converts into debtor's and creditor's relationship between the customer and the bank, respectively, and at the same time, 'Dain'[20] is created on the customer which is equivalent to the Murabaha price.[21]

7.4.4 Shari'ah rulings for price determination

The determination of price through the market forces of supply and demand is not against the teachings of Islam, provided that it takes into account certain conditions[22] imposed by the *Shari'ah*. The permissibility of the price determined by the market is evidenced by the following narration.

> Once Hazrat Bilal went back from the city of Khyber to the city of Madina and presented dates to Hazrat Muhammad Mustafa (PBUH) on which after seeing the dates Hazrat Muhammad Mustafa (PBUH) asked him, the meaning of which is, "Are these kinds of dates being bought and sold in the city of Khyber?" On this question, Hazrat Bilal said, no. He further said, I have exchanged two Saah of the low quality date with one Saah of the high quality dates. On this answer from him, Hazrat Muhammad Mustafa (PBUH) said the meaning of which is as follow. Don't do this Bilal, He further said, Sell the low quality date in the market, get the money and purchase high quality dates.
>
> (Reported by Muslim)

The permissibility of the price determined by the market forces of supply and demand is also evidenced by the following sayings:

> When the prices became high in the Prophet's time and people asked him to fix prices for them, he replied, Allah is the One Who fixes prices, Who withholds, Who gives lavishly, and Who provides, and I hope that when I meet Him none of you will have a claim against me for any injustice with regard to blood or property.
>
> (Reported by Ahmad, Abu Daoud, al-Tirmidhi, Ibn Majah, al-Dari and Abu Y'ala.)

From the aforementioned, one should not be misunderstood that it is a compulsory requirement for every seller to sell his product on the market price; these narrations do not impose the compulsion to follow the market price rather it prohibits external forces to enter into a market and ceil the market price. That is, in general, even the government has no authority to fix the price.[23]

Another important point to consider is that an individual seller can demand more than the market price, less than the market price or equal to the market price for his products after taking into account the aforementioned conditions imposed by the *Shari'ah*. Following verse is the evidence to the fact that any price can be set between the contracting parties with mutual consent.

> The Holy Quran says, "O Believers! Do not misappropriate one another's goods illegally. Indeed, you should undertake transactions by mutual agreement".
>
> (4:29)

7.4.5 Price determination through benchmarking with KIBOR

An individual seller usually sets his product's prices to be competitive with its competitors, failing to do so may cause potential loss and closure of business in no time. For instance, Pepsi-Cola has got all the rights to increase prices for its products but it does not do so, because of the substitution effect towards Coca-Cola. In this connection, Islamic banks are competing with conventional banks in the similar fashion in Pakistan, and both coexist and try to fulfill similar financing needs of their customers. Thus, in order to be competitive in the market, Islamic banks should set their products' prices accordingly. For instance, going back to Mr. A's request for sugarcane financing, a request to the Meezan Bank, for instance, is placed on 15th December, the bank purchases the same in open market and resells it to Mr. A on 17th (taking into consideration all the conditions discussed in Section 4.1.1). However, here lies a huge challenge for the bank to determine the offer price to Mr. A. Although *Shari'ah* allows the bank to charge mutually agreed rate (after taking into consideration all the conditions of profit determination discussed in Section 4.4), they can charge let's say 10%, 20%, etc. However, they should consider an alternative outlook that if Mr. A had gone to a conventional bank, what rate of return they might have charged for that particular transaction? Let's say, if conventional bank had charged 10%, then, so does Islamic bank being the competitor of conventional bank. However, it is noteworthy that merely charging the same rate of return does not render the transaction impermissible in the eye of *Shari'ah*, as one should note that what is being bought and sold, not for how much? Conventional bank here sells money on 10% return, whereas Islamic bank sells sugarcane—a commodity—on 10% return. The transaction of conventional bank here is a loan which stipulates 10% interest that is forbidden in *Shari'ah* evidenced as:

> *Every loan transaction which derives benefit is interest*
>
> Harith ibn Abi Usamah (Musnad)

Thus, the conventional bank's transaction is impermissible because of the benefits drawn on loan transaction, whereas Islamic bank's transaction is permissible because of the benefit drawn on sale transaction which is evidenced by the following Ayah:

> Sale is permissible and riba is impermissible
>
> (2,275)

7.4.6 Difference between the use of KIBOR within both conventional and Islamic banks

Certainty of price is one of the conditions imposed by *Shari'ah*. Thus, once the selling price of the subject matter is determined under the Murabaha transaction, it stays fixed and does not change with the changes in KIBOR regardless of the time period. The AAOIFI puts it in this way:

> The institution's profit mark up in the Murabaha to the purchase orderer must be known, and the mere mention of the total selling price is not sufficient. It is permissible that the profit be determined based on a lump sum amount or a certain percentage of the cost price only or of the cost price plus the expenses. This determination is completed by the agreement and mutual consent of the two parties.

In contrast, conventional banks' rate of return varies as per the variations in KIBOR which creates the de facto difference between the uses of KIBOR in both systems. In short, Islamic banks are not linked with KIBOR particularly in the Murabaha transaction as wrongly inferred by the advocates of conventional finance (see Maclean 2007; Pervaiz 2015; Saeed 2010; Samdhani 2013; Shaikh 2013; Zaharuddin 2013; Zubair & Chaudhry 2014). Had Islamic banks been linked with the KIBOR, their selling prices would have changed with the changes in KIBOR.

7.4.7 Rationale of benchmarking with KIBOR[24]

The foremost reason using KIBOR is being in close competition with conventional banks, Islamic banks charge the same rate of return as that of the conventional banks as stated in Section 4.5. Furthermore, prices of commodities usually differ in different markets, for instance, a cup of tea is charged for Rs. 50 in general, but the same may be charged for Rs. 500 in a 5-star hotel. This gives rise to market pricing, hence, Islamic banks are said to be charging according to the banking market. Moreover, the State Bank of Pakistan (SBP) declares that there are only 5 full-fledged Islamic banks operating in Pakistan compared to 37 conventional banks which constitute a very minimal part of the whole banking industry. Thus, in the present scenario, if Islamic bank charges more than that of conventional counterparts, then most of the customers will rather be wooed towards conventional banks and Islamic banks will be forced to shut down in no time. In contrast, if Islamic banks charge lower than conventional bank then they might not be able to survive due to

a High cost of operations: It is as high as 4.5% compared to 3% for conventional banks. Thus, Islamic banks' spreads are considerably lower and makes it very difficult for Islamic banks to survive on low rates of return.
b Rate of return to investment account holders (IAHs): If Islamic banks receive low financing rates from customers, then it results into low deposit rates to IAHs due to which IAHs would be no more interested to do banking with Islamic banks; consequently, Islamic banks may face the situation of bank run.

7.4.8 Permissibility of benchmarking with KIBOR

To determine the Murabaha price, Islamic banks may choose to adopt any formula or conventional benchmark such as KIBOR or LIBOR. It is not necessary to disclose the formula to the customer but what is important is that the institution has to disclose the amount of cost and profit to the customer. Furthermore, profit should be fixed at the time of execution of the Murabaha transaction, and it will remain unchanged until maturity, as evident by the following clause 4/6 of the AAOIFI.

> It is an obligation that both the price of the item and the institution's profit on the Murabaha to the purchase orderer transaction be fixed and known to both parties on the signature of the contract of sale. It is not permitted under any circumstances to subject the determinate of the price or the profit to unknown variations or variations that are determinable in the future, such as by concluding the sale and making the profit dependent on the rate of LIBOR that will prevail in the future. There is no objection to referring to any other known indicator during the promise stage as a comfort indication to determine the rare of profit, provided that the determination of the institutions' profit at the time of concluding the Murababah to the purchase order is based on a certain percentage of the cost and is not tied up with LIBOR or a time factor.

Moreover, the transaction of Murabaha is based on Islamic principles and fulfills all its necessary requirements, and the rate of profit determined on the basis of the rate of interest will not render the transaction as Haram (see Usmani 2002).

7.5 Concluding remarks

On the basis of the analysis and discussion of the archival data presented in Section 4, it can be concluded that the opinions of Abbas et al. (2014), Beck (2010), Maclean (2007), 4Saeed (2010), and Shaikh (2013) are unsupported by the evidence, and the opinions of Usmani (2002) and Jalil and Rehman (2010) still hold true. Therefore, we conclude that the use of KIBOR in the Murabaha financing for profit determination does not violate any condition of Islamic jurisprudence. However, it is recommended for the Islamic banks to strive for the implementation of Islamic Interbank Offer Rate (IBOR), as the use of conventional benchmark creates misconceptions and misunderstandings in the mind of general public, especially in those regions where Islamic banks coexist with conventional banks.

Notes

1 Islamic Finance Development in Non Traditional Market report. See: http://www.mifc.com/index.php?ch=28&pg=72&ac=160&bb=uploadpdf
2 See the article titled Time Value of Money, dated January 08th, 2007.
3 For example, unborn calf of the cow.
4 A seller is said to have constructive possession of something when the risk of destruction, control, obligations, responsibilities and duties have been transferred on to him.
5 However these conditions are not applicable for Salam and Istisna.
6 There is a difference between the contract of sale and mere promise to sell in *Shari'ah*. In promise, risk of destruction, control of items being sold, liabilities, duties and obligations do not transfer from the promisor to the promisee unlike contract of sale in which all these elements are transferred from the seller to the buyer in instant and absolute terms.
7 It is permissible to sell those things which have both the permissible and impermissible usages.
8 Gharar-e-Kaseer is a major uncertainty within the clauses of the transaction.
9 For example, if Mr. A sells his stolen car to Mr. B. The sale is void as Mr. B may not be able to deliver on his promise.
10 Conditional contracts are those in which the result of one contract is dependent upon the outcome of another contract.
11 Before executing the contract, the bank is bound to disclose the cost as well as profit to the customer. It is noteworthy here that people wrongly argue about the transparency of Islamic banks. In Murabaha disclosure of cost and profit are the requirements in *Shari'ah*' viewpoint. Furthermore, in today's market place, banks purchase the requested items from the supplier identified by the customer leaving no issue of transparency at least in Murabaha financing.
12 Islamic banks in Pakistan prepare a complete set of documents with the name of Master Murabaha Agreement or Murabaha Facility Agreement in order to

execute Murabaha transactions. We, for the readers' facilitation are presenting only those steps or stages which are essential to execute the Murabaha transaction.

13 Refers to *Shari'ah* Non-Compliance Risks (SNCR). See (IFSB, 2016) for details.

14 In Pakistan, usually, the supplier is identified by the customer.

15 In case of customer's refusal, Islamic bank may incur actual loss by in re-selling the sugarcane in open market.

16 Reasons acceptable includes but not limited to the customer's death, insanity, insolvency etc.

17 Islamic bank faces no credit risk when the items can easily be sold in open market with same price, or suppliers provide sale on return basis.

18 It is noteworthy that at the time of contract of agency, the customer has no relation with the bank in *Shari'ah* viewpoint except that of promisor & promisee.

19 During the purchase process, bank being the principal, bears the risk of destruction.

20 When the liability is created through other than loan transaction, it is called Dain'. However, rulings of debt and dain are similar in *Shari'ah* viewpoint.

21 It is immensely important in *Shari'ah* viewpoint that Islamic bank bears the risk of destruction of the item before onward sale to customer.

22 Neither the commodity nor the purpose should be unlawful, Both the buyer and seller must have free consent before entering into a contract, both do not apply coercion, undue influence or commit fraud, there should be no hoardings, no monopoly and no concealment of defects in the goods and the process of price determination should not violate any explicit or implicit rulings of *Shari'ah*. According to the Holy Quran, "When they receive from someone; they receive in full but when they give to others; they defraud" (83:1). In another verse, it is said, "Give the correct quantity and weigh properly and do not cause loss to others" (7:84). Moreover, It has further been directed, "And don't steal the belongings of others" (2:188). The Prophet (PBUH) was asked that which earning is better. He replied; the one which the man earns through his physical labor. (Ahmed). On the issue of hoarding the prophet said; "That who stock the general commodities or items for the sake of maximum benefits and do not supply them in the market is prohibited [Ahmed-Bin-Hanbal: 19802]. "That those who hoard things are sinners. No one hoard in this earth "(Abu Da'ud, No. 2990). "That who import essential commodity into the town for good benefits or hoarding there, Allah's curse upon him." (IbneMaajah, No: 2144).

23 In case of dire need, if the price is too high for ordinary person to buy his livelihood then the Government may ceil the price for a particular period of time. Following is the meaning of the verse which permits the Government to impose such conditions; *"O' believer, obey Allah, and obey prophet, and who has authority over you"*. In this translation of the Aayah, there is a difference between obedience of Allah and His Prophet; and the people of Authority.

24 The State Bank of Pakistan has recently allowed Islamic banks to be de-linked with KIBOR which is a very good development.

References

Abbas, M., Sohaib, A. Q., & Chaudary, N. S. (2014). Is the Current Practice of Murabaha In Pakistan Literally Based on Islam? Al-Adwa, 29(42), 11–20. Shaikh Zayed Islamic Center-University of Punjab.

Beck, K. (2010). "Islamic vs. Conventional Banking: Business Model, Efficiency and Stability, Policy Research" Working Paper 5446. The World Bank, Development Research Group, Finance and Private Sector Development Team.

Bryman, A. (1989). Research Methods and Organization Studies (Illustrated, Reprint, Revised Ed.).

Holden, K. (2007). Islamic Finance: "Legal Hypocrisy" Moot Point, Problematic Future Bigger Concern. *Boston University International Law Journal*, 25, 341, 342–367.

IFSB. (2016). Shari'ah Non-Compliance Risk in the Banking Sector: Impact on Capital Adequacy Framework of Islamic Banks. WP No. WP-05/03/2016.

IFDNTM. (2016). Islamic Finance: Development in Non-Traditional Markets. Retrieved from www.mifc.com/index.php?ch=28&pg=72&ac=160&bb=uploadpdf.

Jalil, M. A., & Rehman, M. K. (2010). Financial Transactions in Islamic Banking are Viable Alternatives to the Conventional Banking Transactions. *International Journal of Business and Social Science*, 01(03), 2010.

Kuran, T. (2004). Islam and mammon. Princeton: Princeton University Press.

MacLean, A. (2007, March 16). Islamic Banking: Is It Really Kosher? Retrieved from www.aei.org/publication/islamic-banking-is-it-really-kosher/

Pervaiz, S. (2015). "Comparison of Islamic and Conventional Finance" whyislam2.wordpress.com/2015/02/05/islamic-finance/

Saeed, S. U. (2010, June 25). Is Islamic Banking Really Islamic? Retrieved from http://blogs.tribune.com.pk/story/194/is-islamic-banking-really-islamic/ The Express Tribune Blogs.

Samdhani, A. E. (2013). Difference between islamic and conventional banking. Karachi: Maktaba Kamilpooray.

Shaikh, A. (2013). Islamic Banking in Pakistan: A Critical Analysis. *Journal of Islamic Economics, Banking and Finance*, 113(913), 1–18.

Dawn (2007, January 08). Time Value of Money in Islamic Banking. Retrieved from www.dawn.com/news/226780/time-value-of-money-in-islamic-banking.

Usmani, M. T. (2002). An introduction to Islamic finance (Vol. 20). Highwood: Brill.

Wahab, A. et al. (2014). A Comparative Study of Islamic Financial System and Conventional Financial System. *Global Business and Economics Research Journal*, 3(5), 15–29.

Zaharuddin, A. (2013). Differences between Islamic Banking and Conventional Banking in Terms of Shari'ah' Ruling Conformity. *Journal of Islamic and Human Advanced Research*, 3(1), 27–40.

Zubair, H. M., & Chaudhry, N. G. (2014). Islamic Banking in Pakistan: A Critical Review. *International Journal of Humanities and Social Science*, 4(2), 161–176.

8 Influence of leverage on ownership structure-performance relationship

A panel data approach of Islamic and conventional banks of Pakistan

Ummara Fatima and Sundas Sohail

8.1 Introduction

Business needs capital to purchase assets and sustain operations. To fill this need business utilizes either from the debt financing or from the equity financing. It is subject to the formation of the company, size and techniques, to take decision whether to pick equity, debt or a mixture of both. Debt and equity make the financial structure of an organization. A good combination of capital structure plays critical part in enhancing profitability of an organization. Capital structure essentially can be alluded to a company's financial framework, the strategy of a firm to finance its assets with a combination of equity, debt or securities (Saad, 2010). An optimal capital structure empowers an organization to proceed effectively on its way to achieve progressive development. Modigliani and Miller (1958) were the first who initiated work on capital structure and introduced broad-spectrum theory of capital structure, which is still under debate (Chakraborty, 2010; Karadeniz et al., 2009). The idea of capital structure became popular after the mainstream of work performed by Miller and Modigliani (1958). In their eminent "theory of irrelevancy of capital structure," it is recommended that in perfect capital market the performance of firm is autonomous of its capital structure. Future, they argued that this relationship can be changed in light of debt as it offers "tax shield advantage" (Modigliani & Miller, 1963).

In theoretical point of view, the ownership structure is defined as the choices that emulate the influence of shareholders in trading those shares at country-level, according to the rules and regulations defined by stock market. The ownership structure is explained through the equity distribution with respect to poll, level of investment and individuality of the equity holders.

Performance determines the core of the firm's efficiency such as maximizing return on assets and maximizing shareholder's benefits (Bauer, 2004; Chakravarthy, 1986; Deesomsak et al., 2004; Marsh, 1982).

Ownership structure significantly affects the firm performance. Berle and Means (1932) started investigation for performance and ownership structure relationship and brought about inconsistent connection between both. Jensen and Meckling (1976) clarified this work through the hypothesis of "agency theory" by presenting "principal-agent framework" featuring the "agency problem between the management and shareholders." The "agency cost" between management and shareholders can be reduced by the use of debt in the capital structure and can also be utilized as an analyzing tool to observe the company managers (Jensen & Meckling, 1976). On the other hand, this "agency cost" can likewise be reduced by increased "managerial ownership" (Jensen & Meckling, 1976) and better capacity of "inside managerial owners" to establish an optimal debt level for firm (Friend & Lang, 1988). Increased ownership of managers increases the performance of the firm because the managers avoid the depletion of assets, and thus, enhanced performance is guaranteed (Smith, 1990).

The history of banking originates in the early world in Babylonia around 2000 BC. Islamic banking originates 1400 years back, and now it is developing quickly around the world. The rules of Islamic financing follow *Shari'ah* standards. Rashid et al. (2017) explored that Islamic banking is initiated in Pakistan in February 1979 to basically wipe out Riba (interest). Islamic banks are allowed by SBP to work in the same capacity as conventional banks, with an essential target to give diversified banking opportunities to construct a sound monetary framework rendering the economic development opportunities through *Shari'ah*-compliant financial operations. In 2002, the exertion of building up the Islamic financial system prompted the foundation of first Islamic bank (Meezan Bank Limited) in Pakistan.

The drive of this chapter is to investigate the impact of "ownership structure" on performance of both Islamic and conventional banks of Pakistan. The previous studies focus only Islamic banks, but this study considers the impact of "ownership structure" on financial performance in comparison to full-fledged Islamic banks and conventional banks listed at PSE (Pakistan Stock Exchange). The study further checks the moderating effect of leverage on ownership structure-performance relation of Islamic and conventional banks simultaneously, which is described below.

Objectives of the study

- Explore separately the effect of ownership structure on the financial performance of Islamic and conventional banks of Pakistan, while considering size, growth and earnings volatility as control variables.
- To investigate the moderating effect of leverage on ownership structure-performance relation of Islamic and conventional banks of Pakistan.

8.2 Review of literature

The segment covers in detail the theoretic groundwork and empirical proofs of the impact of ownership structure on performance, expanding further the moderating role of leverage on the relationship mentioned above.

8.2.1 Ownership structure and performance

The important thing to indicate here is that numerous research scholars have uncovered diverse outcomes for the developed and developing countries. Numerous researchers investigated direct connection between ownership structure and performance of an organization (Berle & Means, 1932; Jensen & Meckling, 1976; Mehran, 1995). Some of them found a nonlinear association (McConnell & Servaes, 1990, 1995; Morck et al., 1988; Pushner, 1995; Short & Keasey, 1999). Some studies explored significant results (Schultz, 2003), whereas others expressed insignificant outcomes (Demsetz & Lehn, 1985; Kamerschen, 1968).

With an increase in "management ownership," performance never increases (Loderer & Martin, 1997), while Cho (1998) and Prowse (1999) have revealed turnaround connection among performance and "managerial ownership." The ownership structure is considered as a piece of the examination to combat the agency issues, which can influence the firm performance of an organization (Jensen & Meckling, 1976). The managers as agent have possession in the company would adjust their interests to different stakeholders and accordingly reduce agency cost; this will serve as a positive influence for the firm valuation. Therefore, the performance and managerial ownership have positive association between them (Jensen & Meckling, 1976). On the other side, when the least managerial ownership exists, the agency conflict is reduced provoking to higher debt level, and then again if there is increased "managerial ownership," it would facilitate the managerial opportunism and along these lines cut down the debt level. Friend and Hasbrouck, (1988) and Friend and Lang (1988) explored a negative association among leverage and managerial ownership and suggested to diminish the level of debt of the firm in order to diminish the default risk.

Another relevant theory is the "stewardship theory" proposed by Donaldson and Davis (1991), which argues that both groups (managers and owners) share common objectives and the executives are stewards of the owners. It means the board of directors have not much authority as proposed by "agency theory." Here, the board performs a supportive role by authorizing the executives which upsurge the performance. The next theory is the "Resource Dependence" (Hillman & Dalziel, 2003), which argues that the existence of board is considered as the provider of resources to their executives to attain the goals of the organization. Even the professional board members can use their skills to train and guide the executives to enhance the performance.

8.2.2 Capital structure and performance

Numerous researchers strongly proposed that decisions about capital structure have significant impact on firm performance (Grossman & Hart, 1986; Jensen, 1986; Mill & Modigliani, 1961; Stulz, 1990; Williamson, 1988). Numerous other studies explore diverse results with respect to capital structure and firm performance relationship. Some studies explore a negative association (Chakraborty, 2010; Huang &Tune, 2006; Karadeniz et al., 2009; Rajan & Zingales, 1995) while others discovered positive relationship (Berger & di Patti, 2006; Khan, 2014).

All of the above examination clarified the use of debt in "capital structure" influences performance of an organization because the organizations frequently agree to fix repayments for a particular period. These installments occur irrespective of the performance of the firm. Equity financing ordinarily keeps away from these repayments yet may expect organizations to provide ownership stake in the organization and agency problem arises.

Agency theory states that as the probability of bankruptcy creeps up, high debt confirms improved performance of the management (Jensen & Meckling, 1976). On the other hand, the "pecking order theory" suggests firms' inclination to internal investment over external investment and the debt over the equity (Myers, 1984). Meanwhile, different theories on capital structure are evolved by numerous researchers over time, effecting or effected by performance. Therefore, theories provide relatively alternate interpretations on leverage-performance relationship. This is when empirical studies are appealed to decide between them. Researchers of the developed and developing economies have discovered the leverage-performance relationship by considering these theories. Yet, the relation between leverage and performance turns to more critical due to the less productive capital markets of the developing countries (Ebaid, 2009). In developing countries, the hostile features are the reason of inverse performance and leverage relation (Alipour & Pejman, 2015; Boadi & Li, 2015).

The research work is not same in nature and distinctive as compared to other studies of Pakistan or anywhere. The study sought to explore first the association between ownership structure and performance of the conventional as well as the Islamic banks of Pakistan and then check the moderated effect of leverage on ownership structure-performance of Islamic and conventional banks separately.

8.3 Hypothesis

- **H1:** Ownership structure has a positive relation with the performance of the conventional banks of Pakistan.
- **H2:** Ownership structure has a positive relation with the performance of the Islamic banks of Pakistan.
- **H3:** Financial leverage moderates the ownership structure-performance relationship of conventional banks of Pakistan.
- **H4:** Financial leverage moderates the ownership structure-performance relationship of Islamic banks of Pakistan.

8.3.1 Framework and methodology

8.3.1.1 Theoretical framework

This section covers the theoretical framework, sample size, data selection and methodology of the research work. The study employed performance measures, i.e. return on equity (ROE) and earning per share (EPS) both as dependent variables. The independent variables include the ownership structure and other control variables, whereas leverage is used as moderating variable. The ownership structure is measured through managerial and institutional ownership. The control variables measured through size, earning volatility and growth. The conceptual framework of the study is described in Figure 8.1:

The sample for this research is the financial sector over nine-year period from 2008 to 2016. The study attempts to explore the comparison between the conventional and Islamic banks of Pakistan. Full-fledged Islamic banks in Pakistan are four. Thus, the study selected four Islamic and four conventional banks for data analysis.

8.3.1.2 Data collection

A panel of secondary annual data of conventional and Islamic banks from 2008 to 2016 is applied in this research. The data is collected from the annual reports of the banks. The further "Financial Statement Analysis" of SBP is utilized to obtain the data.

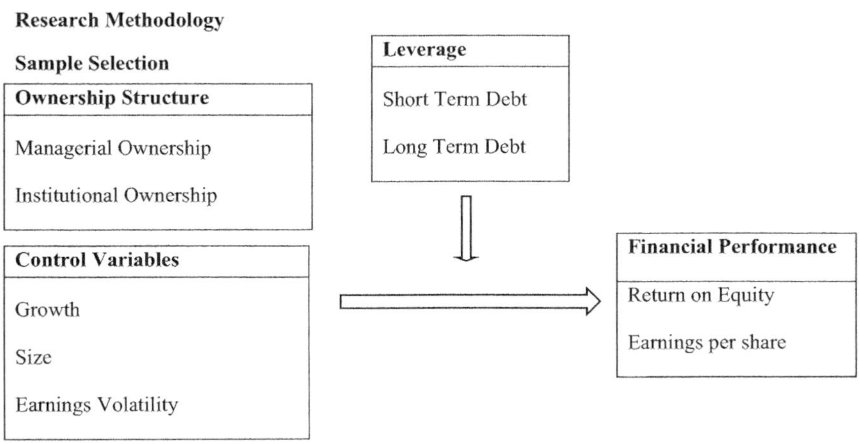

Figure 8.1 The conceptual framework of the relationship between leverage, ownership structure and performance.

8.4 Variables construction

Table 8.1 shows the variables used in the study and how they are measured and operationalized:

8.5 Empirical model

The objective of the study is estimated by the panel regression model with various variables which have been identified as important in the literature (Li, Armstrong, & Clarke, 2014; Singh et al., 2003). The relationship between ownership structure and performance under moderating effect of leverage measured through the following equations:

$$ROE_{it} = \alpha + \beta_1 MO_{it} + \beta_2 SDR_{it} + \beta_3 MO*SDR_{it} + \beta_4 SZ_{it} + + \beta_5 GRW_{it} + \beta_6 EVOl_{it} + \varepsilon_{it} \quad (i)$$

$$EPS_{it} = \alpha + \beta_1 MO_{it} + \beta_2 LDR_{it} + \beta_3 MO*LDR_{it} + \beta_4 SZ_{it} + + \beta_5 GRW_{it} + \beta_6 EVOl_{it} + \varepsilon_{it} \quad (ii)$$

$$ROE_{it} = \alpha + \beta_1 IO_{it} + \beta_2 SDR_{it} + \beta_3 IO*SDR_{it} + \beta_4 SZ_{it} + + \beta_5 GRW_{it} + \beta_6 EVOl_{it} + \varepsilon_{it} \quad (iii)$$

$$EPS_{it} = \alpha + \beta_1 IO_{it} + \beta_2 LDR_{it} + \beta_3 IO*LDR_{it} + \beta_4 SZ_{it} + + \beta_5 GRW_{it} + \beta_6 EVOl_{it} + \varepsilon_{it} \quad (iv)$$

Table 8.1 Measurement of the Study Variables

Variables	*Measurements*	*Notation*
Independent Variables		
Managerial ownership	"Percentage of ordinary shares held by all directors"	MO
Institutional ownership	"Shares owned by the financial institutions/total outstanding common stocks"	IO
Moderating Variable		
Short-term debt ratio	"Short-term debt/total assets"	SDR
Long-term debt ratio	"Long-term debt/total assets"	LDR
Dependent Variable		
Return on equity	"Net profit after tax/total share holders' equity"	ROE
Earnings per share	"Ratio of profit after tax to numbers of ordinary shares"	EPS
Control Variable		
Bank size	"Natural Logarithm of total assets"	SZ
Growth	"(Total assets − Total assets$_{t-1}$)/ Total assets$_{t-1}$"	GRW
Earnings volatility	"(Profit before taxes − Profit before taxes$_{t-1}$)/Profit before taxes $_{t-1}$"	EVOL

Source: Author's own calculations.

8.6 Research findings

8.6.1 Descriptive statistics

Table 8.2 shows the descriptive statistics in terms of mean, maximum, minimum and standard deviation values of dependent and independent variables of conventional banks.

Table 8.3 demonstrates the descriptive statistics summary of the independent, dependent and control variables of Islamic and conventional banks. The table expresses the directions of variables of the model. It depicts that the sampled conventional banks have been received 20% ROE if they get 30% leverage by short-term debt and 3% by long-term debt; which is comparatively less for Islamic banks. Both Islamic and conventional banks are financing more from short-term debt as compared to long-term debt. Kunt and Maksimovic (1999) signify that the firms in emerging countries use considerably less amounts of long-term debt. The table depicts that the institutional investors and managerial shareholders have 2% and 47% ownership, respectively, in case of conventional banks of Pakistan, and 28% and 32% ownership, respectively, in case of Islamic banks of Pakistan, which describes that conventional banks have major contribution in managerial ownership as compared to Islamic banks

Table 8.2 Summary of Descriptive Measures of Conventional Banks

Variable	*OBS*	*Mean*	*Std. Dev.*	*Min*	*Max*
Roe	36	.2030556	.0644014	.03	.29
Eps	36	6.77528	5.460953	6.43	24.47
Mo	36	.4733319	.1261828	.00935	.76
Io	36	.0259434	.0135294	.0049	.0623
Sdr	36	.303505	.0165797	.0016193	.0436644
Ldr	36	.037996	. 0016939	.0014386	.007959
Sz	36	20.11212	1.429869	14.79104	21.64243
Grw	36	.1401111	.0711898	.032	.413
Evol	36	.1270556	.2038313	−.554	.727

Source: Author's own calculations.

Table 8.3 Summary of Descriptive Measures of Islamic Banks

Variable	*OBS*	*Mean*	*Std. Dev.*	*Min*	*Max*
Roe	36	.035	.3160696	−1.34	.71
Eps	36	4.942222	8.960027	−1.25	24.5
Mo	36	.3287583	.2432607	0	.7289
Io	36	.2872072	.4215478	0	1
Sdr	36	.8238889	.1999	0	.93
Ldr	36	.0272222	.0215	0	.11
Sz	36	18.30702	.9443324	16.62113	20.31763
Grw	36	.2720556	.2108203	−.079	.85
Evol	36	.0961111	.5704	−.965	.99

Source: Author's own calculations.

8.6.2 Correlation analysis

Tables 8.4 and 8.5 depict the findings of correlation analysis of the independent variables of both conventional and Islamic banks of Pakistan:

The results depict that there is no issue of multicollinearity, as values of the correlation coefficient are within the range of −1 to 1 and very low.

8.6.3 Panel model regression results

Table 8.6 illustrates the effect of ownership structure on financial performance of conventional and Islamic banks of Pakistan. The study results depict that managerial ownership is showing significant positive relationship with performance (Hill & Snell, 1989) in case of both Islamic and conventional banks, the results are consistent with agency theory (Jensen & Meckling, 1976). Institutional ownership is showing negative significant relationship with ROE (Loderer & Martin, 1997) in case of conventional banks of Pakistan. Bank size is depicting negative significant relationship in case of conventional banks, and in case of Islamic banks it is showing positive significant relationship. Growth and earnings volatility have insignificant relationship with efficiency ratios of Islamic and conventional banks of Pakistan (Tables 8.7 and 8.8).

Table 8.4 Correlation Matrix of Conventional Banks

	io	*mo*	*sdr*	*ldr*	*sz*	*grw*	*evol*
io	**1.0000**						
mo	**−0.3652**	**1.0000**					
sdr	**−0.4495**	**0.3254**	**1.0000**				
ldr	**−0.1087**	**−0.1524**	**−0.3835**	**1.0000**			
sz	**0.2252**	**0.0875**	**0.0057**	**0.0435**	**1.0000**		
grw	**−0.1380**	**0.2004**	**−0.0285**	**0.3161**	**−0.0024**	**1.0000**	
evol	**0.2135**	**−0.0365**	**−0.0129**	**−0.0219**	**−0.0135**	**0.2680**	**1.0000**

Source: Author's own calculations.

Table 8.5 Correlation Matrix of Islamic Banks

	mo	*io*	*sdr*	*ldr*	*sz*	*grw*	*evol*
mo	**1.0000**						
io	**−0.3920**	**1.0000**					
sdr	**0.2543**	**−0.5216**	**1.0000**				
ldr	**−0.3576**	**0.1138**	**−0.1622**	**1.0000**			
sz	**−0.0647**	**−0.4120**	**0.4983**	**0.4100**	**1.0000**		
grw	**−0.0301**	**−0.1093**	**0.0031**	**0.3368**	**0.0452**	**1.0000**	
evol	**0.2013**	**−0.0777**	**−0.2034**	**−0.1427**	**−0.0062**	**−0.2406**	**1.0000**

Source: Author's own calculations.

Table 8.6 Panel Regression Results (Conventional and Islamic Banks)

	Conventional Banks		Islamic Banks	
Variables	*Eq1 ROE Random*	*Eq2 EPS Random*	*Eq1 ROE Random*	*Eq2 EPS Random*
MO	0.57	2.29	1.75	1.82
	0.56	0.00***	0.08**	0.06**
IO	−2.37	3.93	1.80	1.42
	0.01**	0.00***	0.07*	0.015**
Sz	−2.45	−1.78	1.77	3.33
	0.03**	0.07*	0.07*	0.06*
Grw	−0.13	0.04	−0.66	0.43
	0.89	0.96	0.50	0.66
Evol	1.66	−0.63	1.31	1.14
	0.99	0.52	0.19	0.25
Cons	4.02	1.40	−1.96	−3.44
	0.00	0.16	0.05	0.00
No. of Observation	36	36	36	36
No. of Cross-section	4	4	4	4
R-Square	0.55	0.68	0.46	0.60

Source: Author's own calculations.
Robust standard errors in parentheses: *** $p < 0.01$; ** $p < 0.05$; * $p < 0.1$.

Table 8.7 Moderating Effect of Leverage on Ownership Structure-Performance (ROE) Relationship of Conventional Banks

Variables	*Eq1 Random*	*Eq2 Random*	*Eq3 Fixed*	*Eq4 Fixed*
MO	−2.27	1.61	1.91	1.34
	0.02**	0.108	0.06*	0.19
IO	−1.45	−2.70	0.21	1.07
	0.147	0.00***	0.83	0.29
SDR	−2.36		1.83	
	0.01**		0.07**	
LDR		0.87		−0.30
		0.38		0.76
MO*SDR	2.42			
	0.01**			
MO*LDR		−1.48		
		0.139		
IO*SDR			0.33	
			0.74	
IO*LDR				−0.81
				0.42
Sz	−1.70	−2.83	−1.28	−1.82
	0.09**	0.00***	0.212	0.08*
Grw	−0.49	0.100	1.00	1.12
	0.632	0.922	0.32	0.27

(*Continued*)

Variables	*Eq1 Random*	*Eq2 Random*	*Eq3 Fixed*	*Eq4 Fixed*
Evol	1.29	1.94	0.60	0.48
	0.198	0.05*	0.55	0.632
Cons	3.91	4.50	−0.44	2.46
	0.00	0.00	0.66	0.02
No. of Observation	36	36	36	36
No. of Cross-section	4	4	4	4
R-Square	.45	.677	0.752	0.68

Source: Author's own calculations.
Robust standard errors in parentheses: *** $p < 0.01$; ** $p < 0.05$; * $p < 0.1$.

Table 8.8 Moderating Effect of Leverage on Ownership Structure-Performance (EPS) Relationship of Conventional Banks

Variables	*Eq1 Fixed*	*Eq2 Fixed*	*Eq3 Fixed*	*Eq4 Fixed*
MO	−0.36	2.40	1.10	2.00
	0.72	0.05*	0.28	0.05
IO	0.43	0.32	1.60	−1.64
	0.67	0.74	0.12	0.11
SDR	−2.72		−2.90	
	0.04**		0.00**	
LDR		2.18		−1.26
		0.03**		0.22
MO* SDR	0.49			
	0.063*			
MO* LDR		−1.65		
		0.11		
IO* SDR			−1.55	
			0.13	
IO* LDR				2.57
				0.21
Sz	−4.91	−1.75	−3.95	−1.26
	0.00***	0.09***	0.00***	0.21
Grw	0.04	−0.04	0.14	0.24
	0.966	0.972	0.89	0.81
Evol	1.01	1.32	1.11	1.57
	0.323	0.19	0.27	0.12
Cons	3.47	1.14	4.92	2.35
	0.00	0.26	0.00	0.02
No. of Observation	36	36	36	36
No. of Cross-section	4	4	4	4
R-Square	0.74	0.69	0.58	0.65

Source: Author's own calculations.
Robust standard errors in parentheses: *** $p < 0.01$; ** $p < 0.05$; * $p < 0.1$.

The interaction terms of ownership structure and leverage depict interesting results. The results depict that the interaction term of MO*SDR is showing positive significant relation with performance. This shows that short-term debt ratio and managerial ownership both enhance bank performance of conventional banks. The results are consistent with agency theory. In case of institutional ownership, the leverage doesn't have any moderating effect on ownership structure-performance relationship. The results are consistent with Alipour & Pejman (2015) (Tables 8.9 and 8.10).

In case of Islamic banks of Pakistan, the results depict that the interaction term of IO*LDR is showing negative significant relation with performance. This shows long-term debt ratio and institutional ownership both negatively affect bank performance of Islamic banks. In case of managerial

Table 8.9 Moderating Effect of Leverage on Ownership Structure and Performance (ROE) of Islamic Banks

Variables	*Eq1 Fixed*	*Eq2 Random*	*Eq3 Fixed*	*Eq4 Random*
MO	2.39	0.95	2.19	1.58
	0.02**	0.34	0.03**	0.11
IO	−0.67	1.75	−1.51	1.93
	0.51	0.08*	0.14	0.05*
SDR	0.37		−1.50	
	0.71		0.14	
LDR		0.50		2.44
		0.61		0.01**
MO*SDR	−1.29			
	0.21			
MO*LDR		0.57		
		0.56		
IO*SDR			1.36	
			0.18	
IO*LDR				−1.65
				0.09*
Sz	−0.35	1.48	−.28	
	0.72	0.13	0.78	
Grw	−0.73	−0.73	−0.79	−1.00
	0.47	0.46	0.44	0.31
Evol	0.25	1.26	0.21	1.14
	.803	0.20	0.83	0.25
Cons	0.17	−1.57	0.46	−1.83
	0.865	0.11	0.61	0.06
No. of Observation	36	36	36	36
No. of Cross-section	4	4	4	4
R-Square	0.662	0.65	0.79	0.68

Source: Author's own calculations.
Robust standard errors in parentheses: *** $p < 0.01$; ** $p < 0.05$; * $p < 0.1$.

Table 8.10 Moderating Effect of Leverage on Ownership Structure and Performance (EPS) of Islamic Banks

Variables	*Eq1 Fixed*	*Eq2 Random*	*Eq3 Random*	*Eq4 Random*
MO	−0.60	−0.01	1.66	2.08
	0.50	0.99	0.09*	0.03**
IO	0.48	1.11	1.12	2.43
	0.63	0.26	0.26	0.01**
SDR	−1.83		0.52	
	0.07*		0.601	
LDR		0.07		2.88
		0.94		0.00***
MO*SDR	1.44			
	0.163			
MO*LDR		2.29		
		0.12		
IO*SDR			−0.55	
			0.58	
IO*LDR				−2.18
				0.02**
Sz	−0.89	2.61	3.94	2.68
	0.37	0.00***	0.00***	0.00***
Grw	−0.13	−0.03	0.80	0.48
	0.90	0.97	0.432	0.63
Evol	0.23	0.23	0.33	0.86
	0.80	0.30	0.10	0.39
Cons	1.27	−2.43	−3.82	−2.96
	0.21	0.01	0.00	0.00
No. of Observation	36	36	36	36
No. of Cross-section	4	4	4	4
R-Square	0.622	0.54	0.75	0.50

Source: Author's own calculations.
Robust standard errors in parentheses: *** $p < 0.01$; ** $p < 0.05$; * $p < 0.1$.

ownership, the leverage doesn't have any moderating effect on ownership structure-performance relationship. The results are consistent with Alipour & Pejman (2015). In case of Islamic banks, the study results are showing inconsistency with agency theory.

8.7 Conclusion and recommendations

The overall results of the study depict that in case of both Islamic and conventional banks managerial and institutional ownership is showing significant positive relationship with ROE, and other than institutional ownership is showing negative significant relationship with ROE in case of conventional banks of Pakistan. In order to sum up the results of the study, there is no consensus on the moderating effect of leverage on ownership structure-performance relationship of conventional and Islamic banks of Pakistan; further research is called for.

The is a dire need for enhanced statistical justifications for pursuing more corporate governance transformations in ownership structure of the banks, in order to improve the financial strength of the banking sector. The government should improve the ownership structure criteria to get best utilization of funds collected through depositor.

References

Alipour, M., & Pejman, M. E. (2015). The impact of performance measures, leverage and efficiency on market value added: Evidence from Iran. *Global Economics and Management Review*, *20*(1), 6–14.

Bauer, P. (2004). Determinants of capital structure: Empirical evidence from the Czech Republic. *Czech Journal of Economics and Finance (Finance a Uver)*, *54* (1–2), 2–21.

Berger, A. N., & Di Patti, E. B. (2006). Capital structure and firm performance: A new approach to testing agency theory and an application to the banking industry. *Journal of Banking & Finance*, *30*(4), 1065–1102.

Berle, A. A., & Means, G. C. (1932). *The modern corporation and private property*. New York: Harcourt, Brace and World.

Boadi, E. K., & Li, Y. (2015). An empirical analysis of leverage and financial performance of listed non-financial firms in Ghana. *International Journal of Economics and Finance*, *7*(9), 120.

Chakraborty, I. (2010). Capital structure in an emerging stock market: The case of India. *Research in International Business and Finance*, *24*(3), 295–314.

Chakravarthy, B. S. (1986). Measuring strategic performance. *Strategic Management Journal*, *7*(5), 437–458.

Cho, M.-H. (1998). Ownership structure, investment, and the corporate value: An empirical analysis. *Journal of Financial Economics*, *47*(1), 103–121.

Deesomsak, R., Paudyal, K., & Pescetto, G. (2004). The determinants of capital structure: Evidence from the Asia Pacific region. *Journal of Multinational Financial Management*, *14*(4), 387–405.

Demsetz, H., & Lehn, K. (1985). The structure of corporate ownership: Causes and consequences. *Journal of Political Economy*, *93*(6), 1155–1177.

Donaldson, L., & Davis, J. H. (1991). Stewardship theory or agency theory: CEO governance and shareholder returns. *Australian Journal of Management*, *16*(1), 49–64.

Ebaid, I. E. (2009). The impact of capital-structure choice on firm performance: Empirical evidence from Egypt. *The Journal of Risk Finance*, *10*(5), 477–487.

Friend, I., & Lang, L. H. (1988). An empirical test of the impact of managerial self-interest on corporate capital structure. *The Journal of Finance*, *43*(2), 271–281.

Grossman, S. J., & Hart, O. D. (1988). One share-one vote and the market for corporate control. *Journal of Financial Economics*, *20*(Supplement C), 175–202.

Hill, C. W., & Snell, S. A. (1989). Effects of ownership structure and control on corporate productivity. *Academy of Management Journal*, *32*(1), 25–46.

Hillman, A. J., & Dalziel, T. (2003). Boards of directors and firm performance: Integrating agency and resource dependence perspectives. *Academy of Management Review*, *28*(3), 383–396.

Huang, G., & Song, F. M. (2006). The determinants of capital structure: Evidence from China. *China Economic Review*, *17*(1), 14–36.

Jensen, M. C. (1986). Agency costs of free cash flow, corporate finance, and takeovers. *The American Economic Review, 76*(2), 323–329.

Jensen, M. C., & Meckling, W. H. (1976). Theory of the firm: Managerial behavior, agency costs and ownership structure. *Journal of Financial Economics, 3*(4), 305–360.

Kamerschen, D. R. (1968). The influence of ownership and control on profit rates. *The American Economic Review, 58*(3), 432–447.

Karadeniz, E., Kandir, S., Balcilar, M., & Onal, Y. (2009). Determinants of capital structure: Evidence from Turkish lodging companies. *Emerald Group Publishing Limited, 21*(5), 594–609.

Khan, A. (2014). How does stock prices respond to various macroeconomic factors? A case study of Pakistan. *Journal of Management Info, 4*(1), 75–95.

Kunt, A., & Maksimovic, V. (1999). Institutions, financial markets, and firm debt maturity. *Journal of Financial Economics, 54*(3), 295–336.

Li, Y., Armstrong, A., & Clarke, A. (2014). The relationship between corporate governance and financial performance of small corporations in Australia. *Journal of Business Systems, Governance & Ethics, 9(2)*, 25–39. ISSN 1833-4318.

Loderer, C., & Martin, K. (1997). Executive stock ownership and performance tracking faint traces. *Journal of Financial Economics, 45*(2), 223–255.

Marsh, P. (1982). The choice between equity and debt: An empirical study. *The Journal of Finance, 37*(1), 121–144.

McConnell, J. J., & Servaes, H. (1990). Additional evidence on equity ownership and corporate value. *Journal of Financial Economics, 27*(2), 595–612.

Mehran, H. (1995). Executive compensation structure, ownership, and firm performance. *Journal of Financial Economics, 38*(2), 163–184.

Miller, M. H., & Modigliani, F. (1961). Dividend policy, growth, and the valuation of shares. *The Journal of Business, 34*(4), 411–433.

Modigliani, F., & Miller, M. H. (1958). The cost of capital, corporation finance and the theory of investment. *The American Economic Review, 48*(3), 261–297.

Modigliani, F., & Miller, M. H. (1963). Corporate income taxes and the cost of capital: A correction. *The American Economic Review, 53*, 433–443.

Morck, R., Shleifer, A., & Vishny, R. W. (1988). Management ownership and market valuation: An empirical analysis. *Journal of Financial Economics, 20*, 293–315.

Myers, S. C. (1984). The capital structure puzzle. *The Journal of Finance, 39*(3), 574–592.

Prowse, S. (1999). "Corporate Governance in East Asia: A Framework for Analysis", Paper presented at high level Seminar on Managing Capital Flows, Bangkok, 15–16 June 1998. Organized by ADB, IMF, WB and United Nations Economic and Social Commission for Asia and the Pacific.

Pushner, G. M. (1995). Equity ownership structure, leverage, and productivity: Empirical evidence from Japan. *Pacific-Basin Finance Journal, 3*(2), 241–255.

Rajan, R. G., & Zingales, L. (1995). What do we know about capital structure? Some evidence from international data. *The Journal of Finance, 50*(5), 1421–1460.

Rashid, A., Yousaf, S., & Khaleequzzaman, M. (2017). Does Islamic banking really strengthen financial stability? Empirical evidence from Pakistan. *International Journal of Islamic and Middle Eastern Finance and Management, 10*(2), 130–148.

Saad, N. M. (2010). Corporate governance compliance and the effects to capital structure in Malaysia. *International Journal of Economics and Finance, 2*(1), 105–114.

Schultz, E. (2003). The relationship between ownership structure and performance in listed Australian companies. *Australian Journal of Management, 28*(3), 287–305

Short, H., & Keasey, K. (1999). Managerial ownership and the performance of firms: Evidence from the UK. *Journal of Corporate Finance*, *5*(1), 79–101.

Singh, M., Davidson III, W. N., & Suchard, J. A. (2003). Corporate diversification strategies and capital structure. *The Quarterly Review of Economics and Finance*, *43*(1), 147–167.

Smith, A. J. (1990). Corporate ownership structure and performance: The case of management buyouts. *Journal of Financial Economics*, *27*(1), 143–164.

Stulz, R. (1990). Managerial discretion and optimal financing policies. *Journal of Financial Economics*, *26*(1), 3–27.

Williamson, O. E. (1988). Corporate finance and corporate governance. *The Journal of Finance*, *43*(3), 567–591.

9 Dynamic correlation and volatility linkage between stocks and *sukuk*

Masoumeh Shahsavari

9.1 Introduction

The correlation between financial markets that identifies investment risk is regarded as one of the most important ways to be successful in investment. The prediction of the correlation structure and its use to select the best portfolio is considered as a major step in the success of risk and portfolio management. Additionally, monetary policy executives in countries use information and messages in asset prices to anticipate expected inflation rates and economic periods.[1]

As Marquitz and other researchers have shown in their research studies, the greater the when correlation coefficient between the returns of the collection members in an investing portfolio moves to (1-), the risk of portfolio decreases. Portfolio risk is affected not only by the average standard deviation of its members, but also by the diversity of investment and the relationship between the returns of the members. Therefore, looking at the correlation between different financial assets seems to be necessary for investment.

Due to the nature of *sukuk*, which experiments low price fluctuations, holders of these papers will not be exposed to the risk of price fluctuations. In a situation where the risk of price fluctuations in the stock market is detrimental to investors, such as a recession or a sharp drop in prices, the investment in *Sukuk* can be covered by losses from stock price fluctuations.

Despite the importance of correlations between different assets of a portfolio, and the specific features of Islamic financial instruments, there is a few related research studies. Still, some aspects of this market, including its type and its relation with other financial markets of Iran, have not been investigated. Since the investment and diversification of the investment portfolio is of the same importance to the type and extent of the relationship between the various investment instruments, this study tries to use the GARCH family models and the price indices of the *sukuk* market accepted in Iran Fara Bourse and the shares accepted in Tehran Stock Exchange; the behavior of *Sukuk* compared to the shares reviewed and the relationship between the two markets, with the aim of examining the existence or absence of correlation between two time series, should be studied.

Considering the expansion of Iran's debt market and the expansion of Islamic financial instruments in the world, it was necessary to examine the relationship between *sukuk* and other financial instruments in order to understand more precisely the financial markets and the prediction of possible economic situations.

In this research, the GARCH family models and *sukuk* price indices accepted Fara Bourse and the shares accepted in Tehran Stock Exchange have examined the behavior of *sukuk* compared to stock and the relationship between two markets study.

9.1.1 Overview of sukuk features

Sukuk, as expressions of Islamic societies, should comply with religious principles (*Shari'ah*) that govern economic, social and ethical aspects of individuals and institutions (Iqbal and Mirakhor, 2007). Five principles mainly distinguish Islamic financial products: the prohibition on explicit interest rates (*riba*), the prohibition on transactions subject to excessive uncertainty (*gharar*), the prohibition on specific markets or products (pork, alcohol, weapons), a required sharing of profit and loss between contractual parties and a direct link of each operation with the real economy.[2]

We can classify *sukuk* in two categories, with effects on their credit risk exposure:

1 Asset-backed *sukuk*: represents a true sale of assets, since the underlying has been validly transferred to the Special Purpose Vehicle (SPV). In the event of default, therefore, the underlying assets will remain completely separate from the originator. The *sukuk* holders have the full claim over the underlying asset, without any risk of the sale subsequently being inverted by local or *Shari'ah* courts;
2 Asset-based *sukuk*: This is where investors only have a beneficial ownership in the underlying asset instead of legal ownership over the underlying asset. In this structure, assets are generally sold by the originator to the SPV in the form of a trust. The trustee issues certificates showing the investor's ownership interest, while the proceeds are used to purchase the assets. The investor receives a distribution income representing a share of the return generated by the underlying assets or from other sources within the originator. Theoretically, in the event of bankruptcy, investors should have a claim or right to the corporate assets. However, it is unsecured and ranked together with other unsecured creditors, without any priority and rated accordingly.

9.2 Literature review

9.2.1 Literature on conventional portfolio diversification

The interrelationship between markets is a key feature of investor asset allocation because it is instrumental in determining the risk. Estimating the correlation structure and using this to select superior portfolios is a central key point for portfolio and risk managers. Furthermore, monetary policy authorities use information contained in assets prices with the aim of developing expectations in terms of inflation and business cycle conditions. So, understanding the co-movements between stocks and bonds may be useful for their purposes.

Several papers have analyzed the cross-linkage between conventional stock and bond markets. Earlier studies assume a constant relationship between stock and bonds over time. Shiller and Beltratti (1992) find a lower correlation between the two asset classes caused by discount rates. In accordance with the previously mentioned authors, Campbell and Ammer (1993) provide evidence of a similar lower positive correlation, explained by news about future excess stock returns and inflation. Following research studies provided a refinement by analyzing the time-varying correlations: (Li (2004); Cappiello *et al.* (2006); Andersson *et al.* (2008); Chiang *et al.*, (2015); Dimic *et al.* (2016), among others), showing that stock and bond prices tend to move in the same direction, even if there are periods of negative correlations.

Despite the large literature, academic researchers have not reached a consensus about the driving forces behind correlations. Connolly *et al.* (2005) claim that stock-bond market correlation decreases with the increase in stock market uncertainty, suggesting that bonds may be a better hedge against stock market downturns. Kim *et al.* (2006), by analyzing the stock-bond market integration in EMU countries, confirm the negative relationship between stock market uncertainty and stock-bond market correlations. Another strand of literature, investigating the flight-to-quality phenomenon from bonds to stocks, shows negative correlations between those asset classes. Baur and Lucey (2009) reveal that flights occur across countries, enhancing the diversification benefits when they are needed most.

Focusing on macroeconomic driving forces, Li (2004) demonstrates that the uncertainty about expected inflation rates is the primary driver of co-movements between stocks and bonds, whereas unexpected inflation and real interest rates are less influent. Also Andersson *et al.* (2008) confirm that stock and bond prices tend to move together during periods of high inflation expectations, whereas lower level of inflation seems to move prices in opposite direction. Moreover, the authors provide further evidence of a negative relationship between stock market volatility and correlations. Yang *et al.* (2009), by using a large time span that covers 150 years of data at a monthly frequency, recognize that higher stock-bond correlations tend to follow higher short rates or higher inflation rates. Aslanidis and Christiansen (2014) find that macroeconomic fundamentals are the most useful explanatory variables when the stock-bond correlation is largely negative. Christopher *et al.* (2012) stress the importance of sovereign credit ratings on time-varying stock and bond market correlations, while Chiang *et al.* (2015) find evidence that stock-bond correlations are negatively correlated with stock market uncertainty, as measured by the conditional variance and the implied volatility of the S&P 500 index, but positively related to bond market uncertainty.

9.2.2 *Literature review on Islamic finance portfolio diversification*[3]

Despite the exponential growing of *Shari'ah* compliant debt instruments, literature has not yet documented the interdependence between *sukuk* and conventional stocks and the diversification benefits provided by this type of instruments during stock market downturns.

A significant number of studies focus on *sukuk* (Abdulkader and Nathif, 2004; Iqbal and Mirakhor, 2007; Vishwanath and Sabahuddin, 2009), analyzing their structure, features and their different exposure to risks. Rusgianto and Ahmad (2013) examine their volatility through the *Dow Jones Citigroup Sukuk Index* and their relationship with subprime financial crisis shock. They find that precrisis and during-crisis volatility is more sensitive to market events than later. Other authors compare the risk/return profile of *sukuk* with conventional bonds (Zin *et al.*, 2011; Fathurahman and Fitriati, 2013; Mosaid and Boutti, 2014) through a case study analysis (Cakir and Raei, 2007). Najeeb *et al.* (2014) analyze the portfolio diversification opportunities, including *sukuk* in a well-diversified portfolio. They find that returns of local [Gulf Cooperation Council (GCC) and Malaysian] currency *sukuk* have low levels of long-term correlations, allowing gains in portfolio diversification, whereas international currency *sukuk* exhibit high level of long-term correlations.

Recently, several papers explore the interdependencies between *sukuk* and *Shari'ah* compliant stocks. Aloui *et al.* (2015a) assess co-movements between *Shari'ah stocks* and *sukuk* in the GCC countries, finding a strong dependence between them. They also show that Islamic assets don't seem to have a different behavior compared to conventional stock and bond counterparts, with overall portfolio diversification varying across frequencies and time. In a subsequent paper the same authors (Aloui *et al.*, 2015b), investigating the global factors driving the co-movement, show that oil prices and credit event information had a positive relationship during 2008–2013 period. Kim and Kang (2012), using a multivariate GARCH model, document the existence of unidirectional volatility spillovers from *Shari'ah* stocks to *sukuk* during subprime financial crisis.

Those studies are important because they analyze co-movements and dynamic correlations between two different asset classes within Islamic capital markets. Previous literature only investigates the degree of inter-asset class cointegration, among Islamic country stock markets (Marashdeh, 2005; Bley and Chen, 2006; Majid *et al.*, 2007) and the diversification benefits of including *Shari'ah* compliant stock indexes in an international stock portfolio (Achsani *et al.*, 2007; Majid *et al.*, 2009; Karim *et al.*, 2010; Rahman and Sidek, 2011; Saiti 2013, among others).

Finally, Aktar *et al.* (2015) argue that Islamic assets provide substantial diversification benefits during financial crises. In particular, for the period 2007–2010, volatility linkages between Islamic stocks and bonds are lower than volatility linkages between conventional stocks and bonds. Moreover, the characteristics of Islamic financial markets also reduce volatility linkages between Islamic stocks and conventional bills.

Based on the literature, our hypothesis is that *sukuk* have high volatility linkages and high dynamic correlations with conventional stocks, especially during financial crisis, considering their special structure. In fact, the majority of Islamic bonds are issued with an asset-based mode, rather than asset-backed. We consider them as a hybrid financial instrument between conventional bonds and stocks. They shouldn't, therefore, experience the *flight-to-quality* phenomenon, considering their diversity compared to investment grade conventional bonds, and they could have higher co-movements with equity indexes than conventional bonds. But we also expect that dynamic correlations between *sukuk* and conventional stocks are lower than those among stocks, with Islamic bonds providing some diversification benefits.

9.3 Research methodology

In this research, the shares of all companies and securities accepted in Tehran Stock Exchange and also all *sukuk* listed in exchanges in Iran have been selected as the statistical community.

Since the index of top 50 active companies is built of more appropriate combination of stocks from different groups with more efficient weights and is more analytical, the total stock exchange index of Tehran for top 50 active companies has been selected as a sample in this study. So we use its total index stock.

This index, equivalently, is similar to the Dow Jones Index on the New York Stock Exchange, which is the most prominent indicator of the US stock exchange, reflects changes in the price of 50 shares of selected companies from different industries, with the participation of selected companies representing each industry, by including 50 companies, other companies in each industry have been omitted from the combination, and this has led to a significant reduction in the double effect of improving a group's position on the index.

The final price of *Sukuk* listed in Iran Fara bourse and Tehran Stock Exchange Index are the main variables of this research. In the following, we describe them as below:

- *Sukuk* price: The final price of *sukuk* listed in Iran Fara Bourse is collected on a daily basis and based on the database of Tehran Securities Exchange Technology Management Company. There are different kinds of *sukuk* in Iran Fara Bourse like ITBs (Islamic Treasury Builds), musharaka, Murabaha and Ijara.

- Stock price: This index indicates the general trend of the total price of stock companies listed in Tehran Exchange, and shows the general level changes in prices relative to the date of origin. These data are based on information published by Tehran Stock Exchange.

The theoretical domain of this research is to investigate the correlation between *sukuk* and Islamic stocks volatility.

The depth of this market was analyzed for the period of 2015/03–2017/03. In this research, the shares of all companies and securities accepted in Tehran Stock Exchange have been selected as the statistical population. Since the index of 50 companies is more active than the appropriate combination of shares in different groups and is more analytical, Tehran Stock Exchange Index for 50 more active companies has been selected as a sample.

In this research, we try to verify the correlation of *sukuk* accepted in Iran Fara Bourse and shares of companies accepted in Tehran Stock Exchange. For this purpose, in the first step, the *sukuk* weighting index with the final price weight is calculated as follows:

$$CL_t = CL_{t-1} * \frac{\sum P_{t,i} * N_{t,i}}{\sum P_{t-1,i} * N_{t-1,i}} \tag{1}$$

P (t, i): The price of the security i on the date t;
N (t, i): The number of bonds in the ith note market on t;
CL0: The index value on the first day (2015/25/03), which is equal to 100 units.

If a new security lists or expires, the above indicator will be adjusted accordingly:

$$CL_t = CL_{t-1} * \frac{\sum P_{t,i} * N_{t,i}}{(\sum P_{t-1,i} * N_{t-1,i}) + (\sum P_{t,i} * N_{t,i} \text{Accept}) - (\sum P_{t,i} * N_{t,i} \text{Offer})} \tag{2}$$

The *sukuk* price index includes all the *sukuk* accepted in Iran Fara Bourse market.

In the next step, the logarithmic daily returns for the obtained index and also the Tehran Stock Exchange Index are calculated. Daily returns are extracted based on the following logarithmic formula:

$$Y_t = \ln P_t - \ln P_{t-1} \tag{3}$$

Multivariate GARCH models are designed with the aim of study volatilities and correlations co-movements between markets, in order to provide better decision tools in portfolio selection, asset pricing and risk management techniques. Literature has provided several multivariate GARCH models, such as VECH, BEKK, CCC and DCC (dynamic conditional correlation).

Among the several multivariate models, we decided to use the DCC model of Engle (2002); the choice of methodology follows Engle and Sheppard (2008): even using standard univariate GARCH specifications, DCC offers better performance in terms of portfolio allocation among the families applicable to large panel models and therefore is more powerful than the constant correlation estimator developed by Bollerslev (1990).

We implement our DCC model in three steps. First, univariate volatilities are selected by using the Bayesian information criterion (BIC) from a class of GARCH models capable of capturing the common features of financial asset returns variances. We include the following models, all with one lag of innovation and one lag of volatility: GARCH (Bollerslev, 1986) (Equation 4) and EGARCH (Exponential GARCH) (Nelson, 1991) (Equation 5).

Once the univariate models are estimated, the standardized residuals are used to estimate the correlation parameters and the persistence parameters α and β. We implement the asymmetric DCC model, in order to take into accounts the asymmetric return volatility of equity time series (Capiello *et al.*, 2006).

9.3.1 The univariate GARCH model and asymmetric extensions

The GARCH model introduced by Bollerslev (1986) expressed conditional variance as a linear function of the square past values of the series. A generic GARCH (p,q) model can be described as follows:

$$h_t = \omega + \sum_{i=1}^{q} \alpha_i \varepsilon_{t-i}^2 \sum_{j=1}^{p} \beta_j \delta_{t-i}^2 \tag{4}$$

where the α_i and β_j are nonnegative constants and ω is a positive constant.

Since the conditional variance in equation (4) is a function of the lagged residuals and not their signs, the model enforces a symmetric response of volatility to positive and negative shocks.

The EGARCH model is the first that investigate the leverage effects, which refers to the fact that downward movements are more influential for predicting volatility than the upward movements. Nelson's (1991) EGARCH attempts to model fat tails in stock indexes returns by using a generalized exponential distribution; in formula the model can be represented as follows:

$$\log(h_t) + \omega + \sum_{i=1}^{q} \alpha_i \frac{\left|\varepsilon_{t-i}^2\right|}{\delta_{t-i}} + \sum_{i=1}^{q} \gamma_i \frac{\varepsilon_{t-i}}{\delta_{t-i}} + \sum_{i=1}^{q} \beta_j \log \delta_{t-j}^2 \tag{5}$$

Equation (5) allows negative values of ε_t to have different impacts on volatility. Since the coefficient γ_i is typically negative, the model claims for an asymmetric behavior in volatility.

The univariate GARCH models were estimated through the maximum likelihood approach of Bollerslev and Wooldridge (1992), where the log-likelihood function from the Gaussian normal distribution.

9.3.2 The multivariate GARCH model

The DCC model of Engle (2002) is a generalization of the CCC model, which allows the correlation matrix to vary over time rather than requiring them to be constant.

The DCC model of Engle is defined as:

$$H_t = D_t R_t \ D_t \tag{6}$$

where

H_t is a n x n matrix of conditional variances;
D_t is a n x n diagonal matrix of time-varying standard deviations from univariate GARCH models (), in formula:

$$D_t = diag\left(h_{11t}^{\frac{1}{2}} \ldots\ldots h_{NNt}^{\frac{1}{2}} \right) \tag{7}$$

R_t is the correlation matrix defined as:

$$R_t = diag[Q_t]^{-1} Q_t diag \ [Q_t]^{-1} \tag{8}$$

where the n x n symmetric positive definite matrix $Q_t = (q_{ij,t})$ is given by:

$$Q_t = (1-\alpha-\beta)\bar{Q} + \alpha u_{t-1} u'_{t-1} + \beta Q_{t-1} + \gamma\left(g_t g'_t \right) \tag{9}$$

with the standardized residuals $u_t = \varepsilon_{it} / \sqrt{h_{iit}}$, α and β are nonnegative scalar parameters satisfying $\alpha + \beta < 1$ and the vectors g_t are defined as the negative parts of $u_t$as follows:

$$g_{i,t} \equiv \begin{cases} u_{i,t} \ if \ u_{i,t} < 0 \\ 0 \ if \ u_{i,t} \geq 0 \end{cases} = 1,\ldots,N. \tag{10}$$

DCC parameters are estimated by quasi-maximum likelihood by construction because the model is implemented in three different steps: In each of these stages a log-likelihood function is estimated. In the third step, given the results of the Jarque-Bera test of normality, we relax the normality assumption and we adopt a student t-multivariate distribution for the time series returns, which is more suitable and gives better estimation results.

We use a three-stage approach, rather than estimating all the volatility models and correlation model simultaneously, because in practice is more feasible for large portfolios even if the estimator is less efficient.

To test the accuracy of the univariate models, we use the L-Jung Box test using ten interruptions.

According to Hanan Quinn, Schwarz and Akaike and the highest log-likelihood, we apply the best model and apply the output coefficients of the selected model as input to the DCC dynamic multivariate variance model.

To test the accuracy of the DCC model, the Pierce, Hasking and Lee McLeod test will be used. Finally, we look at the output of the model.

9.4 Results and discussion

The time chart shows the stock index of more active 50 companies and the price chart of the *sukuk* price accepted in Iran Fara Bourse is shown in Figures 9.1 and 9.2.

Also the graph of the two time series of the yield of the stock price index of the 50 more active companies and the *sukuk* are shown in Figures 9.3 and 9.4.

As shown in the two above-mentioned graphs, the *Sukuk* index is more stable than the stock index, which can be attributed to the nature of the *sukuk* and its trading volume.

A summary of the statistical characteristics of these two time series is presented in Table 9.1. According to the calculated specification, two time series are not normal.

At next step, the self-correlation of the conditional negation of the series is investigated. The results of our self-correlation, for both time series, show the return on the stock index, and the yield of the *sukuk*, according to Table 9.2, shows a low and positive correlation.

For each of the two time series, 36 average equations with different values of AR and MA are between 0 and 5; among all the above equations,

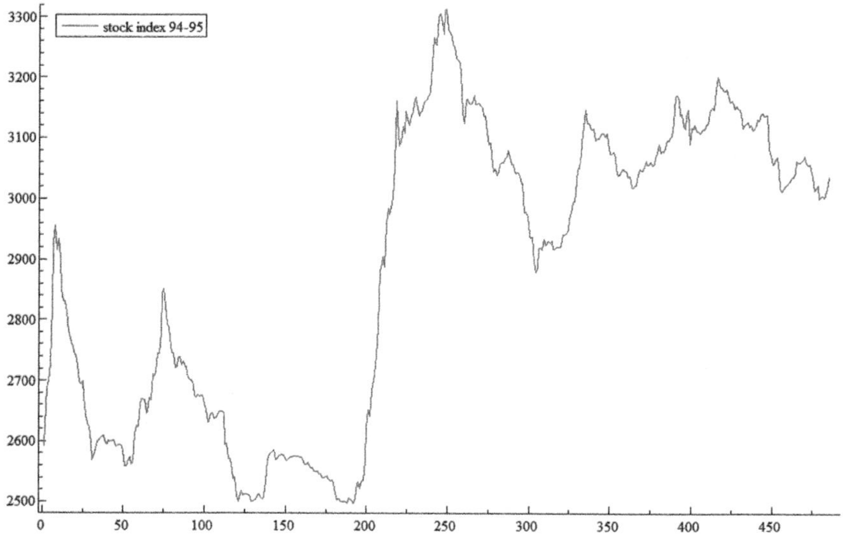

Figure 9.1 Time series of stock index in 2015/03–2017/03.

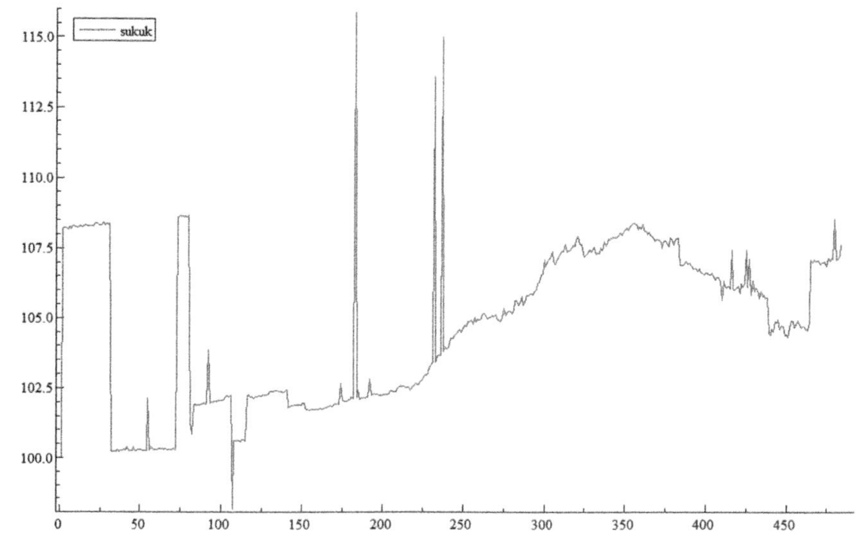

Figure 9.2 Time series of *sukuk* index in 2015/03–2017/03.

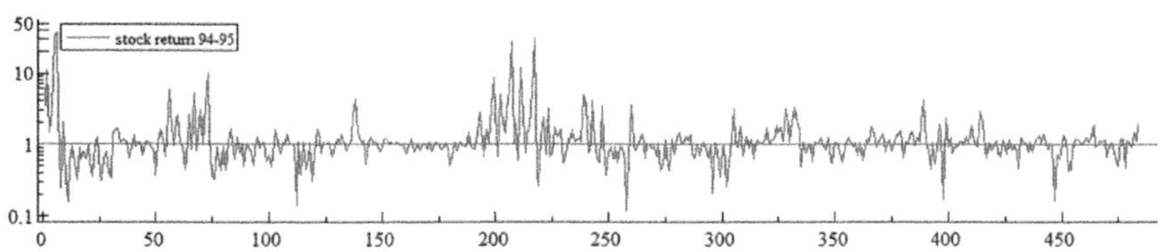

Figure 9.3 Return on the total stock index of 50 active companies of Tehran Stock Exchange in 2015/03–2017/03.

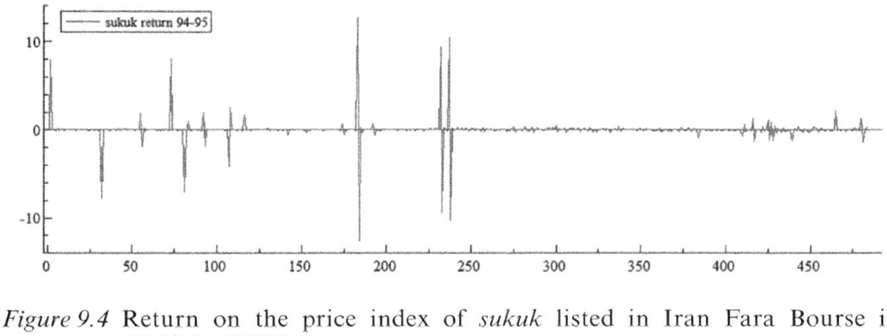

Figure 9.4 Return on the price index of *sukuk* listed in Iran Fara Bourse in 2015/03–2017/03.

which have the best results for Akaike, Hannan-Quinn and Schwarz tests, the mean equation is AR = 2 and MA = 1 because of having the highest LOG-LIKELIHOOD value, is selected

Univariate models with ARMA[4] coefficients are applied on both time series. The results of applying the model are shown in Table 9.3. Based on these results, in the time series of the stock index, there are positive and significant alpha values, indicating a positive and strong correlation between the fluctuations of the index and market shocks. In both models, beta values are also positive and significant. Therefore, in this series of conditional fluctuations, they follow their past. In the EGARCH model, this parameter has a positive and significant gamma parameter that indicates the leverage effect.

Because of asymetric fluctuations of stock and *Sukuk* index and the significant value of γ for both time series, which indicates asymmetric shocks to both variables, the EGARCH model is more appropriate for this study. We will analyze the results of the EGARCH model on this time series. As shown in Table 9.3, all coefficients of the variance equation are significant at 95% confidence level. Therefore, in this time series, the leverage effect is positively correlated with past fluctuations and the reversal of market shocks.

Based on the output coefficients of the models presented in Table 9.3, we can conclude that the sensitivity of *sukuk* to market shocks is less than sensitivity of stock.

To test the significance level of self-correlation of the remaining models, L-Jung Box (1987) tests were used.

Table 9.1 Statistics of the Stock Index and the *Sukuk* Index

Time Series	*Mean*	*Median*	*Maximum*	*Minimum*	*Std. Dev*	*Skewness*	*Kurtosis*
Sukuk	0.015%	0.01%	12.64%	−12.6%	0.014	0.087	48.8
Stock	0.032%	0.02%	36.2%	−21.2%	0.0065	1.42	10.14

Table 9.2 Non-Conditional Correlation of Stock Returns and *Sukuk* Index Return

	Stock	*Sukuk*
Stock	1.00	0.067
Sukuk	0.067	1.00

Table 9.3 Results of Univariate Models

	Mean Constant	*Variance Constant*	α	γ	β
Stock-GARCH	−0.4326	0.04115*	0.2057*	–	0.6752*
Stock-EGARCH	−0.000145	−1.02153*	0.2102*	0.1144*	0.9173*
Sukuk-GARCH	0.004196	0.345117	0.09239	–	0.6796*
Sukuk-EGARCH	0.000329*	−0.8921*	−0.167*	0.4976*	0.8969*

*Significance at the 0.95 level.

The Engle (2002) multivariate (DCC) model for the two time series of the stock index and *sukuk* index is based on the results obtained in previous steps, and the results are presented in Table 9.4. In Table 9.4, the alpha coefficient is not even significant at the 90% confidence level. Therefore, the correlation between the time series of stock returns and the time series of the *Sukuk* returns is not sensitive to market shocks. The beta coefficient obtained at the 95% confidence level is significant. Therefore, it can be concluded that the correlation between *Sukuk* fluctuations and stock fluctuations follows its past.

In Figure 9.5, the correlation between the two time series of the stock index and the *sukuk* index is shown. According to the above diagram, the correlation between these two time series over time has been different. Although two time series have experienced positive correlation in certain periods of the year, in many cases, there is a negative correlation between these two time series.

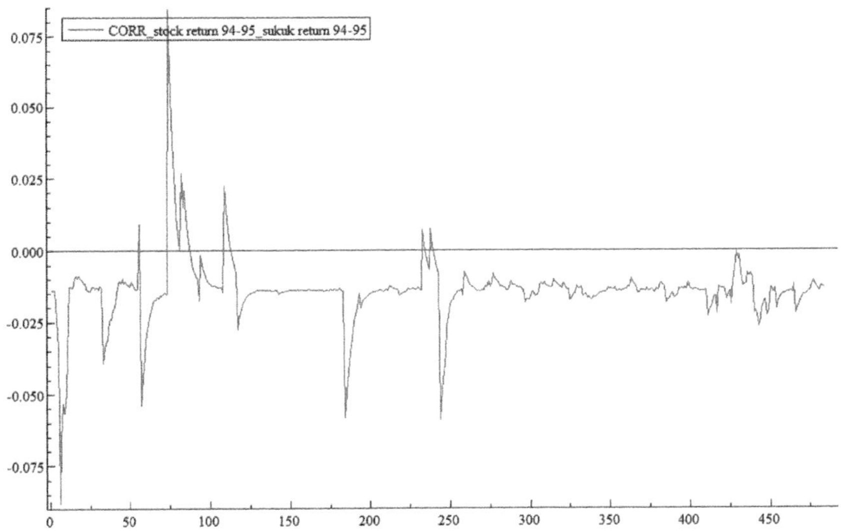

Figure 9.5 Dynamic correlation between stocks and *sukuk*.

Table 9.4 Results of the Multivariate Model

	Constant	α	β	*Log Likelihood*
Stock-*sukuk*	−0.19	0.0096	0.74*	1016.74

*Significance at the 0.95 level.

9.5 Conclusion

This research was carried out using a correlation research method. Data were analyzed in two levels of descriptive statistics and inferential statistics in the form of a table of central indices and dispersion, diagrams and reliability, and normality, self-correlation tests of time series, univariate and multivariate GARCH models. In this research, a fundamental hypothesis found that there is a direct relationship between the stock index fluctuations and the *sukuk* index; according to the results of the research, there is a significant correlation between the two variables that this correlation follows from its past. Therefore, the value of this correlation varies over time. Given the history of correlation between these two time series, despite the observation that there is a positive correlation between these two time series, in most cases, the correlation between these two financial instruments is negative. Therefore, the two financial instruments can be used to diversify the investment portfolio in order to reduce its risk.

9.5.1 Suggestions for future research

- Calculates different and appropriate indices with *sukuk* features

  Due to unique features of fixed-income securities, suitable indicators with this nature are required to take into account the different characteristics of these papers for research, analytical and reporting purposes. In spite of the use and accountability of the price index for fixed-income securities in this study, in order to investigate the price behavior of these securities, it should be noted that the price index will not be accountable for all research because of fixed-income securities with specified maturity and guaranteed coupons. Thus, the price index will not cover all aspects and information about the bonds. And so, we cannot rely on this index to examine the general behavior of the bonds. Therefore, it is recommended that researchers take the necessary measures in this regard.
- Investigation of correlation of *sukuk* with other important economic parameters

  Since the *sukuk* is a young tool in our beloved country, research on this has been a key element. Therefore, it is suggested to carry out several studies on the relationship between this financial instrument and other economic parameters and the discovery of the behavior of this tool at different times.
- Interviews between stocks and *sukuk* for a longer period

  Due to the very low depth of the *sukuk* market in the capital market of Iran in the years prior to 1394, the research has been conducted for two years. But the result of this study will be more reliable over a longer period of time. Therefore, it is suggested that this study should be done for longer periods.

Notes

1 Alex Sclip, Alberto Dreassi, Stefano Miani, Paltrinieri Andrea (8 June 2016). Dynamic correlations and volatility linkages between stocks and *sukuk* Evidence from international markets, *Review of Financial Economics*.
2 Alex Sclip, Alberto Dreassi, Stefano Miani, Paltrinieri Andrea (8 June 2016). Dynamic correlations and volatility linkages between stocks and *sukuk* Evidence from international markets, *Review of Financial Economics*.
3 Alex Sclip, Alberto Dreassi, Stefano Miani, Paltrinieri Andrea (8 June 2016). Dynamic correlations and volatility linkages between stocks and *sukuk* Evidence from international markets, *Review of Financial Economics*.

References

Abdulkader, T., Nathif, A. (2004). Islamic bonds: Your guide to structuring, issuing and investing in sukuk. Working paper: Economy Istitutional Investors.

Achsani, N. M., Effendi, J., & Abidin, Z. (2007). Dynamic interdependence among international Islamic stock market indices: Evidence from 2000–2007. Proceeding of the International Conference of the Islamic Capital Markets. Jakarta, Indonesia. Organized by the Islamic Research and Training Institute, Islamic Development Bank.

Aloui, C., Hammoudeh, S., & Hamida, H. B. (2015a). Co-movement between shariah stocks and sukuk in the GCC markets: S time frequency analyse. *Journal of International Financial Markets, Institutions and Money, 34*, 69–79.

Aloui, C., Hammoudeh, S., & Hamida, H. B. (2015b). Global factors driving structural changes in the comovement between sharia stocks and sukuk in the Gulf Cooperation Council countries. *North American Journal of Economics and Finance, 31*, 311–329.

Andersson, M., Krylova, E., & Vähämaa, S. (2008). Why does the correlation between stock and bond returns vary over time? *Applied Financial Economics, 18*, 139–151.

Aslanidis, N., & Christiansen, C. (2014). Quantiles of the realized stock–bond correlation and links to the macroeconomy. *Journal of Empirical Finance, 28*, 321–331.

Baur, D. G., & Lucey, B. M. (2009). Flights and contagion – An empirical analysis of stock-bond correlations. *Journal of Financial Stability, 5*(4), 339–352.

Bley, J., & Chen, K. H. (2006). Gulf Cooperation Council (GCC) stock markets: The dawn of a new era. *Global Finance Journal, 17*, 75–91.

Bollerslev, T. (1986). Generalised autoregressive conditional heteroskedasticity. *Journal of Econometrics, 31*(3), 307–327.

Bollerslev, T. (1990). Modeling the coherence in short-run nominal exchange rates: A multivariate generalized ARCH model. *Review of Economics and Statistics, 72*, 498–505.

Cakir, S., & Raei, F. (2007). Sukuk vs eurobonds: Is there a difference in value-at-risk?. Working paper: IMF WP/07/237.

Campbell, J., & Ammer, J. (1993). What moves the stock and bond market? A variance decomposition for long-term asset returns. *Journal of Finance, 48*, 3–37.

Campbell, J., & Ammer, J. (1993). What moves the stock and bond market? A variance decomposition for long-term asset returns. *Journal of Finance*, *48*, 3–37.

Cappiello, L., Engle, R., & Sheppard, K. (2006). Asymmetric dynamics in the correlations of global equity and bond returns. *Journal of Financial Econometrics*, *4*(4), 537–572.

Chiang, T. C., Li, J., & Yang, S. Y. (2015). Dynamic stock-bond return correlations and financial market uncertainty. *Review of Quantitative Finance and Accounting*, *45*, 59–88.

Christopher, R., Kim, S. J., & Wu, E. (2012). Do sovereign credit ratings influence regional stock and bond market interdependencies in emerging countries? *Journal of International Financial Markets, Institutions and Money*, *22*, 1070–1089.

Connolly, R., Stivers, C., & Sun, L. (2005). Stock market uncertainty and the stock-bond return relation. *Journal of Financial Quantitative Analysis*, *40*, 161–194.

Dimic, N., Kiviaho, J., Piljak, V., & Aijo, J. (2016). Impact of financial market uncertainty and macroeconomic factors on stock-bond correlation in emerging markets. *Research in International Business and Finance*, *36*, 41–51.

Engle, R. (2002). Dynamic conditional correlation: A simple class of multivariate generalized autoregressive conditional heteroskedasticity models. *Journal of Business & Economic Statistics*, *20*(3), 339–350.

Engle, R., & Sheppard, K. (2008). Evaluating the specification of covariance models for large portfolios. Working paper: New York University.

Eviews.com

Fathurahman, H., & Fitriati, R (2013). Comparative analysis of return on sukuk and conventional bonds. *American Journal of Economics*, *3*, 159–163.

Iqbal M., & Mirakhor, A. (2007). *An Introduction to Islamic Finance: Theory and Practice*. Chichester: John Wiley & Sons.

Karim, B. A., Kassim, N. A. M., & Arip, M. A. (2010). The subprime crisis and Islamic Stock Markets integration. *International Journal of Islamic and Middle Eastern Finance and Management*, *3*, 363–371.

Kim, H. B., & Kang, S. H. (2012). Volatility transmission between the sharia stock and sukuk GII markets in Malaysia. http://search.yahoo.com/search;_ylt=AuynaOiNRkSG9bf6F4qvcFebvZx4?p=volatility%2C+causality.

Kim, S. J., Moshirian, F., & Wu, E. (2006). Evolution of international stock and bond market integration: Influence of the European Monetary Union. *Journal of Banking & Finance*, *30*, 1507–1534.

Li, L. (2004). Macroeconomic factors and the correlation of stock and bond returns. Proceeding of the 2004 American Finance Association Meeting Aldan, PA.

Majid, M., Meera, A. K. M., Omar, M. A., & Aziz, H. A. (2009). Dinamic linkages among ASEAN-5 emerging stock markets. *International Journal of Emerging Markets*, *4*, 160–184.

Majid, M., Yusof, R. M., & Razal, A. N. (2007). Dynamic financial linkages among selected OIC countries. *Journal of Economic Cooperation Among Islamic Countries*, *28*, 25–56.

Marashdeh, H. (2005). Stock market integration in the MENA region: An application of the ARDL bounds testing approach. Working paper: University of Wollongong.

Mosaid, F., & Boutti, R. (2014). Sukuk and bond performance in Malaysia. *International Journal of Economics and Finance*, *6*, 226–234.

Najeeb, S. F., Bacha, O., & Masih, M. (2014). Does a held-to-maturity strategy impede effective portfolio diversification for Islamic bond (sukuk) portfolios? A multi-scale continuous wavelet correlation analysis. Working paper: MPRA, 56956

Nelson, D. B. (1991). Conditional heteroskedasticity in asset returns: A new approach. Econometrica, 59(2), 347–370.

Rahman, A. A., & Sidek, N. Z. M. (2011). Spillover effect of us Subprime crisis on ASEAN-5 stock markets. In Business and Social Science Research Conference. Dubai: World Business Institute Australia.

Rusgianto, S., & Ahmad, N. (2013). Volatility behavior of sukuk Market: An empirical analysis of the dow jones citigroup sukuk index. *Middle East Journal of Scientific Research*, *13*, 93–97.

Saiti, B. (2013). Estimation of dynamic conditional correlations of Shariah-compliant stock indices through the application of multivariate GARCH approach. *Australian Journal of Basic & Applied Sciences*, *7*, 259–267.

Shiller, R., & Beltratti, A. (1992). Stock prices and bond yields. Journal of Monetary Economics, 30(1), 25–46.

Vishwanath, S. R., & Sabahuddin, A. (2009). An overview of Islamic sukuk bonds. *The Journal of Structured Finance*, *14*(4), 58–67.

Yang, J., Zhou, Y., & Wang, Z. (2009). The stock-bond correlation and macroeconomic conditions: One and a half centuries of evidence. *Journal of Baking & Finance*, *33*, 670–680.

Zin, M. Z. M., Sakat, A. A., Ahmad, N. A., Roslan, M., Nor, M., Bhari, A., Ishak, S., & Jamain, M. S. (2011). The effectiveness of sukuk in Islamic finance market. *Australian Journal of Basic and Applied Sciences*, *5*, 472–478.

10 Provision of riba by religious faith

A comparative analysis

Musferah Mehfooz

10.1 Introduction

It remained a definitive goal of all religions in individual or aggregate frame that genuine laws and commandments of God are in certainty for the prosperity of mankind. Doubtlessly, religion always identifies and recognized great or awful, lawful or illicit, and the legitimate and unlawful. Since old circumstances the above examined idea has been known to all humanity. Especially the divine religions clarified the laws and rules to guarantee the individual and collective rights in detail; in this way the uncovered directives enable regard to humankind. Islam underscores these in great detail. As per Muslim's regulation, from human verifiable viewpoint it was the commitment of all dispatchers and furthermore was similar to the divine teachings preached by Moses, Jesus and Muhammad (Peace be upon him).[1]

Islam proclaims to be a continuation of the Abrahamic tradition in the prophetic line of the Near Eastern Prophets. In fact, Moses (*As*) is by far the leading character in the *Qur'ān*, appearing 136 times and dwarfing Muhammad's 4 and Jesus's (*As*) 25. Therefore, by analyzing Islam's religious predecessors (Judaism and Christianity) and the context of their definitions of usury in the Old and New Testaments, the *Qur'ān*'s discussion of riba can be put into greater historical perspective. Islam is a complete religion, which provides complete code of life in every domain of human existence: economic, political, legal, cultural, material, in short collective or individual. Above-mentioned activities are strongly connected with each other, so all economic activities should abide by the given instruction according to Islamic *shari'ah* (law). Holy *Qur'ān* has clear injunctions in business and trading perspective that earnings from trade are permitted in Islam but interest (usury)-related behavior is forbidden.

10.2 Literal meaning of riba

The Hebrew word **"nashek"** is translated as **"usury"** ("interest" in many recent translations). In Leviticus, this Hebrew word **"nashek'** is replaced with **"marbit,"** which denotes a gain on the part of the creditor. This later became the Hebrew word **"ribbit,"** from which the Arabic word **"riba"** was derived.[2] The Greek term used in the New Testament for usury/interest is **"tokos,"** which means "offspring." Significantly, it is in consonance with the earlier Hebraic term "**marbit"** and the later Arabic term in *Qur'ān* **riba**.[3]

In Arabic language, usury is called "riba" and according to *Ibn Manẓūr*, riba is that which is compulsory to be paid by the borrower to the lender along with the prime or actual given amount, which was the basic condition for the loan at the time of debt agreement.[4] *al-Zubaīdī* states: Every loan from which an excess is drawn is riba,[5] and *al-Azharī* states: Every loan from which an excess is drawn or a benefit obtained is riba.[6] Therefore, based on *al-Jazīrī*, he states that according the consensus of all Islamic jurisprudences riba is clearly described as interest without any kind of exception.[7] It means any excess or addition above the principle lent, therefore it includes both interest and usury.[8]

Khurshīd Ahmad, a prominent advocate of Islamic finance in Pakistan, emphasized how riba is to be understood today, and argued that Islam forbids "any premium or excess, small, moderate or large, contractually agreed upon at the time of lending money or loanable funds."[9] Because Islam treats money as a medium of exchange and not a commodity.

10.3 Riba in Old Testament

The medieval Jewish commentator Rashi (Solomon ben Isaac) pointed out that this Hebrew root meant "to bite," from its painfulness to the debtor and commented,

> it resembles the bite of a snake... inflicting a small wound in a person's foot which he does not feel at first, but all at once it swells, and distends the whole body up to the top of his head. So it is with interest.[10]

By this definition the disastrous consequences of riba have wonderfully depicted. And by the definition of St. Ambrose's usury was understood that "it is receiving more than one has given."[11]

The Old Testament included a number of injunctions which protest against any kind of activity that damages the effect of the relationships between the rich and the poor. The manuscript writer of Encyclopedia of social sciences explains: Since the law wished to restrict wealth and to prevent poverty or at least to mitigate it as for as possible, the property less were given the right to share the crops,[12] because sacred text has advised about forgotten sheaves that, it should not be brought in later, but should be left for the gerim and widows.[13] So the Jewish conception from the earliest times has been that the needy are entitled to help, that is the giving of charity is not a virtue but a duty.[14]

Charity is among the virtues that Jewish tradition sets forth as the duty of all. Those who are in need of help are not to be treated as less than equals, and they, too, are the children of God. Judaism holds that charity is more than compassion, that is a form of Justice itself, a restoration of what men have been deprived of as a result of society's shortcomings. Thus, charity in Judaism is called Zedakah, "Justice," which means not only assistance to the needy but righteousness itself.[15]

The Prophet Ezekiel, which are mentioned in Holy *Qur'ān* (21:85) as *Hizqīl*, states that '**The upright man ... oppresses no one, returns pledges, never steals, gives his own bread to the hungry, his clothes to the naked. ... He never charges usury on loans, takes no interest.**[16] Charging of interest was sin in Moses law, and *shari'ah* had strongly condemn this sin and clear commandments were given about it.

In Leviticus commandments of usury had given. It is similar to the statement in Exodus but adds some new information: **"Now in case a countryman of yours becomes poor and his means with regard to you falter, then you are to sustain him, like a stranger or sojourner, that he may live with you. Do not take usurious interest from him, but revere your God, that your countryman may live with you. You shall not give him your silver at interest, nor your food for gain."**[17]

According to Exodus[18], '**If you lend money to any of my people, to any poor man among you, you must not play the usurer with him; you must not demand interest from him.**' Although charging of interest was forbidden for Jews in their laws but they amended the law by using the word "Brother" and specifically extract its meanings "The Jews," and allowed to charge the interest from "Gentile" non-Jews.

According to Deuteronomy, **You shall not deduct interest from loans to your countrymen, whether in money, or food [victuals], or anything else that can be deducted as interest; but you may deduct interest from loans to foreigners. Do not deduct interest from loans to your countrymen, so that the Lord your God may bless you in all your undertakings in the land that you are about to enter and possess.**[19]

Interest on loan to a Jew either in kind or in money was expressly forbidden in Post-Biblical Judaism interoperated this law with extraordinary vigor and forbade any transaction which bores even the remotest resemblance to usury.[20] There was a tendency to forbid all lending at interest, and the Talmud painstakingly forbids even the shadow ('dust') of interest.[21] Judaism strictly forbids interest in any kind of business and trading exchange. Even in Talmud it is strictly prohibited to have a shadow (dust) of interest. This is clearly evident that in ancient Judaism every kind of interest was prohibited because *shari'ah* considered everyone as equal Jews or non-Jews.

The prohibition of interest being of a charitable nature, its violation was not treated as a criminal offense to which any penal sanctions attached. It was only a moral transgression. According to the prophecies of Ezekiel that usury came to be identified with the severest of crimes: it is mentioned in the context of robbery, adultery, killing and other such crimes which are worthy of death.[22]

Lord Stamp illustrates in this reference: It was a sin to charge interest but this only applied strictly to transactions between Jews. To put money with Gentiles could only be compensated by high rate of interest.[23] Paradoxically, Jewish teaching became most well known in the Christian world not through its prohibition on exploiting one's neighbor but through a compromise measure (Deuteronomy 22:21)[24], allowing Jews to charge interest to foreigners – although Jews still had to observe other ethical injunctions in dealing with non-Jews.[25]

The early Fathers of the Church approached this Mosaic Law with contradiction. They were all for community and brotherhood, but not at the exclusion of some other. If they were to remain true to their ideal of universal brotherhood, they could not have allowed usury to anyone, anywhere. Accordingly, there was a consensus in early Christianity that usury did not accord with God's will, and it was, therefore, based on the idea of universal brotherhood, prohibited among Christians.

A development is seen in the laws prohibiting usury: the Old Testament (Lev. 25:35 and Dt. 23:20–21) **forbade interest only among the brethren;** in the Prophets (Ez. 18:8) **all interest-taking is prohibited**; the New Testament takes another step by stipulating: **"Lend to those from whom you can expect nothing in return"** (Luke. 6:34). So, the Deuteronomic prohibition had been universalized by the Prophets and the New Testament, as Christians had been enjoined to treat everyone as "brother."

10.4 Harmful effects of riba on society in Jewish literature

In early rabbinical literature it is concluded that the homes of the Israelites have been delivered to the empire because of four faults:

- On account of those who retain in their possession bills which have been paid (in the hope of claiming them again).
- **On account of those who lend money on usury**.
- On account of those who had the power to protest against wrongdoing and did not protest.
- On account of those who publicly declare their intention to give specified sums for charity and do not give.[26]

The Jerusalem Talmud declares, "Come and see the blindness of those who lend at interest: if anyone calls another an idolater, an incestuous man or a murderer, the other seeks vengeance on his life; but doesn't one who hired a notary and witness and tells them to attest (a usurious contract) deny the Place? This brings out that everyone who lends at interest denies the Principle [of divine authority]".[27]

Aristotle mentioned that "the worst kind of earning wealth with the greatest reason, is usury,[28] because the purpose of money is, to exchange of goods, while here this purpose have an end".[29] He claimed that "usury is against the law of nature and justice".[30] Further according to Early Rabbinical Period, Violation of the prohibition was considered very grave; at times it was seen as equivalent even to the shedding of men's blood and the denial of Yahweh.[31]

St. Augustine (350–430) had described about the usurer that will forever suffer in the hell fire with the devil and his companions.[32] So in Judaism, charging of usury was equal to polytheism, or for committing the adultery, unlawful murder or like many other major sins described in divine teachings, the punishment was hell forever.

10.5 Riba in Christianity

The New Testament has considerably less to say about usury than does the Old Testament. The Gospels consistently mention that loans should not be made with interest. One such example is Luke 6.35, where Jesus (*As*) says to "**lend freely, hoping nothing thereby.**" Jesus recommended lending money to others, even enemies, without demanding any interest. **Love your enemy and do good; lend without expecting repayment. Then will your reward be great. You will rightly be called sons of the Most High; since He Himself is good to the ungrateful and the wicked.**[33]

Basil states that usury must be called tokos (offspring) because of all the evils it engenders. But other offsprings grow only until they reach maturity, whereas usury never ceases to grow, bringing with it ever-increasing sorrow.[34] St. Augustine states that they classified usury, which was synonymous with interest till early 17th century, as theft under the seventh commandment.[35]

10.6 Harmful effects of riba on society in Christian literature

In the medieval Christianity usury was considered a sin because it was a theft of time. Usury was thought to sell the time elapsed between the time of lending and that of collecting. Time, of course, belongs to God, and thus in line with this reasoning usurers were stealing from God Himself.[36]

Moreover, usury was thought of as the sin that never rests. Le Goff vividly depicts how the medieval preachers might have railed against usury. Sisters, and brothers, do you know of a sin that never stops, that is being committed at every moment? No? Of course you do! There is one, and only one, and I will name it. It is usury. Money given out through usury never stops working, it never stops making money. Unjust, shameful, detestable money, but money nonetheless. Brother, do you know a worker who does not stop on Sunday or on holidays, who does not stop working while he is sleeping? No? Well, usury continues working day and night, Sundays and holidays, asleep and awake! Working while asleep? Under Satan's direction, usury, diabolical miracle, succeeds in doing just that. In this too, usury is an insult to God and to His established order. Usury, tireless and endless sin, a chastisement without end, an unflinching henchman of Satan, can only lead to eternal slavery, to Satan, to the endless punishment of Hell![37]

Jacques Le Goff had illustrated the philosophy of strong opposition of prohibition of riba/usury, so it was strongly condemned in Judaism and Christianity.

The component of interest makes leaps in the smooth running of the economy and one of the primary variables which achieves financial emergency. Locke, an eminent political thinker, is of the assessment that high rate of interest rots trade.[38]

10.7 Riba in Islam

Riba/usury is forbidden in *shari'ah* (Islamic law) and had announced amongst the seven major sins (Shirk; Practicing magic; Murder; riba/usury; Unlawfully taking orphans' money; Running away from the battlefield; Accusing chaste, believing women).[39] The *Qur'ān* shapes all matters of life, encompassing the spiritual as well as the physical and the personal as well as the societal. The verb raba (derived noun: riba) has been described in the Qur'an in several general meanings: Economic (increase in wealth),[40] Political,[41] Social and Biological,[42] Theological[43] Botanical,[44] Geological,[45] Hydrological, but[46] mostly this word is described as "an excess," and literally its meaning is an increase or excess in the prime or principle amount, without any effort or sale contract is described in *shari'ah*. It defines that any kind of excess in principal amount or any supplementary benefit upon the prime amount would consider the element of riba.

Basically, the prohibition of riba in *Qur'ān* has occured in four stages which are as follows:

"That which ye given in riba in order that it may increase on (other) people's property hath no increase with Allah; but that which ye give in charity; seeking Allah's countenance, hath increase manifold."[47]

Conventional exegesis holds that *riba* is declared to be deprived of God's blessing in this verse of *Sura-Rum* which is Meccan and believed to be chronologically the first in the *riba* prohibition process, having been revealed around 615 CE. Here *riba is* regarded as simply disapproved, and not yet prohibited. Ibn-e-Arabi states, Arabs were well aware about riba and it was well-known to them. Because when a person sells something on the basis of deferred payment and when the maturity of dealing has occurred, the creditor would demand to the debtor the increase amount on the original debt.[48] So on the first stage made a comparison between those who receive riba and those who give alms to get Allah's pleasure and those who give alms to get Allah's pleasure are given preference in righteousness and are much closer to Him comparatively to those who are receiver of riba. This verse encourages the giving of alms and charity which promotes the sense of brotherhood and the welfare of society, because most of people just consider the apparent quality of riba because it increases their principal amount and they ignore the hidden fatal and disastrous consequence of riba, and they ignore the importance of charity and Zakat, but the Creator wants a happier and prosperous life of His creature in both the worlds.

And further verse revealed in Madinah which explained that those who taking usury or riba shall be punished by Allah Almighty

"That they took riba, though they were forbidden; and that they devoured men's substance wrongfully. We have prepared for those among them who reject faith, a grievous punishment."[49]

On the third stage verse was revealed around the second or third year after Hijrah, which is a strong base for the prohibition of riba by declaring it as forbidden activity. Allah Almighty has clearly announced the people to avoid eating and earning from usury/riba, and it would be a source of their ultimate success.

"O ye who believe! Devour not riba, doubled and multiplied; but fear Allah; that ye may (really) prosper."[50]

The last revelation about prohibition of riba occurred near the completion of the Prophet's (Peace be upon him) mission. It mentioned that Allah Almighty will not show his blessings upon riba-based dealings and he had injunctions to uproot it, because He does not like the violent of his laws, and due to the activities of charity Allah has promised of uncountable blessings.

"Those who devour usury will not stand except as stand one whom the Evil one by his touch Hath driven to madness. That is because they say: 'Trade is like riba'. But Allah hath permitted trade and forbidden riba".[51]

"Allah will deprive usury of all blessing, but will give increase for deeds of charity: For He loveth not creatures ungrateful and wicked". [52]

Allah Almighty has declared the final prohibition of riba in above-mentioned verse. The persons who exercise the activities of riba are like those who are touched by Satan and became poor condition in mind or unsound. Because they thoughtlessly stated that trade is like riba. But by Allah Almighty had declared, trade is permitted and riba is forbidden. Another place it is stated that "O ye who believe! Fear Allah and give up what remains of your demand for riba, if ye are indeed believers." "If you do it not, take notice of war from Allah and His Messenger. But if ye turn back, ye shall have your capital sums. Deal not unjustly, and ye shall not be dealt with unjustly."[53]

The Holy Prophet (Peace be upon him) provided the guidance to mankind which covers all aspects of human life like social, religious and economic activities. In Hadith [speech or saying of Holy Prophet (Peace be upon him)] riba has been discussed repeatedly. Like *Qur'ān* interest-based transactions are strictly prohibited and strongly condemned in Hadith, and the source of it is excess on the principal without any contract of sale.[54]

Punishments for the bad deeds just not to be faced in this world but it follows the life of hereafter. So in this Hadith the riba-based dealings and activities indicate the terrible results. Punishments for those who were engaged in Riba-oriented dealings have been explained by The Holy Prophet Muhammad (Peace be upon him).

"On the night in which I was taken on the Night Journey (Al-Isra'), I came to people whose stomachs were like houses, in which there were snakes that could be seen from outside their stomachs. I said: 'Who are these, O Jibra'il?' He said: 'They are the ones who consumed usury.'"[55]

This Hadith shows the Gravity of the Sin of Riba which socially and morally swear disgrace a person, The Holy Prophet Muhammad (Peace be upon him).

"There are seventy degrees of usury, the least of which is equivalent to a man having intercourse with his mother."[56]

So because of the harmful and vicious impact of riba four parties have been cursed by the Prophet Muhammad (Peace be upon him) and they are receiver, payer, witness and the person who document it. It is evident that in the participated of sin all the parties are equally considered.[57]

The above-mentioned verses and Hadith regarding interest needs to set up a monetary framework where there is no misuse by any means. It builds up equity between the loan specialist and the borrower; the industrialist and the business person prompts fellowship, brotherhood, financial advance and a superior standard of life for all.

10.8 Harmful effects of riba on society in Muslim's literature

Several scholars of the mid- to late-20th century also interpreted riba from a "moral" perspective, away from the literalism that dominates much of the thinking on riba.

Muhammad Asad, a modernist commentator on the *Qur'ān*, maintained that riba involved "an exploitation of the economically weak by the strong and resourceful."[58] *Fazlur Rahmān* argued that the reason of the prohibition of riba was injustice, as was stated in the *Qur'ān* (2:279), and that good natured Muslims with extremely high-minded inner voices earnestly trust that the Qur'ān has restricted all bank enthusiasm for all circumstances in woeful negligence of what riba was verifiably, why the Qur'ān reprimanded it as a gross and savage type of misuse and prohibited it.[59]

Sayyīd Maudūdī says, "Infact usury is the result of selfishness, mercilessness and also accretes these attributes in a human being." Those people who are poor and needy are unable to pay loan, and financiers are sucking their blood. The solution of this atrocious cruelty is that usury should be completely prohibited. That's why the *shari'ah*, which is based on justice and equality, blessing and finesse, rescinds this curse to make those meek people feel free.[60]

Due to the usury-based loans, the finance and economic condition of the whole nation is destroyed, and leaving the harmonious effects on the economic condition of this world. Then due to them they are in-between of malice and enemity; at last due to them the youths of the nation hit with adversity got upset and began to accept extremity and political, cultural and economic philosophy, and began to find the solution of their national difficulties in a bloody revolution, a destructive war. Due to the usury the international pressure enhances and sometimes its intensity became a cause of war.[61]

Sayyīd Qutub illustrates that usury is curse which plays a massive role in localizing wealth in the hands of the moon, and as a result, it promotes selfishness and greediness in society. In the world of business and trade, it sows the seed of dishonesty and atrocity. The debtor has starves in his house, and it doesn't matter for the usurer. His only interest is to take his original amount along usury on accurate time with no concern from someone's sufferings. Even the debtor is forced to sell all his utensils of his home and costumes on his body.[62]

In a nation or country there are only less people who ignore money and give interest. The interest receiver snatch people's possessions from their houses and inflict upon them endless sufferings and financial troubles. Finally, the situation reaches to an end where the money is concentrated in specific hands and families that some poor communities are forced to stand against them and many kingdoms get destroyed because of this. Law and order situation shatters due to these actions. All this is the result of some foolish minds/thoughts.

The original text of the Holy *Qur'ān*, unlike the other Holy Scriptures, is still maintained in its pure form, and it allows trade but forbids riba/interest. In trade, participants make profits or incur losses. Islam, in establishing a socioeconomic justice system, insists that this risk be shared (not always equally) between the two parties.[63]

10.9 Christian and Jewish efforts for promulgation of riba

The important section of the chapter takes an historical view by investigating the change of attitudes toward usury from biblical times to the present. By the 4th century CE, usury was officially prohibited for clergy of the Catholic Church, and by the 5th century the law was extended to all laymen. Usury was not declared a criminal offense until the 8th century, instituted by Roman Emperor Charlemagne. As the anti-usury stance continued, Pope Clement V "made the ban on usury absolute and declared all secular legislation in its favor, null and void."[64]

The Council of Nicea (AD 325), the Council of Laodicea (AD 364), The Second (1139) and Third Lateran Councils (1179) and the Fourth Lateran Council (AD 1205), and later the Councils of Lyon (1274) and Vienna (1311), among others, all protested against usury and that any interest charged on loans for any reason, whatsoever, was a violation of scriptural demands.[65]

Their moneymaking in usury was condemned by the Church, and they were accused of participating in ritual murders. In fact, the famous rabbi Moses Maimonides [1135–1204] and other Jewish legalists interpret the Deuteronomic verses as a positive commandment to take interest on loans to Gentiles.[66]

The high proportion of Jews practicing usury increased their dependency on their neighbors, and it increased social disharmony. Jewish usurers were tolerated as long as there was a need for credit. At the turn of the 12th century, however, a slow deterioration of their condition began to take place in Europe, except where capital or specialized knowledge was still needed.[67]

Jews especially lent money to the clergy, abbeys and knights (the lesser manorial lords) who underwent a significant crisis during the 13th century. It is within this context that Jewish usurers turned over mortgages of knightly property to the magnates for foreclosure.[68] Jews became the symbol (and intermediary) of a power relation between two other socioeconomic rivals, the knights and the magnates.[69]

Katz argues that to set up a monetary framework where there is no misuse by any means. It builds up equity between the loan specialist and the borrower; the industrialist and the business person prompts fellowship, brotherhood, financial advance and a superior standard of life for all.[70]

Martin Luther (1483–1536), who helped start the drift of opinion on usury, wavered on the issue of usury for much of his life. While he was critical of usury, Luther was often willing to excuse it as a product of human moral frailty. He was more critical of those who sought to erase debt altogether and even out the social classes. Luther was also willing to accept civil authority over that of Mosaic or Gospel Law (especially during debtor revolts), even if it meant that usurious activity would continue. Luther rejected this aspect of the concept of universal Christian brotherhood.[71]

The main culprit and a real game changer was John Calvin (1509–64). Calvin stated that economic life was "part of the fallen world,"[72] and he enabled the modern attitude toward interest. Calvin broke with the Greek philosophers and with earlier Church teachings by proclaiming that, in fact, money was not sterile and unable to yield its own fruits.[73] He stated that charging of interest is as reasonable as charging rent for land. Calvin maintained that Luke 6:35[74] had been twisted from its original sense. It merely commands generous lending to the poor. Jesus merely wished to correct the vicious custom of the world, whereby men readily lent to the rich who could pay back and not to the poor. Deut. 23:19[75] was political. The passages in the Old Testament are to be interpreted as requiring only the observance of charity and equity toward the poor, or, if they are to be interpreted more strictly, they still may be considered only as positive political law appropriate for the Jewish economy, but no longer binding today.[76] John Calvin's rejection of the Catholic Church's treatment of usury fed the greed of the emerging class of capitalists.[77]

The condemnation of usury never completely disappeared from Christian thought or from the Christian sphere of influence. It remained important even in the 20th century. Long after Christian usurers had become efficient in competing with Jews, the sin of usury remained associated with Jewish communities. Where Jews were deprived of access to landed property and public office, they developed expertise in usury and banking. The transition to the modern era diminished neither the importance of this pattern of opportunity hoarding nor the denunciation of Jewish usury by the Catholic press, the Protestant clergy, and some socialist and liberal circles.

The growth of finance, industry and land estates led the rabbis to develop concerning contracts, partnerships and legal arrangements to circumvent the biblical prohibition against usury.[78] The traditional mode of life of the Jews enabled them to participate in capitalistic activities, and their religion did not hinder them from exploiting these opportunities, notwithstanding the fact that the spirit of the both of the Old and New Testaments is diametrically opposed to the spirit of capitalism.[79]

After all, the usury which condemned in divine scripture, and if someone charges it, consider the murder of divine law, has become the part of economic system, and many modern economists started to write in favor of usury. Chad Brand argues for the defence of usury that

> In the Western world of today, there are mortgages, retirement investments, car loans, credit cards, and various other situations in which a lender places financial resources into the hands of people who might not pay it back, and situations where people place their money with institutions that use it for investment, with the promise that investors will receive it back with interest. That is today's world. With some exceptions (for instance, Amish communities) people do not live in covenanted enclaves like the people of ancient Israel. This is a place and time in which paying and receiving interest is not only a fact of life but acceptable to most people.[80]

10.10 Conclusion

The purpose of this article was to discuss the usury as censured and restricted in the most grounded conceivable terms. There can be no doubt about the disallowance. When we go to the meaning of usury there is no space for distinction of assessment. Judaism and Islam both contain solid good and lawful prohibitions against the taking of interest. Not surprisingly, to show and avoid the least amount of interest Talmud and Hadith used the similar word "dust." Holy Prophet (Peace be upon him), said, "There will certainly come a time for mankind when everyone will take riba and if he does not do so, its dust will reach him,"[81] and the Talmud painstakingly forbids even the "dust" (least amount) of interest.[82] Both teachings strictly prohibited to have a dust of interest. Allah Almighty forbade riba (interest or usury) because of its hazardous and bad consequences in economic system.

The distribution of wealth in a society becomes unbalanced due to interest. Interest-based loans result in the exploitation of the poor and the needy as it falls out to more poverty, by reducing their future earnings. On the other hand, these interest-based loans make the rich creditors richer and add to their future earnings. Therefore, around 60% of world's resources are controlled and consumed by the 20% rich. So, growing poverty is not the problem of the Third World alone. The advanced countries face this problem too.

If it is important for society to ease the suffering of the poor and allow them to achieve economic self-sufficiency, then it is important to investigate inexpensive lending services as a possible policy tool; for this purpose Islamic banking is introduced which tried the best to exercise according to *shari'ah*-based economic system. Although it has some lacks and not entirely according to *shari'ah injuctions*, but working as interest-free banking and operating in many countries, and also being consider the pleasant addition among the Muslims. But the genuine resolution of the problem of interest will lie in the total enforcement of whole Islamic economic system. Partial or slow enforcement of the Islamic economic system will not work. Therefore, it entered in Islam and established Islamic economic system in full. As mentioned in Quran that:

"O you who have attained to faith! Surrender yourselves wholly unto God, and follow not Satan's footsteps, for, verily, he is your open foe."[83]

And if someone did not abide by the *shari'ah* laws, he is warned in these words in Holy *Qur'ān*.

"But as for him who shall turn away from remembering Me- his shall be a life of narrow scope and on the Day of Resurrection We shall raise him up blind."[84]

Not merely in Islam, also in Bible, there are many passages that confirm the value of a good life. However, the solution to the economic problem, the way to prosperity, like the way to God, is through the Law of Moses. God promises to bless the children of Israel with abundance in the land given that they adhere to the codes of law. For example, the lawgiver proclaims:

Listen to these ordinances, be true to them and observe them, and in return Yahweh your God will be true to the covenant and the kindness he promised your fathers solemnly. He will love you and bless you and increase your numbers; he will bless the fruit of your body and the produce of your soil, your corn, your wine, your oil, the issue of your cattle, the young of your folk, in the land he swore to your fathers he would give you.[85]

It is concluded that riba clashes with mankind's ethics, belief and worldview, and is an economic evil. In spite of appearances to the contrary, it interferes with the balanced growth of man. It destroys the moral life by promoting greed, jealousy, meanness and fraud. Allah would not have prohibited anything if it were essential for human growth, and no evil thing can ever be essential for human life.

Notes

1 Samuel Butler, Elementary Morality, (University of Chicago Press, Chicago1902).
2 Hudson, Michael. The Lost Tradition of Biblical Debt Cancellation. Harvard: Henry George School of Social Science, 1993. Print. 41.

3 Aristotle, The Politics, trans. T. A. Sinclair, revised and re-presented Trevor J. Saunders, (London: Penguin Books, 1992), 87.
4 IbnManẓūr, *Abū'l-FaḍlJamāl al-DīnMuḥammad, Lisān al-'Arab*, (Beirut: Dār Beirut, 1906) vol. 8, p. 23.
5 Muḥammad al-Murtazā Ḥusaīnī al-Zubaidī, *Tājul'urūs: min jawāhir al-qāmūs*, (Beirut: Dār al-Fikr, 1414) vol. 10, p. 142–144.
6 Abū Mansūr al-Azharī, *Tahdhīb al-Lugha, ed., Ibrāhīm al-Ibyārī*, (Cairo: Dār al-Kātib al-ᶜArabī, 1967), vol. 15, p. 473.
7 Jazīrī, *ᶜAbd al-Rahmān. Kitāb al-Fiqhᶜalā al-MadhāhibaI-Arbaᶜa*, (Cairo: al-Maktabat al- Tijārīyyah al-Kubrā, n.d, 6th e), vol. 2, p. 245.
8 Shaikh Mahmud Ahmad, *Economics of Islam*, (Institute of Islamic Culture. 5th Edition, 2005) p. 22.
9 *Khurshīḍ Aḥmad,* Elimination of riba: concept and problems, in Institute of Policy Studies (ed.), Elimination of riba from the economy, Islamabad 1994.
10 Solomon ben Isaac, Commentary on the Pentateuch, Quoted S.Childs, The *Book of Exodus: A critical Theological Commentry*, Old Testament Library, gen. ed. Peter Ackroyd, et al. (Philadelphia, PA: Westminster, 1974), p. 479.
11 St. Ambrose, *Hexameron, Paradise, and Cain and Abel* (The Fathers of the Church, Vol. 42) Translated by John Savage, (Published by: Catholic University of America Press, 1961), p. 269.
12 Encyclopedia of the Social Sciences, (The Macmillan Co., New York, London, 1964) vol. 8, p. 435.
13 Mordical Katz, *Protection of the Weak in the Talmud*, (Columbia University Press, 1925. p. 78.
14 The Slandered Jewish Encyclopedia, (Ed. Cicil Roth, W.H. Allen, London, 1959). p. 427.
15 Collier's Encyclopedia, (The Crowell-Collier Publishing Co., (1963) vol. 13, p. 658.
16 Ezekiel, 18:4–8.
17 Leviticus 25; 35–37.
18 Exodus, 22:25.
19 Deuteronomy, 23:20–21.
20 Encyclopedia of Social Sciences, vol.8, p. 435; Mordical Katz, Protection of the weak in the Talmud, p. 63.
21 The Slandered Jewish Encyclopedia pp. 1344, 1345.
22 Ez. 18:11–13.
23 Lord Stamp, Christianity and Economics, (Published by Macmillan, 1939) p. 12.
24 See Ref No: 19.
25 Nelson, *The Idea of Usury from Tribal Brotherhood to Universal Brotherhood*, (University of Chicago Press, Chicago, 1969, 2nd ed).
26 The Babylonian Talmud, Sukkah, 29 a, b.
27 Gemara of Jerusalem Talmud, Baba **Metzia**, V, II d (Maloney transl. from Bonsirvcn), 462.
28 Aristotle 1258b, Politics.
29 Aristotle. Aristotle in 23 Volumes. Trans. H. Rackham, (Cambridge: Harvard University Press, 1944), Vol. 21, Print: Aristotle: 1952, *Great Books of the Western World*, (Nicomachean Ethics, Politics) (University of Chicago Press, Chicago). Vol. 2.
30 Encyclopedia Americana "Usury" (New York: Americana Corporation, 1967), 824.
31 Maloney Robert Paul, "The Background for the Early Christian Teaching on Usury." (Doctor of Sacred Theology diss., School of Sacred Theology, The Catholic University of America, 1969), p. 135.

32 Buckley, "A theological examination of the religious teachings on 'usury' within the three monotheistic traditions of Judaism, Christianity and Islam, and its relevance for the world today." (Ph.D. diss., Aberdeen University, 1996), p. 97.
33 Luke, 6:35.
34 Maloney, "The Background for the Early Christian Teaching on Usury", p. 148.
35 Buckley, "A theological examination of the religious teachings on 'usury' within the three monotheistic traditions of Judaism, Christianity and Islam, and its relevance for the world today" p. 88.
36 Jacques Le Goff, *Your Money or Your Life: Economy and Religion in the Middle Ages* (New York, 1998), pp. 24–25.
37 Ibid, 30–31.
38 Shaīkh MaḥmudAḥmad, *Economics of Islam, reprinted in 1968* (Lahore: Ashraf Publications, 1952), p. 27.
39 *Al-Saba al- Mubiqat.*
40 *al-Qur'ān*,2:276; 30:39.
41 *al-Qur'ān*, 16:92.
42 *al-Qur'ān*, 17:24; 26:18.
43 *al-Qur'ān*, 69:10.
44 *al-Qur'ān*, 2:265.
45 *al-Qur'ān*, 22:5; 41:39; 23:50.
46 *al-Qur'ān*, 13:17.
47 *al-Qur'ān*, 30:39.
48 Ibn al-ᶜArabī, *Ahkāmal-Qur'ān,* (Beirut: n.p., 1988), vol.1, pp. 320–321.
49 *al-Qur'ān*, 4:161.
50 *al-Qur'ān*, 3:130.
51 *al-Qur'ān*, 2:275.
52 *al-Qur'ān*, 2:276.
53 *al-Qur'ān*, 2:278–279.
54 *Ibn Kathīr, al-Nihāya (an authentic book explaining hadith terminology)*, (Beirut: Dār al-Fikr, 1998).
55 *Ibn Mājah, SunanIbn Mājah*, The Chapters on Business Transactions, Hadith 2359.
56 *Ibn Mājah, SunanIbn Mājah*, The Chapters on Business Transactions, Hadith 2360.
57 *Saḥiḥ Al Muslim,The Book of Musāqah*, Chapter: Cursing the one who consumes riba and the one who pays it, Hadith 3880.
58 Muḥammad Asad, *The message of the Qur'an*, (Gibraltar, 1984), p. 633.
59 Fazlur Rahmān, *Riba and interest, in Islamic Studies* (March 1964) p. 326.
60 Abū'l-'Alā'Maudūdī, *TafhīmulQur'ān*, (Lahore:Islamic publications,2000) vol. 6, p. 175.
61 Muḥammad Ashraf AlīUsmānī, *Shirkat-o-Mazārbat ᶜAsr-e- Hāzir Main*, p. 45.
62 Sayyīd Qutb, *Fī Zilālal-Qur'ān,(Urdu)* (Lahore: Islamī Academy, n.d.), vol.2, p. 70.
63 Zineldin, *The economics of money and banking*. (Stockholm, Sweden: Wicksell International,1990).
64 Birnie Arthur, *The History and Ethics of Interest*, (London: William Hodge, 1958).
65 David Jones, *Reforming the Morality of Usury: A Study of the Differences that Separated the Protestant Reforms* (Dallas, TX: University Press of America, 2004), pp. 31–33.
66 Maimonides, Moses, Mishneh Torah: *The Book of Civil Laws*. Trans. J. J. Rabinowitz (Yale University Press, New Haven, 1949) (1180), p. 77.
67 Moore, *The Formation of Persecuting Society*, (Malden: Blackwell, 2000).

68 Roth, *A History of the Jew s in England*, (Oxford: Clarendon Press 1978, Third Edition), p. 4.
69 Postan, The Medieval Economy and Society: vol. 1 in the Pelican Economic History of England (Harmon'sworth: Penguin, 1972), pp. 152–3, 183–4.
70 Katz Nelson, Periodization and Preferences: Reflections on Purposive Action in Comparative Historical Social Science. In *Comparative Historical Analysis in the Social Sciences*, edited by Mahoney and D. Rueschemeyer (New York: Cambridge University Press, 2003).
71 Nelson, *The Idea of Usury: From Tribal Brotherhood to Universal Other hood*, (University of Chicago Press, Chicago, 1969, 2nd ed.), pp. 29–30.
72 Bruce Garden, Calvin (New Heaven. CT: Yale University Press, 2009), p. 297.
73 Homer and Sylla, *A History of Interest Rates* (Rutgers University Press, New Brunswick, 1991, 3rd ed.), p. 80.
74 But love ye your enemies, and do good, and lend, hoping for nothing again; and your reward shall be great, and ye shall be the children of the Highest: for he is kind unto the unthankful and to the evil.
75 "You shall not charge interest to your countrymen: interest on money, food, or anything that may be loaned at interest."
76 Jean Calvin, Consilia Dc Ususris in Opera, X, cols. 248–249, cited in Buckley, Theological Examination, pp. 127–128.
77 John R. Sutherland, "The Debate Concerning Usury in the Christian Church," Crux, vol. 22 (1986): 3–9.
78 Encyclopedia Britannica, (London, 1962) vol. 22, p. 412.
79 Encyclopedia of the Social Sciences, vol.8, pp. 435–438.
80 Chad Brand, USURY IN SCRIPTURE, Institute for Work, Faith & Economics, 2015, p. 12.
81 *AbūDaᶜūd, SunanᶜAbūDaᶜūd, Kitāb-al-Būyuᶜ, Bāb fi ijtināb-al-Shubukāt,*
82 The Slandered Jewish Encyclopedia pp. 1344, 1345.
83 *al-Qur'ān*,2: 208.
84 *al-Qur'ān*,20:124.
85 Deuteronomy, 7:12–14.

11 Layers of misconceptions about IB

Are Islamic banks threats, challenges and opportunities for investors

Malik Shahzad Shabbir and Awais ur Rehman

11.1 Introduction

The principle of no riba (interest free) is the touchstone of Isslamic banking (IB) and finance industry and it is being practiced in nearly all major religions. This way the principle is expected to be broadly familiar, but the reality is opposite. Knowledge to IB principles is not well known among the society. Even the university students of Islamic countries are not very much aware. Literature has further divulged that the knowledge can synthesize a better and positive perception about IBs (Hamid et al., 2001). This fact can be a point of reference for competitive advantage. The economy of knowledge can be vital for IBs to sustain in an environment of amassed competitive pressure.

This study investigated the behavior and ideas of five layers of misconceptions about the IB system, where the first layer identifies the ideology of laymen about IBs. However, this layman has no any account in interest-bearing and non-interest-bearing financial institutions. During our survey, it is noted that the behavior of layman was absolutely strange about IBs without any strong evidence. When we asked them, why you should show this kind of attitude; they replied straightway that we heard negative observations from other people about Islamic financial system (IFS) that's why we said it is prohibited. However, the misconception behind this layman has personal non-thinking power, lack of observations and misguided ideas about IBs.

In the second layer of misconception, we deal with those investors who have only accounts in Islamic financial institutions (IFI). However, these investors are doubtful about their investment because they still aren't clear about profit earned on their investment was interest-free or not. It is a general observation that whenever some investors will meet each other in any function, they must ask each other's business and consult about new investment in the entire market. In our survey, it is observed that most of account holders of Islamic financial institutions were unable to fetch the exact information to investors of conventional banks (CBs) and also incapable to motivate the other investors to convert their investment in IBs. The misconception behind the second layer of people was about the mechanics and product structure of IBs either on the liability side or asset side (Arouri et al. 2013).

However, recently several studies (Causse, 2010a, 2010b, 2010c; Causse & Abdelhafid, 2010; Causse & Hideur, 2010) investigated the properties of IFI's product development system through a proper analysis of investor's returns, risk sharing and performance in different markets. The third layer consists of conventional economists who know and understand economics very well but they don't have strong knowledge about the Islamic system of financial transactions (Fiqh-ul-Mamo'lat). Mostly, it is observed during our survey that these economists identify and solve the problem of Islamic financial transactions on the basic knowledge of conventional economics. Actually, the third layer of misconception based on solving methods and use of interpretation techniques, which is all most constructed on conventional economics system (Shahzad and Rehman 2015). If the product development team launches any new product or makes new innovations in existing products according to the needs and wants of customers, they get approval from the shari'ah advisory committee of their IFIs before launching product in the market.

The second misconception found in this layer, sometimes it seems that after approval of products from shari'ah advisory committee, when products come to the market, the perception, structure and results are the same as quoted by conventional economists; then these economists argued about IBs are not working according to sharaih complaints in some conferences, seminars and corner meeting. Arbouna (2007) found that IBs used different combinations of sale and trade contracts to meet the legal requirement of shari'ah about the development of new products and services or make necessary innovations in existing products and services of IFIs in order to maintain the desires of investors.

It does not mean that if the results of some products are the same or near to the same then some economists cited that IFI's working and product development methods are the same as the conventional system (Shabbir et al. 2015a). Actually, reason/misconception behinds this issue is the shari'ah scholars of IFIs make sure that every component of this product meets the basic and essential criteria of shari'ah. After completing this whole process, training and development departments of IFIs give training to staff members of banks. During this whole process, the perception and estimated results of economists meet at some extent with that particular product. The conventional economists see the outer look of products and give their final decision in term of neglecting. Actually, they didn't understand the whole process behind this product designing and purifying by the shari'ah advisory committee. Nathan and Rebiere (2007) investigated the performance of IBs through different concepts such as wisdom, faith and knowledge and its impact on investor's behavior through Shari'a Supervisory Boards.

The fourth layer depends upon Islamic economists who have enough knowledge of both economics and Figh-ul-Mamo'lat to understand the Islamic financial systems. These people have only one major misconception about IFIs. According to them, most of the models used by IFIs are adapted from CB, so these people base this issue and comment in such manners that IFIs are not working accurately within the limits of shari'ah. The answer for this misconception is very simple and straight: if IFIs have adapted some models of CB system and used these models after purifying from riba and some other prohibited components, there would not be any shari'ah issue behind these financial models because all they are approved by shari'ah board of IFIs and then launching it in the market. Besides, before designing any model for any product of IFIs one must understand the needs and wants of their target customers. It is observed that IBS is more effective and steadier in a proficient and alteration-free market (Shabbir et al. 2015b).

The second component of misconception of these Islamic economists is valid for some extent. They raised the issue that Islam and its education is most superior in the world from day one but why cannot we make new financial system from starting base for IFIs? They also claimed that more than four decades ago IB was started in Arab countries but why didn't they start from the base point. After conducting survey about this fourth layer, we further communicate with shari'ah scholars, Head of IFIs, training and development department of IFIs and some experts of Islamic finance to resolve this misconception. Jouini and Pastré (2009) examined that Islamic finance is the only choice for investors to reframe their previous finance through its constraints, where risk was controllable and speculation was treated as moderate.

The fifth layer consists of Ulema's and religious/Islamic scholars who have brilliant knowledge about Fiqh-ul-Mamo'lat and worships, but they don't have the same level of knowledge about financial transactions to differentiate between assets driven, liability driven and/or spread, securitization and credit creation according to shari'ah rules and regulations (Shabbir et al. 2016a). Actually, these above-mentioned people of fifth layer are legends of their own work because they spend a lot of time on Fiqh and its related topics, so on the base of this knowledge they neglect the IFS. During our survey, it is observed that some scholars totally disagree with IFS and refer this system as completely prohibited, whereas most scholars consider IFS as partially prohibited and rest of nominal scholars deny to give any kind of remarks about IFS. Aglietta (2010) and Aglietta and Rigot (2009) propose that investors are interested and hopeful to convert their investment in IFIs due to endurance investment in term of returns and risk-sharing factor in IBs.

Now we give a snapshot to differentiate among assets driven, liability driven and other factors. The main source of earning in CBs is the difference between the borrower and lender interest rates. This difference between both interest charge amount is called "spread". The relationship between cost of funds and return on lending is called "liability driven", which refers to CBs. The relationship between return on assets (real estate and automobiles) and investment returns (wadiah, safe custody) is called "assets driven", which refers to IBs. When constraint on leverage conducts then its results convert to credit creation (Jawadi et al. 2014). However, these are the basic knowledge of financial transaction, which will differentiate between both financial systems. If our fifth layer of people is unable to completely understand these basic things then how we can expect from them to realize, review and give decision on complicated financial transactions of IFIs. However, it is noted that IBs treated their customers as partners in order to manage risk and increase the returns on their investment. Whenever IBs enclosed its profit and loss report, then the market will weed incompetent entrepreneurs. This element shows the importance of market discipline and harmony. So depositors select the financial institutions carefully and understand that bank is compactable within the limits of shari'ah about investment perspectives (Chong & Liu, 2006).

11.2 The advantages of IBs as an opportunity for investors

- The strong correlation found in IBs between financial institutions and depositors on liability side, while on the assets side it transfers to financial institutions and its borrowers. It is a beauty of IBs that neither of any participants face unequitable systematic shocks among them. However, conventional capital system of west has found such kinds of unequitable practice of shares/profit among their stakeholders. One of the best examples for understanding of investors about conventional capital system failed in 2007 financial crises especially in-house financing sector of the world economy.
- Return in IB is not merely the collection of a 'spread' between the costs of funds mobilized and the return on funds advanced – conventional debtor-creditor relationships.
- One of the fundamental requirements in Islamic form of intermediation is that financial transactions must be supported by real economic activity. This requirement ensures the financial stability in general.
- Financial innovation in Islamic finance must be within these *Shari'ah* parameters and tested against the *'Maqasid al-Shari'ah'* (*objectives* of the *Shari'ah*). Unnecessary financial engineering led to financial instability in 2008 global financial crisis. Sale of debt against debt is not allowed in Islamic commercial law.
- Just and equitable aspect of distribution is absent in interest-based financing, it may either exploit the debt holder or the financier. This is because the just and equitable aspect of distribution is absent in this way of financing. Inflows (profit) of business are obviously random and are affected by many uncontrollable factors, while outflows (interest payment) are fixed in case of business is financed by debt. If the inflows are zero or less than the outflows it will be detrimental for the businesses. This will certainly lead to bankruptcies, which in turn affect the growth and production cutdowns, and hence result in greater unemployment. On the other side, if businesses make huge revenues then the financier is being exploited as the financing earned less than its actual share.

However, in equity-based financing there is always just distribution of revenues and both parties get their equitable share in both above-mentioned scenarios.

- Debt-based financing always caters the needs of those segments of the society who are able to give safe and fixed repayments. Financing only well-secured businesses and giving less weightages to profit-potential projects lead to income and wealth inequalities and misallocation of resources. This security-oriented approach is fatal for the growth of small business enterprises which may have enormous potential to grow and hence have greater potential to contribute more to the gross national product (GNP) but failed to provide an assurance of repayment to financial institutions. The overreliance on pledges, securities and collateral leave very small room for small-scale entrepreneurs to benefit from these financing which is a great obstruction to the growth of economy.
- Islamic finance promises to enhance the discipline that contributes towards ensuring growth and financial stability.
- Interest-based system leads to income and wealth inequalities and misallocation of resources.

11.3 Ethical theory of IB

The decision to use IB services is not only based on profits but also on obtaining the blessings of Allah (SWT). One way to obtain these blessings is to support programs to improve and expand Muslim communities. In this regard, IBs function on an interest-free basis. Their wealth creation is considered as expanding Muslim communities, and Muslims who help these banks are consequently considered as those who should attain salvation. Profit and investment affect customers' behaviors when they are making decisions. Their choices are not only based on instant current financial returns. They are also factors in long-term returns hereon.

Ethics are the moral behavior that underpins every human act. Every human being has behavior traits, and Islam emphasizes the need for good behavior. Religion defines moral behavior. To understand the meaning of Islamic ethical behavior more fully, ethics are related to temperament, and human behavior is found in people's actions. According to Al-Ghazali (505H), ethics are inherent in the nature of human souls and are born from deeds done without hesitation, without thinking of oneself and without prior reflection. Ibn Miskawaih (2010) has stated that ethics are a condition of themselves that guide people to pursue numerous modes of behavior without thought or consideration. Mawardi (2011) wrote in his book entitled *Adab al-Dunya wa al-Din* that ethics are not only controlled by the Al-Quran and the Sunnah but they are in fact based on thoughts concerned with three behavioral aspects: religious behavior, world behavior and individual behavior. Religious behavior mostly leads to understanding, knowledge and religion. World behavior, second behavioral form, focuses on the behavior of the world and individual ethics. Individual behavior refers to human virtues such as humility, good behavior, simplicity, self-control and trust. Based on an observation of a number of previous studies, only one has defined Islamic ethical behavior, which was that by Awan and Azhar (2014). Their study, based in Pakistan, examined how customers chose IB products because the banks offered good products and services without interest, which is prohibited in Islam. Most customers preferred their banks because of their religious motives for securing the confidentiality of their customers, which led to there being a crucial ethical distinction drawn that was based on the Al-Quran and the Sunnah. The study focused more on religious obligations since there was a lack of definition on what constituted Islamic ethical behavior.

Humans, as vicegerents of the divine on earth, have the ability to learn, gain knowledge and make rules and policies based on their knowledge to develop further knowledge and improve practices based on what has been learned (Bunzel, 2015). Humans have the freedom to choose what is best for them, and, at the same time, they must follow the rules of Allah (SWT). For example, humans have to work to earn salaries that enable them to live their own lives while helping others. The salaries received could be used for many contingencies, and any excess could be saved in bank accounts. Moreover, Islam encourages Muslims to keep investing their money so that the income from such investments may be used for good causes (Nurrachmi et al., 2012). Once humans have chosen banks with which they would want to save their money, they need to understand their roles as depositors. According to Bollen (2010), depositors are defined as people who make others intermediaries, who expect those intermediaries to repay them the amount they have deposited on demand, although the amounts deposited need not have the same real currency value when withdrawn as when initially invested. This establishes debtor and creditor relationships between intermediaries and depositors. In addition, the main sources of money at IBs come from their depositor facilities (Amin, 2013). Depositors have the right to choose to deposit their savings either in CBs or in IBs, but Muslims are obliged to choose the sort of intermediaries who will not harm or become a burden to them.

11.3.1 The ideal banking system

In order to create environments conducive to the development of the IB, the development of the banking system should start with the development of a concept for ideal IB. Below are the explanations on how such concept can be established. The idea is to create a structure which can accommodate the creation of double-tier Mudarabah banking through employing project finance and asset securitization schemes which are widely known in CBs. However, IB is part of the broader concept of Islamic economics which aims at the introduction of value system and ethics of Islam into the economic sphere. Because of this ethical foundation, the concept of IB for the follower of Islamic faith is more than merely a concept on how to do banking. It is the embodiment of the submission to Allah (SWT) since following the Islamic precepts is a religious obligation (Shabbir et al. 2016b). Based on this tenet, the IB can be elaborated as a system of banking which provides just financing, is free from factors unlawful to Islam and offers benefits not only to the shareholders of the bank but also to the stakeholders of the bank. The IB should avoid the potential huge divergence between real assets and real liabilities which may be translated into a profit and loss sharing (PLS) banking with some elements of morality and justice. In practice, the IB consists of PLS and non-PLS mode of financing in assets side. However, heavy reliance on the non-PLS mode often attracts sarcastic criticisms that most Islamic financing techniques used at present bear no difference in substance compared to the conventional finance and that the superficial distinction of the Islamic finance and conventional finance is mainly centered in the use of Arabic names and in the disguised trade transactions for conventional transaction which are substantially similar to those of conventional finance. Even though this notion can be refuted by the development of myriad *Shari'ah* justifications for a restricted scope of application of some conventional techniques, it is sufficient to say that effort should be directed toward the revival of the early concept of IB, the double-tier Mudarabah, in order to minimize the effects of the above-mentioned sarcastic criticisms (Shabbir et al. 2015a).

The two-tier Mudarabah model, where the depositors will place their fund as a Mudarabah deposit in the bank, which in turn invest the fund through Mudarabah in several projects. The investment Mudarabah (the second tier) is structured as a non-recourse project finance transaction using leasing as a main vehicle where the repayment of the financing was convened only to actual revenue generated by the project. Then, each individual project is securitized and sold back to the bank. Because all projects are converted into marketable quasi-equity security, the risk of maturity mismatch between the first tier Mudarabah and the second tier Mudarabah can be avoided. In this juncture, the viable alternative to this is an instrument which is created through securitizing the assets of such an institution or any subsidiary thereof. While the mobilization of resources does not need to be conducted through securitization, it can be demonstrated that this vehicle is the most suitable one in case of developing Islamic financial instruments in conventional environment. One of the arguments for the suitability of the securitization is the clarity of the source of the stream of income (Marliana et al. 2011).

11.4 Literature review

Interest-free financing became a conceptual issue, and it has been primarily focused by Ahmed (1981) through IBs around the world because strong conceptual ideas of the investors left a good image for the rest of investors. However, it is noted that the existing literature is unable to completely cover the main factors such as facilitation of transactions, pool risk and mobilized saving of IBs, which show the exact growth and viability of IBs. While some studies exclude the interest from IFIs through their strategy consequence (Khan 1986, Khan and Mirakhor 1987 and Bashir 2000), IFIs face new challenges as well as know some new realities of market after deregulation and topical trends of financial liberalization. These trends create competitions between interest-free and non-interest-free financial institutions after global financial markets combination. IFIs consider this competition as an opportunity, and it starts to design innovational models according to the needs and wants of their target customers in domestic and international markets. After gaining this opportunity by IFIs, it gets more investment prospect from the market within the viable retune rates and regulatory degree of risk (Bashir et al. 1993, Bashir 1999, Zaher and Hassan 2001, Samad and Hassan 1999).

Muslim and non-Muslim are two main types of investors in IFIs, where satisfaction is a basic and essential element of the any investor. Non-Muslim investors get satisfaction by maximizing their profits, and still this increment of profit remains in their accounts continuously. Some of non-Muslim investors don't believe on Islamic faith; for their perspectives IBs are reasonably a new concept, and it may become an opportunity for them as new investor in existing market. However, the satisfaction levels of Muslim investors are different from non-Muslim investors because Muslims investors got maximum utility from absolute relation with Allah (SWT) and well deed behavior with his human beings. However, the Muslim investors and consumers also face restrictions on what to invest and consume and where to invest and consume according to shari'ah, respectively. However, Quran gives a clear indication about this perspective because charity is a function of "good deeds" too (Qur'an, 46:15; 18:46), it is the one best form of good deeds. Allah (SWT) admired disbursements on charity (Qur'an, 63:10). Actually, Islam teaches us how to manage and allocate your resources, different activities of capital market, wealth and income distribution system and how to manage production and consumption system (Asutay, 2008).

It is a general concept of Islamic economics that risk of venture will be beared by mutual understanding of borrowers and lenders because success or failure of venture is uncontrollable by them. Dar and Presley (2000) found some theoretical models like PLS (Mudarabah) and joint venture (Musharakah) concepts are mostly used in IB. Gait and Worthington (2008) investigate some obstacles exist to investors of IBs such as different risk-sharing conditions, complications among management and unfamiliar business situations. It is also noted that financing method of IBs is related with visible risk of its capital. Metwally (1997) and Rosly and Zaini (2008) highlighted some of the difficulties about risk arising, classifying, observing and computing through the financing instruments of IFIs. *"All intellectual, practical, political, constitutional and legal efforts undertaken to enforce an interest-free system were not meant in earnest and therefore they inflicted a serious damage to the cause of Islam as well as IB"* (Khan and Bhatti, 2006, p. 145).

The Malaysian investors received 1.16% through return on Mudarabah deposits (ROMD) which is less return on equity (ROE) rather than USA fixed deposit holders. It shows an opportunity for the investors of IFIs.

However, 11.82% gap found between ROE and ROMD of IBs of Malaysia is higher than 8.61% return of USA interest-based banks. An internally snapshot of ROMD with others Islamic modes of financing in Malaysia shows that an average of ROMD was 7.56 times higher than the Malaysian IBs through their capital share. When we designed the rank of Malaysian banks on the basis of ROMD then we come to know the highest position got by Bank Islam Malaysia Berhad with 11.47 times higher than its share of capital, and the lowest position got by Maybank of Berhad with 2.9 times higher than its capital share of market (Rosly and Zaini 2008).

However, IBs found an exclusive institution for investor's perception to provide financial products and services permitting the needs and wants of their target customers within the limits of Islamic principles; IFIs also took risk management as special challenge to compete this risk and it had showed a positive effect on new and existing customers to easily motivated them for more investment in IBs. After the global challenges and financial crises damaged the international market, the priority of international investors had converted from conventional to IBs globally because when all big brand names had become the victim of crises and continuously declined their market values, in that particular time IFIs are not only stable in their position in the market but also have rapid growth in its market value. This is the main cause, which pushes the minds of all kinds of investors but especially non-Muslim investors to think about their investment and decide, are they continuously facing this decline process or should they change their banks (Sundararajan and Errico 2002)? *"Today we have reached a tipping point, which leaves us only one choice: change or face continued decline and misery"* (Chairman World Economic Forum 2010).

11.5 Methodology

This research is based on primary data. It includes the opinion of investors, layman, educationists and customers of different types of IBs. The respondents belong to different age groups, educational and occupational background, irrespective of gender. However, some branches of IB were selected at random from Lahore city; we also interviewed some investors and academician from Lahore to make our study more valuable and strong in this regard, whereas 132 questionnaires were distributed among investors, customers and other people of the society. The investors and academician were interviewed on a structured questionnaire through experienced enumerators. We took 5% as level of confidence in data analysis. The sample remained unweighted in respect to gender to avoid any bias. The areas of questions consists of the following: Personal information, Preference for bank selection, Opinion about shari'ah compatibility of IBs, Knowledge of investors about Islamic financial practices and products, Level of satisfaction about service quality of banks and Islamic scholars or Ulema understand the basic concepts of IB such as asset driven, liability driven and spread; IB is an opportunity or thread or challenge for the investors; and IBs give opportunities and information about usage of services and facilities to their investors. Questions were designed by keeping these areas in mind and to confirm the objectives of the study.

A pilot survey was conducted, and necessary adjustments were made in the questionnaire. However, we used adjusted sample and 5% level of confidence in our study. On the average, it took 15–20 minutes of enumerator to interview respondent investors. Furthermore, ANOVA and LSD (least significant difference) tables explain the results of interview. The responses of the questionnaires were summarized in SPSS software. Cross-tabulation was done for getting the overall results of the research. All the results were then converted into percentages/proportions.

11.6 Data analysis and discussion

Table 11.1 shows the mean values of all the variables in the questionnaires. However, the purpose of mean values is to determine the center of tendency in all the values given in the data. The maximum and minimum values of mean are 2.772 and 1.184, respectively, in the above table, whereas the difference between maximum and minimum value is 1.588. Most of the values are near to maximum value of mean, and there is no negative value found in the whole table, which shows that the positive relationship among all the mean values. For overall IBs, if the highest mean values occur with the magnitude of 2.772 for both of these variables, do common investors know about the procedure of products of IB like car and house financing? As per the questionnaire used

Table 11.1 Mean Values

Descriptions	*Mean*
Do Islamic scholars or Ulema understand the basic concepts of IB such as asset driven, liability driven and spread?	1.538
Do you think IB is a threat for the investors?	1.636
Do you think IB is a challenge for the investors?	1.409
Do you think IB is an opportunity for the investors?	1.184
How would you rate your level of satisfaction with IB?	2.453
Do you ask from your banks about the Shari‘ah compatibility of the bank operations?	2.363
When you have a problem, your bank shows a sincere interest in solving it for motivation of their investors?	2.646
IBs give opportunities and information about usage of services and facilities to their investors.	2.415
What is your opinion about profit of IBs?	2.363
What is your opinion about Shari‘a compliant banking system?	2.061
Normally no IB approached common investors.	2.469
Procedure of opening an account is difficult in IB for laymen.	2.430
How many Islamic religious scholars understand the mechanism of IBs such as financial transactions?	2.484
How much investors know that deposits are used and distributed in IBs?	2.484
Do common investors know about the procedure of products of IB like car and house financing?	2.772

to collect this data, the value 1 was representing highly disagree state and the 5 is for highly agree response. Hence, mean value of 2.772 shows that most of the investors are agree in both of these cases. If the lowest mean value occur at 1.184, do you think IB is an opportunity for the investors?

Table 11.2 divulges the results generated by the independent sample T-test. The data was processed under this test with the aim of comparative analysis

Table 11.2 Group Mean Variables (* indicates less than 5% significance level)

Group Means Variables	*Bank Type*	*Mean*	*Means Diff*	*Sig. (2-tailed)*
Do Islamic scholars or Ulema understand the basic concepts of IB such as asset driven, liability driven &spread?	CB	1.606	0.106	0.262
	Islamic	1.538		
Do you think IB is a threat for the investors?	CB	1.575	−0.102	0.238
	Islamic	1.677		
Do you think IB is a challenge for the investors?	CB	1.393	0.006	0.937
	Islamic	1.387		
Do you think IB is an opportunity for the investors?	CB	1.212	0.112	0.087
	Islamic	1.1		
How would you rate level of satisfaction with IBs?	CB	2.424	−0.162	0.211
	Islamic	2.586		
Do you ask from your banks about the Shari'ah compatibility of the bank operations?	CB	2.484	0.226	0.105
	Islamic		2.258	
When you have a problem, your bank shows a sincere interest in solving it for motivation of their investors?	CB	2.606	−0.127	0.349
	Islamic	2.733		
Banks give opportunities and information about usage of services and facilities to their investors.	CB	2.272	−0.394*	0.005
	Islamic	2.666		
What is your opinion about profit of IBs?	CB	2.363	0.041	0.738
	Islamic	2.322		
What is your opinion about Shari'ah compliant banking system?	CB	2	−0.129	0.242
	Islamic	2.129		
Normally no IB approached common investors.	CB	2.424	−0.059	0.693
	Islamic	2.483		
Procedure of opening an account is difficult in IB for laymen.	CB	2.393	−0.107	0.477
	Islamic	2.5		

(*Continued*)

Group Means Variables	*Bank Type*	*Mean*	*Means Diff*	*Sig. (2-tailed)*
How many Islamic religious scholars understand the mechanism of IBs financial transactions?	CB	2.636	0.282	0.056
	Islamic	2.354		
How much investors know that deposits are used and distributed in IBs?	CB	2.424	−0.092	0.522
	Islamic	2.516		
Do common investors know about the procedure of products of IB like car and house financing?	CB	3.06	0.609*	0.000
	Islamic	2.451		

of challenges, opportunities and threads in the way of correcting the misconceptions for society about IBs. The significant differences between the mean values were observed at the variables of how would you rate your level of satisfaction with IBs; IB is a threat for the investors; when you have a problem, your bank shows a sincere interest in solving it for motivation of their investors, your opinion about Shari‘a compliant banking system; banks give opportunities and information about usage of services and facilities to their investors; normally no IB approached common investors; procedure of opening an account is difficult in IB for laymen and how much investors know that deposits are used and distributed in IBs.

The significant value shows that these IBs observe statistically different results under the variables of banks to give opportunities and information about usage of services and facilities to their investors: Do common investors know about the procedure of products of IB like car and house financing? While between these variables the biggest mean difference occurs and the common investors know about the procedure of products of IB like car and house financing with the mean difference of 0.609. However, positive mean difference is the evidence to state that this problem is present at a bigger level in Islamic counterparts. It means that the CBs' management in Pakistan is not as much concerned with the service quality as the IB management. This issue is due to the new entry of IBs in the financial industry for the investors.

11.6.2 Analysis of variance (ANOVA)

For the multiple comparisons, in order to observe the change in the investors' perception with respect to religious education conducted, Table 11.3 describes the results of one way ANOVA. As evident through data analysis, the investors' perception of taking the IB as threat undergoes insignificant difference with the change in religious education of significance value at 0.064, while the results are vice versa with the variables of challenge and

Table 11.3 ANOVA – Analysis (* indicates less than 5% significance level)

Description	*Sum of Squares*	*DF*	*Mean Square*	*F-stat*	*Sig.*	*p-Value*
Threat	Between groups	2.145	4	0.536	2.326	0.064
	Within groups	17.757	77	0.231		
	Total	19.902	81			
Challenge	Between groups	3.15	4	0.788	3.706*	0.008
	Within groups	16.362	77	0.212		
	Total	19.512	81			
Opportunity	Between groups	5.014	4	1.253	9.548*	0.000
	Within groups	10.108	77	0.131		
	Total	15.122	81			

opportunity. Henceforth, the variable of threat was not taken to the further test of LSD and vice versa for challenge and opportunity.

Table 11.4 entails the statistics generated for LSD. Here, the group difference becomes significant as the religious education goes from 1 to 2, with significance value at 0.09 and the mean difference at −0.466. This negative mean difference is representative of the fact that the investors' perception goes towards "No". However, we say that increase in investor's religious education from Amma to Khasa (primary to secondary level) makes them less in taking the IB investments as a challenging one. When religious education goes from 2 to 1 all the results are the same as discussed above with positive mean difference value (0.466). Whereas, in the same dimension 3, the results are different when religious education goes from 2 to 3 with mean difference 0.416 at 0.001 level of significant. It means that investor perception is positive about IB as a challenge. In dimension 2, religious education spirits from 3 to 2 with negative mean difference (−0.416) form at the above discussed significant level (0.001), and all the results are converted into inverse form.

In opportunity table, when religious education moods from 1 to 3 and 1 to 4, the group difference becomes positively significant with 0.337 and 0.400 at 0.012 and 0.009 significant levels, respectively. These positive signs represent that IBs are an opportunity for investors. However, in dimension 2, when religious education transferred from 1 to 2 and 1 to 3, the differences in mean values are 0.337 and 0.400 with significant levels of acceptance 0.012 and 0.009, respectively. In dimension 3, the relationships among religious education find positively significant from 2 to 3, 2 to 4 and 2 to 5 with their mean values 0.520, 0.583 and 0.583 at different levels of significant 0.000, 0.000 and 0.032, respectively. The results of this correlation among the variables represent that investors want to invest more in IBs through their portfolio investment. In dimensions 3, 4 and 5, it has found negative correlation among the variables as from 3 to 1 and 3 to 2, 4 to 1 and 4 to 2, and 5 to 2 with mean difference values (−0.337, −0.520, −0.400, −0.583 and −0.583) at altered affirmative level of significant values (0.012, 0.000, 0.009, 0.000 and 0.032).

Table 11.4 Religion Multiple Comparisons LSD (* indicates less than 5% significance level)

Dependent Variable	*(I) Education Religious*	*(J) Education Religious*	*Mean Difference (I-J)*	*Std. Error*	*Sig.*
Challenge	1	2	−0.466*	0.173	**0.009**
Dimension 3		3	−0.050	0.167	0.765
		4	−0.228	0.190	0.235
		5	0.2	0.357	0.577
Dimension 3	2	1	0.466*	0.173	**0.009**
		3	0.416*	0.124	**0.001**
		4	0.238	0.155	0.129
		5	0.667	0.339	0.053
Dimension 2	3	1	0.050	0.167	0.765
		2	−0.416*	0.124	0.001
Dimension 3		4	−0.178	0.147	0.230
		5	0.250	0.335	0.459
Dimension 1	4	1	0.228	0.190	0.235
		2	−0.238	0.155	0.129
Dimension 3		3	0.178	0.147	0.230
		5	0.428	0.348	0.222
Dimension 3	5	1	−0.200	0.357	0.577
		2	−0.667	0.339	0.053
		3	−0.250	0.335	0.459
		4	−0.428	0.348	0.222
Opportunity	1	2	−0.183	0.136	0.183
		3	0.337*	0.131	**0.012**
Dimension 3		4	0.400*	0.150	**0.009**
Dimension 2		5	0.400	0.280	0.158
	2	1	0.183	0.136	0.183
Dimension 3		3	0.520*	0.097	**0.000**
		4.00	0.583*	0.121	**0.000**
		5.00	0.583*	0.266	0.032
Dimension 3	3.00	1.00	−0.337*	0.131	**0.012**
		2.00	−0.520*	0.097	**0.000**
		4.00	0.062	0.116	0.592
		5.00	0.062	0.264	0.814
Dimension 3	4.00	1.00	−0.400*	0.150	**0.009**
		2.00	−0.583*	0.121	**0.000**
		3.00	−0.062	0.116	0.592
		5.00	0.000	0.273	1.000
Dimension 3	5.00	1.00	−0.400	0.280	0.158
		2.00	−0.583*	0.266	**0.032**
		3.00	−0.062	0.264	0.814
		4.00	0.000	0.273	1.000

11.6.3 ANOVA – Analysis

In relative comparisons among three variables as threat, opportunity and challenge in order to observe the change in the investors' perception with respect to religious education conducted, Table 11.5 describes the results of one way ANOVA. As evident through data analysis, the investors'

Table 11.5 ANOVA – Analysis of Religiosity (* indicates less than 5% significance level)

Description	*Sum of Squares*	*Df*	*Mean Square*	*F-stat*	*Sig.*	*p-Value*
Threat	Between groups	0.755	4	0.189	0.805	0.524
	Within groups	29.79	127	0.235		
	Total	30.545	131			
Challenge	Between groups	4.742	4	1.186	5.543*	0
	Within groups	27.167	127	0.214		
	Total	31.909	131			
Opportunity	Between groups	2.169	4	0.542	3.896*	0.005
	Within groups	17.4	125	0.139		
	Total	19.569	129			

perception of taking the IB as challenge undergoes significant difference with the change in religious education of significance value at 0.000, while the results of opportunity are the same as challenge but result of threat is different which shows insignificant value at 0.524 level of significant. Henceforth, the variable of threat was not taken to the further test of LSD and vice versa for challenge and opportunity (Table 11.5).

Table 11.6 entails the statistics generated for LSD. Here, the group difference becomes significant as the religious education goes from 1 to 3, with significance value at 0.02 and the mean difference at −0.833. This negative mean difference is representative of the fact that the investors' perception goes towards "No". However, we say that increase in investor's religious education from Amma to Khasa (primary to secondary level) makes them less in taking the IB investments as a challenging one. When religious education goes from 2 to 3 all the results are the same as discussed above with positive mean difference value (−0.833). Whereas, in the same dimension 3, the results are different when religious education goes from 3 to 1 with mean difference 0.833 at 0.02 level of significant. It means that investor perception is positive about IB as a challenge. In dimension 2, religious education spirits from 3 to 2 with negative mean difference (0.833) form at the above discussed significant level (0.02), and all the results are converted into inverse form.

When religious education moods from 3 to 4, 3 to 5 and 5 to 4 the group difference mean values become positively significant with 0.583, 0.333 and 0.250 at significant levels of 0.000, 0.024 and 0.004, respectively. Whereas, in dimensions 3 and 1, variables show negative mean values with magnitude of −0.583, −0.250 and −0.333 at significant level values (0.000, 0.004 and 0.024), where religious education transferred from 4 to 3, 4 to 5 and 5 to 3, respectively. In the table of multi-comparisons of LSD test for opportunity variable, religious education goes from 4 to 5 with value of mean difference 0.267 at significant level 0.000. This positive sign represents that IBs are an opportunity for investors. However, in dimension 3, when religious education transferred from 5 to 4, the difference in mean value is −0.267 with significant level of acceptance 0.000.

Table 11.6 CB Multiple Comparisons LSD (* indicates less than 5% significance level)

Dependent Variable	*(I) Education CB*	*(J) Education CB*	*Mean Difference (I-J)*	*Std. Error*	*Sig.*
Challenge Dimension 3	1	2	0	0.462	1
		3	−0.833*	0.353	0.02
		4	−0.250	0.332	0.454
		5	−0.500	0.332	0.135
Dimension 3	2	1	0	0.462	1
		3	−0.833*	0.353	0.02
		4	−0.250	0.332	0.454
		5	−0.500	0.332	0.135
Dimension 2	3	1	0.833*	0.353	0.02
		2	0.833*	0.353	0.02
Dimension 3		4	0.583*	0.147	0
		5	0.333*	0.146	0.024
Dimension 3	4	1	0.25	0.332	0.454
		2	0.25	0.332	0.454
		3	−0.583*	0.147	0
		5	−0.250*	0.085	0.004
Dimension 3	5	1	0.5	0.332	0.135
		2	0.5	0.332	0.135
Dimension 1		3	−0.333*	0.146	0.024
		4	0.250*	0.085	0.004
Opportunity	1	2	0	0.373	1
		3	−0.167	0.284	0.56
Dimension 3		4	−0.333	0.268	0.217
		5	−0.067	0.268	0.804
Dimension 3	2	1	0	0.373	1
		3	−0.167	0.284	0.56
		4	−0.333	0.268	0.217
		5	−0.067	0.268	0.804
Dimension 2	3	1	0.167	0.284	0.56
		2	0.167	0.284	0.56
Dimension 3		4	−0.167	0.119	0.164
		5	0.1	0.117	0.398
Dimension 3	4	1	0.333	0.268	0.217
		2	0.333	0.268	0.217
		3	0.167	0.119	0.164
		5	0.267*	0.069	0
Dimension 3	5	1	0.667	0.268	0.804
		2	0.667	0.268	0.804
		3	−0.100	0.117	0.398
		4	−0.267*	0.069	0

11.7 Conclusion

This study investigated the behavior and ideas of five layers of misconception about Islamic financial system, where the first layer identifies the ideology of layman about IBs. However, this layman has no any account in interest-bearing and non-interest-bearing financial institutions. However, rest of four layers consist of account holder of IBs, Islamic economists, conventional economists and religious scholars or Ulema's. In this study, we find that IB is an opportunity, challenge and threat for investor perspective. The results of this study show that two variables such as opportunity and challenge out of three are positively significant and rest of one as threat is insignificant. Results of individual mean values express that most of the values are near to origin and where the maximum and minimum values are as 2.774 and 1.184, respectively. T-test represents the individual significant and insignificant results of model, and we elaborate all the individual values on base of significant levels. Whereas F-test denotes the significant level as an acceptance or rejection of the whole model. The table of multi-comparison of LSD tests shows hybrid results in terms of positive and negative which are based on dimensions, difference in mean values, standard errors, both religious education (I, J) and significant levels.

Whereas, it is also noted in our survey that most of investors are not well educated and they are unable to differentiate between function of asset and liability side of balance sheet. In our survey, some investors share their views that investors of CB system told us that IB will not work or exist more in the global market. This news will draw bad effects on the new IBs investors as well as the existing. So, it is suggested that IFIs should publish small booklets in national/local language to motivate clients. The IFIs will also organize corner meetings with their all investors but especially with long-term investors. These facts must reduce the misconception of investors, and it also promoted the IFS in the world as an opportunity for new investors.

Based upon the findings the study puts forward the following suggestions. It was observed that the investors are not well to bear the knowledge of Islamic finance; moreover, the more knowledgeable individuals were akin to have a positive association towards Islamic finance. The lower level of empathy received by IB employees is the fuel to the fire of this scarcity of knowledge. Hence, the banks are encouraged to work on the principles of economy of knowledge by instilling a better knowledge both among the general public by arranging seminars and among employees by enhancing the IB trainings. It was seen that the investors' perception was strong to take Islamic investments as an opportunity to invest. This fact be tailored in the marketing strategy of IBs, and the investors are encouraged to opt for Islamic investments to diversify their portfolios.

Suggestions for the father research can be granted in the way that this study was questionnaire based by the nature of its methodology, and the results can be compared while arching the future research upon experimental methods. The sample can be diversified as well, and the impact of knowledge can be investigated upon different and larger samples. Study also suggested that the bank employees are not well knowledgeable to guide with empathy. A dedicated study can be conducted on IB employees to further spearhead the significance of trainings and the level of employees' knowledge. Bank accounts were taken as the proxy for investments the future research can opt for the different proxies like Islamic stocks and *sukuks*.

References

Aglietta, M. (2010). *La crise: les voies de sortie* (p. 15). Paris: Michalon.

Aglietta, M., & Rigot, S. (2009). *Criseetrénovation de la finance*. Odile Jacob.

Ahmad, K. (1981). *Studies in Islamic Economics*. Leicester: Islamic Foundation.

Amin, H. (2013). Some viewpoints of IB retail deposit products in Malaysia. *Journal of Internet Banking and Commerce, 18*(1), 1–13.

Arbouna, M. B. (2007). The combination of contracts in Shariah: A possible mechanism for product development in IB and finance. *Thunderbird International Business Review, 49*(3), 341–369.

Arouri, M. E., Ben Ameur, H., Jawadi, N., Jawadi, F., & Louhichi, W. (2013). Are Islamic finance innovations enough for investors to escape from a financial downturn? Further evidence from portfolio simulations. *Applied Economics, 45*(24), 3412–3420.

Asutay, M. (2008). IB and finance: Social failure. *New Horizon*, 169, 1–3.

Awan, A. G., & Azhar, M. (2014). Consumer behaviour towards IB in Pakistan. *European Journal of Accounting Auditing and Finance Research, 2*(9), 42–65.

Bashir, A. (1999). "Risk and profitability measures in Islamic banks: The case of two sudanese banks. *Islamic Economic Studies, 6*(2), 1–24.

Bashir, A. (2000). Determinants of profitability and rates of return margins in Islamic banks: some evidence from the Middle East. Grambling State University Mimeo.

Bashir, A., Darrat, A. F., & Suliman, M. O. (1993). Equity capital, profit sharing contracts, and investment: Theory and evidence. *Journal of Business Finance & Accounting, 20*(5), 639–651.

Bollen, B. R. (2010). What is a deposit (and why does it matter)? [Electronic Version], available at: http://ssrn.com/abstract=1756073 (accessed 2 March 2016).

Bunzel, B. C. (2015). From paper state to caliphate: The ideology of the Islamic state. Brookings Institution Analysis Paper No. 19, Brookings Institution, Massachusetts Ave., NW Washington, D.C.

Causse, G. (2010a). La finance Islamique. *La revue du financier*, Juin, No. 182–183, 6–180.

Causse, G. (2010b). La finance Islamique: les principes et les principales opérations. *La revue du financier*, Juin, No. 182–183, 23–44.

Causse, G. (2010c). Le système financier Islamique: nature et perspectives de développement. *LA REVUE DU FINA La revue du financier*, Juin, No. 182–183, 169–78.

Causse, G., & Abdelhafid N. (2010) Produits dérivés Islamiques: de l'utilisation implicite à la standardisation. *Revue Banque*, Juin, No. 275, 51–54 [4pp.].

Causse G., & Hideur N. (2010). La gestion des risques dans les banques Islamiques. *La Revue du Financier*, Juin, No. 182–183, 73–88.

Chairman World Economic forum. (2010).*The Global Competitive Report 2010–2011*.

Chong, B. S., & Liu, M. (2006). IB: interest-free or interest-based? *Pacific-Basin Finance Journal, 17*, 125–144.

Dar, H. A., & Presley, J. R. (2000). Lack of profit loss sharing in IB: Management and control imbalances. *International Journal of Islamic Financial Services, 2*(2), 3–18.

Gait, A., & Worthington, A. (2008). An empirical survey of individual consumer, business firm and financial institution attitudes towards Islamic methods of finance. *International Journal of Social Economics, 35*(11), 783–808.

Hamid, A. H. A., & Nordin, N. A. M. (2001). A study on IB education experience and the strategy for the new millenium-A Malaysian Evidence. *International Journal of Islamic Financial Services*, *2*(4), 1–10.

Jawadi, F., Jawadi, N., & Louhichi, W. (2014). *Does Islamic finance outperform conventional finance? Further evidence from the recent financial crisis* (No. 2014–279).

Jouini, E., & Pastré, O. (2009). *La Finance Islamique-Une solution à la crise?*

Khan, M. (1986). Islamic interest free banking: A theoretical analysis. *IMF Staff Papers*.

Khan, M. S., & Mirakhor, A. (1987).The framework and practice of IB. *Theoretical Studies in IB and Finance, The Institute for Research and Islamic Studies, Texas*.

Mansoor Khan, M., & Ishaq Bhatti, M. (2006). Why interest-free banking and finance movement failed in Pakistan. *Humanomics*, *22*(3), 145–161.

Marliana, A., Shahimi, S., and Ismail, A. G. (2011). Operational risk in Islamic banks: examination of issues. *Qualitative Research in Financial Markets* 3:2, 131–151.

Mawardi, A.H.A.I.M.I.H. (2011). Kitab Adab al-Dunya w'al-Din (The ethics of religion and of this world), Nabu Press, South port.

Metwally, M. M. (1997). Differences between the financial characteristics of interest-free banks and conventional banks. *European Business Review*, *97*(2), 92–98.

Miskawaih, I. (2010). Tahdzib al-Akhlaq wa Tathhir al-A'raq, Maktabah al-Thaqafah al-Diniyyah, Cairo.

Nathan, S., and Ribiere, V. (2007). From knowledge to wisdom: The case of corporate governance in IB. *The Journal of Information and Knowledge Management Systems*, *37*(4), 471–483.

Nurrachmi, R., Fathia, M., Mad-ahdin, A., Radenarmad, N., & Akhtar, R. (2012). Time value of money in Islamic perspective and the practice in IB implications. MPRA Paper No.46818, INCEIF.

Rosly, A. S., & Zaini, A. M. (2008). Risk-return analysis of Islamic banks' investment deposits and shareholders' fund. *Managerial Finance*, *34*(10), 695–707.

Samad, A., & Hassan, M. K. (1999). The performance of Malaysian Islamic bank during 1984–1997: An exploratory study. *International Journal of Islamic Financial Services*, *1*(3), 1–14.

Shabbir, M. S., Ghazi, M. S., & Akhtar, T. (2015a). The viability of Islamic finance and its impact on global financial stability: Evidence from practical implications. *European Journal of Economics, Finance and Administrative Sciences*, *5*(85).

Shabbir, M. S., Khalil ur Rehman, A., & ur Rasool, A. (2015b). Does Islamic finance industry manage Shariah complaint risk in transactions? *European Journal of Economics, Finance and Administrative Sciences*, *3*(83).

Shabbir, M. S., Ghazi, M. S., & Akhtar, T. (2016a). The relationship between traditional as well as modern modes of financial instruments for international market through Islamic finance. *Journal of Internet Banking and Commerce*, *22*(3).

Shabbir, M. S., Rehman, A. K., & Akhtar, T. (2016b). The role of Islamic leading organizations for the promotion of Islamic finance in Western countries. *The Journal of Internet Banking and Commerce*, *21*(1).

Shahzad, M., & Rehman, A., (2015). Barriers to service quality in the banks of Pakistan: A comparative study of Islamic and conventional banks. *Business and Economics Journal*, *6*(4), 178.

Sundararajan, V., & Errico, L. (2002). *Islamic Financial Institutions and Products in the Global Financial System: Key Issues in Risk Management and Challenges Ahead* (Vol. 2). International Monetary Fund.

Zaher, T. S., & Hassan, M. K. (2001). A comparative literature survey of Islamic finance and banking. *Financial Markets, Institutions & Instruments, 10*(4), 155–199.

12 Overview of progress in Islamic commercial and social finance in Pakistan

Salman Ahmed Shaikh, Mohd Adib Ismail, Abdul Ghafar Ismail, Shahida Shahimi and Muhammad Hakimi Mohd. Shafiai

12.1 Islamic banking in Pakistan

Financial institutions facilitate intertemporal finance between savers and investors by providing efficient delegated monitoring and portfolio management services (Diamond, 1984). Financial credit institutions enable consumers to access their potential lifetime resources when they are not readily available in earlier stages of their lives. People can use their current endowments or future stream of expected incomes as collateral to access credit facilities in the present (Kahf, 1996).

Islam allows financing and investments, but without the element of interest. Islam aims for circulation of wealth and pursuit of the productive enterprise for earning a livelihood. On the other hand, providing a fixed return to money capital leads to continuous accumulation and concentration of wealth among the wealthy capitalists. Islamic finance makes it necessary that money capital cannot get stipulated returns unless it participates in the productive enterprise by undertaking the risk. This enables circulation of capital, full employment of resources and avoids the ills of the concentration of wealth, economic stagnation, unemployment and simultaneous existence of unused resources and unmet needs. Islamic teachings discourage idleness of capital by disallowing any stipulated increase to the lending of money capital and by levying *Zakāt* on idle capital. This ensures capital circulation in the real economy so that financial intermediation contributes to socioeconomic development by having a direct and compulsory link with the real sector of the economy.

The idea of Islamic banking was first materialized in the area of social finance. In Egypt, El-Naggar in 1963 launched Mit Ghamr Islamic Savings Bank. In addition to that, Tabung Haji (Pilgrims Fund Corporation) began its operations in 1963 to enable Malaysian Muslims to save funds for the journey of Hajj (Chachi, 2005). On the other hand, contemporary Islamic banking started with the launch of Dubai Islamic bank in 1979.

After humble beginnings, Islamic financial institutions were launched globally in Muslim majority regions of Asia, Africa and even Europe. According to the Global Islamic Finance Report (2018), global Islamic finance assets reached $2.43 trillion in 2017. Majority of the global Islamic financial assets are held by Islamic banks and conventional banks with Islamic banking windows as they enjoy the share of 75% of the total global Islamic banking assets. Looking at the market shares of Islamic banking in different countries, it is revealed that Islamic banking share in overall banking in Saudi Arabia, Kuwait, Bahrain, Qatar, the UAE, Malaysia and Pakistan remains at 51.2%, 45.2%, 29.3%, 25.8%, 21.6%, 26% and 15%, respectively (Ernst & Young, 2016).

During the early years after independence from British India, masses in Pakistan had a keen interest in introducing Islamic socioeconomic institutions in the country. However, political instability became a hurdle in making swift progress towards that end. The interest reemerged after the increased focus in the 1970s around the Muslim countries to develop an indigenous Islamic financial system. In Pakistan, the country's constitution passed unanimously in 1973 clearly mentions in Section 38(f) that *Ribā* should be eliminated as early as possible. This paved the way for Islamic banking on the legal front. Furthermore, the Council of Islamic Ideology in its report in 1980 on the elimination of *Ribā* from the economy conclusively defined *Ribā*. The report emphasized that concrete steps should be taken to introduce Islamic banking in place of *Ribā*-based banking. The report gave the following conclusive definition of *Ribā*:

> The term *Ribā* encompasses interest in all its manifestations irrespective of whether it relates to loans for consumption purposes or for productive purposes, whether the loans are of a personal nature or of a commercial type, whether the borrower is a government, a private individual or a concern, and whether the rate of interest is low or high.

Finally, the verdict on interest by the Supreme Court of Pakistan in 1991 further consolidated the progress in paving the way for Islamic financial institutions. With these legal developments, Islamic banking in Pakistan made humble beginnings first in the 1980s, and then, the real impetus came with the launch of the first full-fledged Islamic bank in Pakistan in the year 2002. As of now, Islamic banking is an established industry with 15% and 15.6% market share in total banking assets and deposits, respectively, as of March 31, 2019. By end-March 2019, the total Islamic banking assets in Pakistan stood at Rs. 2.79 trillion ($23.25 billion), while total Islamic banking deposits stood at Rs. 2.20 trillion ($18.33 billion). With increased participation of conventional banks in the Islamic banking industry, the branch network has swelled to 2,689 branches by end-March 2019. Nonetheless, the country's share in global Islamic banking industry remains at a meager 1% despite hosting 12% of global Muslim population.

However, the scope of scaling up and finding new customer base is significant. According to National Financial Inclusion Strategy by State Bank of Pakistan (2015b), only 10.3% of adult population in Pakistan has a bank account, whereas the average for South Asia and lower middle-income countries is 33% and 41.4%, respectively. The savings also do not channel through financial institutions as out of 36% of adults who save, only 4% of the people save in financial institutions. On the other hand, according to State Bank of Pakistan's Knowledge, Attitude and Practices Survey, 98% people who do not operate bank accounts believe in the prohibition of interest. Furthermore, more than 93% people overall consider bank interest as prohibited (State Bank of Pakistan, 2015a).

12.2 Islamic capital market in Pakistan

12.2.1 Equity market in Pakistan

By and large, the capital market in Pakistan has provided competitive returns as compared to the low-risk fixed-income investments historically. Most of the people with investment motive and having adequate risk appetite prefer capital market investments in the secondary market due to higher expected return and greater liquidity. Figure 12.1 gives a snapshot of how the broad market index (KSE-100) has moved during 1998–2018. It can be seen that the growth had been consistent with a break during 2008–2010. The twin peak is observed since the stock market fell substantially in response to the global financial crisis which also had the contagion impact on the domestic capital market.

Figure 12.2 shows the index values of the Karachi Stock Exchange Al-Meezan Index (KMI-30) during 2009–2018. From plotting the KSE-100 index values for comparison, it is evident that KMI-30 index has steadily increased ever since its launch.

Nonetheless, there had only been 28 new long-term corporate debt instruments issued during 2011–2018. From the perspective of savers, the corporate bonds do not generate much interest in Pakistan partly because of

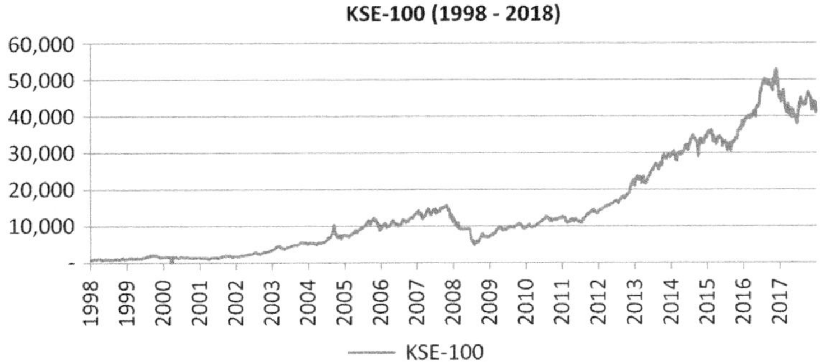

Figure 12.1 KSE-100 index daily values (adjusted closing) for 1998–2018.

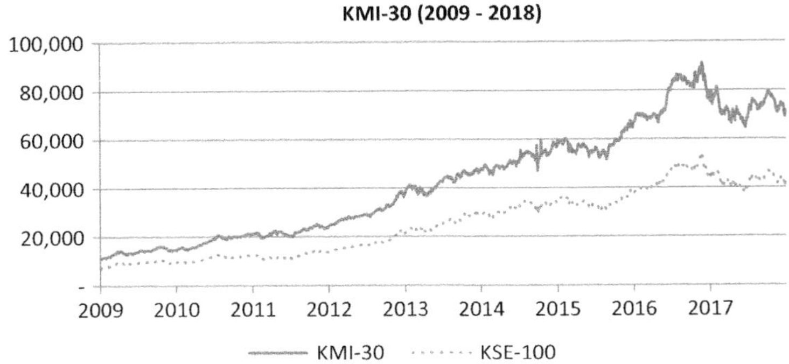

Figure 12.2 KSE-100 and KMI-30 index for 2009–2018.

alternative high-yielding sovereign national savings scheme instruments which have no default risk and enjoy tax exemption of returns. On the other hand, the government of Pakistan minimally uses Islamic modes of financing for its budgetary needs. As a result, there are fewer Islamic investment instruments as a substitute for sovereign investment instruments.

On the other hand, the corporate sector itself is facing stiff competition globally for sustaining its exports. The security and energy crisis has depleted firm-level competitiveness; hence, very few long-term big investments have come in the country after the nationalization in the 1970s. Furthermore, indirect taxation and removal of import barriers had also reduced the competitiveness of local producers following the Structural Adjustment Programs of the World Bank and the IMF.

12.2.2 Sukuk market in Pakistan

For Muslim investors looking for regular long-term income, *Sukuk* investments are a *Shari'ah* compliant alternative to corporate and treasury bonds. *Sukuk* certificate represents the *Sukuk* holder's ownership in real assets. Since Islamic law allows sale as well as the lease of real assets, the income earned in the form of profit on the sale or rents on the lease of assets is permissible.

Sukuk market in Pakistan is limited just like corporate bonds. As of 2018, more than 100 *Sukuk* had been issued in the last decade or so by the corporate sector and by the government of Pakistan. Innovative structures have also appeared in recent years to issue *Sukuk* in the service sector companies. For example, airtime-based *Sukuk* using Ijarah and Sub-Ijarah of services have been issued which use airtime (minutes) represented by prepaid calling cards and identified by the serial number of each card as the underlying assets. In recent years, some of the corporate *Sukuk* have also got listed on the exchange.

12.3 Islamic mutual funds

Islamic mutual funds like their conventional counterparts provide portfolio management services to risk-averse and risk-neutral investors. Islamic mutual funds have to follow *Shari'ah* compliance criteria in their portfolio selection and revision. Furthermore, they also have to purify their non-compliant portion of income from the total earnings to make their income *Shari'ah* compliant. The screening methodology approved by the *Shari'ah* advisors in Pakistan is explained below.

12.3.1 Business of the investee company

First and foremost, the business of the company should be *Halāl* (permissible). Thus, investments in common stocks of interest-based banks, conventional insurance companies, interest-based leasing companies and in companies which provide prohibited goods or services, such as liquor, drugs and weapons, are not permissible. Stocks of these companies cannot be included in the portfolio. Once the qualitative screening on the nature of the business is passed, then the screening is done on quantitative indicators related to business processes, such as the use of interest-based leverage, investments and share of the non-compliant portion of income.

12.3.2 Ceiling on interest-based debt

Interest-based debt must be lower than 37% of the total assets of the company. Interest-based debt includes borrowing through bonds, finance lease and commercial paper, for instance. It also includes interest-based conventional banking products, such as interest-based loans, capital lease and hire purchase agreements.

12.3.3 Ceiling on interest-based investments

The *Shari'ah* screening criteria specify that disallowed investments must be less than 33% of the total assets of the company. Investments in T-bills, conventional funds, corporate bonds, sovereign bonds, national savings scheme instruments and interest-based derivatives are impermissible. If a company is declared as non-compliant due to a violation of any of these principles, investments in such company would also be considered impermissible.

12.3.4 Cap on Shari'ah non-compliant income

The non-compliant portion of income must be less than 5% of the consolidated total revenue of the company. The definition of total revenue is as follows:

$$\text{Total Revenue} = \text{Gross Sales} + \text{Total Other Income} \tag{1}$$

The prohibited income includes interest income from financial investments and overdue receivables. It also includes income from prohibited goods and services, such as gambling, prostitution, casinos, tobacco and liquor. Dividend income from such businesses is regarded as non-compliant income.

12.3.5 Minimum requirement of illiquid assets

The *Shari'ah* screening criteria further stipulate that non-liquid assets must be 25% or more of the total assets of the company. Non-liquid assets are defined as follows:

$$\text{NonLiquid Assets} = \text{Total Assets} - \text{Liquid Assets} \tag{2}$$

Liquid assets comprise cash, advances, trade receivables and prepayments. Non-liquid assets include inventory, plant, equipment, machinery and furniture. Non-liquid assets can be traded above or below par value.

12.3.6 Minimum price of a share as per Shari'ah

The financial worth of the company equals at least the monetary value of liquid assets it holds. Thus, the minimum price per share is represented by net liquid assets per share:

$$\text{Per Share Net Liquid Assets} = \frac{\text{Total Assets} - \text{Illiquid Assets} - \text{Current Liability} - \text{Long-term Liability}}{\textit{Total Outstanding Shares}} \tag{3}$$

Other than these screening principles, the rules of sale in Islamic jurisprudence also have to be followed which prohibit short selling, options, forward sale and futures sale. In order to provide a contrast in the screening methodology applied in Pakistan as compared to globally, a summary of the quantitative screens followed in three major indices globally is provided in Table 12.1.

Next, some developments and indicators related to the Islamic asset management sector in Pakistan are presented. As of September 30, 2018, there are 245 mutual funds in Pakistan, out of which 126 are Islamic funds and 119 are conventional funds. Table 12.2 reports total assets under management (AUM) in Islamic mutual funds in each category of funds. It can be seen that most funds are invested in equity. Compound Annual Growth Rate (CAGR) for Islamic equity funds during 2011–2018 had stayed at 40.27%, while the CAGR for Islamic income funds had been clocked at 5.93% during the same period.

Table 12.3 presents the market share distribution of Islamic and conventional funds in each category of funds. Islamic funds have 38% market share as compared to 62% market share of conventional mutual funds as at December 31, 2018. In asset allocation, balanced, commodities, fund of

Table 12.1 Screening Criteria of Global Indices

Quantitative Screens	*S&P*	*Financial Times Stock Exchange*	*Dow Jones*
Leverage	Debt to equity (12-month average) must be less than 33%.	Debt should be lower than 33% of the total assets.	Debt to equity (24-month average) should be lower than 33%.
Liquidity	Accounts receivables to equity (12-month average) should be lower than 49%. Cash plus interest-bearing securities to equity (12-month average) should be lower than 33%.	Cash plus interest-bearing investments should be lower than 33% of the total assets. Accounts receivables and cash should be lower than 50% of the total assets.	Cash plus interest-bearing securities divided by equity (24-month average) should be lower than 33%. Accounts receivables divided by equity (24-month average) should be lower than 33%.
Revenue	Non-compliant income other than interest income to revenue should be lower than 5%.	Non-compliant income should be less than 5% of the total revenue of the company.	–
Dividend purification	$Dividends\left(\frac{NonCompliant\ Income}{Total\ Revenue}\right)$		

Table 12.2 Assets under Management in Islamic Funds (in million Rs.)

Category	*2011*	*2012*	*2013*	*2014*	*2015*	*2016*	*2017*	*2018*
Equity	7,027	8,104	15,349	23,363	51,167	67,215	92,788	75,095
Income	20,888	29,944	36,414	36,783	21,028	29,692	31,508	31,273
Fund of funds	–	–	699	927	3,269	23,679	61,411	45,585
Asset allocation	1,264	1,120	870	1,116	4,784	10,818	31,193	29,088
Fund of funds – CPPI	–	–	–	11,533	20,671	9,168	379	14,006
Money market	6,353	7,762	7,088	5,189	13,483	5,920	7,337	8,927
Balanced	2,289	2,334	2,538	6,955	3,493	4,822	9,516	7,843
Aggressive income	725	688	1,178	2,253	2,157	3,209	1,105	796
Capital protected	724	443	1,304	2,972	3,015	1,771	244	127
Index tracker	–	289	901	1,176	1,159	881	1,881	1,687
Commodities	–	–	–	–	–	321	457	243
Total	39,270	50,684	66,341	92,267	124,226	157,496	237,819	139,575

Source: Mutual Funds Association of Pakistan.

Table 12.3 Market Share in Mutual Funds Industry – 2018

Category	*Conventional (%)*	*Islamic (%)*
Aggressive fixed income	91	9
Asset allocation	32	68
Balanced	35	65
Capital protected	94	6
Commodities	0	100
Equity	67	33
Fund of funds	8	92
Fund of funds – CPPI	3	97
Income	65	35
Index tracker	21	79
Money market	93	7
Voluntary Pension Schemes	36	64
Total	62	38

Source: Mutual Funds Association of Pakistan.

funds and index tracker categories, Islamic funds have a greater market share as compared to conventional mutual funds.

12.4 Islamic microfinance in Pakistan

The share of Muslim population in global poverty pool is almost two times as much as their share in the total global population. Conventional microfinance involves interest which is prohibited in Islam. Non-use of financing services due to the prohibition of interest in the Islamic faith is also another reason why conventional microfinance reach is low in Muslim majority regions.

Like conventional microfinance, Islamic microfinance targets people who face liquidity constraints and who are otherwise non-bankable due to their low, unstable or unverifiable income and non-ownership of assets that can be used as collateral. Among the populous Muslim majority countries, most of the poor population resides in Nigeria, Bangladesh, Pakistan and Indonesia. Along with Bangladesh, Pakistan, Nigeria and Indonesia are the other countries where there are more than a million microfinance clients. However, apart from Bangladesh, the outreach gap computed as the difference between the number of poor people and the existing number of microfinance clients exceeds 90% in Pakistan, Nigeria and Indonesia.

There are two categories of Islamic microfinance models, i.e. non-market-based not-for-profit models and market-based for-profit models (Obaidullah, 2008). The former model uses *Qard-e-Hasan*, *Waqf* and *Zakāt* funds for providing financing. Market-based commercial models provide microfinancing using *Murabaha*, *Ijarah* and *Salam*.

Qard-e-Hasan-based financing ensures that there is no additional stipulated increase paid over the principal amount. Thus, it enables the borrower to benefit from the loan and repay the same amount of money. This increases the chances of taking benefit of the loan and enabling socioeconomic mobility rather than getting trapped in interest-based compounded debt. This form of financing also protects the lender since the principal amount of money has to be repaid. Thus, while *Qard-e-Hasan* provides ease in repayment burden for the borrower, it also protects the lender from moral hazard. *Qard-e-Hasan* is a useful instrument to enable the poor client to survive and graduate to a non-poor status by providing funds which can be utilized for personal consumption needs as well as for purchasing the raw materials, tools and business inventory for productive enterprise.

The economics of Islamic microfinance literature shows Islamic Microfinance Institutions (IMFIs) benefit from the social capital derived from Islamic values and principles. Ahmed (2002) reasons that IMFIs can reduce high monitoring costs and moral hazard problem since Islamic modes of financing involve a real transaction. Komi and Croson (2013) find significantly higher compliance rates for the Islamic-compliant contracts (profit-sharing and joint venture) than for the traditional contract (interest-based). Ashraf et al. (2014) in an empirical study provide evidence that high religious orientation is associated with financial responsibility and completion of contract obligations among the clients. Samad (2014) emphasizes that IMIFs are responsible and do not encourage clients to overburden themselves in indebtedness. He argues that if Islamic microfinance is offered in India, the mass suicides committed especially by the Indian farmers can be contained to a great extent. However, institutionalizing and establishing Islamic microfinance at large scale is needed to realize the benefit of these structural benefits and positive externalities.

An estimated 58.7 million people in Pakistan are living in multidimensional poverty, mostly in rural areas (Naveed and Ali, 2012). Comparing this figure with a number of people served with microfinance shows a huge potential outreach gap. Table 12.4 gives facts about microfinance in Pakistan.

Currently, only 5.5 million people are served with microfinance in Pakistan. The share of Islamic microfinance segment in active borrowers and gross loan portfolio stands at 16% and 7%, respectively, in 2017 (Source: Pakistan Microfinance Network). Table 12.5 presents the province-wise

Table 12.4 Stylized Facts about Microfinance in Pakistan

Key Indicators	*2010*	*2011*	*2012*	*2013*	*2014*	*2015*	*2016*	*2017*
Number of borrowers (million)	1.6	1.7	2.0	2.4	2.8	3.8	4.6	5.5
Gross loan portfolio (bln Rs.)	20.2	24.8	33.1	46.6	61.1	92.9	136.9	200
Active women borrowers	0.8	0.9	1.3	1.4	1.6	2.1	2.5	2.7
Branches	1,405	1,550	1,460	1,606	1,747	2,960	3,220	3,533

Source: Pakistan Microfinance Network.

Table 12.5 Microfinance Outreach – Province Wise

Key Indicators – Province Wise	*Sindh*	*Punjab*	*Balochistan*	*KPK*
Offices – fixed	651	2,284	17	107
Offices – mobile	26	14	2	–
Active borrowers	904,892	3,449,902	5,577	97,239
Potential microfinance market	2,400,000	12,600,000	500,000	500,000
Penetration rate (%)	37.7	27.4	1.1	1.9%

Source: Pakistan Microfinance Network.

outreach statistics. It can be seen that the penetration ratio is the lowest in two of the most underdeveloped provinces of Pakistan, i.e. Balochistan and Khyber Pakhtoon Khwah.

One would expect Islamic finance to have a greater focus on social finance given the general level of higher incidence of poverty and since the philosophy and theoretical basis of Islamic finance are rooted in the socio-ethical framework of Islam. Nevertheless, Islamic finance has not been able to translate that potential and promise into practice substantially as yet.

12.4.1 Islamic microfinance institutions and operations

The prominent organizations that provide Islamic micro-financial services include Akhuwat, Kashf Foundation, Wasil Foundation, Islamic Relief Pakistan, Muslim Aid Pakistan, Kawish Welfare Trust, Esaar Foundation and Naymet Trust.

One of the recent success stories has been the *Qard-e-Hasan* model of Akhuwat. This institution with humble setup and uncomplicated procedures has provided financing to 3.4 million clients with a nearly 99% recovery rate as of May 31, 2019. Kashf Foundation is another organization with a sizable outreach with 237,573 clients served with a staff of 2,210 as at end-December 2016. The microcredit loan portfolio stands at Rs. 5.9 billion ($57 million) as at December 31, 2016.

Wasil Foundation provides financing using Islamic modes of financing which enable it to generate profits on sale and lease of assets. In the reported statistics for 2010, the gross loan portfolio stood at Rs. 210 million ($2.1 million) with a 91% recovery rate. Naymet Trust provides financing using *Qard-e-Hasan* and *Murabaha* with 60% and 40% shares, respectively, in 2016. The total assets of the trust as at June 30, 2016, stood at Rs. 22.3 million ($213,000). Total credit portfolio was recorded at Rs. 11.3 million ($107,619) with *Murabaha* portfolio of Rs. 4.6 million ($44,000) and *Qard-e-Hasan* portfolio of Rs. 6.7 million ($64,077).

Islamic Relief is an example of an incorporated microfinance institution in Pakistan operating since 1992 with a presence in all four provinces of Pakistan, especially in the northern areas of Pakistan. Their microcredit portfolio stood at Rs. 38 million ($0.36 million) as at December 31, 2014.

The institution has helped some 11 million families over its 25-year journey in Pakistan with various programs including rehabilitation of internally displaced persons, disaster risk reduction, climate change adaptation, water and sanitation, food security and health programs.

In the next and last section of the chapter, a brief review of the use and contribution of Islamic redistributive institutions is provided to show that how much vibrant these institutions are in complementing the purchasing power of poor people to meet the basic needs in Pakistan.

12.5 Role of redistributive institutions

Besides the financial institutions, Islamic redistributive institutions also have ample potential to achieve resource redistribution at the household level. There are various institutions in the Islamic framework that can play an effective role in income and wealth redistribution. Effective use of these redistributive institutions can help in the fulfillment of basic needs for all members of the society, especially the underprivileged poor people who face net endowment deficiency (Zarqa 1988). The two most prominent such non-market-based redistributive institutions include *Zakāt* and *Waqf*.

12.5.1 Institution of Zakāt in Pakistan

In Islam, *Zakāt* is a religious obligation to pay a portion of net wealth and production over the amount of *Nisāb* to the specified heads (*Al-Qur'an*, Chapter Tauba 9: 60). The specified heads of *Zakāt* ensure the welfare of poor, needy and weaker segments of society as well as provide collective funds for public welfare and social protection.

The empirical studies on welfare potential of *Infāq* (charity) in Pakistan show considerable potential to alleviate poverty in Pakistan. Malik et al. (1994) use household data and establish that *Infāq* (charity) has a significant effect on reducing the poverty gap. In a cross-country study, Shirazi and Amin (2009) estimate that Pakistan needs 1% of GDP for poverty elimination under \$1.25 a day and needs 6.77% of GDP for poverty elimination under \$2.00 a day. Previous estimates by Kahf (1989) show that *Zakāt* to GDP ratio between 1.6% and 4.4% is needed to fill the poverty gap. In another study, Azam et al. (2014) establish that *Zakāt* significantly enhances the welfare of households in Pakistan. Finally, Akram and Afzal (2014) argue that *Zakāt* disbursement among the poor, needy, destitute, orphans and widows has played a significant role in poverty alleviation. The results reveal an inverse relationship between poverty and *Zakāt* payment in the short run as well as in the long run.

Nevertheless, *Zakāt* collection at the federal and province level is very low in Pakistan as can be seen in Figure 12.3. In the year 2015, Rs. 5.74 billion (US\$54 million) *Zakāt* was received by the central public *Zakāt* agency. Lack of trust between the government and the people is one major reason

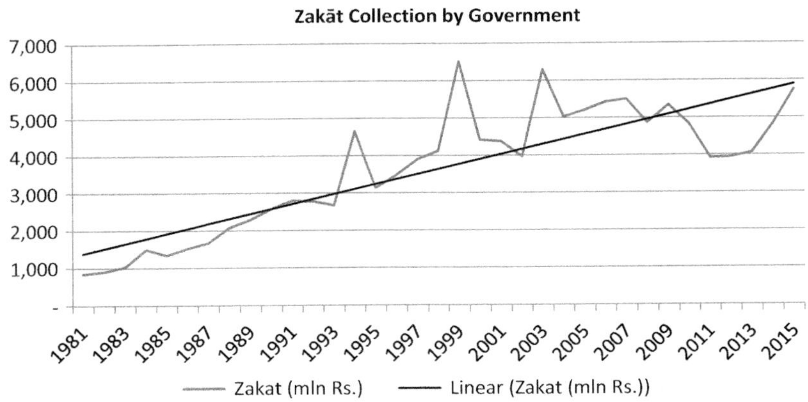

Figure 12.3 Zakāt receipts (in million Rs.).

behind low *Zakāt* collection at the federal level in Pakistan. Due to the limited availability of *Zakāt* funds collected by *Zakāt* and *Ushr* department, the scale of providing assistance to the poor is very low. The most vibrant *Zakāt* and *Ushr* department is in Punjab province, but even that is also catering to a very limited section of poor people. For instance, through the Sustainable Economic Empowerment Program (SEEP), annually 30,000 young people are imparted technical and vocational training. In addition to that, scholarships to some 2,000 students are provided annually by Punjab's *Zakāt* and *Ushr* department. However, these programs do not sufficiently fill the gap in the country amidst 22 million out of school children between the ages of 6 and 15. The total *Zakāt* budget for 2016/17 for Punjab was Rs. 4.15 billion ($40 million). In addition to that, the total *Zakāt* budget for 2016/17 for Sindh was Rs. 249 millions ($2.4 million).

Most people usually disburse *Zakāt* obligation privately. They also pay *Sadqāt* individually to the poor people or to the organizations working for the welfare of the poor people. According to the Pakistan Center for Philanthropy, the total estimated charitable giving in Pakistan stands at Rs. 300 billion ($2.8 billion) in 2015. In the provincial studies, the amount contributed in the year 2013 stood at Rs. 67.9 billion ($0.65 billion) in Sindh (Pakistan Center for Philanthropy, 2013). Additionally, the amount contributed in the year 2010 stood at Rs. 103.69 billion ($1 billion) in Punjab (Pakistan Center for Philanthropy, 2010). A recent estimate by Pakistan Peace Initiative (2017) contends that people in Pakistan pay around Rs. 554 billion ($5.31 billion) in charity every year.

To give just a glimpse of how important the third sector is in the sociodemography of Pakistan, a few major success stories are mentioned. The Sindh Institute of Urology and Transplantation (SIUT) is a privately funded dialysis and kidney transplant center in Karachi. It is the country's largest public sector health organization providing services free of any cost. Shaukat Khanam Cancer Hospital and Research Center is the country's largest cancer hospital with an annual budget of Rs. 10 billion ($96 million). The hospital was built through private donation drive in 1994. Edhi Foundation, which originated from Karachi, holds the world record for the "largest volunteer ambulance organization". Indus Hospital in Karachi provides free of cost treatment. It is a private hospital working on donations and has treated 2.3 million patients during 2007–2016. Among the numerous food distribution centers, Saylani Welfare Trust provides meals twice a day to more than 50,000 people in the city of Karachi alone free of cost.

12.5.2 Institution of Waqf in Pakistan

Waqf implies donating identified physical assets by the donor (*Waqif*) for the continuous benefit of the community or a specified group of beneficiaries. A Cash *Waqf* is "the confinement of an amount of money by a founder(s) and the dedication of its usufruct in perpetuity to the welfare of society". Donating a piece of land for construction of masjid, school or hospital is an example of *Waqf*. *Mutawalli* or *Nazir* is the trustee who safeguards the asset and ensures that the asset is used for the intended purposes and the benefits are enjoyed by the specified beneficiaries. Table 12.6 summarizes the distinctive features of *Zakāt*, *Waqf* and *Sadaqah*.

In history, *Awqaf* provided several public goods and services, such as roads, water and sewage system. Educational institutions and hospitals were also established using the model of *Waqf* (Kuran, 2001). Even in current times, *Awqaf* can help in capacity building and wealth creation through building all forms of capital including human (education and health institutions and services), physical (roads and infrastructure) and financial capital (*Waqf*-based microfinance and banks).

Table 12.6 Distinctive Features of Islamic Philanthropy

Zakāt	*Waqf*	*Ordinary Sadaqah*
• Compulsory • Heads of **Zakāt** are specified in Holy Qur'an. • Specific financial flows.	• Voluntary • Beneficiaries can be anyone. • The flow of benefits on a sustained basis.	• Voluntary • Beneficiaries can be anyone. • Specific financial flows.
• Transfer of ownership to a living Muslim is necessary. Hence, allocation and disbursement are usually contemporaneous.	• Naturally open to institutionalization due to the donation being of an asset that remains intact or has potential to grow.	• May or may not be open to institutionalization depending on the nature and value of *Sadaqah*.

The legal framework for *Waqf* in Pakistan allows *Waqf* administrations headed by a Chief *Waqf* Administrator in all provinces. The Chief *Waqf* Administrator exercises complete powers in all matters relating to *Waqf*. In Pakistan, *Waqf* is mostly used in establishing mosques and maintaining shrines and, in some cases, Muslim graveyards. In the province of Punjab, *Awqaf* Department maintains a hospital and 14 dispensaries. At Data Darbar hospital, Rs. 28 million ($270,000) per annum is spent on healthcare. In the 14 dispensaries, the poor and needy patients are treated freely. In addition to that, Sindh government owns 31 *Waqf* properties in the Sindh province. In Pakistan, corporate *Waqf* is uncommon, except for Hamdard Laboratories. The main reason for the dormant *Waqf* sector in Pakistan owes to the negative effects of nationalization of public property during the 1970s (Malik, 1990). Table 12.7 summarizes the regulatory framework for *Waqf* administration around the world including Pakistan.

12.6 Conclusion & recommendations

Islamic finance in Pakistan is penetrating steadily in different financial sectors of Pakistan. Islamic banking market share is 15% in the overall banking assets, and the market share of Islamic mutual funds is 38% of the overall mutual fund industry. More than 100 *Sukuk* had been issued to date, and the government of Pakistan also meets its fiscal needs by issuing *Sukuk*. Nonetheless, Islamic microfinance is yet to realize its true potential, and there is a significant need for micro-financial services so that Islamic finance could facilitate consumption smoothing for net endowment-deficient poor people in Pakistan. Islamic redistributive institutions have potential, but their use and focus in policymaking are limited. Lack of trust between public and government has resulted in the very limited mobilization of *Zakāt* funds through the official government agencies in Pakistan. In addition to that, nationalization in the 1970s and non-standardization of rules have resulted in lower interest in the institution of *Waqf*. In light of this overview, we present following recommendations for the promotion of Islamic finance in Pakistan including both Islamic banking and Islamic social finance sector.

12.6.1 Policy recommendations for mainstreaming Islamic banking

- Islamic banks need to allow hassle-free account opening at banks for self-employed technicians, small entrepreneurs, tutors, housewives and students to increase their outreach among the general masses. Sustained growth in branchless banking is required to allow more outreach and to avoid the scale disadvantage in underprivileged areas.
- Given the fact that Islamic banks mobilize around 35% of their total deposits from customers in the form of *Qard*, it is important to emphasize that they shall provide at least 20% of their non-remunerative deposits

Table 12.7 Comparison of Regulatory Framework in Regional Countries

Attributes / Countries	*Malaysia*	*Indonesia*	*Singapore*	*India*	*Pakistan*	*Bangladesh*
Permanence	Temporal, perpetual	Temporal, perpetual	Perpetual	Perpetual	Perpetual	Perpetual
Creation	Only for one-third of assets. *Waqf*-Khas needs Sultan's permission. No private Mutawalli.	Permission to create. Registration required. Un-registration not punishable.	Only for one-third of assets. Registration necessary, else a fine.	Permission to create. Registration required. Un-registration not punishable.	Permission to create. Registration required. Un-registration not punishable.	Permission to create. Registration required. Un-registration not punishable.
Donor	Muslims and non-Muslims	Muslims and non-Muslims. Individuals as well as organizations.	Muslims	Muslims and non-Muslims	Muslims	Muslims and non-Muslims
Endowed assets	No mention of financial assets.	Specification of immovable and movable assets (including financial).	No specification of financial assets.	No specification of financial assets.	No specification of financial assets.	No specification of financial assets.
Beneficiary	Family *Waqf* not recognized.	Family *Waqf* not recognized.	Family *Waqf* not recognized.	Family *Waqf* recognized.	Family *Waqf* not recognized.	Family *Waqf* recognized.
Ownership and administration	*Waqf* is registered under the name of the Islamic Religious Council, which acts as a proprietor.	Badan Wakaf Indonesia does not own or manage the assets, but supervise.	Majlis Ugama Islam Singapura administers all *Waqf*.	State supervises, but does not own or manage assets.	State supervises. Chief Administrator appoints a manager to control, manage and maintain *Waqf* assets.	State supervises. But, the Chief Administrator can assume responsibility for administration by notification.
Trustee	Islamic Religious Council or Majlis is the sole nazir or trustee.	Private entities can be a trustee.	Private entities can be a trustee, but with a limited role.	Private entities can be a trustee.	Chief Administrator appoints a manager. Mosques/ shrines have religious purposes committee.	Private entities can be a trustee.

as *Qard* to the small farmers. This initiative will enable them to showcase their contribution to social development and impact the lives of underprivileged people more directly.

- Since agriculture provides employment to more than one-third of the people in the labor force, Islamic banks need to increase their financing share in agriculture, which is 0.4% of their financing mix as compared to the industrial average of 4.1% as at March 31, 2019 (Islamic Banking Bulletin March 2019, State Bank of Pakistan).

12.6.2 Policy recommendations for scaling up Islamic social finance

- To encourage the creation of *Waqf* other than in dormant real estate, private entities shall be incentivised to establish, manage and administer *Waqf* with the role of Chief Administrator being a monitor and supervisor. The Chief Administrator can oversee the preservation of *Waqf* assets, but the development function shall rest with independent managers who have the authority to make decisions.
- To retain public confidence, the Chief Administrator shall not have the right to appropriate property unless through the court of law if there is usurpation or abuse by the trustees. Minimal intervention in the routine administration is necessary in order to encourage the private establishment of *Waqf* on the demand side and for financial institutions and corporations to offer wealth management services, especially in Cash *Waqf*, on the supply side.
- The contributions to these *Waqf* by individual and corporate donors shall be made eligible for tax credit like it is the case with other recognized institutions in Section 61 of the Income Tax Ordinance 2001.
- If a donor dedicates real estate to an existing *Waqf* or establishes a new *Waqf*, the taxes related to registration and transfer of property shall be exempted.
- There should be a balance between development and preservation. To encourage private participation, there should be flexibility in the use of *Waqf* assets for investment in the form of leasing and financial investments. Furthermore, it is important to have risk management guidelines to ensure the preservation of *Waqf* assets.
- Provisions should be added in the existing laws regarding *'ibdāl'* (exchange) and *'istibdāl'* (substitution) of *Waqf* assets in order to revive the old *Waqf* assets, revitalize the existing ones and ensure sustainable existence and utility of *Waqf* assets.

12.6.3 Policy recommendations for financing social development by IFIs

- Islamic banks can facilitate the development of old *Waqf* assets by way of diminishing *Musharakah*, Sale and Leaseback and *Istisnā* in order to rebuild and renovate *Waqf* property for improved post-financing valuation as commercial buildings.

- Microenterprise *Waqf* can be established by Islamic banks to mobilize people's social savings in the form of Cash *Waqf* donations and then disburse these funds to the poor micro-entrepreneurs in the form of *Qard-e-Hasan*. Initially, these funds can be disbursed to shortlisted projects approved by business incubations centers at top business schools in the country.
- Family *Waqf* shall also be recognized in the law and can be offered by financial institutions, providing private wealth management services, such as by Takaful companies.
- Islamic banks like other banks collect donations for hospitals and educational institutions. Such institutions can mobilize funds through Cash *Waqf*, and the Islamic banks can become the collection, payment and investment agents. If a special tax credit is allowed to those who donate to Cash *Waqf* through banks, it will help in financial inclusion and documenting the philanthropic third sector activities.
- The government can mobilize the funds through Cash *Waqf* for the shortfall in the annual Public Sector Development Program (PSDP) by engaging Islamic banks as the collecting agent to gain wide public participation and engagement.
- *Waqf*-based IMFIs can be established where the seed capital can be mobilized through Cash *Waqf*. Islamic banks can use their existing resources, capacity and infrastructure to integrate financially excluded micro-borrowers into the financial system through this mechanism.

12.6.4 Policy recommendations for central bank for financial inclusion

- State Bank shall subsidize the financing cost of building and renovating old *Waqf* assets by employing Islamic banks for financing the building and renovation cost. The subsidy in financing cost will pay off in terms of post-financing valuation of *Waqf* property as commercial buildings. Malaysia has successfully used *Waqf* for building commercial malls and hotels, such as Pantai Puteri (Malacca), Regency Seri Warisan (Perak), Grand Puteri (Terengganu) and Klana Beach Resort (Negeri Sembilan). Such activity will increase employment in the construction sector which is interlinked with many other sectors.
- Since the contributors in Cash *Waqf* do not have commercial motives and repayment expectations from the financial institution, the State Bank shall allow opening microenterprise *Waqf*-based credit subsidiaries under Islamic banks with a reduced minimum paid up capital of Rs. 100 million instead of Rs. 300 million which is the lowest paid-up capital requirement for district-wide microfinance banks at the moment.
- In using the Family *Waqf* model, a special account for family members shall be allowed to be offered in banks in which the deposit will be kept

in safe custody by the bank and only withdrawable by nominated family members after a certain time lapse. As an investment agent, the Islamic bank would be allowed to use and invest these funds and be paid a fee for this service. For providing further incentive, Takaful coverage can also be offered simultaneously. This will help in financially including those individuals who save their money at home or in Bisee system (a kind of forced savings plan without any return) for the future needs of their family members.

- Agency fee income for managing payments and disbursements related to Cash *Waqf* shall be exempted or charged a reduced tax rate in order to route charitable spending through banks.
- State Bank shall allow and promote impact investing accounts where the donors will open a non-checking Cash *Waqf*-Am (General) account in which the proceeds will be invested by the bank and any returns on investments will top up the amount in Cash *Waqf*. The bank's fees will be proportionate to the returns generated. Periodic disbursements from the Cash *Waqf* account will be credited to the identified welfare institutions. The float money will provide liquidity to the bank and financial system. Routing payment inflows and outflows through banks will provide transparency to the individual donor.
- Since *Waqf*-based IMFIs have donor clients which do not have the primary motive of impact rather than profits, State Bank shall devise flexible rules regarding debt burden ratio, collateral and percent of financing allowed as a ratio of existing capital held by the micro-entrepreneur in the prudential and risk management guidelines.

References

Ahmed, H. (2002). Financing Micro Enterprises: An Analytical Study of Islamic Microfinance Institutions. *Islamic Economic Studies, 9*(2): 27–64.

Akram, M. M., & Afzal, M. (2014). *Dynamic Role of Zakāt in Alleviating Poverty: A Case Study of Pakistan*. Germany: University Library of Munich, 1–46.

Ashraf, A., Hassan, M. K., & J. Hippler III, W. 2014. Performance of Microfinance Institutions in Muslim Countries. *Humanomics, 30*(2): 162–182.

Azam, M., Iqbal, N., & Tayyab, M. (2014). *Zakāt* and Economic Development: Micro & Macro Level Evidence from Pakistan. *Bulletin of Business and Economics, 3*(2): 85–95.

Chachi, A. (2005). Origin and Development of Commercial and Islamic Banking Operations. *Journal of King Abdul Aziz University: Islamic Economics, 18*(2): 3–25.

Council of Islamic Ideology (1980). Report of the Council of Islamic Ideology on the Elimination of Interest from the Economy, CII, Pakistan.

Diamond, D. W. (1984). Financial Intermediation as Delegated Monitoring: A Simple Example. *Review of Economic Studies, 51*(3): 393–414.

Ernst & Young (2016). World Islamic Banking Competitiveness Report. Ernst & Young Group.

Global Islamic Finance Report (2018). Global Islamic Finance Report. London: Edbiz Consulting Group.

Kahf, Monzer. (1996). The Demand Side or Consumer Behavior: An Islamic Perspective. http://monzer.kahf.com/papers/english/demand_side_or_consumer_behavior.pdf.

Kahf, M. (1989). *Zakāt*: Unresolved Issues in Contemporary Fiqh. *Journal of Islamic Economics, 2*(1): 1–22.

Komi, M. E., & Croson, R. (2013). Experiments in Islamic Microfinance. *Journal of Economic Behaviour & Organization, 95*: 252–269.

Kuran, T. (2001). The Provision of Public Goods under Islamic Law: Origins, Impact, and Limitations of the *Waqf* System. *Law and Society Review, 35*(4): 841–898.

Malik, S. J. (1990). *Waqf* in Pakistan: Change in Traditional Institutions. *Die Welt Des Islams, New Series, 30*(1/4): 63–97.

Malik, S. J., Hussain, M., & Shirazi, N. S. (1994). Role of Infāq in Poverty Alleviation in Pakistan. *Pakistan Development Review, 33*(4), 935–952.

Naveed, A., & Ali, N. (2012). *Clustered Deprivation - District Profile of Poverty in Pakistan*. Social Development Policy Institute.

Obaidullah, M. (2008). *Role of Microfinance in Poverty Alleviation: Lessons from Experiences in Selected IDB Member Countries*. Jeddah: Islamic Research Training Institute - Islamic Development Bank.

Pakistan Center for Philanthropy (2010). Individual Philanthropy in the Punjab, Pakistan Center for Philanthropy.

Pakistan Center for Philanthropy (2013). Individual Philanthropy in the Sindh, Pakistan Center for Philanthropy.

Pakistan Peace Initiative (2017). Pakistan Peace Collective Project, Federal Ministry of Information and Broadcast.

Samad, M. A. (2014). Islamic Microfinance: Tool for Economic Stability and Social Change. *Humanomics, 30*(3): 199–226.

Shirazi, N. S., & Amin, M. F. (2009). Poverty Elimination through Potential *Zakāt* Collection in the OIC-member Countries: Revisited. *Pakistan Development Review, 48*(4): 739–754.

State Bank of Pakistan (2019). Islamic Banking Bulletin, March 2019.

State Bank of Pakistan (2015a). Knowledge, Attitude and Practices of Islamic Banking of Pakistan, State Bank of Pakistan, Karachi, Pakistan.

State Bank of Pakistan (2015b). National Financial Inclusion Strategy. A Strategy for Building a Dynamic and Inclusive Financial Sector to Support Pakistan's Growth in the 21st Century, State Bank of Pakistan, Karachi, Pakistan.

13 Translation of economic verses by Shaykh-ul-Islam Muhammad Tahir-ul-Qadri in the light of translation studies

Comparison with other translators

Shair Ali Khan

13.1 Introduction

Text transfer is a material movement as Anthony Pym mentioned (2010:13–14), considering translation a 'semiotic activity' which can represent and misrepresent its materiality. According to Pym, the complexity between the material and semiotic levels passes through various theoretical registers from culture to culture changes. This change, surely, has lasting effect on the target readers. Translation is the most difficult complex and serious text transferring activity. It needs full commands and high degree of bilingual competencies. Translation does not mean to deliver the meaning of the source text but it means to capture the linguistic, rhetorical, cultural and suprasegmental features. This text transfer activity becomes the most serious and dangerous while transferring the sacred word of God. Because God is beyond human faculty, due to which God selected His messengers to inculcate His divine deep-structured words to the human faculty. Every word of God is of great significance in terms of containing various kinds of meanings which the human intellectual cannot convert into other languages with the same rhetorical, linguistic and cultural backgrounds. Translation studies opened new horizons in the field of translation by introducing new theories, applying new principles and practicing (Nida & Taber, 1969) various types of translation strategies in a diversity of text types (Reiss, 1977). Quran translation is one of the complex and challenging fields of translation studies because it is the only book in the actual words of Allah. Quran is miraculous, and no such book can be produced by all the genius, intellectual and wise human; similarly, it is miraculous in its translation, and according to accepted views of scholars "the word of God cannot be translated by the word of human" (Hussain Abdulrauf).

13.2 Objectives of the study

The study aims at elaborating the translational strategies used by Dr Tahir-ul-Qadri in his translation in comparison with the translations of three renowned legendary translators of Quran. They are Muhamad Asad, M. Pickthall and

Abdullah Yousaf Ali. It, as well, aims to analyze the structural level of both source language and target language, the level equivalence in terms of terminologies specifically of economic nature.

13.3 Limitation of the study

The study is limited to the verses containing economic data. Five verses of economic dealings have been selected randomly. The translations of Dr Tahir-ul-Qadri along with three other renowned translators, i.e. Pickthall, Muhamad Asad and Abudllah Yousaf Ali, were selected.

13.4 Theoretical frame of the study

Theoretically, the study has applied the shifts of Catford (1965:73), i.e. level shifts and category shifts and the translation strategies by Viney-Darbelnet (Venuti 2000:84), Lawrence Venuti and Newmark (Newmark 1998:68–91).

13.5 Methodology

The study is descriptive and analytical in nature. For counting the words of verses, manual method has been applied, and for the translated words of the verses, the word count of Microsoft Word has been used.

13.6 Quran translation

The Quran is the ultimate source of guidance in all spheres of life. Economy is the power in the current world which is used by the big powers for terrible games with the poor communities. Since the time of Pharaoh till day the wealth is the source of ruling over the world. The Quran, looking to its critical role in human life, mentioned the wealth as 'qiyaam' (Nisa 4:5). The translation of the Quran is the most challenging task as compared to the translation of other religious texts as it is, by intention, extraordinarily structured to make it distinguished from the literary creation of human faculties. A slight deviation from the intended meaning of Allah, surely, damages the true sense of the Quran.

Scholars of high faculty tried, since its revelation, to transfer the message and meaning of Quran for the purpose of preaching and communication. So the companions of Prophet Muhammad (PBUH) who were sent to the kings and leaders applied the communicative approach of translation to convey the divine and prophetic messages.

The blessed and rewarded personalities tried to convert this text into other languages using their linguistic competencies and proficiencies. They rendered it by utilizing a range of translational strategies, principles and methods.

13.6.1 Quran translation of economic verses

Economy is the backbone of human progress. Conveying a clear concept of divine economic principles in target translation is essential and of great importance in today's human trans-culturalism and multi-socialism. Quran presented the principles and rules of economic justice, the use of wealth and dealings relating to trade and transactions. All these divine concepts need to be translated clearly with the same linguistic, rhetorical, aesthetic and spiritual senses.

13.6.2 Translational and linguistic analysis of economic verses

Example No. 1: Chapter 59: Verse 7

كَيْ لَا يَكُونَ دُولَةً بَيْنَ الْأَغْنِيَاءِ مِنكُمْ

No.	*Translators*	*Translations*	*Analysis*
1	Dr Mohammad Tahir-ul-Qadri https://www.islamawakened.com/quran/59/7/default.htm	This distribution system is to ensure that (the whole wealth) may not circulate (only) amongst the rich of you (but should circulate amongst all the classes of society).	The key singular word "doolatan" occurred as noun of the copula verb has been shifted to single verb "circulate" with mentioning the hidden and pre-mentioned subject of the copula verb at the beginning of the sentence and the additional linguistic contents to domesticate the Arabic sentence for target readers. The word "aghniya" has been translated semantically with "rich".
	M. M. Pickthall http://www.islam101.com/quran/QTP/QTP059.htm https://www.islamawakened.com/quran/59/7/default.htm	That it become not a commodity between the rich among you.	The singular noun has been translated with a single noun "commodity", the style is of old English, and type of translation is literal. No translation strategy has been applied. The word "aghniya" has been translated semantically with "rich". Formal equivalence is found.

No.	Translators	Translations	Analysis
	Muhammad Asad	So that it may not be [a benefit] going round and round among such of you as may [already] be rich.	The key singular word "doolatan" has been translated with a phrasal verb with four words, with two additional words to sublime the translation according to the Arabic text. The word "aghniya" has been translated semantically with "rich".
	Yusuf Ali (Saudi Rev. 1985) http://www.islam101.com/quran/yusufAli/QURAN/59.htm https://www.islamawakened.com/quran/59/7/default.htm	In order that it may not (merely) make a circuit between the wealthy among you.	The key word has been translated with verbal phrase of three words "make a circuit". The word "aghniya" has been translated lexically with "wealthy".

Analysis

According to the science of translation studies Dr Qadri has applied the strategy of shift (category shift), the strategy of annotation (explanation of related meanings) and the strategy of addition to convey the hidden interrelated linguistic features in his translation for the target readers applying the literal approach of translation. Whereas Pickthal did not apply any translation strategy with a formal equivalence at sentence level remaining close to the sentence structure of the Quran producing semantic translation. Muhammad Asad as well applied the strategy of shift (category shift) and addition and communicative. Yousaf Ali applied the strategy of addition only along with literal type of translation keeping in view the source sentence structure.

V.No.1	Translator	Strategies	No	Verse Words	Translated Words
	Dr Tahir ul Qadri	Shift Annotation Addition Literal translation Formal equivalence at sentence level	5	8	28
	Pickthal	Semantic translation Formal equivalence	2	8	11

(*Continued*)

V.No.1	*Translator*	*Strategies*	*No*	*Verse Words*	*Translated Words*
	Asad	Shift Addition Communicative translation	3	8	21
	Ali	Addition Literal translation Formal equivalence	3	8	15

Example No. 2

يَمْحَقُ اللَّهُ الرِّبَا وَيُرْبِي الصَّدَقَاتِ وَاللَّهُ لَا يُحِبُّ كُلَّ كَفَّارٍ أَثِيمٍ (بقرة-276)

S. No.	*Translator*	*Translation*	*Strategies*
	Dr Mohammad Tahir-ul-Qadri	Allah **eliminates** *usury (i.e., deprives usurious profits of prosperous growth)* and **multiplies alms gifts** (i.e., increases blessings of clean wealth manifold through charity donations). And Allah does not like anyone who is ungrateful and disobedient.	Two explanation strategies, Sentence/formal equivalence: Present sentence Semantic translation: Eliminate: semantic features.
	M. M. Pickthall	Allah hath **blighted** usury and **made almsgiving fruitful**. Allah loveth not the impious and guilty.	Semantic translation: Blight contains the semantic features covering Quranic meaning. Perfect tense, no sentence equivalence
	Muhammad Asad	God **deprives usurious gains** of all blessing, whereas He **blesses** charitable deeds with manifold increase. And God does not love anyone who is stubbornly ingrate and persists in sinful ways.	Formal equivalence Communicative translation
	Yusuf Ali (Saudi Rev. 1985)	Allah **will deprive** usury of all blessing, but **will give increase** for deeds of charity: For He loveth not creatures ungrateful and wicked.	Formal equivalence Communicative translation

Analysis

The verse contains two economical terminologies (الربا و الصدقات) in objective case preceding two verbs of present and future features (يمحق و يربي). Dr Qadri and Pickthall translated the first verb with single equivalent verbs "eliminates" and "blighted", the first term with "usury", whereas the other two translators explained the meaning of the Arabic first verb. Asad translated the first term with explanatory words, whereas Ali translated with one word as Dr Qadri and Pickthall have done. Dr Qadri translated the second verb "يربي" with one verb "multiplies", Pickthall used two words "made fruitful", Asad used four words "blesses with manifold increase" and Ali used two words "give increase". Dr Qadri and Asad used present indefinite tense whereas Pickthall used present perfect tense and Ali used future tense. Dr Qadri used strategy of explanation and addition in brackets inside the text to remove the ambiguity from the verbs that contain connotative religious and spiritual meanings. Dr Qadri and Pickthall focused on the semantic aspect of the verbs, whereas the other two translators focused on the explanatory aspect of the verbs and terms.

V.No.2	*Translator*	*Strategies*	*No of Strategies*	*Verse Counts*	*Translated Words*
	Dr Tahir ul Qadri	Explanation Formal equivalence Semantic translation	3	13	34
	Pickthall	Semantic translation	1	13	15
	Asad	Formal equivalence Communicative translation	2	13	30
	Ali	Formal equivalence Communicative translation	2	13	23

Example No. 3

وَلَا تَأْكُلُوا أَمْوَالَكُم بَيْنَكُم بِالْبَاطِلِ وَتُدْلُوا بِهَا إِلَى الْحُكَّامِ لِتَأْكُلُوا فَرِيقًا مِّنْ أَمْوَالِ النَّاسِ بِالْإِثْمِ وَأَنتُمْ تَعْلَمُونَ (بقرة-188)

S. No.	*Translator*	*Translation*	*Strategies*
	Dr Mohammad Tahir-ul-Qadri	And do not **eat up** one another's **wealth** amongst yourselves through **injustice**, nor take wealth to **the authorities** (as a bribe) so that, this way, you may (also) **swallow** a portion of others' **wealth** unfairly, whilst you are aware (that this is a sin).	Addition Literal translation Shift of meaning: specific 'hukkam' to general: authorities Formal equivalence
	M. M. Pickthall	And **eat not up** your **property** among yourselves in **vanity**, nor seek by it to gain the hearing of **the judges** that ye may knowingly **devour** a portion of the **property** of others wrongfully.	Semantic translation Shift of meaning: general 'hukkam' to specific: judges
S. No.	*Translator*	*Translation*	*Strategies*

Muhammad Asad	AND **DEVOUR** NOT one another's **possessions wrongfully**, and neither employ **legal artifices** with a view to **devouring** sinfully, and knowingly, **anything** that by right **belongs to others**.	Communicative translation Shift of meaning: general 'hukkam' to 'legal artifices' specific
Yusuf Ali (Saudi Rev. 1985)	And do not **eat up** your **property** among yourselves for **vanities**, nor use it as **bait for the judges,** with intent that ye may **eat up** wrongfully and knowingly a little of (other) people's **property.**	Addition Semantic translation Shift of meaning : 'hukkam' as 'judges'

Analysis

The verse discusses economic dealings with one another in a social set up. The key words are 'eat up, devour, swallow', 'wealth or property or possessions' and 'authorities, judges and legal artifices'. These words are open for various interpretations due to their ambiguous nature. Three translators use the word 'eat up' for the first verb, whereas one of them used the word 'devour' for the word 'أموال'. Dr Qadri used the world 'wealth', two translators used the word 'property' and one used the word 'possession'. The verbs 'eat up or devour' with 'property' and 'possession' are not familiar as these cannot be eaten. But the word 'wealth' has a semiotic relation with eating because wealth is the source of all the edibles. Dr Qadri's translation tries to familiarize the word of God to the general public by selecting a semantically acceptable word. The translation of "الحكام" is as well open to various interpretations. Dr Qadri translated it as "authorities", two translators translated as "judges" and one of them translated as "legal artifices". The word 'judges' is specific but used by some exegetes such as Qushairi,[1] Ibni Abbas,[2] Jalalain,[3] while the word 'authorities' is more comprehensive and used in exegeses such as Kashani[4] that covers all sorts of judgments issued by the tribal and communal systems in various societies and cultures.

V.No.3	*Translator*	*Strategies*	*No of Strategies*	*Verse Counts*	*Translated Counts*
	Dr Tahir ul Qadri	Addition Literal translation Shift of meaning Formal equivalence	4	26	44
	Pickthall	Semantic translation Shift of meaning	2	26	34
	Asad	Communicative translation Shift of meaning	2	26	27
	Ali	Addition Semantic translation Shift of meaning	2	26	35

Example No. 4

يَا أَيُّهَا الَّذِينَ آمَنُوا لَا تَأْكُلُوا أَمْوَالَكُم بَيْنَكُم بِالْبَاطِلِ إِلَّا أَن تَكُونَ تِجَارَةً عَن تَرَاضٍ مِّنكُمْ وَلَا تَقْتُلُوا أَنفُسَكُمْ إِنَّ اللَّهَ كَانَ بِكُمْ رَحِيمًا (نساء-29)

Dr Mohammad Tahir-ul-Qadri	***O believers***! Do not **devour** one another's **wealth unlawfully** amongst yourselves unless it is a **trade** by your **mutual agreement** and *do not* ***kill*** *yourselves*. Surely, ***Allah*** is Kind to you.	Class Shift: translation of vocative sentence with one noun. Literal translation Adaptation: Allah
M. M. Pickthall	***O ye who believe!*** **Squander** not your **wealth** among yourselves in **vanity**, except it be a **trade** by **mutual consent**, and **kill** not one another. Lo! ***Allah*** is ever Merciful unto you.	Literal translation Adaptation: Allah
Muhammad Asad	***O YOU who have attained to faith***! Do not **devour** one another's **possessions wrongfully** – not even by way of **trade** based on **mutual agreement** – and do not **destroy** one another: for, behold, **God** is indeed a dispenser of grace unto you!	Literal translation Shift of sentence: vocative past indefinite into present prefect
Yusuf Ali (Saudi Rev. 1985)	***O ye who believe!*** **Eat not up** your **property** among yourselves in **vanities**: But let there be amongst you **Traffic and trade** by **mutual good-will**: Nor kill (or destroy) yourselves: for verily ***Allah*** hath been to you Most Merciful!	Literal translation Addition strategy Adaptation: Allah

Analysis

The verse contains key concepts of economic dealings in Quranic specific terms such as "الباطل تراض و تجارة وأموال". All these terms contain, in their semiotic dress, rules and principles of Islamic economics. In addition to these terms, it contains vocative expression, proverbial expression in negative imperative forms which need to be translated carefully. From translational point of view Dr Qadri used the strategy of shift while translating the first vocative phrase. He used the strategy of adaptation in translating the word of dignity "Allah" and a literal method for translating the proverbial expression. Pickthall and Ali translated the vocative phrase in literal method, whereas Asad translated the vocative past indefinite into present prefect form in a literal method which is a shift of category. Pickthall and Ali adapted the Arabic word "Allah". Pickthall and Ali adopted the literal method keeping in view the structure of

Quranic sentence, whereas Dr Qadri and Asad adopted the structure of target language in order to make the translation faithful but they both translated the proverbial expression in literal method.

V.No.4	*Translator*	*Strategies*	*No of Strategies*	*Verse Counts*	*Translated Counts*
	Dr Tahir ul Qadri	Class Shift Literal translation Adaptation: Allah	3	29	31
	Pickthal	Literal translation Adaptation	2	29	32
	Asad	Literal translation Shift of sentence	2	29	43
	Ali	Literal translation Addition strategy Adaptation	3	29	39

Example No. 5

وَأَوْفُوا الْكَيْلَ إِذَا كِلْتُمْ وَزِنُوا بِالْقِسْطَاسِ الْمُسْتَقِيمِ ذَٰلِكَ خَيْرٌ وَأَحْسَنُ تَأْوِيلًا (بني إسرائيل 35)

Dr Mohammad Tahir-ul-Qadri	And **measure in full** *whenever* you measure out **(anything),** and ***(when you weigh anything)*** weigh with a **straight balance**. This **(honesty)** is better, and much better **with regard to its consequence (as well).**	Strategy of addition Strategy of explanation Modulation Communicative translation
M. M. Pickthall	**Fill the measure** <u>*when*</u> ye measure, and weigh with a **right balance**; **that is meet,** and better in the **end.**	Semantic translation Formal equivalence
Muhammad Asad	And **give full measure** <u>*whenever*</u> you measure, and weigh with a **balance that is true**: this will be ***[for your own]*** good, and best in the end.	Strategy of addition Class Shift: translating noun in a sentence Faithful translation
Yusuf Ali (Saudi Rev. 1985)	Give full measure <u>*when*</u> ye measure, and weigh with a **balance *that is straight***: that is **the most fitting** and the most **advantageous in the final determination.**	Class Shift: single noun with a sentence Strategy of explanation Communicative translation

Analysis

The verse contains very important economic and trade dealings that have far effects on the social life. The worthy translators tried their best to convey the true sense of God's message. They applied various translational strategies for this purpose. Dr. Qadri and Asad applied the strategies of addition within the holy text to remove the ambiguity and make the text cohesive and coherent, whereas Asad and Ali both applied the strategy of category (class) shift. Along with that Dr Qadri and Ali applied the strategy of explanation. Pickthall kept in consideration the sentence level of the source text while translating, where Dr Qadri, on the other hand, applied the strategy of modulation in translating the first imperative verb and object where he converted the object "الكيل" as verb "measure" and the verb "اوفوا" as prepositional phrase "in full". Dr Qadri used the strategy of explanation as the word "تأويلا" in many words "**with regard to its consequence (as well)". Ali's example of explanations is 'most advantageous in the final determination'.** The translation of Pickthal and Asad is economical in words, whereas Dr Qadri and Ali's translations are less economical.

Grammatically Dr Qadri, Pickthall and Asad used the cohesive devices to make the text coherent inside the text. Dr Qadri used the punctuation mark 'full stop' at the end of two consecutive commands, de-connecting the following sentence and used the strategy of addition by adding the word 'honesty' putting an abstract noun in brackets for the actions of weighing, whereas Pickthall used semicolon (;) for connecting the following sentence with the previous two commands. Asad and Ali both used colon (:) for showing the connection between the commanding sentences and the resulting sentence (Figure 13.1).

V.No. 5	*Translator*	*Strategies*	*No of Strategies*	*Verse Counts*	*Translated Counts*
	Dr Tahir ul Qadri	Strategy of addition Strategy of explanation Modulation Communicative translation	3	14	33
	Pickthal	Semantic translation Formal equivalence	2	14	20
	Asad	Strategy of addition Class Shift Faithful translation	3	14	27
	Ali	Class Shift Communicative translation	2	14	27

13.6.3 Translational strategies/methods analysis

No.	*Translators*	*Total Used Strategies*	*Total Verse Count*	*Translated Count*
1	Muhammad Tahir ul Qadri	18	90	170
2	Muhammad Marmaduk Pickthal	9	90	112
3	Muhammad Asad	12	90	148
4	Abdullah Yousaf Ali	12	90	139

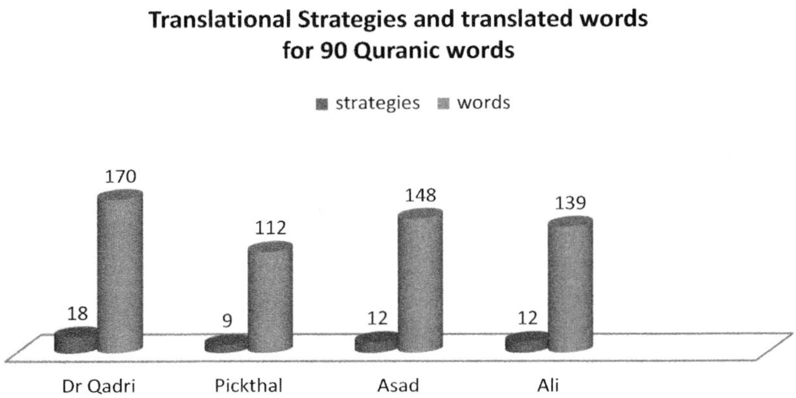

Figure 13.1 Translational strategies and translated words for 90 Quranic words.

13.7 Conclusion

The Quran is the word of God, full of literary and linguistic sciences. The translator spent their full faculty to transfer this linguistic and literary treasure into the world languages. During their translating activity they applied various kinds of strategies to translate the text and transfer the words with their semiotic feature faithfully. The discussion can be concluded in the following points:

Findings

- All the four translators used various kinds of strategies in their translation.
- They used the strategies of addition within the holy text to remove the ambiguity and make the text comprehendible for the common readers.

- They have produced literal, semantic and faithful types of translations.
- They have applied the strategy of adaption for the words which need to be adapted because the semantic meaning of the adapted word cannot be rendered.
- Some of the translators applied the strategies of shifts of category and level.
- The strategy of modulation is as well observed in the selected examples.
- The strategies are found in the translation of the verses.

Final Remarks

- Dr Qadri translations contain more translational strategies than other translations including the strategies of addition, modulation, shifts and explanation to remove the ambiguity from the text in order to familiarize it to the general public. Sometime Dr Qadri adopted literal method of transition but most of the time he remains faithful in his rendering by using cohesive devices. Dr Qadri served his full faculty to convert the word of God: the most complex text of the world that is why his translation is less economical.
- Pickthall translation is an example of keeping full consideration of sentence structure of Quran. It, sometimes, forms very literal type of translation due to remaining close to the Quranic structure. He used the punctuation markers as cohesive devices for streamlining the meaning of the Quran. His translation is very much economical.
- Muhamamd Asad translation is as well economical but he sometimes uses strategies to make the text coherent. He used the strategies of addition, explanation and shifts. He sometimes adopts a semantic style of translation.
- Abdullah Yousaf Ali as well used strategies for removing the ambiguities from the text and making it cohesive and coherent. His translation is less economical in words. He used the strategies of shifts, addition, explanation, adaptation and literal translation.

Notes

1 www.altafsir.com/Tafasir.asp?tMadhNo=3&tTafsirNo=108&tSoraNo=2&tAyahNo=188&tDisplay=yes&UserProfile=0&LanguageId=2
2 www.altafsir.com/Tafasir.asp?tMadhNo=2&tTafsirNo=73&tSoraNo=2&tAyahNo=188&tDisplay=yes&UserProfile=0&LanguageId=2
3 www.altafsir.com/Tafasir.asp?tMadhNo=1&tTafsirNo=74&tSoraNo=2&tAyahNo=188&tDisplay=yes&UserProfile=0&LanguageId=2
4 www.altafsir.com/Tafasir.asp?tMadhNo=2&tTafsirNo=107&tSoraNo=2&tAyahNo=188&tDisplay=yes&UserProfile=0&LanguageId=2

References

Asad, M. 1980. ***The Message***. Dar ul Andalus: Gibralarter.

Ali, Y. 1983. *The Holy Quran: The Translation and Commentary*. Beirut: Dar Al- Arabia.

Catford, J.C. 1965. *A Linguistic Theory of Translation*. London: Oxford University Press.

Islamawakened.com

Example 1: https://www.islamawakened.com/quran/59/7/default.htm
Example 2: https://www.islamawakened.com/quran/2/276/default.htm
Example 3: https://www.islamawakened.com/quran/2/188/default.htm
Example 4: https://www.islamawakened.com/quran/4/29/default.htm
Example 5: https://www.islamawakened.com/quran/17/35/default.htm

Newmark, P. 1998. *A Text book of Translation*. London: Printice Hall.

Nida, E.A., & Taber, C.R. 1969. *The Theory and Practice of Translation*. Leiden: E. J. Brill.

Pym, A. 2010. *Translation and Text Transfer: An Essay on the Principles of Intercultural Communication*. Tarragona: Intercultural Studies Group.

Qadri, Mohammad Tahir ul. 2012. The Glorious Quran. Online Link: http://www.irfan-ul-quran.com/quran/english/index.html

Reiss, K. 1977. Text Types, Translation Types and Translation Assessment, translated by A. Chesterman, ed. (1989), in *Readings in Translation Theory*, pp. 105–15. Helsinki: Finn Lectura.

Venuti, L. 2000. *Translation Studies Reader*. London: Routledge.

14 Drawing inferences from Ali ibn Abi Talib's Teachings on social and collective responsibility for a fair and just economy

Najam Abbas

14.1 Introduction

14.1.1 Ali ibn Abi Talib's teachings for a just economic conduct of the government

There are several reasons to focus on Ali ibn Abi Talib and his reign as the last among the four rightly guided caliphs. Ali was the closest male member among all the Prophet's relatives as cousin and as a reminder of support the Prophet received from his uncle and Ali's father Abu Talib. Ali's five years as the caliph (r. 35–40/656–660) marked a crucial transition phase in economic and social dynamics of that time. That is why a close examination of Ali's vision about how economic affairs ought to run in the society, how he assumed the role of a spiritual leader and exercised his authority, and his words comes in a mentor's voice when issuing instruction and entailing correction of the waywardly.[1]

When looking for Ali ibn Abi Talib's teachings for a just economic conduct of government, it is important to see how Ali ibn Abi Talib perceived the causes of poverty. He noted three major flaws, namely, absence of freedom, equal opportunity and fair access to resources which creates both poverty and disparity. Ali ibn Abi Talib pursued genuine justice, fair and equal distribution since for him the objective of rule was the pursuit and promotion of justice. Hence, he viewed deprivation and disparity as injustice.

The chapter shows how – in his guidance about the ideal conduct of the Islamic government concerning economic matters through his theoretical elaborations, specific advice and practical actions – Ali ibn Abi Talib teaches us to look at poverty in a comprehensive and holistic manner to address its broad multifold dimensions encompassing economy, polity and society. That is why we find Ali ibn Abi Talib pursuing a three-track approach consisting of (1) persuading the people through rhetorical appeals and persuasion to encourage positive practices in society at large, combined with (2) attempts to set ethical standards for senior state administrators to follow, backed by (3) practical measures to curb negative traits and tendencies among public officials to ensure they do not deviate from their social and collective responsibilities.

14.1.1.1 Vision of value-based governance

This chapter highlights how Ali ibn Abi Talib's deliberations show a clear commitment to comprehensive justice. Ali ibn Abi Talib not only addressed the symptoms of injustice but treated their roots as part of an all-encompassing effort covering legal, social as well as economic aspects of life.

This analysis of Ali ibn Abi Talib's vision and action will cover several important aspects: (1) the standards Ali ibn Abi Talib wished for his authorities to meet; (2) the reforms Ali ibn Abi Talib proposed for the ruling authorities; and (3) the qualities, objectives and values he required of his officials to help enable the delivery of economic justice.

14.1.2 The tools Ali ibn Abi Talib devised for addressing economic injustice

With the intention of providing guidance about the rights of the ruler and the ruled over, Ali ibn Abi Talib put forward the guidance for reforming the individuals, instruments and institutions of administration along with laying down a code for ethical practices and professional conduct for all members of society.

This chapter explains that Ali ibn Abi Talib not only provided theoretical policies but also spelled out measures for their practical implementation. Ali ibn Abi Talib observed that tax collectors and revenue administrators tend to pursue a short-term approach for fulfilling immediate needs for quick gains. He instead encouraged them to depart from such a practice and broaden their perspectives to consider long-term gains which can be accrued by applying taxes more considerately in order to contribute towards much wider economic gains. In this manner he helped the treasury officials to get their overall perspective rights. He attempted to shift the prevalent approach from a narrow focus on revenue collection to a wide-ranging vision for growth, development and collective progress.

Concrete guidelines were provided concerning all fiscal and economic matters and appropriate mechanisms to address them. The practice of not withholding public money implied that it was disbursed when the need arose and not held back to enrich the state. Ali ibn Abi Talib set up a clear framework for a just and fair economy by promoting a sense of trusteeship to treat natural resources as a responsibility for the larger and lasting interests of not only present but also future generations.

14.1.2.1 Muslims' public treasury: approaches for raising state revenues

For Ali ibn Abi Talib the collection of tax revenues was a means rather than an end. He was very clear that the priority was not raising funds but ensuring the overall well-being of the larger Muslim community.

14.1.2.2 Promoting positive practice in the market

This chapter also discusses how Ali ibn Abi Talib took practical measures to ensure fair practice in the market (not as a one-off step but as a regular exercise). This reflects the significance and the priority he attached to a fair and just running of the market as something which touches the lives of the common people on a daily basis. His direct interaction and close contact with the people was aimed to encourage them to deal fairly. His regular check-up visits to Kufa's markets too served as a reminder of the sense of ethical and moral accountability present and alive in the society generally and among the traders specifically.

14.2 Review of selected literature on Ali ibn Abi Talib's teachings about justice through approach, attitude and action

In recent years, contemporary scholars of Islamic economics and Islam's distributive justice are drawing pertinent guidance from the primary sources such as Nahj al-Balagha (in Arabic, Farsi and English). Furthermore, secondary sources comprising of contemporary publications published from Iran, Iraq and Lebanon offer a more contemporary rendering of what inferences could possibly be drawn from Ali ibn Abi Talib's sermons, letters and axioms.

In addition to guidance directed at government functionaries, Ali ibn Abi Talib also issues instructions to individuals through his sermons and advice to the common man. The overall purpose was to improve the mindset, inculcate correct attitudes, as well as to cultivate a purpose-driven and principle-led way of life for members of the community both individually and collectively. Taken together, these teachings encourage people to uphold and exercise justice in a just and responsible manner. In both his speech and conduct, Ali ibn Abi Talib paid due attention to the importance of economic production and has set his own example as one of the active participants in economic activities: encouraging others to take full advantage of available opportunities, putting skills to productive purposes, donating wealth to the poor and using resources to serve the Muslim community.

In his doctoral thesis Depiction of Ali in Jahiz's works, Adrian J De Gifis notes, 'Alī's eloquence is characterized by lucidity, concision and moral intention. As a historical phenomenon, ancient wisdom designates a distinctive cultural tradition and intellectual activity in the history of the Middle East. One set of his sayings appeals to reason and conscience, and others cater to the followers' desire for knowledge and understanding. This is evident in varying forms found in Ali ibn Abi Talib's sayings, whose primary objective was to educate using the sentence, wise saying or proverb; the admonitory precept; or maxim and meditative advice.[2]

Most of Ali ibn Abi Talib's sayings which were later collected in writing form have in common the theme of wisdom as a distinct virtue of life and thought employing a characteristic vocabulary. Prominent among his principle methods of teaching are instruction and counsel or persuasion.

As a crucial component of preaching, eloquence has the power to persuade its audience tacitly. Since brilliant exposition delivered in a beautiful language can prove quite effective, hence, Ali ibn Abi Talib "attempted to stir the hearts and minds of his audience with his verbal artistry, rhythmically compounding his lessons in cadenced parallelisms and vivid metaphors".[3]

Ali ibn Abi Talib's sayings are often marked by alliteration or assonance and are made memorable by vivid imagery or witty expression. It is noted by Walter Ong that in an oral culture verbal expression is mnemonic. "In a primary oral culture, to solve the problem of retaining and retrieving carefully articulated thought, you have to do your thinking in mnemonic patterns, shaped for ready oral recurrence".[4]

For Arabs, a way of thinking and an attitude to life traditionally emphasized an experience, reasoning, morality and general human concerns. Its audience was both its individuals and their wider social settings (community, society or nation).

Parallelism, "the hallmark of Ali's verbal creations, produces a strong acoustic rhythm, and pity sentences, repetition, assonance, and prose-rhyme augment this rhythm", notes Qutbuddin. She further points out a number of features of oral-based verbal production are discernible including vivid imagery, testimonial citation, additive rather than subordinate phrases, aggregative rather than analytic expositions, an agonistic tone and closeness to the human lifeworld, shown through the use of mundane objects and daily activities as metaphors physically showcasing abstract ideas.

14.2.1 Teaching and practice to encourage productive participation

One of the most important characteristics of Ali ibn Abi Talib was his attention to economic production. During the lifetime of the Prophet Muhammad and afterwards he remained engaged in different productive activities.

In the years after the migration to Medina, he is reported to have worked as a wage earner in the garden, pulling water from wells for brick making in order to support himself as well as the Prophet. At times, he would fetch one bucket of water in exchange for one date. Repetitively pulling water buckets from the well would cause blisters on his hands. But upon earning his day's wage he would collect his portion of dates and share them with the Prophet. Ali ibn Abi Talib discouraged an indolent attitude towards mundane work and said: "A man who is inert in his worldly matters would be even less active in improving his Hereafter".

14.3 Research methodology

This chapter analyses a selected range of works to help understand the views of Ali ibn Abi Talib regarding the idea of equitable economic distribution put to action as just practice. This chapter takes a critical approach to texts which can be descriptive or polemical. The methodology of this research is based on the analysis of historical descriptions as an approach employed as the primary means for the case study method. This then refers to the descriptive material assembled by the writers and commentators of history to shed light on the development of specific events. This chapter presents a set of guidelines which Ali ibn Abi Talib provided during his reign as the caliph from 35–40 A.H./656–661 A.D.

Scholars of Islamic Studies and History have written at length about Ali ibn Abi Talib's biography and about *Nahj al-Balagha*, i.e. the collection of his sermons, sayings and letters which is considered to be an apex work of eloquence. In recent years however, scholars and writers of social sciences have attempted to see what inferences relevant to today's society, such as economic equality and distributive justice, could be drawn from earlier history. Without going into deeper details, this chapter draws attention to examples citing attempts made by Ali ibn Abi Talib to inculcate and implement notions of economic justice.

A survey of contemporary literature in Arabic, Persian and Urdu helps us discern some useful guidelines comprising the following dimensions: (1) salient features of Ali ibn Abi Talib's vision towards a fair economy which is to be run with just practices; (2) the attitudes, morals and pressures necessary to put such a system in order; (3) ethical prerequisites to ensure justice which also entails observing and (4) specific criteria for value-based governance when appointing government functionaries.

The chapter looks at the guidance issued by Ali ibn Abi Talib, as communicated formally in writing through edicts and decrees, as well as verbally through maxims, sermons and instructions. It then focuses on classifying such guidance under different themes in order to analyse and interpret the motivations and objectives behind the texts and establish what possible linkages could be made between the caliph's overall vision and the instruction communicated by him. Step 1 in this study was to select and translate from Arabic and Persian texts relevant to the topic. Step 2 was to classify them under specific themes, while Step 3 was to conduct an analysis to understand the broader thinking behind the measures proposed, as well as their possible implications. Pursuing such analysis at further levels could help reveal the circumstances under which those guidelines were issued.

The selected examples serve as a case study of both the guidance offered and challenges linked to the prevalent social situation of the time. The descriptive method allows the cases to be placed in their fuller context, to reflect the conditions which existed at that time. The descriptive method enables the interpretation of historical statements as well as ascertains their present relevance. Using the method of exposition helps in analysing and explaining what motivated Ali ibn Abi Talib to invite the people to change the practices prevalent at that time. In this respect the main research method used in this chapter is the textual analysis of historical accounts and statements to present the social reality of those times, and thus to help draw inferences for the present day.

14.4 Results and discussion: vision of value-based governance

Ali ibn Abi Talib gave a vision to ensure the administrators he appointed aspired to meet the following objectives:

The first basis of such vision is to take steps against financial wrongdoing and administrative misconduct, and inculcate a culture of a clean and stable governance system based on integrity, equality and prevention of injustice.

According to Ali ibn Abi Talib, prerequisites for a good governance to flourish involve building it on the foundations of ethical values as well as laying down rules and regulations essential to run the system successfully. It ensues, first, raising awareness and consciousness for the fight against financial and administrative corruption for a sound cultural upbringing of society and the stable foundation of the economy. Ali ibn Abi Talib inculcated a care for protecting the wealth of the community as an important priority to ensure that it reached all who really deserved it.

A criteria for public officials is that (1) the appointee should be truthful with the people and himself and not to use deal-making as an end, (2) the official works to serve the common people and win their goodwill instead of working for their comrades and cohort's sake and (3) an individual who takes a bold stand to get rid of injustice and to be strict with those who mess with people's properties.[5]

14.4.1 Setting a moral compass

According to the Lebanese writer George Jurdaq: [Ali] neither showed pride nor humiliated himself unnecessarily. He presented himself as he was without any pretentions or artifice. He was free from affectation and hypocrisy. It is difficult to find a straightforward man like him. Once he purchased a bagful of palm-dates and was carrying them home. Some persons observed this and volunteered to carry the bag for him. He, however, told them politely that it was more appropriate for the head of the family to carry it by himself.[6]

In the recommendations made by him to his sons, Hasan and Husayn, he said: "Be enemies of the oppressors and supporters of the oppressed". He further said: "Be enemies of the oppressor even though he may be your near relative and support the oppressed person even though he may not be related to you and may be a stranger".[7]

Historical and traditional sources from both Sunni and Shia point out that Ali ibn Abi Talib was not inclined to either favour or discriminate against anyone when it came to distribution of wealth from the treasury. There was no priority given to those who had embraced Islam earlier than others, participated in more military campaigns than others, or by way of a relationship were closer either to the Prophet Muhammad or to Ali ibn Abi Talib. Thus, when shares from the treasury were distributed, nobody was treated preferentially on the basis of the tribe to which they belonged or whether they were an Arab or a non-Arab.[8]

When distributing funds, Ali ibn Abi Talib handed out an equal share to everyone, without favouring one individual over the other. A non-Arab slave would get a same share as his Arab master. When some people raised this issue with Ali ibn Abi Talib, he picked up a small twig from the ground, held it in between two fingers and said: I have gone through the whole Quran but couldn't find if even this much preference is mentioned there for Banū Isma'īl over Banū Isḥaq.[9]

14.4.2 Practice of not withholding public money

On occasions when Ali ibn Abi Talib inspected the treasury and found that the wealth deposited there was yet to be distributed, he would thus address the people: "I cannot spend a night in peace, if there is even a dirham left unspent from the treasury".

At times when some wealth arrived at the treasury, he would distribute it among the people declaring: I am not to act as a watchman to guard stored wealth locked for safekeeping.

In all matters, Ali ibn Abi Talib followed the Prophet Muhammad and his tradition. For him it was not possible to divide the shares except on the basis of equality. When the caliphate was transferred to Ali ibn Abi Talib, those who had enjoyed such privilege expected to benefit as before. However, Ali ibn Abi Talib refused to continue those practices and decreed that everybody must benefit equally from the public treasury, and it made some upset. In response to the request of such people the Imam gave a sermon to explain his principled position. It included the following points:

1. The end does not justify the means, although it was quite possible to win the backing of some people by awarding them a large amount to support a cause which was right in the first place, but Ali ibn Abi Talib did not agree to serve a noble cause by pursuing an unjust approach.
2. Public property and national wealth should not be used to win the approval and support of a few.
3. Those who support a cause motivated by the promise of monetary gains are quick to withdraw their support should their gains dry up.[10]

14.4.3 Muslims' public treasury: approaches for raising state revenues

From Ali ibn Abi Talib's instructions to his deputies in the provinces it could be deduced that governors were advised never to worry over pursuing a lenient approach to tax collection, because it serves as an indirect investment in developing the towns and provinces, and eases the burden over the people. This is because fair treatment of the people will win them over and will lead them to extend their increased support.[11]

14.4.4 Status for financial audit

Ali ibn Abi Talib reminded the tax collectors of their roles that as the treasurers of the people, they were also representatives of the community and the ambassadors of the Imam.

> The honour and status of revenue collectors attributes to the dignity, worth and dignity of the treasury. Until the credibility of the public treasury is established, the administrators cannot expect to earn importance and respect in the eyes of the people.

In his commentary on this matter, Ibn Abi al-Hadid offers three points: (1) The tax authorities are the trustees of the people's collective assets.[12] (2) They look after the interest of the community.[13] (3) The tax authorities are the government's emissaries to the people.[14]

14.4.4.1 The characteristics and functions of financial auditors

One of the main objectives of Islam is ensuring even justice for all members of the community. The realization of such a cause depends on numerous factors, among them the most important being the character displayed by the revenue collectors in terms of their beliefs, morals and behaviour. Therefore, Ali ibn Abi Talib on many occasions emphasizes the need to employ the most appropriate for the task. This, in some cases, such as tax collection, had an even greater significance.

Because the tax officer will collect the fruit of people's savings, and their labour and profit. It is necessary that such a person must possess a number of competencies.

14.4.4.2 Principle of fairness

Ali ibn Abi Talib has enumerated the following attributes and duties of the tax collectors: In relation to the collection of the taxes, exercise fairness and lenience in carrying out your duties. The significance of fair handling will result in taxpayers' satisfaction.

In Ali ibn Abi Talib's view a person who served others and shared their burden was the best and perfect individual. Ali ibn Abi Talib himself participated in many activities which contributed to lessen the burden of the poor and the needy.[15] He set an example for others and declined to live in lodgings far bigger than one's actual need.[16] Ali ibn Abi Talib wanted to set with his own example, a model of conduct for others to exercise moderation, and applied exacting standards on himself far more than demanding from others.[17]

In Ali ibn Abi Talib's view an ideal society is one in which everyone, especially those with less income, is able to meet their basic needs. The strategy to reach such an aim is that those with higher income refrain from extravagant expenditure over food items which can lead to wastage of excess food by some and shortage for those who can't afford to buy much.

14.4.4.3 Discouraging leaving the means of production idle

Ali ibn Abi Talib paid priority consideration to the universal provision of life's basic necessities.

Once a person saw Ali ibn Abi Talib carrying a load of palm kernels and asked what he intended to do with that. In response Ali ibn Abi Talib said: God willing, these kernels will produce 100,000 date trees. He then went on to sow them all, and each one of them grew into a date tree.[18]

When it came to distributing his own wealth, Ali ibn Abi Talib helped those in need, beginning with ones related to him. Yet, Ali ibn Abi Talib did not make any distinction between acquaintances and strangers and distributed an equal share among them. In this manner he set an example of how to serve the two ideals, namely, justice and unity in the community.[19]

Ali ibn Abi Talib toiled on the lands to make them useable and later donated them for helping the needy people. At the time of death, all he had left was his share of 700 dirham received from the public treasury.[20]

With a shovel in his hands as he dug hard, a well sprung out on the land of Yanbu. Those who witnessed this fortune cried that it is time of glad tidings for Ali's inheritors. However, this is how Ali ibn Abi Talib reacted on this occasion: "Tell this good news to all my inheritors that I am donating all this to the needy, poor and destitute". Ali ibn Abi Talib followed a similar conduct regarding all of his properties.[21]

Most of Ali ibn Abi Talib's income came from the lands, date palms and the wells as a result of his own hard work in putting those resources to productive use. Much of the revenue generated came as a result of him developing them from barren pieces of land abandoned by others owing to the difficult conditions faced and hardships involved.[22]

Ali ibn Abi Talib was not in favour of leaving any sources of production idle. In his view, wealth and other resources were meant to benefit the people, and hoarding them was tantamount to unjust use of such resources.[23]

14.4.5 Looking after the needy ones

In Ali ibn Abi Talib's opinion fulfilling the needs of a needy person is one of the foremost responsibilities and one that cannot be ignored under any circumstances. This remained an overriding concern throughout his life but even more so after he took over the caliphate's responsibility. He always kept thinking if there was any destitute who still struggled to find a loaf of bread.[24]

14.4.5.1 Monitoring the economic activities of the close ones

Although Ali ibn Abi Talib choose to lead a simple life as a role model, he considered it pertinent to caution his appointed authorities to beware of the deeds of their associates and relatives and remain mindful of possible consequences of such deeds.

In a perfect model of an Islamic state it was necessary to conduct comprehensive economic reforms. In this regard, when Ali ibn Abi Talib was informed that a relative of one of his appointees had confiscated a piece of land inappropriately, the Imam reminded the appointee of his obligations and ordered him either to get the property returned to its rightful owners or face his sword. Ali ibn Abi Talib took serious corrective and reformative measures to narrow the gap between the rich and the poor, for the social uplifting of the poor and to elevate their dignity.

14.4.5.2 Putting the priorities right

Below are the few examples highlighting some instances where Ali ibn Abi Talib is noted reminding both government officials and tradesmen and common folk of their social and collective responsibilities. He often reminded that it is the duty of governors to make the subjects prosperous in the first instance and then to think of collecting the revenue.

Once Ali ibn Abi Talib passed by a heap of garbage and pointed out that it had ended up here as the result of the miserly withholding excess stuff to themselves. If it were given out to the poor it would have contributed to the betterment of the society.

14.4.5.3 Promoting positive practice in the market

Ali ibn Abi Talib used to begin his day in Kufa by making the rounds from one market to another. He would stand at the entrance and thus address the people of each market:

O traders fear Allah Almighty; Extend the good and seek blessing by being easy on others; Adorn yourself with courtesy and refrain from swearing; Stay away from lies and wrongdoing and do justice to the oppressed; Do not deal in usury; Keep your balances accurate; Do not devalue people nor their possessions and do not cause mischief on the ground as spoilers.

He used to make the rounds in all the market places and would then sit with the people.

Ali ibn Abi Talib took practical measures to ensure fair practice in the market not as a one-off step but as a routine. This reflects the significance and the priority attached to a fair and just running of the markets as something which touches the lives of common people on a daily basis. His direct interaction and close touch with the people encouraged them to deal fairly. His regular check-up visits to Kufa's markets also kept the sense of ethical and moral accountability present and alive in the society and specifically among traders.

14.4.6 Ali ibn Abi Talib's dedication to social reform, economic governance and development

In its essence and purpose, the government following ideals of Imam Ali was (Alavi) was founded to pursue comprehensive reforms, especially economic, as it declared this to be a priority goal in its planning and policy. The Alawi government's reform programs in this sphere can be noted to be pursuing an outline of five fundamental objectives: (1) To end discrimination in the distribution of public funds, (2) Recovery of misappropriated public assets, (3) Prevention of amassing excessive wealth in the new government, (4) To strive for effort for developing lands for greater prosperity and (5) Social Cover for the disabled and the disadvantaged.

The first three are corrective measures to undo past wrongs which were preventing equity and growth. While the next two are initiatives aimed at alleviating poverty and addressing disparities between different sections of the society.

These measures were aimed to reduce the burden of the people and provide economic justice for the welfare of the individual. This is because the rule of Ali ibn Abi Talib considered it as a divine obligation and a religious necessity.

Thus, it is not limited to ensure material progress, but also to improve the quality of life at both individual and collective levels.[25]

Ali ibn Abi Talib's letters to a number of his officials serve as valuable historical documents evident of how he commanded the political, religious elements in his government to uphold the establishment of the rule of justice in the face of all temptations.

Ali ibn Abi Talib discouraged the amassing of wealth and accumulation of assets by officials or their close associates, from which no doors shall be opened under any excuse or religious justification.

14.4.6.1 Discouraging harmful practices

Alongside Ali ibn Abi Talib's sayings to encourage the desired economic practices, we find clear instructions and teachings of what practices to avoid. There are clear teachings discouraging unethical trade practices such as adulteration, cheating and fraud: Look after the traders' affairs before yourself or wherever they may be in your area. Know, along with this, that most of them are very narrow-minded, and awfully avaricious. They hoard goods for profiteering and fix high prices for goods. This is a source of harm to the people and a blot on the officers in charge.

Ali ibn Abi Talib issued clear instructions discouraging misleading or deception in day-to-day trade: "So give full measure and weight and do not defraud, diminish [the value of], people's goods, and do not work corruption in the earth, by way of unbelief and acts of disobedience, after it has been set right, through the sending of messengers [thereto]. That, mentioned, is better for you, if you are believers, [if you are] seekers of faith, so hasten to it" [Tafsir Jalalayn 7: 85].

The Imam said, however cheating rises in trade, loss and poverty follow. This is what the traders tend to indulge in but it causes poverty because cheating in the balance reflects negatively on the poor people directly. According to the Imam, remaining idle in the world negatively affects one's religious dimension, whereas engaging in "productive work and earning a livelihood helps in a person's pious life".

14.5 Conclusion

The passages referring to the selection of sayings (which encourages to adopt virtue and abandon vice) offer a series of precepts to illustrate how the moral order is realized at the levels of thought, speech and behaviour concerning the following:

a The contrasting way of life of the contended and the greedy persons;
b The appropriate rewards and retribution in store for each, respectively;
c The qualities and behaviour of the righteous as evoking admiration;
d Correcting the person focus of pursuits in the world;
e Encouragement to lead a purposeful, productive and pro-active life.

When referring to social responsibility a good research needs to acknowledge and appreciate where the teachings took their origins and evolved forth. It is in that context that a retrospective look will enable researchers to realize how Ali ibn Abi Talib's teachings sharpen the individual's conscience by encouraging them to embrace particular virtues and shun specific vices. The teachings are targeted at developing sound moral foundations for improving ethical standards to build the character of individuals and communities who are prepared in order to promote justice and counter injustice. In this regard, the teachings also draw attention to the question what it means to be productive for a person individually, for a family, community and a member of society at large. The guidance about the desired way of living points to (1) the desired approach to strive for one's well-being and (2) the need to admonish procrastination, and offers (3) encouragement for the pursuit of an active and productive life.

For a fuller appraisal of history, it is equally important to list those factors owing to which ideals on social and collective responsibility provided by Ali ibn Abi Talib could not find their way into practice. It is therefore essential to shed light on factors which impeded or prevented the implementation of those ideals that will encourage and enable the new researchers to a holistic and more meaningful appraisal of the economic vision, the guidelines for the just distribution and the challenges to efforts to implement those ideals on collective responsibility over the past centuries.

Notes

1 For a detailed biography detailing Ali ibn Talib and his vision of and pursuit for justice see Shah-Kazemi 2005.
2 De Gifis 2010.
3 Qutbuddin 2013, p. xvii
4 Ong further points out: Your thought must come into being in heavily rhythmic, balanced patterns, in repetitions or antitheses, in alliterations and assonances, in epithetic and other formulary expressions, … in proverbs which are constantly heard by everyone so that they come to mind readily and which themselves are patterned for retention and ready recall, or in other mnemonic form. Serious thought is intertwined with memory systems. Mnemonic needs determine even syntax. p. 34
5 It may also be added that upon summoning an official for accountability Ali ibn Talib reminded him: "It is not for you to be oppressive towards the ruled". This implies that an official should interact with the common people as per specified rules and regulations. This also implies that he is not superior to others by any exemption except for the authority vested in him to carry out his responsibilities.
6 Jordac 2010: 72
7 Jordac 2010: 66.
8 Yusufi 2008: 79
9 With reference to Ali ibn Talib's practice, it has been reported that whatever wealth was deposited in the treasury, he always distributed it among the people without favouring one over the other. When the two Ṭalḥa b. Abdullah and Zubayr b. al-Awam objected to equal distribution, Ali ibn Talib pointed out: "Didn't the Prophet of God distribute the wealth equally among the Muslims?" He further told them that it wasn't something that he decided himself or on his own wish: "You and I both know well that this practice was introduced and carried out by the Prophet himself".
10 Nūrī Hamadānī. 'Bayt al-Mal dar Nahj al-Balagha', *Sālnāma Al-Nahj*, vol. 19–20/Autumn/1385/2006.
11 Ayatollah Hassanzadeh thus elaborates: Paying sympathetic attention to the people's complaint and offering them tax concessions makes a positive impression of the government and hence in this way the rulers have little to lose. Because, first, developing the cities contributes to a rise in the revenues and profits; second, development of idle land improves the government's image; third, it causes people to praise and trust their government as they trust in their government's justice and fairness; and fourth, under the circumstances when the government needs to borrow from people and needs them to make some sacrifice financially or physically, they will respond readily (Rahmani 2000: 17 and 321).
12 Ali ibn Talib, letter 51.
13 Ali ibn Talib, letter 51.
14 Ali ibn Talib, letter 51.
15 Husayni 2007: 88.
16 Husayni 2007: 74.

17 Husayni 2007: 7.
18 Husayni 2007: 63.
19 Husayni 2007:95–96.
20 Husayni 2007: 97.
21 Husayni 2007: 97–98.
22 Husayni 2007: 112.
23 Husayni 2007: 116.
24 Husayni 2007: 92.
25 The above lines draw from Mustafa Jafar Pisha-Fard, Hukumati Alawi wa Ihtimam ba Istilahat Ijtimai Iqtisadi tuse wa rafah, Retrieved 12 November 2017 from http://tinyurl.com/MJpisha1

References

De Gifis, Adrian J. (2010). *The Theory of Virtuous Leadership in the Works of al-Jahiz*, Ph.D. Thesis, University of Chicago. Illinois: Chicago.

Husayni, Syed Rida. (2007). *Sirah Iqtisad Ali ibn Abi Talib*, Tehran. 1386 Shamsi.

Jordac, George. (2010). *The Voice of Human Justice*. Karachi: Islamic Seminary Publications.

Nūrī Hamadānī. Bayt al-Mal dar Nahj al-Balagha. *Sālnāma Al-Nahj*, vol. 19–20/ Autumn /1385/2006.

Pisha-Fard, Mustafa Jafar. (2000). Hukumati Alawi wa Ihtimam ba Istilahat Ijtimai Iqtisadi tuse wa rafah. *Hukumat-i Islami*, vol. 18, No. 4 (1379 Shamsi), pp. 56–97, Retrieved 12 November 2017 from http://tinyurl.com/MJpisha1

Qutbuddin, Tahera. (2013). *A Treasury of Virtues: Sayings, Sermons, and Teachings of Ali, edition and translation of the Dustur ma'alim al-hikam compiled by al-Qadi al-Qudai, with the Miat kalimah (One Hundred Proverbs) attributed to al-Jahiz*. New York: New York University Press.

Rahmani, Muhammad. (2000). Bayt al-Mal dar Nahj al-Balagha. *Hukumat-i Islami*, vol. 17, No. 3 (1379 Shamsi), pp. 315–346.

Rishad, Ali Akbar. (2000). *Danish-nama-i Ali ibn Abi Talib*, Vol. 7, Iqtisad (1380 Shamsi).

sssShah-Kazemi, Reza. (2005) *Justice and Remembrance—Introducing the Spirituality of Imam Ali*. London: I. B. Tauris.

Yusufi, Ahmad Ali. (2008). *Nizam Iqtisad Alawi, mabani, ahdaf wa usul rahbardi*. Tehran: 1387 Shamsi.

15 Pricing anomaly

Tale of two similar credit-rated bonds with different yields[1]

Mohamed Ariff, Alireza Zarei and M. Ishaq Bhatti

15.1 Introduction

This chapter is about what to expect as per the bond pricing theory, considering the market practices and the actual yields as observed in the normal bond market for two apparently similarly rated bonds. Type A bond is the mainstream bond, and Type B is a new bond instrument designed and traded under the product name *Sukuk* certificate. Both government bodies and corporations raise funds by issuing either type of bonds since these are marketed as equivalent instruments. There are several fixed income markets worldwide, where Type B securities are traded alongside Type A securities, so the research issue addressed in this chapter has global relevance to several other bond markets. About 65% of the Type B bonds are traded in Malaysia, so we chose this market given the data availability to test the pricing behavior in this country.

There is strong historical evidence and theory-based reasoning to expect returns to be identical for the two portfolios of bonds we study. *A priori* reasoning suggests similarly rated bonds with same tenor ought to be priced to yield the same returns to investors, especially since the issuers are known to decide to offer either one as a matter of choice: identical companies are known to raise money by issuing both types of bonds. Despite some argument that the two types of bonds have different contractual – indenture – provisions,[2] the price-relevant characteristics are the same. For example, a AAA-rated mainstream Type A bond issued with a ten-year tenor should be priced by investors to yield the same return to investors as an equivalent AAA-rated Type B bond with the same tenor. Hence, a Type B, the *Sukuk* certificate, should give investors equivalent return, on average, if the tenor and ratings are the same, despite one being the mainstream bond and the other being a new instrument that has begun trading just in the recent 20 years. Applying the existing debt pricing theory (Williams, 1938) as is widely used in the industry, investors would expect returns to be the same for both types of bonds. There is also literature-based evidence that equity market equivalent securities (see Hassan, 2001) and equivalent mutual funds (see Mansor, Bhatti, & Ariff, 2015, etc.) traded as Type A and Type B securities are priced to yield the same returns.

We explore the research question as to whether the debt markets for the mainstream bond and the new bond instruments behave differently as reported in Safari, Ariff, and Mohamad (2013). Since existing market practices relate to them as equivalent funding instruments, it is an interesting research question to verify if the claim of significant differences can be verified in this study using newer data with newer methodology. This is the motivation for undertaking this research to evaluate the pricing behavior of a new emerging market while the mainstream bond has been around for centuries.

15.1.1 Research issue

This study provides a report on how two equivalent pairs of Type A and Type B debt market securities are traded in the largest bond market in Malaysia. Since risk is involved in the case of corporate bonds, the returns of any pair of corporate bonds with treasury must have higher returns as predicted by the liquidity premium theory (Hicks, 1946; Keynes, 1930; Lutz, 1940). Hence, one should observe risk-free securities to have lower returns than the risky corporate ones across both types of bonds. Treasury bonds of lower tenor would have lower returns compared to treasuries of higher tenor; *a priori*, Type A and Type B securities should have the same returns to investors. On a similar reasoning, a AAA-rated firm issuing a mainstream bond and the same firm issuing a AAA-rated Type B bond with the same tenor (and with the same order of claim to payments under bankruptcy rules) should be priced such that the returns to investors of these equivalent securities ought to be the same. Market players believe this is the case as they go about trading in equivalent instruments, and the practice in the marketplace from our discussions with market participants suggests that they consider the pairs of equivalent instruments as substitutes fulfilling the same funding requirements of the issuers.[3] Conventional market practices and the current concepts in the bond markets as well as the scant literature on the pricing of Type B instruments also suggest that both types of bonds are substitutes that would yield identical returns to investors.

There are 16 other financial centers, where Type B securities (government bonds and AAA corporate bonds) are listed and traded as matching securities. The interesting facts about the two types of securities are that (i) the common debt securities and (ii) the new *Sukuk* debt certificates are traded side by side in the same markets.[4]

The mainstream bonds pay pre-negotiated interest payments in the form of ordinary annuity on semi-annual and/or quarterly intervals to common bondholders, while the Type B bonds pay similar fixed payments although the payments are called dividend distribution (based on profit-sharing) as ordinary annuity to investors. Conversations with scholars or industry people on this topic suggest that the two forms of returns to investors (coupons and dividends paid to fund providers) are apparently close and that they are unlikely to be any significant different in terms of rewards. The long-run relationship between the dividend distribution and mainstream bond returns is an unanswered question as well. There is a market perception, indeed an assumption, that the two yields are somehow interrelated, but not much is addressed about the long-run relationship. Moreover, this research efforts to also verify if the casual relationship of similar behavior is in fact observable in carefully structured tests. Third, data series are also available on corporate Type B yields. Thus, in the case of the zero-risk treasury bonds and the AAA corporate bonds, there should be a test with longer-dated and new data available.

Tests employed in this study are meant to examine the mean and median differences between the return series of respective securities.[5] The obtained statistics from test on the difference are expected to provide evidence for or against a significant difference in all the series. We also document a significant long-run equilibrium relationship (or cointegration) and Granger causality as existing between the respective variables. Therefore, our findings suggest that the pricing behavior of the two types of bonds is converging to a long-run equilibrium with a testable speed of adjustment or error correction. These appropriate tests applied to this topic are meant to produce more accurate test results on the topic. We provide useful information to estimate a fully specified model using an autoregressive distributed lag (ARDL) approach with lag orders being identified and optimized properly, after performing many iterations of regression equations.

The rest of the chapter is organized as follows. The next two sections cover relevant literature and test methodology. The results are presented in Section 4 on zero-risk treasury securities and AAA corporate bonds. The final section is a summary in Section 5.

15.2 Literature review

The literature is scant on Type B instruments as compared to the mainstream debt instruments. Safari et al. (2013) show that there is a significant difference across the two types of bonds and the difference ranges from 6 to about 56 basis points. A study by Mansor et al. (2015) suggests that the Type A and Type B securities have identical returns to investors across the samples of mutual funds. There is broad agreement that Type B financial instruments yield about the same return as the common share instruments. Overall, there seems to be no conclusive evidence for Type B (new) securities to have higher or lower yields. One argument receiving wide support why the two types of securities have similar yields is the empirical reality at this stage of development of Type B financial services industry, where market makers are simply cloning existing common old instruments to become the new Type B instruments by some simple design differences. However, the results of this study on two equivalent debt markets are about significant differences in matched pairs of bond instruments.

There is extensive literature on Type A bonds with studies going back to several decades. The relevant studies are those relating to rating, returns to investors, valuation models on bond pricing, and liquidity preference theory.

Williams (1938) and Lucas (1978) are relevant for the valuation model, which is used for computing the yield to maturity. The model is specified as:

$$V_0 = \sum_{t=1}^{\infty} \frac{CF_t}{(1+r)^t} \quad (1)$$

where

V_0: the value of the bond at time 0,
CF_t: the stream of expected cash flows at time t, normally the coupons and face value as the CFs, and
r: the discount or required rate of return.

Another theory is relevant for comparing the yields over time with different times to maturity. Lutz (1940) suggested that the difference is due to the time to maturity being a yardstick for how long the investors in the bond market are losing liquidity. For parting with liquidity, investors require higher yields to be offered by bond issuers for longer time to maturity.

While searching for data for this study, we noted that the Type B bonds are evaluated using Williams' model in the belief that investors treat the Type A and B bonds as equivalent for fair price calculation. Thus, Equation (1) is relevant for yield estimation while the idea of liquidity premium theory enables us to test if the yields of short-tenor bonds are lower than those of the medium- and long-term tenor bonds of Type A and B. Hence, the bond valuation theorem and the liquidity preference theories are directly relevant to this study. The support for the predictions of these theories is quite strong, so these ideas are generally accepted for bond price behavior. As for the evidence to support liquidity preference of investors, all standard finance books have references to studies that maturity of bonds determines the size of the investor returns (example, Bodie et al., 2018).

The final set of literature relates to bond rating and investor returns. It is widely known in the marketplaces that the yields of treasury bonds are lower than the yields of corporate bonds because the corporate bonds are riskier than the treasury bonds. This too is found in any standard textbook with citations to the empirical literature. Thus, the relevant literature on the two types of bonds is leaning towards the main idea that the yields of similarly rated bonds with a given maturity ought to provide the same returns to investors.

15.3 Methodology

The data used in this study are on treasury bonds and AAA corporate bonds. We group the instruments as matched pairs of two classes as described in the earlier section. In the case of treasury or corporate bonds, we match common Type A and the new Type B treasury bonds. Corporate issues are grouped as follows: the medium term if tenor is five or fewer years, and long term for tenors above five years. So, each pair relates to the Type A common bonds and the Type B bonds. We test six pairs of observations with the data covering ten-year period of issues.

The data series are collected from the central bank of Malaysia, the Bond Pricing Agency (BPA), which is a private vendor and investment advisor on debt securities. We also sourced some data from the Thomson Reuters DataStream. The yields are computed on monthly basis, as reported in the databases. If there is lack of trading in the monthly data on one instrument, then the instrument is excluded. The yields are from traded data at the exchange. The total number of monthly observations amounts to 424, and the total number of instruments is 52 (26 × 2) over the test period for each type.

A paired-sample-type mean difference test is applied to verify the existence of significant yield differences in the pair of matched samples using the average and median series in the yields between the two types of securities as to whether the difference is significantly higher (premium) or lower (discount). Once the difference is computed, a test of difference can be done using the mean and median differences. Mean and median difference formulae are:

$$t = \frac{Mean}{\sqrt{\frac{\sigma^2}{n-1}}} \tag{2}$$

$$t = \frac{Median}{\sqrt{\frac{\sigma^2}{n-1}}} \tag{3}$$

where the mean and median refer to the computed returns of each of the Type A and Type B yields. The standard error shown as the denominator is computed from the differenced series. The t-values are expected to be significant when the differences in the several paired series are tested. Test on median is done to satisfy the criticism that yields may not be normally distributed (as per the central limit theorem).

As stated before, this study also investigates the evidence of long-run and short-run relationship between the two types of securities using the cointegration and causality analyses. The literature on econometric time series suggests several approaches to estimating the dynamics of variables with varying assumptions. The linear time series models using the early versions of time series cointegrating estimators as the vector autoregressions (VARs), proposed by Sims (1980), are found to have robust statistical properties subject to the presence of no parameter restrictions. It is important also to note that the selection of series to be included as Y_t as in the following equation and the choice of lag order plays a crucial role to satisfy the preliminary conditions for appropriate estimation.

$$Y_t = \mu_t + A(L)Y_{t-1} + \varepsilon_t \tag{4}$$

The choice of lag orders can be achieved using information criteria but is subject to adjustment by performing iterations. There has been a wide array of applications of VARs in empirical economic and finance literature. Examples are studies by Bates and Granger (1969), Granger and Newbold (2014), Stock and Watson (2004), Clark and McCracken (2005), and Smith and Wallis (2009). Nevertheless, there still exist some limitations in the VAR approach pertaining to distortions in impulse responses resulted from the effects of omitted variables and measurement errors or misspecifications being embedded in the residuals which eventually leads to misinterpretation of the obtained statistics. Moreover, the VAR models are a-theoretic, that is they are not based on any economic theory, given there is no restrictions on any of the parameters under estimation.

A significant issue relating to poor performance of the VAR or equivalent models is generally due to formal misspecifications of the models such as spurious relationship between variables, results from non-stationary processes, as in Clements and Hendry (1998). Accordingly, the issue of variable stationarity and cointegration analysis has been extensively investigated since the early 1980s by many scholars including Granger (1981); Granger and Weiss (1983); Granger (1986); Engle and Granger (1987); Johansen (1988); Johansson, Douglas, and Nonaka (1985); Banerjee, Dolado, and Mestre (1998); and Harris, McInish, Shoesmith, and Wood (1995).

Given the non-stationary property of most economic time series, as can be verified from their stochastic trend behavior, investigation of a genuine long-run relationship in their trended behavior plays a significant role. This approach calls for determination of the validity of the cointegrating series by investigating the order of integration of the variables, which by definition should be similar. As a precondition, all the variables must be integrated of order 1 (i.e. I(1)) to be estimated in the model. Alternatively, the so-called ARDL bound testing of Pesaran, Shin, and Smith (1999) and Pesaran, Shin, and Smith (2001) employs a single equation setup wherein a combination of I(0) and I(1) series can be taken into consideration. Further, different variables can be assigned different lag lengths as they enter the model. An ARDL (p, q) regression model takes the following form:

$$y_t = \beta_0 + \beta_1 y_{t-1} + \ldots + \beta_k y_{t-p} + \alpha_0 x_t + \alpha_1 x_{t-1} + \alpha_2 x_{t-2} + \ldots + \alpha_q x_{t-q} + \varepsilon_t \quad (5)$$

where ε_t is a random "disturbance" term. The model follows an autoregressive representation, where y_t is explained by lagged values of itself and employs distributed successive lags of the x_t explanatory variable. Using this approach, the time series properties concerning serial correlation of residuals and dynamic stability of the model will be controlled. The presence of significant long-run relationship between the variables can be verified using the *so-called* bound testing approach. Hence, the model is robust to the conventional cointegration techniques. The ARDL has been extensively used in the empirical economics and finance literature by many scholars, reasons being more application and flexibility of test modeling for economic time series estimation and forecasting. Examples are studies by Narayan (2005); Duasa (2007); Rapach and Strauss (2010); Barhoumi, Darné, Ferrara, and Pluyaud (2012); and Ariff and Zarei (2014).

A verified cointegrating relationship leads to error correction estimation to identify the speed of adjustment of conventional and Type B securities, respectively, as in the following specifications:

$$\Delta TYPE\ A_t = \alpha_i + \sum_{i=1} \delta_1 \Delta TYPE\ B_{t-i} + \sum_{h=0} \theta_1\ \Delta \mathrm{TYPE\ A}_{t-h} + \lambda_1 \left(TYPE\ A - \hat{\alpha}_i - \hat{\delta}_1\ TYPE\ B_{t-i} \right) + e_t \tag{5a}$$

$$\Delta TYPE\ B_t = \alpha_i + \sum_{h=1} \delta_1 \Delta TYPE\ A_{t-h} + \sum_{i=0} \theta_1\ \Delta \mathrm{TYPE\ A}_{t-i} + \lambda_2 \left(TYPE\ B_{t-i} - \hat{b}_i - \hat{\theta}_1\ TYPE\ A_{t-h} \right) + e_t \tag{5b}$$

where the coefficients of λ_1 and λ_2 are used to measure the speed of adjustment of the dependent variables to the long-run equilibrium, and the terms in the brackets are representative of the long-run relationship, while other variables are differenced used to measure the short-run dynamics.

15.3.1 Variables and hypotheses

There are four hypotheses developed for testing. These are identified and described in Table 15.1. The short-run dynamics analysis is conducted using causality test with F-test on lagged values of the independent variables. The cointegration analysis is performed using the ARDL bound testing approach. The lag optimization process is followed using the Akaike Information Criteria (AIC) with a maximum of 12 lags allowed for each model. The short-run Granger causality test is then employed by imposing restrictions on the differenced independent variables within the equation which imposes the error correction term (ECT) as the long-run component, after the optimum lags are determined and specified. In this way, the results can be further extended to include the causality of short-run and long-run components.

The hypotheses developed are meant to identify if the Type B (new) debt instruments in the exchange provide the same yields to investors as predicted by theory and by the limited research on mutual funds and equity of two types of instruments. Our prior is to assume no difference exists and observe the results by rejecting the null hypotheses. Hence, the results we expect to get may have quite significant implications either way. There is no reason for a significant difference to exist for the yields on Type A and the

Table 15.1 Test Hypotheses Developed for Testing Differences in Deposits and Zero-Risk Yields

Hypotheses	
H1	There is no significant difference between Type B Risk-free Treasury bond yields and Type A Risk-free common Treasury bonds: medium and long terms.
H2	There is no significant difference between the yields of the Type B corporate bonds and the yields of common corporate bonds, AAA-rated bonds.
H3	The yields of Risk-free Treasuries of Type B instruments and the common Treasuries of Type A bonds are not cointegrated in the long run.
H4	The yields of risky Type B AAA corporate bonds and the yields of AAA corporate bonds are not cointegrated.

Type B (new) contracts. This appears to suggest that if the same functions are fulfilled by two equivalent instruments as in these debt markets, then the results must be the same. Hence, there are strong theoretical grounds on which we suspect that the earlier report needs to be carefully retested.

The hypotheses related to the test on long-run relationship are for a close relationship between the two series, meaning that the series are cointegrated, even if significant average differences are evidenced or not evidenced. We have mean/median difference tests, cointegration tests, and short-run as well as joint (long-run) causality tests. The results are expected to show that there could be similar behavior of the two-matched series, meaning no statistically proven differences. This would suggest that the two contract modes are meant to fulfill the same function. If there is evidence of significant differences, plus a lack of cointegration or lack of evidence of causality, then the debt market behavior is peculiar enough for us to term this puzzle since we do not know why there is difference between the identical pairs.

15.4 Findings

The findings on the sets of interrelated tests are reported and discussed in this section. Table 15.2 is a summary of descriptive statistics on the variables used in this study. The results in the table are descriptive statistics on treasury securities of both Type B (new) and the common Type A grouped as (i) medium term for up to 5 years and long-term yields for above 5 years. This time-based classification allows us to have subsamples of observations to ensure accurate results for classes (for a discussion on yearly yield tests please see the cited paper in the first section). Panel B is a summary on AAA corporate bond yields of both types.

One regular pattern seen is that the yields of zero-risk treasuries are increasing with increases in tenure of the bonds: this is in line with the liquidity

Table 15.2 Descriptive Statistics of the Series Used in the Tests

This table reports the descriptive statistics of Islamic and conventional government, corporation (AAA), and agency bond rates as in panels A, B, and C, respectively. Accordingly, the series are divided into three different terms to maturity including short, medium, and long terms.

Types	*Mean*	*Median*	*Max*	*Min*	*Std. Dev.*	*Skewness*	*Kurtosis*	*Obs.*
Panel 1: Government Bond Rates								
Medium-term Type A	3.35	3.34	4.58	2.20	0.40	−0.02	3.76	318
Medium-term Type B(new)	3.42	3.40	4.65	2.30	0.39	0.03	3.68	318
Long-term Type A	4.06	4.01	5.18	2.91	0.43	0.35	2.71	424
Long-term Type B(new)	4.11	4.07	5.18	3.00	0.41	0.29	2.55	424
Panel 2: Corporations (AAA) Bond Rates								
Medium-term Type A	4.07	3.97	5.44	3.32	0.41	1.04	3.89	318
Medium-term Type B(new)	4.01	3.93	5.40	3.30	0.38	0.91	3.72	318
Long-term Type A	5.08	4.99	6.73	3.92	0.59	0.37	2.52	424
Long-term Type B(new)	5.08	4.97	6.69	3.88	0.65	0.42	2.34	424

Note: Islamic denotes *Sukuk* issues in the same market. Some series are slightly skewed, and the normality tests fail to support normal distribution. Our tests are also done on medians for robustness checks.

preference theorem (Hicks, 1946), in which results are similar to the results long since known. The short-term mean is about 3%, whereas the long-term mean is about 4%. Thus, this means that the two markets are able to price the duration of the instruments correctly for both the Type A and the Type B common bonds.

The differences for the Type B vs. common Type A AAA-rated are as follows: −0.06 or 6 basis points for medium term and 0.02 or 2 basis points for the long term. Hence, the AAA-rated Type B corporate bond instruments have *lower* returns to investors (discount). These numbers are yet tested.

In the cases of AAA Type A bonds, we find the opposite results. Note that the medium-term and long-term common corporate bonds have anywhere between 2 and 4 basis point higher differences. Hence, the descriptive statistics in this table provide an initial indication on the existence of differences between the two types of securities. These differences are yet tested as will be done later, but there is no good reason to suggest why there are differences. Figure 15.1 is a graph of the series over the test period. Plots show that the Islamic zero-risk and the risky yields appear to dominate the conventional yields across all maturities, short-, medium-, and long-term bonds. There is a systematic higher yield for shari'ah-compliant securities, which should be tested to see if these are statistically significant.

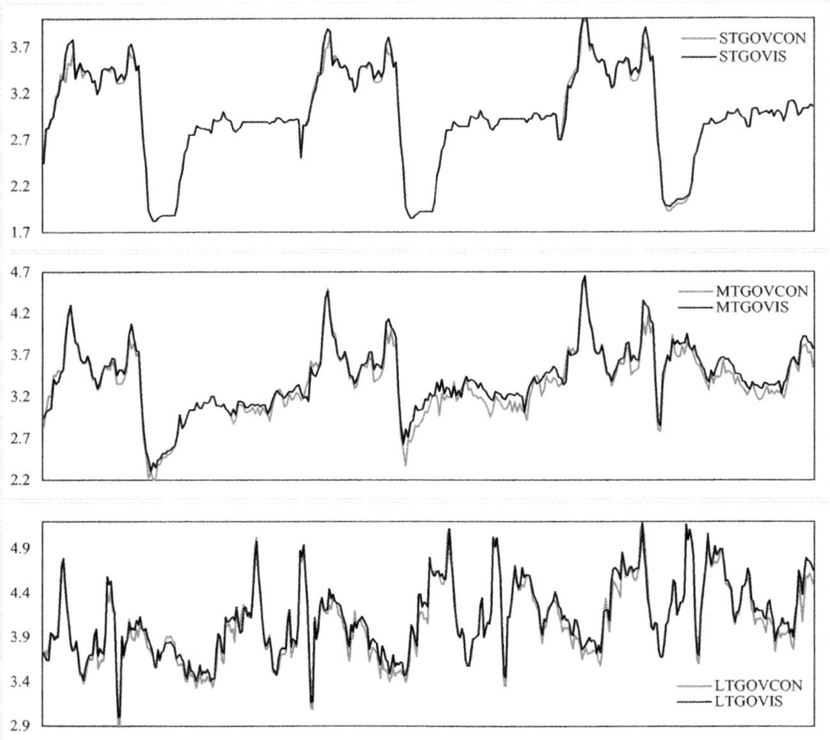

Figure 15.1 Zero-risk common bond vs. *Sukuk* bond yields.

Notes: Dotted line: Islamic rates, solid line: conventional rates. Upper graph: short-term government bond yields, middle graph: medium-term government bond yields, lower graph: long-term government bond yields.

Figure 15.2 provides the plots of the investment returns on AAA bonds for identical term, risk, and issuers: the term of the Type B issues does not have as many as the conventional issues. Hence, there are breaks in the series. It is mildly evident that there is slightly *higher* yields, which may or may not be much different across the time until a test is done. However, in the case of medium-term Type B, the difference appears to be much larger than is the case for the other maturities. Only tests could show if these differences are premium or discounts.

15.4.1 Test on differences in returns

Table 15.3 is a summary of the findings on the important issue of whether there is observed systematic yield differences to the investors in the two types of debt instruments. These tests are two-sided tests done on mean and median differences in the paired samples of conventional and securities. The maintained hypothesis is that the differences in means and the medians

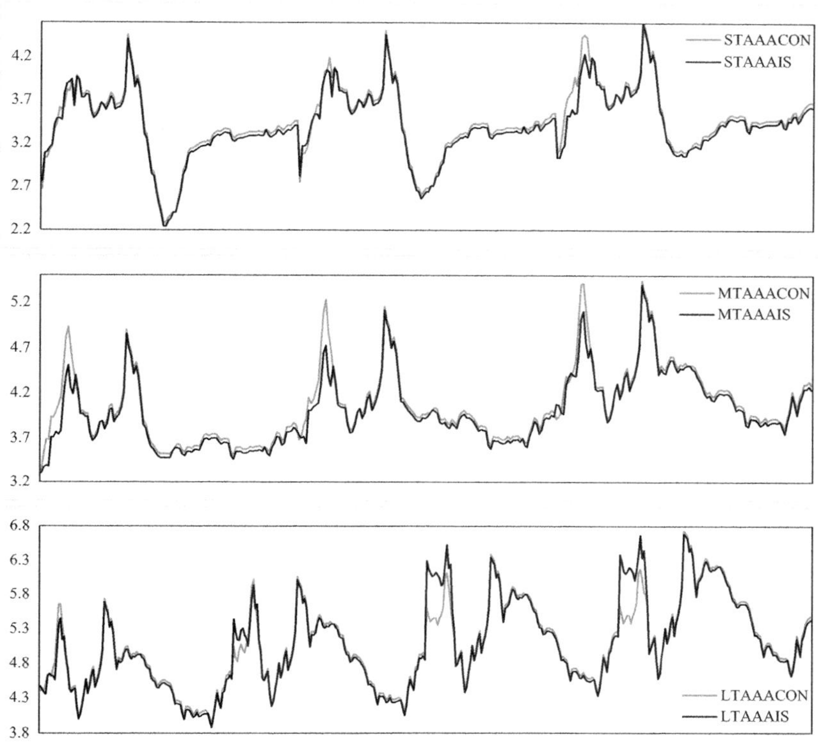

Figure 15.2 AAA common bond vs. AAA *Sukuk* bond yields for identical issuers.

Notes: Dotted line: Islamic rates, solid line: conventional rates. Upper graph: short-term government bond yields, middle graph: medium-term government bond yields, lower graph: long-term government bond yields.

Table 15.3 Mean and Median Difference Test Statistics on Islamic and Conventional Yields

This table reports the test statistics for the mean and median of conventional and Islamic government securities. The number of observations in each test is about 400 monthly yields.

Type		*Mean*	*Median*	*Comment*
Government, Agency & Corporate Securities				
Medium-term treasury bonds	Difference	−0.065	−0.060	Islamic higher
	(t-stat)	(−13.45)***	−12.28***	
Long-term treasury bonds	Difference	−0.054	−0.045	Islamic higher
	(t-stat)	(−14.48)***	(−11.86)***	
Medium-term AAA bonds	Difference	0.060	0.040	Conventional higher
	(t-stat)	11.75***	7.798***	
Long-term AAA bonds	Difference	−0.008	0.040	Conventional higher
	(t-stat)	(−1.08)	4.92***	

Note: The t-values are significant at or higher than 0.01 probability. Where the entry is "0" in the case of the median tests, the two series had the same medians, so no test is needed.

are not significantly different from zero. The number of observations is close to about monthly yields in tested data set pairs. Most of them have several trades in each observation period, and some had continuous trade as evidenced by noting the volume of trades.

The t-tests on the means and on the medians all show that there is a significant difference in the returns to investors in the paired securities. The first two tests (medium term and long term) show that there is a significant difference between the yields of the pairs of Risk-free *Treasuries*. The t-values exceeding 4.423 indicate that the investment returns on common debt instruments are lower than in the Type B security yields maturities, medium vs. long. This level of significance is acceptable at or above 0.01 probability, which suggests to the reader the existence of a strong significant return difference in the treasury market prices.

The returns for the medium-term AAA corporate markets are *lower* for the Type B (new) bonds although the investor return is higher only for the longer-term Type B (new) bonds against the longer-term Type A bonds. It is only in the cases of bonds with less than five-year maturities where we find no difference, so we have some with no difference, some with higher, and some with lower returns. This is an anomaly compared with all other trends showing a Type B (new) security having a premium, which is significantly higher than zero. Interestingly, thus, the private sector-led Type B (new) listed bond markets have lower returns compared to the observed *higher* returns in the cases of Type B (new) securities in the government-led Treasuries instruments.

15.4.2 The long-run dependence of the both yield series

The results on the cointegration and causality tests are presented in this subsection, as tests of long-run equivalence in the Type A and Type B behavior, that is the behavior of conventional and Islamic assets. The test results help to answer a central pricing issue in the dual bond market. Measured as monthly yields of debt instruments, there is sufficient evidence of a higher yield for treasury issues by the government. In the cases of private sector-based corporate debt instruments, the returns for Type B (new) instruments are lower than those for Type A common debt instruments. As we described in the early part of this study, the two debt types are perceived in the market place as being fundamentally substitutes because firms and governments could use either to fund themselves, except that one such assets are priced using pre-agreed interest payments, and the other is based on post-profit distribution of returns earned by issuers, which presumably depends on risk and maturity differences. Hence, the two series, at least in the long run, have to be cointegrated, which is what we are testing.

Table 15.4 is a summary of statistics from cointegration test on the pairs of returns to investors in the government debt instruments. The test procedure applied in this study incorporates a fully specified model with optimum lags – after performing a large number of iterations of regression equations – to be verified from high R-squared statistics and the absence of serial correlation. The optimal lag specification is reported in the third column of the table, which is used in our subsequent tests. The significant f-statistics obtained for all models under the so-called bound testing approach of Pesaran et al. (1999) and Pesaran et al. (2001) indicates the presence of significant long-run relationship between the variables.

This fact can also be implied by the ECT statistics reported in the sixth column of the table. The test requirement is that the sign on ECT should be negative and be significance for at least one out of the two regression models being investigated. There is evidence of significant long-run relationship between the respective pairs. The ECT also measures the speed of adjustment to the long-run equilibrium following any structural instabilities in the behavior of either variable in the regression equation. For instance, the short-run Type A treasury securities tend to adjust to the long-run equilibrium level with the Type B securities of the same type over a 3-month period,

Table 15.4 Result from Cointegration Test (Treasuries)

This table provides statistical report from the ARDL cointegration test with variables being fully optimized using the AIC, as can be verified from the substantial R-squared statistics reported in the last column of the table. The obtained F-statistics of the bound testing approach in column 4 as well as the ECT in column 6 affirm the presence of significant long-run relationship between conventional and *Sukuk* government bond yields.

Type				*Wald Test F-Statistics*		
DV	*IV*	*ARDL Lag Specification*	*Bound Test (f-statistics)*	*Long-run Coefficient (t-statistic)*	*ECT (t-statistic)*	R^2
ST A	ST B	(7,10)	15.07***	0.949	−0.355	0.996
			k=1	(66.81)***	(−4.85)***	
ST B	ST A	(10,7)	18.92***	1.031	−0.445	0.995
			k=1	(91.74)***	(−5.96)***	
MT A	MT B	(4,4)	12.79***	0.952	−0.294	0.969
			k=1	(22.83)***	(−4.75)***	
MT B	MT A	(12,11)	6.50**	1.019	−0.259	0.973
			k=1	(18.98)***	(−3.30)***	
LT A	LT B	(11,12)	7.06**	1.061	−0.239	0.982
			k=1	(25.40)***	(−3.71)***	
LT B	LT A	(7,8)	11.98***	0.883	−0.247	0.982
			k=1	(23.95)***	(−4.42)***	
Pesaran et al. (2001) Critical Value (k=1)				*Lower Bound I(0)*	*Upper Bound I(1)*	
			99% level	6.84	7.84	
			95% level	4.94	5.73	
			90% level	4.04	4.78	

Note: The figure in parenthesis (...) represents optimum lag length selected based on AIC. The reported R-squared values are for the general regression equation with respective ARDL parameterization of the lag components.

while the short-run Type B securities, that is Islamic securities, tend to have faster speed of adjustment to the long-run equilibrium which is equivalent to 2.25 months (1/0.445).

Assets with longer-term maturities are found to have relatively slower adjustments, which is nearly four months, compared to the two- to three-month adjustment of short-term Treasury securities. The adjustment speed for Treasuries is due to its greatly superior liquidity in the market. Corporate bonds have very low liquidity since most investors hold to maturity.

Results reported in Table 15.5 are for the causality test between the two-type treasury securities. We have implemented two tests of causality for identification of short-run as well as joint (long-run) causality, by restricting, from the obtained error correction mechanism (ECM): (i) the several lags of differenced independent variable for the short-run causality and (ii) short-run and long-run (that is the ECT) components to examine if the restriction null hypothesis is rejected using Wald-type F-statistic procedure. This is a standard approach of the Granger causality test often applied in economic and financial studies.

The test results show bidirectional causality. In such cases, the results reported in the last two columns of Tables 15.3 and 15.4 help us to verify evidence in support of significant bidirectional causal relationship between Type A and Type B bond yields. Therefore, both types of securities are found to have contemporaneous feedback on each other despite the fact that there is a long-run cointegration between two instrument types, which is

Table 15.5 Results from Causality Test (Treasuries)

This table provides statistical report from tests of Granger causality for identification of long-run and short-run dynamics. The obtained statistics affirm the presence of significant short run and joint causality between conventional and Islamic government bond yields.

Type		*Wald Test F-Statistic*	
DV	*IV*	*Short-run Causality (p-value)*	*Joint Causality (p-value)*
ST-A	ST B	329.06*** (0.00)	299.14*** (0.00)
ST B	ST A	402.89*** (0.00)	356.17*** (0.00)
MT A	MT B	251.69*** (0.00)	204.26*** (0.00)
MT B	MT A	78.72*** (0.00)	72.36*** (0.00)
LT A	LT B	312.02*** (0.00)	312.02*** (0.00)
LT B	LT A	475.15*** (0.00)	426.35*** (0.00)

consistently an evidence for arguing that the two instruments are equivalent in terms of investor returns.

Table 15.6 reports statistics on the cointegration analysis for the two type corporate AAA securities. Given the full specification of models with large number of lagged variables, there is again evidence of significant long-run relationship between the two pairs of assets, as can be verified from the bound test and the ECT test statistics.

The speed of adjustment being significant and negative is relatively slower for the longer maturity corporate securities than is the case for the short-term assets. Further, the yields on Type A securities are found to adjust slower to the long-run equilibrium than those on the Islamic or Type B securities, especially for the long-term assets, by about 4 months difference (that is 11 months of adjustment of the Type A compared to 7 months of the Type B securities).

Table 15.6 Result from Cointegration Test (Corporate Securities)

This table provides statistical report from the ARDL cointegration test. The obtained F-statistics of the bound testing approach in column 4 as well as the ECT in column 6 affirm the presence of significant long-run relationship between conventional and Islamic government bond yields.

Type				*Wald Test F-Statistic*		
DV	*IV*	*ARDL Lag Specification*	*Bound Test (f-statistics)*	*Long-run Coefficient (t-statistic)*	*ECT (t-statistic)*	R^2
ST A	ST B	(10,12)	14.53*** k=1	0.995*** (40.80)	−0.272*** (−5.31)	0.993
ST B	ST A	(12,10)	14.50*** k=1	0.980*** (42.85)	−0.281*** (−5.36)	0.993
MT A	MT B	(7,12)	22.54*** k=1	0.995*** (37.89)	−0.307*** (−6.66)	0.989
MT B	MT A	(12,11)	16.63*** k=1	0.971*** (36.99)	−0.295*** (−5.76)	0.988
LT A	LT B	(11,12)	6.59** k=1	0.956*** (15.82)	−0.090*** (−3.57)	0.990
LT B	LT A	(12,12)	11.64*** k=1	0.973*** (18.22)	−0.131*** (−4.64)	0.989
Pesaran et al. (2001) Critical Value (k=1)				*Lower Bound I(0)*	*Upper Bound I(1)*	
			99% level	6.84	7.84	
			95% level	4.94	5.73	
			90% level	4.04	4.78	

The figure in parenthesis (...) represents optimum lag length selected based on AIC. The reported R-squared values are for the general regression equation with respective ARDL parameterization of the lag components.

The asterisks ***, ** and * indicate significance at 1%, 5% and 10%, respectively.

Table 15.7 Results from Cointegration and Causality Test (Corporate Securities)

This table reports statistics from short run as well as joint (long run) causality test on conventional and Islamic corporate debt securities. The results affirm the presence of bidirectional causality between the two variables.

Type		*Wald Test F-Statistic*	
DV	*IV*	*Short-run Causality (p-value)*	*Joint Causality (p-value)*
ST A	ST B	260.21*** (0.00)	244.31*** (0.00)
ST B	ST A	334.62*** (0.00)	308.16*** (0.00)
MT-A	MT-B	142.25*** (0.00)	131.53*** (0.00)
MT-B	MT-A	149.90*** (0.00)	147.86*** (0.00)
LT-A	LT-B	176.16*** (0.00)	163.90*** (0.00)
LT-B	LT-A	195.08*** (0.00)	181.35*** (0.00)

The asterisks ***, ** and * indicate significance at 1%, 5% and 10%, respectively.

Results pertaining to the short- and long-run causality are reported in Table 15.7. Likewise, there is evidence of significant joint causal relationship between the variables in all six models. This indicates a contemporaneous or simultaneous causal effect from each variable on the other. That is, in the corporate conventional bond and Type B bond markets (where we found the Type B instruments offer lower returns to investors) both types appear to affect each other in terms of causality. Nevertheless, the earlier discussion pointed to the long-run cointegration between the two, which means that the two are equivalent in terms of generating the investor returns. We further provide results from a correlation analysis between variables in Table 15.8 in the appendix.

15.5 Conclusion

Our study started with the aim of providing comprehensive testing to establish if the two types of debt securities popularly called conventional – Type A and Type B debt instruments are yielding higher (lower) returns to investors in a dual market where these are traded in some 17 markets worldwide: our study of one market has implications for 16 others. The issue at stake is whether debt markets provide differential returns to otherwise equivalent debt instruments being invested in. A related test we did is to establish if the two types of instruments are equivalent by testing for cointegration and causality.

The results can be summarized as providing confirmatory statistics on these issues. Examining the cointegration between the two return series suggests that mostly the series are causally related and there is cointegrated in the short and long runs. The yields on almost all Type B securities are determined by their conventional pairs over the long run, which is an important contribution of this study, lending support for the idea that the present Type B (new) instruments are clones of the older Type A instruments. This is evident that, even if the returns are significantly different, the two instruments appear to be substitutes for investment purposes as they have long-run dependence on each other. Second, we found that (i) government issues of securities appear to have higher returns to investors in Type B securities and (ii) the private sector-originating conventional debt instruments have significant higher returns to investors compared to the Type B in the private sector and in the banks. Finally, in terms of causality, most of the tests suggest the conventional series cause the other series to change: that is Type A Granger-causing Type B. However, in the cases of Type A corporate bonds and Type B corporate instruments the causality turns both ways, meaning the two series are affecting each other.

The results would have us argue that there is a systematically and significantly higher returns to investors in Type B instruments issued by government, whereas contrarily corporate bond yields in Type A bonds are higher than those in the Type B instruments. That the two types appear to be equivalent as substitutes for investors are held up via the evidence of cointegration between the two. Finally, returns on conventional instruments appear to Granger-cause the returns in Type B instruments: this is a direct evidence supporting the recent published finding that the interest rates serve as benchmark to the Type B profit-and-risk-sharing instrument returns. In the cases of corporate bond and Type B securities, both series are causally related (bidirectional). If, indeed, the differences are due to yet-undiscovered structural features of the Type A and/or Type B bonds, it beckons further research.

While stock market and mutual funds market yields to investors in Type B and conventional Type A equity-like instruments provide about the same returns to investors, our evidence is contrary when it comes to debt instruments. There is differential returns to investors in the dual-type debt market instruments. What are the factors associated with the evidence of differential returns to investors need to be researched in future research. As data sets become available on debt instruments from other countries, more research is encouraged to replicate our results in some of the other 16 dual markets where Type A and Type B debts are traded.

Appendix A

Correlation Table

Table 15.8 Correlation of the Common Bond and *Sukuk* Bond Yields

	ST-A	*ST-B*	*MT-B*	*MT-B*	*LT-A*	*LT-B*	*ST-A*	*ST-B*	*MT-A*	*MT-B*	*LT-A*	*LT-B*	*ST-A*	*ST-B*	*MT-A*	*MT-B*
Panel A: Govt. Bonds																
ST-A	1.00															
ST-B	1.00	1.00														
MT-A	0.87	0.88	1.00													
MT-B	0.85	0.87	0.98	1.00												
LT-A	0.11	0.14	0.50	0.52	1.00											
LT-B	0.10	0.13	0.48	0.52	0.98	1.00										
Panel B: AAA Bonds																
ST-A	0.90	0.91	0.78	0.80	0.15	0.15	1.00									
ST-B	0.91	0.91	0.79	0.81	0.16	0.15	1.00	1.00								
MT-A	0.54	0.57	0.74	0.78	0.67	0.67	0.70	0.71	1.00							
MT-B	0.51	0.54	0.68	0.74	0.61	0.62	0.71	0.71	0.96	1.00						
LT-A	−0.02	0.01	0.32	0.36	0.80	0.80	0.15	0.15	0.78	0.76	1.00					
LT-B	−0.03	0.00	0.31	0.35	0.79	0.79	0.13	0.14	0.75	0.75	0.99	1.00				
Panel C: Agency Bonds																
ST-A	1.00	1.00	0.87	0.85	0.11	0.10	0.90	0.91	0.54	0.51	−0.02	−0.03	1.00			
ST-B	1.00	1.00	0.88	0.87	0.15	0.13	0.91	0.92	0.58	0.54	0.02	0.00	1.00	1.00		
MT-A	0.55	0.55	0.64	0.63	0.22	0.20	0.52	0.54	0.43	0.38	0.09	0.10	0.55	0.55	1.00	
MT-B	0.57	0.58	0.67	0.67	0.23	0.22	0.55	0.56	0.45	0.41	0.11	0.12	0.57	0.58	0.99	1.00

Note: ST-A: short-term common bond, ST-B: short-term bond, MT-A: medium-term common bond, LT-A: long-term common bond, LT-B: long-term *Sukuk* bond.

Acknowledgment

We acknowledge, with sincere gratitude, the help provided by Meor Amri, the CEO of Bond Pricing Agency of Malaysia, who gave access to their extensive data series for this research and the University of Putra Malaysia for help in data collection via DataStream. We are also grateful for the constructive comments from Duc Nguyen and the participants of the fourth Paris Financial Management Conference. Some of the contents in this chapter is based on Ariff, Chazi, Safari, and Zarei (2017) and Ariff, Zarei, and Bhatti (2018).

Notes

1 This paper was adapted from the article "Test on yields of equivalently-rated bonds" published by Mohamed Ariff, Alireza Zarei, Ishaq Bhatti on International Journal of Islamic and Middle Eastern Finance and Management, 2018.

2 For example, Type B bonds have real asset backing, distributes the coupons from profits of the assets backed with specific provisions of risk-sharing, etc.

3 The research team conducted face-to-face interviews to assess the attitude to the two types of bonds. We found that the investors as well as the investment advisors consider the two types as being equivalent. The stakeholders use the standard algorithms to price both types of bonds.

4 Please refer to the following publications for definition of profit-shared contracting and other details on certificates (Ariff & Iqbal, 2011; Ariff, Iqbal, & Mohamad, 2012).

5 The tests were done with both means and medians in order to avoid spurious test results if the distribution of returns is non-normal.

References

Ariff, M., Chazi, A., Safari, M., & Zarei, A. (2017). Significant difference in the yields of Sukuk bonds versus conventional bonds. *Journal of Emerging Market Finance*, 16(2), 115–135. doi: 10.1177/0972652717712352

Ariff, M., & Iqbal, M. (2011). *The Foundations of Islamic Banking: Theory, Practice and Education*. Edward Elgar Publishing.

Ariff, M., Iqbal, M., & Mohamad, S. (2012). *The Islamic Debt Market for Securities: The Theory and Practice of Profit Sharing Investment*. Edward Elgar Publishing.

Ariff, M., & Zarei, A. (2014). The US exchange rate behavior: An advanced test on price parity theorem. *Pertanika Journal of Social Sciences & Humanities*, 22(S), 107–125.

Ariff, M., Zarei, A., & Bhatti, I. (2018). Test on yields of equivalently-rated bonds. *International Journal of Islamic and Middle Eastern Finance and Management*, 11(1), 59–78. doi: 10.1108/IMEFM-02-2017-0040

Banerjee, A., Dolado, J., & Mestre, R. (1998). Error-correction mechanism tests for cointegration in a single-equation framework. *Journal of Time Series Analysis*, 19(3), 267–283.

Barhoumi, K., Darné, O., Ferrara, L., & Pluyaud, B. (2012). Monthly GDP forecasting using bridge models: Application for the French economy. *Bulletin of Economic Research*, 64(s1), s53–s70.

Bates, J. M., & Granger, C. W. (1969). The combination of forecasts. *Or*, 20(4), 451–468.

Bodie, Z., Kane, A., and Marcus, A. J., (2018). Investments (11th ed.). McGraw-Hill Education.

Clark, T. E., & McCracken, M. W. (2005). Evaluating direct multistep forecasts. *Econometric Reviews*, 24(4), 369–404.

Clements, M. P., & Hendry, D. F. (1998). Forecasting economic processes. *International Journal of Forecasting*, 14(1), 111–131.

Duasa, J. (2007). Determinants of Malaysian trade balance: An ARDL bound testing approach. *Global Economic Review*, 36(1), 89–102.

Engle, R. F., & Granger, C. W. J. (1987). Co-integration and error correction: Representation, estimation, and testing. *Econometrica*, 55(2), 251–276.

Granger, C. W. (1981). Some properties of time series data and their use in econometric model specification. *Journal of Econometrics*, 16(1), 121–130.

Granger, C. W. (1986). Developments in the study of cointegrated economic variables. *Oxford Bulletin of Economics and Statistics*, 48(3), 213–228.

Granger, C. W. J., & Weiss, A. A. (1983). Time series analysis of error-correction models. In S. Karlin, T. Amemiya, & L. A. Goodman (Eds.), Studies in Econometrics, Time Series, and Multivariate Statistics (pp. 255–278): Academic Press.

Granger, C. W. J., & Newbold, P. (2014). *Forecasting Economic Time Series*. Academic Press.

Harris, F. H., McInish, T. H., Shoesmith, G. L., & Wood, R. A. (1995). Cointegration, error correction, and price discovery on informationally linked security markets. *Journal of Financial and Quantitative Analysis*, 30(04), 563–579.

Hassan, M. (2001). *Risk, Return and Volatility of Faith-Based Investing: The Case of DJIM*. Paper presented at the Fifth Harvard University Forum on Islamic Finance, October 6.

Hicks, J. R. (1946). Value and Capital (2nd ed.). Clarendon Press, Oxford.

Johansen, S. (1988). Statistical analysis of cointegration vectors. *Journal of Economic Dynamics and Control*, 12(2), 231–254.

Johansson, J. K., Douglas, S. P., & Nonaka, I. (1985). Assessing the impact of country of origin on product evaluations - a new methodological perspective. *Journal of Marketing Research*, 22(4), 388–396.

Keynes, J. M. (1930). *A Treatise on Money*. JSTOR.

Lucas, R. (1978). Asset prices in an exchange economy. *Econometrica*, 46(6), 1429–1445.

Lutz, F. A. (1940). The structure of interest rates. *The Quarterly Journal of Economics*, 55, 36–63.

Mansor, F., Bhatti, M., & Ariff, M. (2015). New evidence on the impact of fees on mutual fund performance of two types of funds. *Journal of International Financial Markets, Institutions and Money*, 35, 102–115.

Narayan, P. K. (2005). The saving and investment nexus for China: Evidence from cointegration tests. *Applied Economics*, 37(17), 1979–1990.

Pesaran, M. H., Shin, Y., & Smith, R. J. (2001). Bounds testing approaches to the analysis of level relationships. *Journal of Applied Econometrics*, 16(3), 289–326.

Pesaran, M. H., Shin, Y., & Smith, R. P. (1999). Pooled mean group estimation of dynamic heterogeneous panels. *Journal of the American statistical Association*, 94(446), 621–634.

Rapach, D. E., & Strauss, J. K. (2010). Bagging or combining (or both)? An analysis based on forecasting US employment growth. *Econometric Reviews*, 29(5–6), 511–533.
Safari, M., Ariff, M., & Mohamad, S. (2013). Do debt markets price and conventional bonds differently? *Journal of King Abdulaziz University Islamic Economies*, 26(2), 113–149.
Sims, C. A. (1980). Macroeconomics and reality. *Econometrica: Journal of the Econometric Society*, 48, 1–48.
Smith, J., & Wallis, K. F. (2009). A simple explanation of the forecast combination puzzle. *Oxford Bulletin of Economics and Statistics*, 71(3), 331–355.
Stock, J. H., & Watson, M. W. (2004). Combination forecasts of output growth in a seven-country data set. *Journal of Forecasting*, 23(6), 405–430.
Williams, J. B. (1938). *The Theory of Investment Value* (Vol. 36). Harvard University Press.

16 Resolving Islamic finance disputes through arbitration in the Middle East[1]

Maria Bhatti

16.1 Introduction

During the past three decades, the Islamic Middle East has experienced rapid economic growth and become a significant player in the international commercial system. A growing interest has emerged in alternative forms of financial and economic institutions in different parts of the world due to commercial globalisation. The rapid development of commercial activity in the Islamic world has also led to a growing interest in laws and procedures regulating Islamic finance disputes, and the potential tension between the Western model of commercial arbitration and Islamic legal principles.[2]

The majority of Islamic finance assets, according to the Thomson Reuters Report notes that the majority of Islamic Finance assets are held by Saudi Arabia, Malaysia, Iran and the UAE as per Figure 16.1.[3] Furthermore, a report by Standard & Poor's Rating Services titled, 'Islamic Finance Outlook 2016 Edition' reports that Islamic banks in the GCC were growing faster than conventional banks between 2008 and 2014 (Figure 16.2).[4] For this reason, Ayub observes that

> Islamic principles of economics and finance...have already proved their ability to attract policymakers and practitioners from all over the world to develop the edifice of an efficient financial a system...Islamic finance has been developing so vigorously that it has evolved from a nascent industry to a global market, where Muslim and non-Muslim are working together and learning from each other for the development of relevant products and services.[5]

Consequently, the arbitration of Islamic finance disputes becomes relevant. Islamic traditions influence arbitration in the Middle East, and therefore, Islamic jurisprudence plays a crucial role when trying to understand and analyse the function of international commercial arbitration in resolving Islamic finance disputes. This tension has the effect of rendering the Arab world as an unpopular place for arbitration, and this may be due to the lack of confidence the international world has in the arbitration laws of the Arab countries.

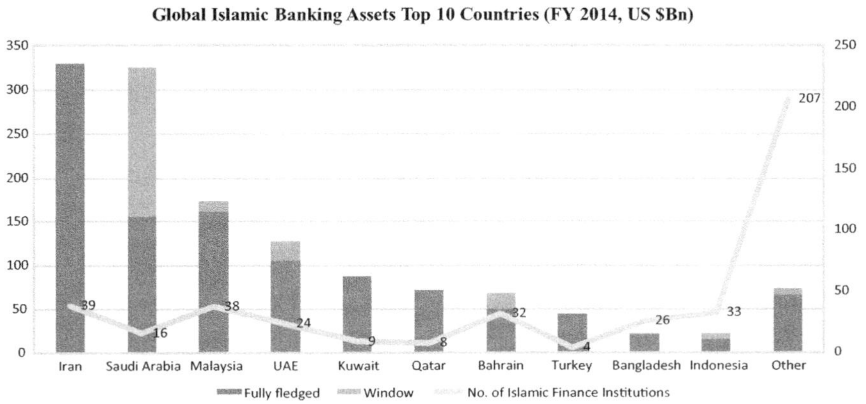

Figure 16.1 Global Islamic banking assets top 10 countries (2014).
Source: Thomson Reuters Islamic Finance Development Report 2015, page 6.

From 1998 till 2006, only 206 out of 8,085 arbitrators were Arab.[6] Furthermore, in 2006, 62 cases registered at the International Chamber of Commerce involved at least one Arab party, and among these cases, only 11 had the seat of arbitration in an Arab country.[7] This article will argue that in order for the Arab world to excel in the international commercial world, it is vital for countries from the Islamic Middle East to consistently recognize and enforce arbitral awards as per the New York Convention and ensure Shari'a laws are in harmony with dominant international legal conventions and practices. In this way, arbitration will become a useful dispute resolution mechanism for Islamic finance disputes.

16.2 Arbitration in the Middle East

It is evident that the Middle East is beginning to make an effort to expand their economic opportunities by attracting investors. For example, many countries are now joining the World Trade Centre and registering at the International Chamber of Commerce.[8] Many new arbitration centres have also been established, including the Euro-Arab Chambers of Commerce, the Cairo Regional Centre for International Commercial Arbitration, GCC Commercial Arbitration Centre, Dubai International Arbitration Centre, Abu Dhabi Commercial Conciliation and Arbitration Centre and the International Islamic Centre for Reconciliation and Arbitration.[9] Since the early 1990's, many Arab countries have moved towards modernizing their arbitration legislation and codifying laws and regulatory systems regarding commercial arbitration.[10]

An increasing number of Arab states have chosen to draft their arbitration laws modelled on the UNCITRAL Model Law on International

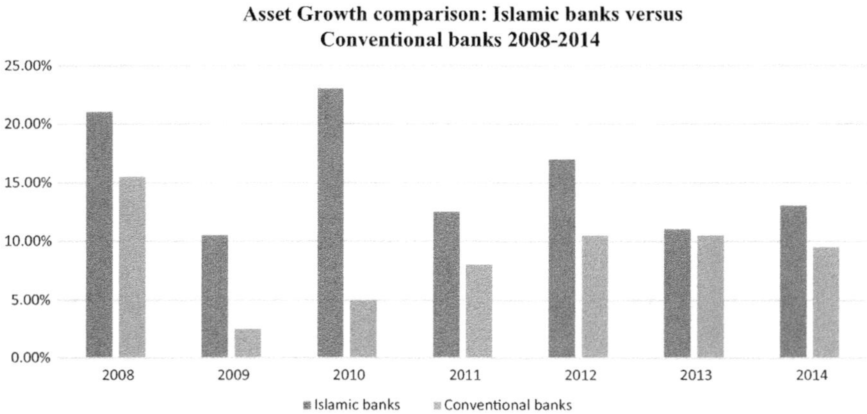

Figure 16.2 Asset growth comparison: Islamic banks versus conventional banks 2008–2014.

Source: Standard & Poor's Ratings Services: McGraw Hill Financial, Islamic Finance Outlook 2016 Edition, (2016), page 40.

Commercial Arbitration. This includes countries, such as Bahrain, Egypt, Jordan, Oman, and Tunisia. Furthermore, Kuwait and the UAE are also considering introducing modern arbitration legislation based on the Model Law.[11] On the other hand, Algeria, Lebanon, and Morocco have adopted the French approach.[12]

The international community has become more globalized concerning its consensus on substituting international arbitration for domestic litigation in areas of international investment and commercial disputes. The community has also provided space for fair and effective international dispute resolution and encourages the role of states in establishing an international and national legal environment as well as a supportive reciprocal relationship between national courts and arbitral tribunals.[13] For this reason, many Arab countries have also ratified the New York Convention. These countries include Algeria, Bahrain, Djibouti, Egypt, Jordan, Kuwait, Lebanon, Mauritania, Morocco, Oman, Palestine, Qatar, Saudi Arabia, Syria, Tunisia, and the UAE.[14]

16.3 Public policy

The notable Islamic scholar, Abu Hamid al-Ghazali (d. 1111) wrote in length about the concept of public interest (*maslahah*) in his works, *Shifa al-Ghalil* and *al-Mustasfa*.[15] Although Ghazali was generally critical about the concept of *maslahah*, he thought of it as a valid concept if it promoted the *maqasid* (higher objectives) of Shari'a. Ghazali defined the five higher objectives of Shari'a: faith, life, intellect, lineage, and property and emphasized the protection of the objectives as a matter of absolute priority.[16] The reason why this is important in the area of arbitration is that parameters, such as the higher objectives of law and life after death, are not recognized under secular law.[17] Therefore, the fact that countries such as Saudi Arabia are signatories to the New York Convention does not provide security for foreign companies regarding the enforcement of arbitral awards.[18] Article V (2) of the New York Convention provides that recognition and enforcement may be refused if (a) the subject matter of the difference is not capable of settlement by arbitration under the law of that country, or (b) the recognition or enforcement of the award would be contrary to the public policy of that country.[19] Signatories can, therefore, avail themselves of Article V (2) (b) and not recognize an arbitral award on the basis that it is contrary to public policy. This is an issue in Saudi Arabia as public policy is determined by reference to Shari'a (including the common good of humanity) as opposed to just the parties that are involved in the dispute.[20]

Arguably, the public policy referred to under Article V (2) (b) is international public policy, which refers to laws relating to exchange control, illegal activities such as arms traffic and counterfeit currency, or the protection of tenants.[21] However, the national courts of some Islamic nations do not recognize foreign awards due to public policy under Shari'a law.[22] For example, Article 2 of the UAE Civil Code states, "one shall resort to the rules and principles of the Moslem fiqh in the construction of the laws," and Article 27 provides that "the provisions of all the laws which would be against the Moslem Shari'a, public order or good morals of the State of the United Arab Emirates shall not be applied."[23]

Public policy under Shari'a relates to a procedural and substantial aspect. The procedural aspect does not cause many issues as they require:

1 strict equal treatment of parties to the arbitral action;
2 Prohibition against the arbitrator deciding without listening to both the plaintiff and defendant;
3 Prohibition against an arbitrator from making an award without giving the parties the opportunity to submit their evidence, please and defence.[24]

However, in regard to the substantive aspect, as mentioned above, two main differences may arise: (1) the Shari'a prohibition of interest (*riba*) and (2) uncertainty/risk (*gharar*). This may cause tension between public policy under secular law predicated on individual rights and public policy under Shari'a, which is more focused on collective rights.[25] It also worries many scholars such as Mallat, who have a more cynical approach: 'whether rejected openly by legislation or hampered by administrative means, the uselessness in Lebanon of an arbitration clause...is true of Bahrain, of the UAE, of Kuwait, of Jordan and Oman.'[26]

Similarly, Akaddaf states, "although Saudi Arabia ratified the New York Convention....the Saudi legal system does not recognize or enforce agreements of foreign jurisdictions."[27] On the other hand, Al-Baharna argues that Kuwait and Syria have routinely enforced the New York Convention, and cites *Merrill Lynch v Behbehani* (1985).[28] In this case, an English arbitrator issued a $1,314,484.896 award against Behbehani. Roy views Kuwait's willingness to enforce an arbitral proceeding against itself as a positive step in embracing the New York Convention.[29] On the other hand, Roy argued that

> [a]s Saudi Arabian law and policy is diametrically opposed to the rules and laws of many member nations, Saudi Arabian courts may find it easy to reject non-domestic arbitral awards pursuant to New York Convention Article V (2)(B). In essence, Saudi Arabia may not be required to enforce any more non-domestic arbitral awards than it did prior to its 1994 accession to the New York Convention.[30]

The lack of enforcement is concerning as it ends up defeating the objective of the New York Convention and in turn, the arbitration processes itself.[31]

16.4 Recent Reforms

Nevertheless, the new Saudi *Arbitration Law 2012* introduced in 16 April 2012 reforms arbitration laws in Saudi Arabia to make them more compatible with international law. Saudi Arabia has also introduced the Enforcement Law 2013 to ensure that arbitral awards are enforced as per international standards. Although this is a step in the right direction, it still unclear whether these new reforms will achieve these goals. Interestingly, the *Saudi Arbitration Law 2012* under Article 2 states '[w]ithout prejudice to the provisions of Islamic law and the provisions of international conventions in which the Kingdom is party, the provisions of this regulation are applied to every arbitration.' Therefore, the new law is aiming to adhere to both Shari'a as well as international conventions. According to academics Nesheiwat and Al-Khasawneh, '[t]he drafters of the New [Saudi] Law made a conscious decision to base it on the *UNCITRAL Model Law* in order to create a legal framework for arbitration that is more in tune with international standards. At the same time, the drafters sought to maintain the essential principles of *Shari'a* and local practice, thus creating a hybrid set of rules that simultaneously deviate from a converge with the *UNCITRAL Model Law*.'[32] It will be interesting to see how these objectives are met.

Another new development in the area of Shari'a arbitration is the introduction of institutional arbitration rules, known as the *i-Arbitration Rules* 2012 where the "i" indicates compliance with *Shari'a*.[33] These rules were developed by the Asian International Arbitration Centre (formerly known as the Kuala Lumpur Regional Centre for Arbitration). The benefit of institutional arbitration rules is that they can be used by parties internationally and are not limited to national boundaries. The i-Arbitration rules are consistent with international conventions and include a clause which allow the arbitrator to use Shari'ah-based penalties in the event of late payment (as opposed to interest), known as *gharamah or the concept of* compensation (*ta'widh*). One difference between interest and compensation is the reference to the Islamic money market as established by the Bank Negara Malaysia when calculating the profit rate awarded.[34]

16.5 Conclusion

In recent times, measures are being taken to address the alienation of the Islamic world and the dismissive attitude toward Shari'a in the field of international commercial arbitration in the Islamic Middle East. Countries in the Islamic world are making more of an effort to expand their economic opportunities and harmonize their commercial legal systems with the international world, in order to attract investors. According to Professor A.S. El-Kosheri, the increasing popularity of international arbitration suggests that

> Arbitration will become the natural justice in business communities inside and outside the Arab world. Nowadays, complicated transactions take place, and there is substantial inward and outward investment, which means that we need to find a good forum for resolving disputes.[35]

This is evident by the fact that growing number of countries from the Islamic Middle East are ratifying the New York Convention, and numerous countries have also based their arbitration laws on the UNCTRAL Model Law on International Commercial Arbitration. Nevertheless, even after the ratification of international conventions, the Arab world is seen as an unpopular place for arbitration due to the lack of confidence that the international world has in the arbitration laws of the Arab countries. This is because Shari'a law is highly complex and depending on the country, huge variations exist regarding the incorporation and application of arbitration laws and the practice and procedure in enforcing the arbitral awards.[36] Complications arise due to the complex interaction between secular law and Shari'a law depending on the amount of influence each law plays in a particular country. Moreover, the fact that a country has ratified the New York Convention does not guarantee the enforceability of the award due to the public policy carve-out exemption.

In light of the global financial crisis, it is vital for the Middle East to become a more popular destination for commercial arbitration. For this to occur, the arbitration framework should recognize the rich Shari'a jurisprudence and its growing international emergence in the international commercial world as well as the current dominant international legal conventions and practices. Shari'a law can no longer be dismissed as a backward form of legal system with no modern application because it is a matter of conscience that plays a huge role in influencing the mindset of individuals living in the Middle East. However, at the same time, jurisprudential tools from within the Shari'a, such as the concept of *maqasid* (higher objectives of Shari'a law) consisting of *maslaha* (public interest), *ijtihad* (independent reasoning), and re-interpretation should be used in order to harmonize Shari'a law more effectively with the international system of arbitration. It is crucial for countries from the Islamic Middle East to consistently recognize and enforce arbitral awards as per the New York Convention. A more consistent form of 'public policy' in accordance with Shari'a law needs to be set out and applied as a standard throughout the Islamic Middle East in order to give Islamic Commercial Arbitration more legitimacy.

Notes

1 This article forms part of the author's LLM research at the University of Melbourne.
2 See generally, Maria Bhatti, *Islamic Law and International Commercial Arbitration* (Routledge, 2018).
3 Islamic Corporation for the Development of the Private Sector (ICD) - Thomson Reuters, Islamic Finance Development Report 2015: Global Transformation (2015). www.zawya.com/mena/en/ifg-publications/241115073158K/, 6.
4 Standard & Poor's Ratings Services: McGraw Hill Financial, Islamic Finance Outlook 2016 Edition (2016). www.spratings.com/documents/20184/86966/Islamic_Finance_Outlook_2016_v2/4d9d6fd9-3b11-4ae2-9168-13ee2543b73b, 40.
5 Muhammad Ayub, *Understanding Islamic Finance* (Wiley, 2007), 15.
6 Lara Hammoud and Sami Houerbi, 'ICC Arbitration in the Arab World' (2008) 25 *Journal of International Arbitration* 231, 234.
7 Ibid.
8 Lara Hammoud and Sami Houerbi, 'ICC Arbitration in the Arab World' (2008) 25 *Journal of International Arbitration* 231.
9 Shaistah Akhtar, 'Arbitration in the Islamic Middle East: Challenges and the Way Ahead' (2008) *International Comparative Legal Guides* 11 at www.iclg.co.uk/index.php?area=4&show_chapter=2201&ifocus=1&kh_publications_id=83
10 Lara Hammoud and Sami Houerbi, 'ICC Arbitration in the Arab World' (2008) 25 *Journal of International Arbitration* 231, 235.
11 Ibid.
12 Ibid.
13 Charles Brower and Jeremy Sharpe, 'International Arbitration and the Islamic World: The Third Phase' (2003) 97 *The American Society of International Law* 643, 647.
14 Lara Hammoud and Sami Houerbi, 'ICC Arbitration in the Arab World' (2008) 25 *Journal of International Arbitration* 231, 235.
15 Mohammad HashimKamali, *Shari'ah Law: An Introduction* (Oneworld Publications, 2008), 124.
16 Ibid 125.
17 Faisal Kutty, 'The Shari'a Factor in International Commercial Arbitration' (2006) 28*Loyola of Los Angeles International and Comparative Law Review* 565, 602.
18 See generally, Maria Bhatti, *Islamic Law and International Commercial Arbitration* (Routledge, 2018).
19 *1958- New York Convention on the Recognition and Enforcement of Foreign Arbitral Awards*, art V(2)(b),7 June 1959 at www.uncitral.org/uncitral/en/uncitral_texts/arbitration/NYConvention.html

20 Faisal Kutty, 'The Shari'a Factor in International Commercial Arbitration' (2006) 28*Loyola of Los Angeles International and Comparative Law Review* 565.
21 Samir Saleh, 'Recognition and Enforcement of Foreign Arbitral Awards in the Arab Middle East' in Julian DM Lew, *Contemporary Problems in International Arbitration* (1987) 349, 347.
22 Faisal Kutty, 'The Shari'a Factor in International Commercial Arbitration' (2006) 28 *Loyola of Los Angeles International and Comparative Law Review* 565, 603.
23 Abdul Hamid El-Ahdab, *Arbitration with the Arab Countries* (Springer, 1990), 742.
24 Samir Saleh, 'Recognition and Enforcement of Foreign Arbitral Awards in the Arab Middle East' in Julian DM Lew, *Contemporary Problems in International Arbitration* (1987) 349, 347.
25 Faisal Kutty, 'The Shari'a Factor in International Commercial Arbitration' (2006) 28 *Loyola of Los Angeles International and Comparative Law Review* 565, 603.
26 Chibli Mallat, *Introduction to Middle East Law* (Oxford University Press, 2007) 349.
27 Fatima Akaddaf, 'Application of the United Nations Convention on Contracts for the International Sale of Goods (CISG) to Arab Islamic Countries: Is the CISG Compatible with Islamic Law Principles?' (2001) 13 *Pace International Law Review* at www.cisg.law.pace.edu/cisg/biblio/akaddaf.html
28 Husain M. Al-Baharna, 'The Enforcement of Foreign Judgments and Arbitral Awards in the GCC Countries with Particular Reference to Bahrain' (1989) 4 *Arab Law Quarterly* 332, 337.
29 Kristin T. Roy, 'The New York Convention and Saudi Arabia: Can a Country Use the Public Police Defense to Refuse Enforcement of Non-Domestic Arbitral Awards?' (1994) 18 *Fordham International Law Journal* 921, 937.
30 Ibid 954.
31 Shaistah Akhtar, 'Arbitration in the Islamic Middle East: Challenges and the Way Ahead' (2008) *International Comparative Legal Guides*, 11 at www.iclg.co.uk/index.php?area=4&show_chapter=2201&ifocus=1&kh_publications_id=83
32 Faris Nesheiwat and Ali Al-Khasawneh, 'The 2012 Saudi Arbitration Law: A Comparative Examination of the Law and Its Effect on Arbitration in Saudi Arabia' (2015) *Santa Clara Journal of International Law* 13(2), 445.
33 Kuala Lumpur Regional Centre for Arbitration, 'KLRCA Arbitration Rules (Revised 2013)' (2013). http://klrca.org/rules/arbitration/.
34 Global Arbitration Review, 'KLRCA to unveil Islamic Arbitration Rules', *Global Arbitration Review* (online), 17 September 2009. http://globalarbitrationreview.com/article/1031606/klrca-to-unveil-islamic-arbitration-rules.
35 'Aseel Al-Ramahi, 'Sulh: A Crucial Part of Islamic Arbitration' (Working Paper # 12, London School of Economics and Political Science, 2008) 20.
36 Shaistah Akhtar, 'Arbitration in the Islamic Middle East: Challenges and the Way Ahead' (2008) *International Comparative Legal Guides* 11 at www.iclg.co.uk/index.php?area=4&show_chapter=2201&ifocus=1&kh_publications_id=83

17 Formation of tangible capital from intangible capital and venture philanthropy

An innovation in Islamic finance

Toseef Azid, Osamah Al Rawashdeh, and Muhammad Omer Chaudhry

17.1 Introduction

Nobel Laureate Friedrich Hayek (1967, 1976, 1978, 1979, 1988) used "the world of gift" and "the world of commerce" when he explained the term of "extended order." Aftermath a number of questions were raised, for example: what if there is any difference between gifts and commerce? Is it possible for us to distinguish between "commercial sector" from a "philanthropic sector (voluntary sector)," or a "market economy" has different values and norms than a "gift economy," or "commercial transaction" has different basis than a "gift"? Is it possible for us to find the relationship in between commerce and philanthropy? Is the commercial and non-profit sectors more efficient when they perform philanthropic activities? Or in a concise way one can ask in this manner: "Is it better to have a market society in which all transfer payments are defined by law in terms of rights and obligations, or one in which they are gifts that depend exclusively on the benevolence of individuals?" (Birner 2009, p.147).

From Hayek analysis, one has the impression that philanthropy is impacting less than the market process and philanthropy is counterproductive in the modern global economy. In his view market mechanism teaches us that how to give the benefits to others, and he proposed to use the term market economy instead of "catallaxy[1]". According to him,

> The morals of the market, is do lead us to benefit others, not by our intending to do so, but by making us act in a manner which, nonetheless, will have just that effect. The extended order circumvents individual ignorance … in a way that good intentions alone cannot do—and thereby does make our efforts altruistic in their effects.
>
> (Hayek 1988, p. 81)

According to Hayek, it is better for us not to know that who is getting the benefits of the economic/social activities. Though, in contrast many of the social scientists have the different opinion, for example, Mises (1949) said, "the ultimate end of action is always the satisfaction of some desires of the acting man" (p.19), and similarly Frank Knight perceived,

> it is a fundamental error to take the individual as the exclusive datum because some sort of family life, and far beyond that, some kind of wider group into which the individual is also born and develops and to which he or she is, in varying degrees, loyal are also data for our understanding of human action.
>
> (1982[1947], pp. 84–86)

Tönnies is in opine that we have two distinctive types of actions to the social relations to the community, i.e., "natural or essential will and rational or arbitrary will" (1940[1887], pp. 119–173).[2] It means that rational or arbitrary will is always inspired by the thought and the same applied to philanthropic attitude towards one's fellow human beings. However, according to Hayek that we are continuously adjusting our different dimensions of lives (actions, thoughts and emotions) with respect to different kinds of orders and rules, i.e., altruism vs. extended order of market. Mauss defines the process of philanthropy as "to give something is to give part of oneself" (1967 [1925], p. 10). Approaches of Muass and Hayek have their own logic regarding the issue of market and philanthropy.[3]

However, in the Islamic literature philanthropy has its own methodology which we will discuss in detail in the next section. In Islamic system there are two types of almsgiving, i.e., compulsory (*Zakah, Ushaer, Fitrana*) and voluntary (any type of charity other than compulsory one). Moreover, philanthropy is the fifth pillar of Islam, and it has its own significance for the Muslim *Ummah*. Holy *Qur'an* mentioned a number of times about the charity and its reward from Allah (SWT) in this life and life hereafter. The teaching of Islam guides us that philanthropy is a complementary set to the market set. And both have their own impact on the productivity and efficiency on the system of a moral economy.

Asutay (2013) explained the scenario of market and non-market as:

> As an extension of self- interest and private enterprise assumptions, Islamic moral economy institutionalizes the market as the institutional framework for exchange in the economic sphere. However, the market mechanism is also filtered so that social priorities are served alongside individually oriented utility and profit- maximizing motives. Thus, a moral filter is expected to regulate the market. It should also be noted that as a result of the moral filter system, to overcome the market and government failure, Islamic moral economy relies on third- sector institutions such as waqf (voluntary organizations, pious foundations) and zakah in serving the welfare needs of society.
>
> (p. 62)

According to the spirit of Islam that moral economy is started from the philanthropy. It has not only tangible impact but has the intangible effects, it purifies the soul, it increases the degree of brotherhood and enhances the social network, it strengthens the sense of belonging among the member of the community, it is a universal instead of local phenomenon and it increases the bond and building the trust among the Muslim *Ummah*.

The structure of the present study is as follows: Section 2 discusses the concept of philanthropy in the conventional as well in the Islamic periphery; Section 3 presents the concept of tangible and intangible capital formation in pure economic, social, psychological, human and religious framework; and Section 4 explains the theory and practice of venture philanthropy. At the end, study concludes the whole discussion and also gives some policy suggestions.

17.2 Philanthropy in the conventional literature

Yet we do not have a standardized definition of philanthropy; however, Dobuzinskis (2009) "defines the philanthropic order broadly, including not merely the activities of donors and foundations but also a whole range of processes that allocate material and symbolic resources through nonmarket mechanisms fuelled by more or less explicitly altruistic motivations." He further added, "even gifts offered for self-centred reasons can generate a sequence of reciprocal actions that evolve into deeper interpersonal or social relationships. Trust is usually built in that way, for example" (2009, p.131). Tocqueville defined as "to sacrifice a part of his interest to save the rest" (p.503). Generally, most of the economists, on the one hand, give the attention to the process of exchange as market phenomenon but, on the other hand, do not consider the altruism and philanthropy in a proper manner, i.e., individuals those are giving charity without any expectations and do not want any reward. However, some economists emphasize on the concept of Pareto optimality[4] like Kolm (2006) discussed this very concept and said that "Vilfredo Pareto's forgotten distinction between utilities and ophelimities" (Kolm 2004, pp. 16–23; 2006). In his view

> the latter are estimations of individuals' material welfare, whereas the former take into account mutual interactions: my utility is a function at the very least of your welfare, if not in a more complex (reflexive) manner of your other-regarding utility.
>
> (Dobuzinskis 2009, p. 136)

Dobuzinskis (2009) argued that market process and the philanthropy are moving parallel to each other and provide the stability of the Hayek's great society. "Gifts exist only at the margin of the market economy" (Dobuzinskis 2009, p. 119). Karl Polanyi argued in *The Great Transformation* (2001[1944]) about the double movement, i.e. one is regulated by the market without any intervention of the external forces, whereas the other is the reaction of this dimension and providing the protection of the economic and social agents from the selfish behaviour of the market. In his opinion the existing system of capitalism is the product of this double movement. Philanthropy belongs to that sphere where collective, public and club goods are directly transferred to the individuals. It redistributes the income and wealth based on the choice of the donors without there being any rights or on the part of the receivers.

Carnegie in 1899 gave the idea of "indiscriminate almsgiving." His emphasis was on the deserving and non-deserving people. Deserving are those who are poor not because of their own fault but because of their fortune and lack of opportunities despite their best efforts. On contrary, some are poor because of their own decisions. He emphasizes that reward should be for those who show the behaviours such as effort, industry and persistence and not to those who show the behaviour of carelessness, negligence and lethargy.

Islam condemns the non-deserving people and emphasizes almsgiving to the deserving people. There is an authentic saying of the Prophet Muhammad (SAW) that on the day of judgement he does not want to see the sign of begging on the forefront of any Muslim. He also taught that giving hand is better than the receiving hand. But, on the other hand, it is also emphasized that does not forget the deserving members of the community. Also Islam encourages the Muslims to work hard instead of receiving the philanthropy, and halal earnings are considered as someone is participating in the holy war. Keeping that in view one cannot assume the existence of non-deserving people in the true and pure Islamic society.

Sometimes a question is raised if no one is contributed then what will be the situation? It has been observed in the conventional system there is no compulsion on any individual to participate in the process of philanthropy especially at the giving end. However, in the Islamic system, the situation is not as the same as we have in the conventional environment. As it is mentioned above, in the Islamic system, compulsory charity is the one of the five pillars of Islam, and this is the duty of the Islamic state to develop an administrative system for the collection of this religious duty. The real question is when and why? Islam provides guidance for this question. Furthermore, Islam accepts the right to receive payments transferred from other Muslim Brothers. In *Surah Tauba*[5] it is clearly mentioned that the categories where this compulsory philanthropy must be distributed. The more one gives in the way of Allah (SWT), in fact, the more reward he will receive in the life hereafter. Islamic norms are so strong if they are implemented in their true sense then charity is not for the individuals but for the development of the society. Historically, it has been observed at the time of second Caliph Umar bin Khatab that in the Capital of Islamic state people could not be able to find anyone who was willing to receive the charity so they deposited it in the treasury (*Bait-ul-Ma'al*).

17.3 Formation of tangible capital from intangible capital

Generally capital formation refers to a net addition of capital stock. It is realized that higher the capital formation of an economy, the faster its growth and increases its production capacity, i.e., producing more goods and services can lead to an increase in the level of national income. In the old conventional literature, only traditional economic capital was discussed; however, in the current literature different varieties of capital are discussed, i.e., human, social, cultural, psychological and religious capital. All these are known as intangible capital. Quite a number of social scientists discussed the importance of intangible capital and its impact on the national income and welfare of the community.

Traditionally, economic capital (both financial and tangible assets such as plant and equipment) has received all the attention.[6] But enlightened managers today recognize the importance not only of tangible assets, data and physical resources, but also of intangible capital, i.e., religious, social, psychological and human capital (intellectual capital)—"human" which includes all the workforce works for all the ranks of the organization, and the economic term "capital" includes all those resources which are used for investment.[7]

In Innaccone (1990) opinion that concept of religious capital is derived from the theories of different types of intangible capital emerged, i.e. theories of social, cultural and human capital. He added all these are originated from the social capital, i.e. the investment and participating of the people in their social groups.[8] It is observed that through religious capital, the religious practices and satisfaction are produced (Iannaccone 1990; Finke 2003). Contrary to that Smith (2003) says that the natural foundations of human behaviour are belief and moral values. Finke (2003, p.3) argued, "Religious capital consists of the degree of mastery of an attachment to a particular religious culture." Finke's definition of religious capital is based on social capital, human capital and economic behaviour of household (Finke 2003, pp. 2–3). In general people through their practices are enhancing and protecting their religious capital (Stark and Finke 2000, pp. 120–121). Verter found that through religious capital, one can gain the cultural capital.[9] However in his opinion, if religious/spiritual capital was not invested properly then it may disturb the other types of intangible capital (Verter 2003).

However in the periphery of Islam the generation of capital is started from the economic capital but it is based on the God-fearing behaviour (*Taqwa*). The whole community is developed on the basis of religion. All behaviours towards the worldly affairs are dependent on the virtuous which society has. Islam plays a very important role in building the character of the Muslim individuals. God-fearing person (*Muttaqi*) is spending more in the way of *Allah* (SWT) and expecting more reward from *Allah* (SWT) in the life hereafter. So the foremost capital which is generated is religious capital.

The desired behaviour is good intention, honesty, kindness, moral attitude, virtuous behaviour, honours for others and towards brotherhood among the members of the society, and the undesired behaviour is dishonesty, cheating, theft, jealousy, backbiting, dishonour and so on. This boosts up the psychological state of the charity giver. In this scenario of Islamic economy, out of religious capital the psychological capital generates and provides the foundations of social capital. The term "psychological capital" is discussed in detail in the different studies of economics, business, psychology, investment and sociology. A renowned psychologist Martin Seligman challenged the prevailing understanding of the subject and introduced the concept of positive psychology, i.e., changed the whole scenario from wrong to right, bad to good, specifically, weaknesses to strengths, health and life rather than illness and death. Seligman (2002) said, "when we are engaged (absorbed in flow), perhaps we are investing, building psychological capital for our future" (cited in Luthans et al. 2004, p. 46).

In the words of Luthans et al. (2004, p. 46), "Applied to the workplace, this 'flow' can be restated in terms of personal and organizational goal alignment and job fit." It depicts in Table 17.1 that psychological capital generates after religious capital while social and human capital lying beyond psychological capital. In contrast, basically psychological capital consists of "who you are" rather than what you believe and what or who you know. Explicitly, desired behaviour consists of "confidence, hope, optimism, and resilience—four states that have also been used by Stajkovic (2003) in his core confidence factor for work motivation" (Luthans et al. p. 46).

Through positive organization behaviour (POB) or positive psychology we can measure these types of capacities, more paths for the development, more chances for the management and also the more efficient and effective work. Luthans (2002a, 2002b) drawn an axiom from POB that with the generation of psychological capital more efficiency and productivity can be enhanced. However, these four states have the positive impact on the work performance, which prevails in the workplace and enhances the POB, i.e., higher level of productivity, better customer service and more employee retention.

Similar to religious and psychological capital, social capital is considerably more vague and unquantifiable and generally not easy to measure. Particularly, it is based on the trust among the members of the society, members' personal relationship and network of the contacts. Table 17.1 describes religious capital as "what you believe," on the other hand social capital is defined as "who you know." It is worthwhile to note that social capital has both dimensions, i.e. inside a firm ("Whom can I turn to for help in solving this problem?") and outside the firm ("Who can advise me on finding the best price and quality in making this purchasing decision?"). Social capital is generally measured and evaluated by the different dimensions of the network, i.e., size, structure and its composition. Adler and Kwon (2002) after surveying the literature on social capital have concluded that social capital has a significant positive impact on the human resources[10] and organizational areas.[11] Similar to other intangible capital, the investment on social capital has positive impact both in the future and present on the success, performance, efficiency and competitive advantage of the company.

On the contrary, most of the conventional literature argued that social capital generates the cultural capital and then ultimately preparing the foundations for the religious capital. However like Smith (2003) some are in opine that beliefs and moral are the core value of human behaviour.

In the Islamic mythology the behaviour are developed on the basis of the degree of piousness, i.e., how much one feels fear from God? The desired behaviour from social capital in the Islamic culture is good relationship, network of contacts among the pious members of the society, environment of brotherhood, good environment of friendship, helping others without selfish behaviour and so on. However, these three intangible types of capital generate the another intangible capital known as human capital. Becker (1975) defines "human capital as a means of production, similar to other means of production." In the system of Islam, human capital can thus also be built through religious values, social network and psychological state of the community. The ingredients of human capital are rituals, knowledge, and moral attitude that come from religious capital; hope resilience, optimism, and efficiency that are taken from psychological capital; and relationship network of contacts, friends, and brotherhood that are added from social capital. After adding the recipe of education, training and healthcare, it emerges as the human capital. In a nutshell, ethical milieu needs an advancement in knowledge and the desire to learn knowledge (not like a statue, it is flexible and dynamic), improvement in experiences and skills, learning effectively the market strategies and how to survive in the current state of market, behaviour, psychological state, social interaction and skill, and all of these collectively defined as "human capital". Thus, in the current scenario, human capital is the most significant factor for the success of continuous performance of the firms.

Experts are differentiating religious capital and social capital from the religious human and social human. It is a well-recognized phenomenon that human capital plays a significant role in increasing the human efficiency and productivity, whereas the role of social capital is also recognized the relationships in production. Social networks have their own impact on the economic and social life of the members of the society, e.g., from better job, tension-free work place and social gatherings with the friends to happier marriage. It is concluded by Putnam (2001) that religious communities and the phenomenon of attending the church play a very important role in the creation of social capital in USA. Because the source of the most of social activities is based on the religious activities and hence is developing the social capital. It can be seen in Table 17.1.

Intangible capital other than human capital "can be measured in ways similar to human capital – years of experience, practice and levels of knowledge and skills" (Iannaccone and Klick 1993, p.6). In a nutshell, intangible capital cannot be evaluated as monetary capital; however, it is the degree of "mastery or attachment."

However, the transformation of these intangible capitals is extremely different than economic capital, i.e., transformation cannot be purchased, is irreversible, is a continuous process and has no limits because it creates energy. However, it is interesting to note that the inherent feature of transformation is that it is uncertain phenomenon. There is a clear-cut difference between transformation and transaction, i.e. transformation is a universal, wide spread and general phenomenon. Transformation has a number of challenges to the expectations and patience because it is not continuous, it has its own ways and own patterns and it may occur in steps. Transformation does not have homogenous impact on its participants, it is asymmetric and its impact varies among the individuals. When we are considering scenario of charity, it seems to have a multiplicative impacts on the participants. It has an empowering impact on the individual intellect ability. We can assume the same process of transformation whenever we consider the impact of philanthropy on the above intangible capitals. In the Islamic environment transmission of capital among the family members and generations is very much desired. It is observed from the different *Qur'anic* verses[12] and sayings of Prophet (SAW)[13] that this type of transmission has its own impact on the building of moral society, consequently which has the impact on the growth of the economy and society.

Table 17.1 Formation of Intangible Capital from Tangible Capital in Moral Economy

Type of Capital	Traditional Economic Capital	Religious Capital	Psychological capital	Social Capital	Human Capital	∑ (End Result)
Traits	What you have ↓	What you believe ↓	What you are ↓	What you know ↓	What you have ↓	Development of the personality ↓
Nature of capital	Finance Tangible Assets (plant, equipment, patents, data)	Belief Intentions Practice Rituals	Confidence Hope Optimism Resilience	Relationship Network of Contacts Friends (Brotherhood)	Experience Education Skills Knowledge Ideas Healthcare	Incremental change in capital through moral economy
Change →	Philanthropy →	Generation of Resources	Generation of Resources →	Generation of Resources →	Generation of Resources	New Resources
Expected return	Profit →	Reward in the life hereafter	Happiness →	Satisfaction	utility →	*Falah* in both of the lives
Motivation to maximize gains (compassion, or some kind of inner fulfilment) while minimize the losses						

Source: Rawashdeh et al. (2017).

17.4 Venture philanthropy

This is the John Rockefeller III who first introduced the term of "venture philanthropy" in 1969; the objective is to fund those causes which are not very much popular in the society but these causes extremely need the attention of the society. However, this idea got more popularity in 1990. This concept and term of venture philanthropy approached to that community who wants to solve the social problems with its wealth and business wisdom. Venture philanthropy is defined as "a field of philanthropic activity where private equity/venture capital models are applied in the non-profit and charitable sectors with the overall objective to maximize social impact." It is categorized into six key factors: "engaged partnership," "tailored financing," "multi-year support," "provision of non-financial services", "assistance to build organizational-capacity" and "performance measurement" (Ochs 2008[14]). It is also worthwhile to note that venture philanthropy is not only dealing with the charities or also not only works in earning the profit. It works with different organization with vast varieties. These may be social organizations, social industrialists, trading and business charities, and socially driven commercial organizations. Venture philanthropy filled a gap in between "traditional grants for non-profit" and "commercial market rate equity and loans." Some objectives of investment are similar to the commercial organizations, i.e., sustainability and economies of scale. They are also trying to use traditional business tools for promoting the start-up, enhancing the growth, taking the risk for certain social ventures and building sustainable operating capacity, close relations in between donors and recipients and clear target for the expected performance. These all are the sustainable features of the best philanthropy. These are playing a very important role in the diversification of capital market for not-profit and social organizations. In comparison with the small organizations, venture philanthropy is more efficient because it creates higher degree of expertise and level of skill. It is generally offering a long-term projects and core operations. The term venturing is an approach which emphasized on determination, flexibility, ability and the creativity which is required for the start-up venture to get the success in the social and economic market. Moreover, it has a very important distinct feature, i.e., the venture philanthropist is always ready to take the responsibility for success and also ready to take the risk on his shoulders, and even always ready to play an effective role in the board of the organization (Table 17.2).

Generally, it is observed that social- and grant-based organizations are comparatively more risk-taking; however, the venture philanthropy has different characteristics and has a different policy for entry and exit. It is also observed there is always conflict and tension in between the financial and social returns on investment. So it is a big challenge for the venture philanthropist that how to match the different distinctive cultures with the different economies, how to provide the human services and expertise and also how to provide the capital. And on the reciprocal basis it is also necessary

Table 17.2 Traditional vs. Venture Philanthropy

Features	*Traditional Philanthropy*	*IFIs as Venture Philanthropists*
High engagement	Investors: not-engaged, gift givers, not involved beyond the grant and not in the process, want to know how resources are used, least concerned with effectiveness.	Always ready to take an active role in the growth, development and expansion of the project and/or also committed and dedicated to a person whom they are supporting.
Tailored financing	Finance: conservative, form of a grant/gift, no payback.	Flexible, revenue-generating social enterprises; funds for infrastructure; project delivery with growth, scale and quality.
Multi-year support	May commit to a multi-year project funding, no concern beyond that point, long-term project "dependent on grant funding", tested and proven projects may end prematurely.	Venture philanthropists engage on a multi-year basis with the view toward the project becoming self-sufficient.
Non-financial support	Non-profits leaders and organizations are usually responsible for finding their own service providers are on an as-needed basis.	An engaged partnership with a venture philanthropist means the delivery of non-financial services, e.g., *musharakah* or *mudharabah*.
Organizational capacity-building	Supporting organizations that "do good", focus is on the reach and delivery.	Needs to succeed to deliver its services in the most effective way possible support for organizational set up.
Performance-based measurement	In traditional philanthropy, the evaluation stageconcentrates on the initial project proposal screening. Performance-based measurement goes beyond reporting and compares the achieved outcomes with the intended outcomes.	To work closely with the person leading the project to develop targets, metrics, and tracking methods, not only for internal performance but also for impact assessment.

Source: Constructed by authors, information from Ochs(2008).

for the social organizations to learn from the venture capital community, i.e., how to get the new ideas from the engagement of the venture philanthropist in social issues, how to get the reputation in the community and how to recruit the different factors of production. In the business, a number of businesses are emerged which consider a lot of business opportunities in the social innovation, i.e.

> for growing brand equity (through association with well-known charities or social enterprises); attracting talent (particularly younger people who want to believe that their employer has a social conscience); and to stimulate cultures of innovation in the mainstream business through engagement with different types of organization.

In the business world one can see a significant growth of social organizations/social entrepreneurship. They have dual objective, i.e., earning profit with focusing on the social goals. It creates a distinctive challenge for the social enterprise, on the one side, they are trying to preserve their commercial position, whereas, on the other side, they are committing with their social goals. Most of them are small in size and deficient in economies of scale and scope. Due to this reason whenever they have a successful innovation, the large business organizations are trying to capture their market and ultimately enjoying the innovation of the social entrepreneur. However, there is also a new trend that social enterprises are developing a network which enabled them to enjoy the facilities and services similar to the large enterprises. Currently it has been observed that the number of social enterprises is increasing. At present one can see a significant financial investment trend in the social enterprises. However, limited resources are allocated for the development of human resources, whereas it is the dire need of the growth and development of the social entrepreneurship and social innovation.

Keeping all the above challenges, it is considered that philanthropic grants are ideal funding for the social innovations. Because in real terms donors are not interested in the high level of returns as they have in the private sector as well as they are able to handle the high level of risk. Even though we have a lot of philanthropic funds but still there is not too much funds allocated for the support of social innovations, there is not too much attention about the mix of funding for individuals, how these enterprises can work at optimal level or how to get the maximum benefits from these funds. It is expecting that in future there will be more awareness and will be more chances for the philanthropist to create more tools for hybrid ventures with the combination of grants, equity and loans. Venture philanthropists often place great importance on the role of the "social entrepreneur," the person not only with the vision but also with skills to carry out the project of change.

In most of the developing countries and particularly in the Muslim countries, the issue of "brain drain" is getting a lot of attention especially in the context of economic development, and most of their human capital is working outside of the country of their origin. Islamic Financial Institutions (IFIs) (and also as venture philanthropists), as being the ethical institutions, should engage the skilled labour force in the different projects and also provide the necessary skill to the unskilled workers. This skill should be transferred to the community for the sustainable development. Additionally, life-threatening, chronic illnesses such as HIV/AIDS and Hepatitis C are impacting the work force or shortening the amount of time that one is able to work. Long-term sustainability of a project requires local talent. IFIs can play a significant role in this direction also while playing the role of venture philanthropist. Social capital and networks are very much important for the development of the community and economy. IFIs as venture philanthropists can bring social capital and networks to the projects and regions in which they work, so their interaction with the local context could be useful.

Islamic finance has extraordinary uniqueness in the financial market. At present it is approximately US$2.2 trillion industry. It is trying to meet the banking requirements and needs of faith-conscious of the members of Muslim *Ummah*. Those are avoiding the interest and other non-*halal* transactions and products. It is also very important to note that approximately 1,407 IFIs all over the world. But unfortunately they are not able to provide sufficient services to the Muslim *Ummah*. It may be due to the size of this sector which is comparatively still small to conventional finance. Because less than 1% of the total world financial assets are *shari'ah* compliant. However by using the philanthropy which is a significant in amount can be used by these institutions (according to one survey that almost £371 each Muslim on average pays charity), they can serve the *Ummah* in a better way. Keeping the above in view, in the present study we are proposing that Islamic venture philanthropy can use the basic tools of conventional philanthropy. It may be in the format of tailored financing. Islamic venture philanthropy may ask the professional financial advisors for their advice and assistance for establishing the strong building of the community. It is assumed that the wealth of philanthropist is used for the *shari'ah* compliant financial activities, and the profits of these activities can be reinvested for the development of the larger communities. This proposed model will establish the strong network among the IFIs and the local investors and philanthropists. This will provide an opportunity for sharing the risk and profit which have the well-defined development objectives. And it also has its financial and social impact through the venture philanthropy in the local as well as Muslim community at large. For more understandings, Table 17.3 depicts the different types of venture philanthropist.

The Islamic banks should invest socially and ethically. It is explained by Asutay (2013) as:

> IBF is a society- oriented financing proposition, as it aims to serve the communities and not markets. Since IME aims to create a framework of developmentalist financing, instruments of poverty reduction are an inherent part of IBF. For this, in addition to Islamic financing of economic activity for development, zakah and qard hasan can be mentioned.
>
> (p.64)

IFIs in this context can perform their ethical duty on the following framework: open their doors for every type of ethical finance, deal with the

Table 17.3 Types of Venture Philanthropist

Actors	*In Conventional Setting*	*In an Islamic Setting*
Investors	Funds for social purposes (loans, grants, equity financing), social, financial, and ecologic returns, blended value, blended model.	Funds for social purpose but on the condition of *Mudharabah/Musharakah*, benevolence loans, *Shari'ah* compliant products.
Incubators	Quite different from the venture capital incubator, sweat equity, own concept project.	Sweat equity and own concept project but in the periphery of *shari'ah*.
Ally	Supports the social entrepreneur, or the person, rather than a social enterprise or organization.	Supports the individuals those are more pious but also social entrepreneurs, and creating the ideas for the projects but under the umbrella of *Shari'ah*.
Broker	an organization that provides services by bringing together the social entrepreneur and the philanthropist.	The same as we have in the conventional set up
Nominator	Nominating possible organizations, projects, or social entrepreneurs to receive sponsorship, but is not in and of itself a venture philanthropist.	Nominating those organizations those have a high degree of goodwill in term of their efficiency, provider of social services and have the high degree of moral values.

Source: Constructed by authors, information from Ochs (2008).

noneconomic results of economic action, are responsible for the efficiency and equity of these funds, improve the common well-being of all the members of the society/community through profit which is produced by the ethical investment funds. There should be transparent process in all the business and financial activities, and active involvement of the representative of the set of philanthropist in the process of decision-making should be encouraged. These are some relevant points to be followed in addition to the above points. So in this way they can emphasize on their social, financial and religious goals. We are expecting that after observing the efficient performance of the IFIs, these philanthropists (also known as business angles) will provide more funds for the social ventures, will provide their advisory service and also will persuade the other investors for the potential projects. They will also be able to convince the other investors about the benefit of these projects with the reference to this world and life hereafter.

Currently all over the world, there is a growing development in the IFIs based on their ideology, and they can play a very important role in diversifying the capital market, i.e., tangible and intangible. In that way they can also efficiently promote the activities of social purpose organization. Because their basic structure is different than the commercial bank, they can offer

Table 17.4 Venture Philanthropy in Context

<table>
<tr><td colspan="2">Primary driver is to create societal values</td><td colspan="5">Blended Societal and Financial Values
←→</td><td colspan="2">Primary driver is to create financial values</td></tr>
<tr><td colspan="6">Special Purpose Organizations (SPOs)</td><td colspan="3"></td></tr>
<tr><td colspan="2">Charities</td><td colspan="3">Revenue generating social enterprises</td><td>Socially driven Business</td><td colspan="3">Traditional Business</td></tr>
<tr><td>Grants only not trading</td><td>Trading revenue and grants</td><td>Potentially sustainable > 75% trading revenue</td><td>Breakeven all income from trading</td><td>Profitable surplus reinvested</td><td>Profit distributing socially driven</td><td>CSR</td><td>Company allocating percentage to charity</td><td>Mainstream Market Company</td></tr>
<tr><td colspan="2">Impact only</td><td colspan="4">Impact First
Impact first investors seek to optimize social impact with a floor of financial returns</td><td colspan="2">Finance First
Financial first investors seek to optimize financial return with a floor of social impact</td><td>Financial only</td></tr>
<tr><td colspan="6">Venture philanthropy focus</td><td colspan="3"></td></tr>
<tr><td colspan="2">Grant making</td><td colspan="4">Social investment focus</td><td colspan="3"></td></tr>
<tr><td colspan="3"></td><td colspan="5">Impact investing</td><td></td></tr>
</table>

Source: Balbo et al. (2010, p.18).

those packages which are the blend of social and financial returns. It is well worth to note that skill and training of the human resources are very much important for the growth of the social sector. However, it has been observed that in most of the Muslim countries labour market is not well developed. And also sufficient resources are not devoted for the development of these resources. Regarding this issue IFIs through venture philanthropy can promote the enterprise of the social sector. Venture philanthropy and its related impacts are summarized by Balbo et al. (2010) (see Table 17.4).

17.4.1 Status of venture philanthropy under the umbrella of Shari'ah

In the Islamic jurisprudence, the approach that is adopted by all school of thoughts is based on *the Qur'anic* principle of facilitation, i.e., inclusive accommodation and flexibility. *Qura'an* guides us as "Allah desires ease for you and does not desire hardship for you" (2:185), and "He has chosen you, and has not laid upon you any hardship or constriction in the matter of Din" (28:78). "Allah does not want to make things hard for you" (5:6). And Allah's messenger said, narrated by A'isha (may Allah be well pleased with her): "Never was Allah's Messenger (blessings and peace be upon him) presented with two options except that he would choose the easier of the two, so long as it was not a sin." And narrated by Anas b. Malik (may Allah be well pleased with him), the Prophet (blessings and peace be upon him): "Make things easy and do not make things difficult. Give glad tidings and do not make people feel averse." Similarly 'Allama Ibn Qudama from Hanbali school said, "If a jurist is approached for an edict and his edict remains devoid of openness and flexibility because of his rigidity the edict-seeker should be guided towards some other jurist who is open-minded and flexible." So it is consensus among the jurists if there is need of time, then we can adopt accommodating reasoning than the jurists' reasoning. For example, al-Sarakhsi narrated:

> If two people entrusted a person with gold coins (dinar), silver coins (dirham), clothes, riding beasts and servants, and then one of them went back to reclaim his possessions from him, according to Imam Abu Hanifa it would not be permitted for him to do so unless both are present. Whereas according to Imam Abu Yusuf and Imam Muhammad, he will be ordered to divide the property and pay him his rightful share.

Imam Muhammad said, "The verdict of Imam Abu Hanifa is closer to juristic reasoning *(aqyas),* while the verdict of Imam Abu Yusuf is more accommodating (*awsa'*)." Other school of thoughts have the same opinion that accommodating has more preference. On the basis of the above discussion we have the opinion about the venture philanthropy, its structure should be based on the views of accommodating (*awsa*).

Keeping the above in view that venture philanthropy has no any conflict with the basic laws of Islam, and there is more ease for the public. If the charity for the public interest is accommodating, then it can be used by the IFI as venture philanthropy and can be used for the other purposes which will enhance the welfare of the Islamic society.

17.5 Conclusions

The integration market and non-market institution can be established in the system of Islam. Especially in the context of philanthropy and IFIs, this idea is more practicable. Philanthropy is desirable and necessary for filling the gaps of the Muslim countries. It also creates the bindings among the members of the Muslim *Ummah*. Simultaneously, it gives the strength to the brotherhood among the givers and receivers. From the religious point of view it gives the more utility to the givers as *Qur'an* says that spend in the way of Allah (SWT) which is beyond to your needs. It is very much important to note that in the process of philanthropy the benefits to both the parties (givers and receivers) increase the relationship between them.

We observed in the different studies that philanthropy has the positive impact on the development and growth of the personalities of the givers and receivers. For example, receivers feel the importance of the philanthropy, its influence on the society/community and its goodness, and then will try to become on the side of givers. This will give him the sense of sharing which ultimately increases the new resources and generates the tangible and intangible capital of the economy as well as society. It also creates the strong motivational framework. However, the aspect of life hereafter and accountability are very much significant, and without considering these factors we cannot be able to explain this phenomenon. Similarly, IFI will be able to fill that gap which remains in the society even after the tremendous efforts of public sector. Here venture philanthropy is the best tool which can be used for the stability and solidarity of the community and society. And also IFIs through venture philanthropy can integrate market and non-market institutions.

We are aware that the needs of the Muslim *Ummah* are diverse and vary significantly between countries and even within any specific region. Nevertheless, there are certain needs that are global, the first of which is education. Intangible capital is the essential element for development, and is used as one of the key criteria when assessing an investment opportunity. When we look at investment in intangible capital, especially in the Muslim world, data tells us that there is a significant underinvestment, especially at the lower levels of the socio-economic stratum. Investment in venture philanthropy through IFIs within local institutions can generate significant return on both the financial and social levels.

One more important aspect will be informal activities of IFIs. They can involve themselves if there is any natural disasters, such as floods or earthquake. It has been observed that the performance of Muslim philanthropist and philanthropic organization is significantly more rapid and efficient than the typical government agencies, for example, the quick help they provided to the Indonesian victims during the tsunami and victims of earthquake in Pakistan in 2005.

At the country level, profit will be directed towards the building of social infrastructure such as healthcare, community care, education, training, environmental programs and provision of accommodation that is affordable to people on low income. IFIs with their local counterpart will also arrange funding for these services.

Islam requires us, and in fact blesses us, with the obligation to give to others. We can assert that this *Shari'ah* compliant venture philanthropy program in leveraging *Zakat* and *Sadaqah* can satisfy the development demands of the poor communities of the different Muslim countries and simultaneously can generate the financial returns and growth in the financial sector.

This combined approach based on wealth creation and transfer, and new ways and paths for the commercial approaches for the social change could be able to attract the high level of new financial resources. Furthermore, there will be better community development through Islamic venture philanthropy. Islamic venture philanthropy that integrates with modern and merging approaches for social investment will be enabled to increase the social capital; this will perform more than the traditional philanthropy and will play a very significant role for the growth and development of oriented models. It is suggested that Islamic finance industry which is offering an alternative to the conventional finance system can serve more humanity particularly to the Muslim communities than its conventional counterpart, and Islamic venture philanthropy can offer a sophisticated amended Islamic finance which can fulfil the objective of social innovation.

Notes

1 (*katalattein* or *katalassein)* which has Greek rootsmeans both "to exchange" and "to receive into the community" or "to turn from enemy into friends."
2 "*wesenwille* (natural or essential will) and kürwille (rational or arbitrary will). This distinction turns on the character of deliberation, between, on the one hand, where the action (or the will) unavoidably includes thinking, and, on the other, where thinking directs action (or the will). *K*ürwille is a form of action motivated by the thought (thus, prior to the action) of satisfying one's own need, hence, the prototypical social relation is that of exchange. Characteristic of kürwille is the individual's orientation toward the attainment of what is desired by that individual, and as such it does not, according to Tönnies, encompass a 'positive' (or, philanthropic) attitude towards one's fellow human beings" (Tönnies 1940 [1887], pp. 119–173; Cited in Steven 2009, pp.5–6).
3 "The differences between Hayek's and Mauss's approaches are clearly illustrated by their ideas on the emergence and function of credit. For Mauss, financial credit as we know it has evolved out of a system of giving, accepting, and reciprocating gifts that serve as a provision for the future for individuals. Gift-giving, while creating cohesion, is not deprived of elements of self-interest. For Hayek, on the contrary, credit is the result of the spontaneous emergence of partial-reserve banking in a market economy. Not only did it make it possible for individuals to permanently live beyond their means, it practically forced them to do so, producing ever more in order to be able to pay their debts, thus making credit one of the causes of economic growth" (Birner 2009, p.150).
4 Pareto optimality, is a state of allocation of resources in which it is impossible to make any one individual better off without making at least one individual worse off.
5 Chapter Tauba Verse 60.
6 "Consider the millionaire who continues to use his capital actively in enterprises which give employment and develop the resources of the world. He who manages the ships, the mines, the factories, cannot withdraw his capital, for this is the tool with which he works such beneficent wonders; nor can he restrict his operations, for the cessation of growth and improvement in any industrial undertaking marks the beginning of decay" (Carnegie 2006, p. 50, cited in Otteson 2009, p.25).
7 "Bill Gates has been known to comment that the most important assets in his company walk out the door every night. In other words, he recognizes that the collective knowledge, skills, and abilities of his employees represent a distinctive competency that has created value and set Microsoft apart from its competitor" (Luthans et al. 2004, p.45).
8 "Rodney Stark and Roger Finkefurther developed the concept and have written extensively on the subject, amongst other well-known sociologists of religion such as Christian Smith, Jerry Z. Park, Wade Clark Roof, and Nancy Ammerman" (Albaugh, p.2 available at nazarene.org/files/docs/albaugh_ryan_paper. visited on 10 November 2015).
9 It is a well-recognized phenomenon that if someone from any group of clergy, people is listening him very carefully and giving him more prestige and honour.

10 Success in career, turnover in jobs, compensation for the executives, and help in searching jobs.
11 I exchange of resources among the different units, entrepreneurship, relations with the suppliers, networks among the set of regional production units, and learning from the different companies.
12 Surah Al Tour.
13 Saying of Prophet.
14 Table 17.2 portrays the more detail.

References

Adler, P. S. and Kwon, S-W.2002. "Social Capital: Prospects for a New Concept" *The Academy of Management Review*, 27(1), pp. 17–40.

Albaugh, R. Analyzing the "Religious Capital" Approach to Religious Participation, Point Loma Nazarene University, (available at nazarene.org/files/docs/albaugh_ryan_paper, visited on 10 November 2015)

Asutay, M. (2013) *Islamic Moral Economy as the Foundation of Islamic Finance in Islamic Finance in Europe: Towards a Plural Financial System*. Cheltenham, UK: Edward Elgar.

Balbo, L., Heneberger, L., Mortell, D. and Oostlander, P. 2010. *Establishing a Venture Philanthropy Organisation in Europe: A Practical Guide*. Knowledge Centre: European Venture Philanthropy Association.

Becker, G. S. (1975). Front matter, human capital: a theoretical and empirical analysis, with special reference to education. In *Human Capital: A Theoretical and Empirical Analysis, with Special Reference to Education*, Second Edition, pp. 22–0. NBER.

Birner, J. 2009. "Comment on Putting Philanthropy Order." *Conversations on Philanthropy*, VI, pp. 115–139. Donors Trust.

Carnegie, A. 2006. *The Gospel of Wealth and Other Writings*. New York: Penguin Classics.

Dobuzinskis, L. 2009. "French Perspectives on the Origin and Logic of the 'Philanthropic Order': A Critical Account." *Conversations on Philanthropy*, VI, pp. 115–139. Donors Trust.

Finke, R. 2003. "Innovative Returns to Tradition: Using Core Beliefs as the Foundation for Innovative Accommodation." *Journal for the Scientific Study of Religion*, 43, pp. 19–34.

Hayek, F. A. 1967. "Opening Address to a Conference at Mont Pérèlin," in *Studies in Philosophy, Politics, and Economics*, edited by F. A. Hayek. Chicago, IL: University of Chicago Press, pp. 148–159. (Orig. pub. 1947.)

Hayek, F. A. 1976. *Law, Legislation, and Liberty, Volume II: The Mirage of Social Justice*. Chicago, IL: University of Chicago Press.

Hayek, F. A. 1978. *New Studies in Philosophy, Politics, Economics and the History of Ideas*. Chicago, IL: University of Chicago Press.

Hayek, F. A. 1979. *Law, Legislation, and Liberty, Volume III: The Political Order of a Free People*. Chicago, IL: University of Chicago Press.

Hayek, F. A. 1988. *The Fatal Conceit: The Errors of Socialism*. Edited by W. W. Bartley III. Chicago, IL: University of Chicago Press.

Iannaccone, L. R. 1990. "Religious Practice: A Human Capital Approach." *Journal for the Scientific Study of Religion*, 29, pp. 297–314.

Knight, F. H. 1947. *Freedom & Reform: Essays in Economics and Social Philosophy.* New York and London: Harper & Bros.

Kolm, S.-Ch. 2004. *Macrojustice: The Political Economy of Fairness.* Cambridge, MA and London, England: MIT Press.

Kolm, S.-Ch. 2006. "Reciprocity: Its scope, rationales, and consequences", Chap. 7 in *Handbook of theEconomics of Giving, Altruism and Reciprocity*, edited by S.-C. Kolm and J. Mercier Ythier.Amsterdam: North-Holland, pp. 371–541.

Luthans, F. 2002a. "The Need for and Meaning of Positive Organizational Behavior." *Journal of Organizational Behavior*, 23(6), pp. 695–706.

Luthans, F. 2002b. "Positive Organizational Behavior: Developing and Managing Psychological Strengths." *Academy of Management Executive*,16(1), pp. 57–72.

Luthans, F., Luthans, K.W. and Luthans, B.C. 2004. "Positive Psychological Capital: Beyond Human and Social Capital." *Business Horizons*, 47(1), pp. 45–50.

Mauss, M. 1967. *THE GIFT: Forms and Functions of Exchange in Archaic Societies*, Norton Library, New York: Norton.

Mises, L.V. 1949. *Human Action: A Treatise on Economics.* Albama: Ludwig von Mises Institute.

Ochs, K. 2008. Social Innovation and Education: Examining the Venture Philanthropy Model of International Development, presentation to the Philanthropy SIG, American Educational Research Association Meeting.

Otteson, J. R. 2009. "Comments on 'the gospel of wealth' and true Philanthropy." *Conversations on Philanthropy: Identity, Interests, & Philanthropic Commerce*, 6(8), pp. 21–26.

Park, J. Z. and Smith, C. 2000. "'To Whom Much Has Been Given...': Religious Capital and Community Voluntarism Among Churchgoing Protestants." *Journal for the Scientific Study of Religion*, 39, pp. 272–286.

Polanyi, K. 2001. *The Great Transformation: The Political and Economic Origins of Our Time*, 2nd ed. Foreword by Joseph E. Stiglitz; introduction by Fred Block. Boston, MA: Beacon Press.

Putnam, R. (2001). Social capital: Measurement and consequences. *Canadian Journal of Policy Research*, 2(1), 41–51.

Rawashdeh, O. H., Azid, T. and Qureshi, M.A. 2017."Philanthropy, Markets, and Islamic Financial Institutions: A New Paradigm." *Humanomics*, 33(4), pp. 563–578.

Seligman, M. E.P. 2002. *Authentic Happiness: Using the New Positive Psychology to Realize Your Potential for Lasting Fulfillment.* New York: Free Press.

Smith, C. 2003. *Moral, Believing Animals: Human Personhood and Culture.* New York: Oxford Press.

Stajkovic, A. D. 2003. Introducing Positive Psychology to Work Motivation: Development of a Core Confidence Model. Paper presented at Academy of Management national meeting, Seattle, Washington (August).

Stark, R. and Finke, R. 2000. *Acts of Faith: Explaining the Human Side of Religion.* Berkeley: University of California Press.

Steven, G. 2009. "Philanthropy and Human Being" *Conversations on Philanthropy*, VI, pp. 1–14. Donors Trust.

Tönnies, F. 1940. *Fundamental Concepts of Sociology.* New York: American Book Company.

Verter, B.2003. "Spiritual Capital: Theorizing Religion with Bourdieu against Bourdieu." *Sociological Theory*, 21(2), pp. 150–174.

18 Theoretical, practical vis-à-vis legal development in Islamic banking

A case of Pakistan

Hussain Mohi-ud-Din Qadri

18.1 Introduction

A system sought by any society is an organic manifestation of its members' beliefs and perception on and of life, its purpose and their role in this world. Thus, the social system can never be separated from its doctrinal roots. The term "system" incorporates a set of relations, subsystems, beliefs and institutions activated in the life of people, as well as the activities, policies and laws that underline their governance.

In order to transform the philosophy of the science of economics into a practical form capable of addressing man's needs and its implementation in the society, economic systems are created. Based on the definitions given above, we have four economic systems that are currently in vogue today:

- The capitalistic economic system
- The socialistic economic system
- The mixed economic system
- The Islamic economic system

18.1.1 The Islamic economic system

> Islamic economics is the knowledge of injunctions and rules of the *Shari'ah* that prevent injustice in the acquisition and disposal of material resources in order to provide satisfaction to human beings and enable them to perform their obligations to God and the society.

As is generally understood, the objective of any economic activity is satisfaction of human wants, needs and desires. But in Islam, this is not an end in itself. A man is not supposed to live for himself or for his kin only. His obligations as a social being are much larger than this. He has obligations and responsibility towards the needy of the society. A Muslim earns a living not merely to satisfy his own and his family's wants, but also to discharge his obligations towards society at large. This is what God has ordained for him, and this is an objective, which also makes his earning a pious act ('ibadat), in the sight of God.

18.2 Historical background of Islamic economics and banking in the world

The formation of financial institutions without Riba as a landmark of Islamic bank was tried in the 1940s in Malaysia, but was unsuccessful (Erol and El-Bdour, 1989). In the 1960s, the formation of Islamic banking has become a reality in the world; it does not mean that concept of banking did not exist before the arrival of Islam (Joni and Hadenan, 2006). Riba-based banking was operational when Islam was introduced as a civilization. In those days, Arabs used to lend their money to other parties for trading through the methods of al-Qirad or al-Mudarabah for the sake of making interest-based profits. These methods were popular among both the Qureshi Arabs and the Jewish community (Karim, 1996). In the pre-Islam era, the city of Mecca was the center of trade and was considered one of the main routes for traders traveling from north to south. Facilities like money deposits and business loans were popular among the traders in those days (Mohamad, 2013).

Even before the prophet hood was announced, Holy Prophet Muhammad (pbuh) was famous for his moral demeanors such as honesty and veracity. The Arabs of his time selected him as their wealth keeper until he migrated to Medina (Hamoud, 1985). On the other hand, during the time of the Holy Prophet (pbuh) there was a man (Al-Zubayr al-Awwam) who assumed the role of banker and saved the deposits of other people. However, he modified this form of money keeping into loans.

The origin of Islamic banking can be traced back to the time of the Prophet Muhammad (pbuh), especially after his migration to Medina (Qadri, 2008). The formation of the institution of "Bayt al-Mal" is an example of the method of central banking in the Islamic state of Medina. Bayt al-Mal contributed significantly while eradicating the poverty for the society of Medina. The first office of Bayt al-Mal was established in the Prophet's mosque in Medina.[1] However, the Caliph Umar bin al-Khattab (634–644 AD) professionalized the operations of Bayt al-Mal by making it an autonomous body.[2] There were two main sources of revenue for the Bayt al-Mal. The primary source was the zakat (alms collected for the poor or wealth tax), kharaj (land tax), jizyah and donations. The secondary source included property without an owner, the assets of apostates and the properties of individuals without legal heir (CIFP, 2006).

All these funds were spent in two ways. The first expense was for the defense of the state and the salaries of government employees. The second expense was for community and infrastructural development, such as the construction of roads and an irrigation system (CIFP, 2006). In the early days of Islam, the Finance Ministry of the country came under the command of the Bayt al-Mal. Facilities like money deposits and money lending were initially restricted. However, during the Caliphate of Umar bin al-Khattab, these policies were relaxed and a limited number of individual business loans were made available. For example,

> The sons of Caliph Umar bin al-Khattab, Abd Allah and Ubayd Allah received business loans from the Bayt al-Mal prior to their business trip. Caliph Umar stated that the transaction that took place between his two sons and the Bayt al-Mal was based on the Mudarabah principle and he asked his sons to give a share of their profits to the Bayt al-Mal.
>
> (This episode is recorded in the Muwatta' Imam Malik) (CIFP, 2006)[3]

During the early days of Islam, money orders and bills of exchange were also used. Ibn al-Abbas once took a money deposit and notified Kufah of its receipt (CIFP, 2006). Meanwhile, in the history of the Islamic banking system, according to Al-Yaqubi (d. 897c), Umar bin al-Khattab, was the first to draw cheques and to put his seal underneath and sign them[4] (Mohamad, 2013). A similar statement was made by Al-Jahashiyari (d. 942 CE) in respect to Harun Ar-Rashid, "Al-Fadhl asked him (Ar-Rashid) to draw a cheque in his own hand with regards to the sum of money". Ibn Miskawaih (d. 1030) in his Tajarib al-Umam also mentioned that the wages and salaries of the army were paid via cheques and that one of the major charges made against Muhammad bin Dawud was that he paid the army in cash instead of cheques. So, the custom of using cheques became a common practice among the general populace. Thus, centers of money exchange were established by the Muslim merchants in different parts of Muslim world and beyond. Muslim states and dynasties all over the world embraced this well-established banking and finance system, scrupulously avoiding Riba in all shapes and forms.

The formation of Islamic banks has been sanctioned by divine revelation, which allowed trade and the functioning of banking that was free of Riba (Lee and Detta, 2007). K. H. Mas Mansur first formulated the argument that the interest (Riba) charged by conventional bank was illegal (haram) because it was based on extortion (Rahardjo, 1998; Karim, 2001).

The development of global sharīʻah-compliant assets, however, is estimated at USD 1 trillion with a growth rate of 15%–20% per annum (Abdul Kadir, 2009). In the 1980s, Islamic banks have started operations in non-Muslim countries like Europe, America and Australia (Ebrahim and Joo, 2001). Moreover, Islamic banks established in the UAE, Kuwait, Qatar, Oman, Saudi Arabia and the adjoining countries were more profitable than the conservative banks (Qadri, 2008). In the 1970s, Islamic banking started to prosper after the launch of the First International Conference on Islamic Economics organized by King Abdul Aziz University in Mecca, Saudi Arabia, and after the foundation of first commercial Islamic Bank, Dubai Islamic Bank (DIB), in the UAE. After this initiative, Saudi Arabia established many private and semi-private commercial Islamic banks. Later on, similar banks were established in Egypt, Sudan, Kuwait, Bahrain and so on. The aim was to make Islamic banking an effectual and dynamic means of financial mediation between surplus and deficit economic units.

18.3 Islamic banking and finance: a case of Pakistan

Khan and Bhatti (2006, 2008) pointed out the reasons why Islamic banking failed in Pakistan while it succeeded in other Muslim countries. In their 2008 book, the case of Pakistan's complex geopolitics associate with Islamic faith and sectorial division are discussed. This section links the literature with Khan and Bhatti's work with those of Chapra (2001) and Haron and Yamirudeng (2003), among others who reported that the development of Islamic banking in a particular economy is influenced by the support of Muslims and the government. Pakistan was one of the first nations to introduce Islamic banking in society. These efforts began in the mid-1960s in response to both religious and economic needs in the country. Presently, Islamic banking has been set up as an industry with a share of 13% of the market. This development has been made possible with the assistance of the State Bank of Pakistan (SBP). Other factors have also assisted the rise of Islamic banking such as new regulatory measures supporting the banking industry as well as the increase of foreign investors and population growth.

18.3.1 Pakistan's economy at a glance

Pakistan is a country with a rapidly developing business sector within the Organization of Islamic Cooperation (OIC). In 2015, it was thought that Pakistan would be the next economic success story (Runde, 2015). As the second largest economy in South Asia, Pakistan is anticipated to be the world's fastest developing Muslim economy in 2017, ahead of Indonesia, Malaysia, Turkey and Egypt (Zahid, 2017). Pakistan benefits from investment in the China Pakistan Economic Corridor (CPEC) initiative[5] which is equivalent to USD 45 billion in infrastructure development projects including roads, railways and power plants. The economic corridor provides a link between the Xinjiang province in China and Gwadar, which is a port on the south coast of Pakistan west of Karachi.

With the multibillion dollars of infrastructure proposed under CPEC, opportunities to offer *sukuk* for infrastructure and demands for Islamic project financing are expected to increase. The first CPEC transaction was a USD 1.95 billion loan syndication, which was financed for the most part by large Chinese banks. But the deal featured two Shari'ah-compliant branches worth a combined Pakistan rupees 16 billion extended by Faysal Bank, Meezan Bank and Habib Bank (Vizcaino, 2016). The IMF predicts that the CPEC will support the Pakistan economy[6] to develop the gross domestic product by more than 5% by 2020. By 2050, the gross domestic product is forecast to reach USD 4.2 trillion from the current USD 988 billion. The CPEC provides Pakistan with a chance to develop Islamic finance.[7]

18.4 Regulations governing Islamic banking and finance in Pakistan

Islamic or Riba-free banking was introduced in Pakistan in the late 1970s through several pioneering legal and regulatory initiatives that called for the elimination of Riba from the banking system and for the full Islamization of the country's economy. These included changes to Banking Companies Ordinance (BCO-1962) to accommodate non-interest-based transactions, the Mudarabas Ordinance in 1980 to introduce Mudaraba as a two-level fund structure for undertaking Shari'ah complaint businesses (GIFR, 2017).

In spite of the fact that there is no enabling legislation for Islamic banking in the country, Pakistan has made special arrangements under the general market direction for Islamic finance by the ruling of the Federal Shariat Court (FSC) in (November 1991) that declared the procedures adopted by banks to be un-Islamic. However, these changes had very limited success because of the inadequate infrastructure and the absence of skilled human resources (HR). The greatest step towards promoting Islamic banking in the country was the introduction of the Islamic Banking Policy in December 2001 (GIFR, 2017). This policy was adopted to develop a policy according to which banks were allowed to offer Islamic financial services in three forms: (i) full-fledged Islamic banks, (ii) Islamic banking subsidiaries of conventional banks and (iii) independent Islamic banking branches (IBBs) of conventional banks. Under this policy, the first full-fledged Islamic bank, "Meezan Bank", was established in 2003.[8] This became the foundation stone for the second era of Islamic banking in Pakistan.

Detailed directions for profit and loss distribution and pool management in Islamic banking institutions were issued in 2012,[9] replacing the 2008 "Instructions & Guidelines for Shari'a Compliance in Islamic Banking Institutions". These directions required Islamic banking institutions to set up a well-defined pool management framework for administration purposes. Each pool was to have distinct targets and risk reward features, which were to be managed as virtual enterprises having clearly identifiable resources, liabilities, incomes and expenses. These directions were required to bring transparency and standardization across the banking industry and to safeguard investors' interests.

Conventional banks charge interest in their operations. Islamic financial institutions avoid interest and utilize more than one key instrument as the basis for their intermediary activities (Ayub, 2007). In order to encourage conventional banks to set up Islamic subsidiaries, the initial least capital requirement for a subsidiary was brought down from Rs. 10 billion to Rs. 6 billion. In this manner, Meezan Commercial Bank was granted a license from the SBP (State Bank of Pakistan) to set up the first Islamic banking subsidiary. New standards for the operation of Islamic banking windows were issued by SBP in 2014,[10] which expected banks to get composed endorsement from the central bank before opening each Islamic window, as well as providing the regulator with additional details on staffing, training and marketing arrangements.

A second five-year plan to increase support for the advancement of Islamic finance in Pakistan was launched by SBP in 2015. The purpose of the SBP's five-year strategic plan was to set a common direction for Pakistan's

Islamic banking industry to augment the existing growth momentum and to lead the industry to the next level of development. Key concentration areas of the plan, which were supposed to run from 2014 to 2018, include policy environment, Shari'a governance and compliance, awareness, capacity-building and market development. The strategic plan expected the banking business to increase to the amount of 15% of the country's overall banking system by 2018. Since then SBP has introduced numerous new principles and guidelines, the most recent one being IBD Circular No. 01 of 2016 dated September 7, 2016. With this circular, Islamic banks are currently permitted to benchmark their products based on participatory modes – known as Musharaka and Mudaraba – and Wakala-based agency, with respect to an index other than the Karachi Inter Bank Offered Rate (KIBOR). However, they are required to plot their alternative pricing mechanism for participatory financing schemes. This decision by the central bank is expected to enable Islamic banking to be more Shari'a authentic and prepare for the improvement of a Shari'a-consistent evaluating benchmark by Islamic banking institutions in the near future.

18.4.1 Islamic banking in Pakistan

The Islamization of the financial system of Pakistan paralleled the global revival of the Islamic banking in the late 1970s (Akhtar, 2007). On September 29, 1977, the process was initiated by the presidential order to the national Council of Islamic Ideology (CII). The council was asked to develop a plan for an interest-free banking system. The purpose was to eliminate Riba from the financial system of Pakistan. This report is considered to be a milestone towards the Islamization of the banking system in Pakistan. Practical steps taken after the release of this report are given below:

- Practical measures included the operation of specialized financial institutions such as HBFC (House Building Finance Corporation), ICP (Investment Corporation of Pakistan) and NIT (National Investment Trust) in July 1979 and that of the commercial banks from January 1981 to June 1985.
- On June 26, 1980, the legal framework of Pakistan's financial and corporate system was amended in order to permit the issuance of interest-free corporate financing, which was called Participation Term Certificate (PTC). An ordinance was publicized to permit the formation of Mudaraba companies and the issuance of Mudaraba certificates for risk-based capital. The BCO of 1962 was also revised to cover the provision of bank finance through profit and loss sharing (PLS), the markup in prices and hire and leasing purchase.
- In 1981, distinct interest-free counters started operating in all the nationalized commercial banks, and one foreign bank (Bank of Oman) started accepting deposits on a PLS basis.

- In 1982, banks were permitted to offer finance on a selective basis under the practice of Musharaka in order to meet the working capital requirements of trade and industry.
- In 1985, finance to all entities comprised of individuals had to be made according to specified interest-free modes.
- In 1985, all commercial banking in Pakistan rupees was made interest-free and banks in Pakistan no longer accepted interest-bearing deposits. All existing deposits were considered on the basis of PLS. Current deposits continued to be accepted but no interest or share in profit or loss was allowed for any of these accounts. Conversely, foreign currency deposits in Pakistan continued as before.
- In 1991, the FSC declared the process known as 'markup' technique with or without 'buy-back arrangement' to be unacceptable for Islam.
- In 2000, the Commission for the Transformation of Financial System (CTFS) was established in SBP and a task force was established by the Ministry of Finance of Pakistan to eradicate Riba from government financial transactions.
- The CTFS report stated that a number of prior arrangements should be made in preparation for changes in the financial system. The fundamentals of Shari'ah-compliant modes of financing and a draft seminal law called "Islamization of Financial Transactions Ordinance 2001" as well as model agreements for key modes of financing were also identified. With regard to assets and liabilities, the Commission was responsible for dealing with the major products of banks and financial institutions, such as letters of credit or guarantee, bills of exchange, Term Finance Certificates (TFCs), State Bank's Re-finance Schemes, Credit Cards, Interbank transactions, underwriting, foreign currency forward cover and various kinds of bank accounts.

The Islamic banking industry in Pakistan has shown significant advancement since its launch in 2001. Today it consists of 5 full-fledged Islamic banks and 16 Islamic branches of conventional banks with some 2,322 outlets. In 2016, two Islamic banks – Burj Bank Limited and Al-Baraka Bank (Pakistan) Limited – merged into a single entity under the name Al-Baraka Bank (Pakistan) Limited. On December 2016, there were 1,220 Islamic banking windows operated by 9 conventional banks with separate IBBs. Together they held 11.7% of market assets and 13.3% of deposits in the total banking industry after recording PKR 1,853 billion and PKR 1,573 billion in assets and deposits, respectively. The rapid development of Islamic banking is reflected in the increasing share of Islamic banking in assets, deposits and the financing of the banking industry as shown in Figure 18.1. On the basis of the development ratio noted in 2016, it is expected that the development rate will have the capacity to accomplish the 15% target market share by 2018.

Both total assets and deposits have recorded consistent growth with a compounded annual growth rate (CAGR) of 32% and 34% from 2006 to

2016, respectively (Figure 18.2). In addition, the CAGR for financing and investment reached 34% during the period 2006–2016. The diminishing Musharaka remained the main mode of finance, followed by Murabaha and Musharaka (Figure 18.3). However, Murabaha as a mode of finance has become increasingly unpopular. The percentage share of Murabaha financing was 16% in 2016, down from 41% in 2013 (Figures 18.3–18.6). Istisna became consistently preferred as a mode of finance, reaching the figure of 8.4% of the total number of Islamic banking institutions in 2016 as compared to 5.6% in 2013 (Figures 18.3–18.5).

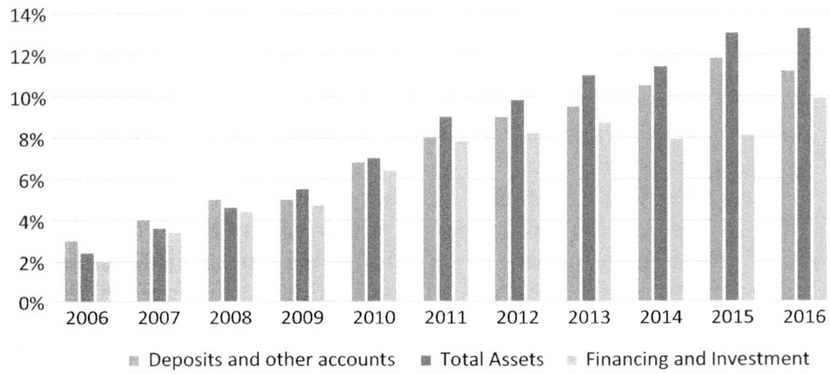

Figure 18.1 Market Share of Assets, Deposits and Financing and Investment of Islamic Banking Sector (%).

Source: State Bank of Pakistan.

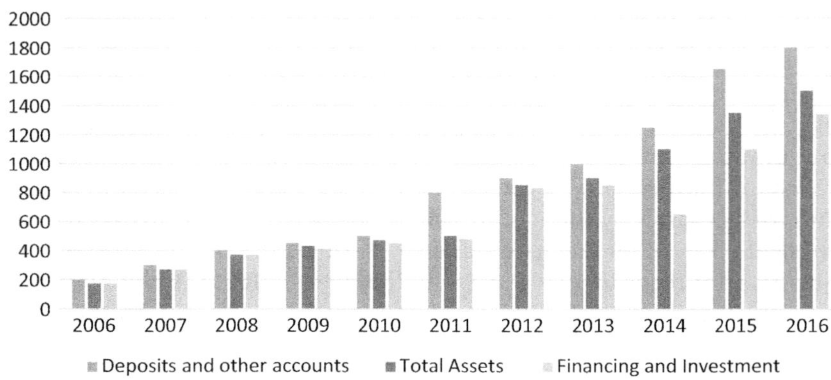

Figure 18.2 Total Assets, Deposits and Financing and Investments of Islamic Banking Sector (PKR Billion).

Source: State Bank of Pakistan.

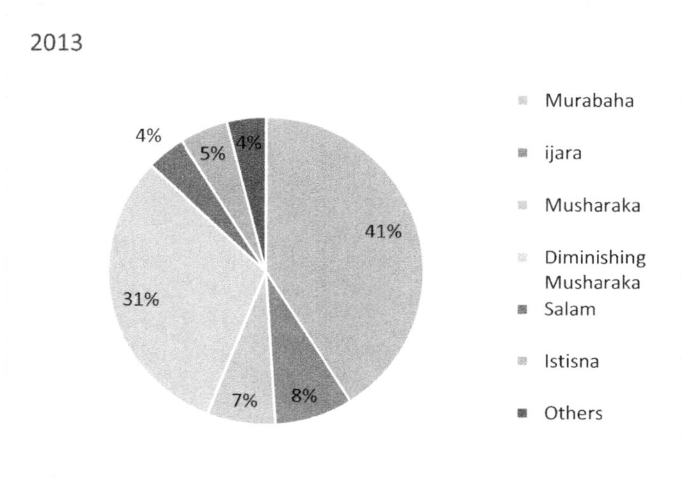

Figure 18.3 Financing mix (% Share).
Source: State Bank of Pakistan.

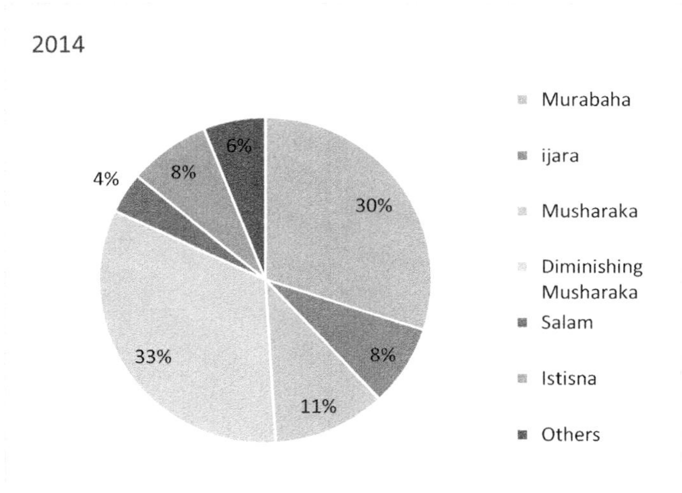

Figure 18.4 Financing mix (% Share).
Source: State Bank of Pakistan.

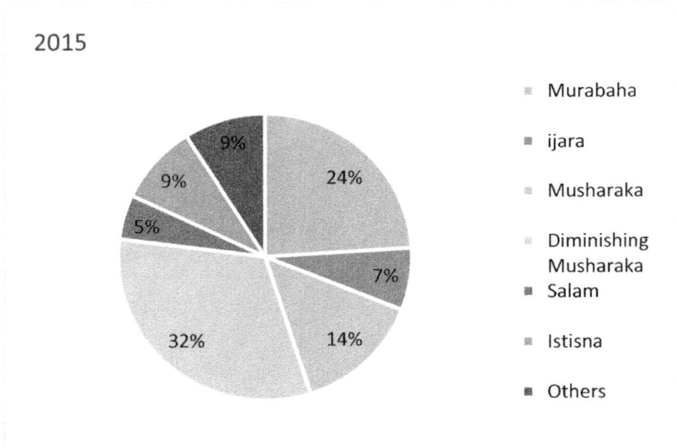

Figure 18.5 Financing mix (% Share).
Source: State Bank of Pakistan.

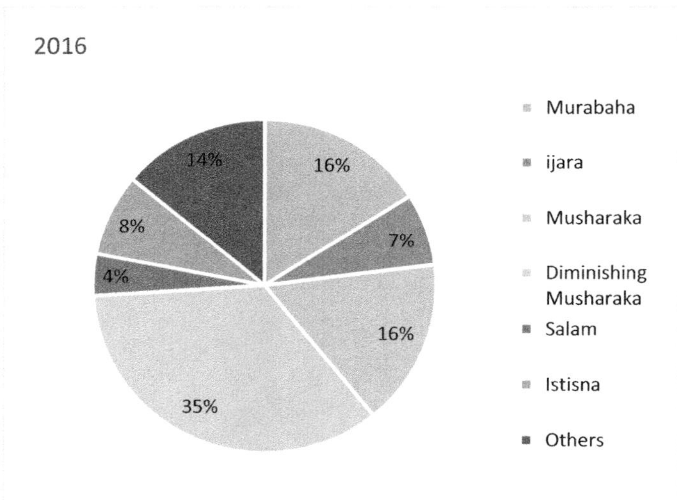

Figure 18.6 Financing mix (% Share).
Source: State Bank of Pakistan.

18.5 Theoretical development of Islamic banking in Pakistan

In the late 1970s, Islamic banking and finance has built up substantial momentum in the Muslim world. Most Muslim countries have brought their Islamic banks into the private sector. So far, however, the economy of no single country has completely accepted the terms of an Islamic economy. Major steps for Islamic banking in Pakistan were taken in 1977 when the President of Pakistan, Mohammed Ziaul Haq, directed the CII to develop a plan to Islamize Pakistan's economy within three years. The CII was founded in 1957 under Articles 197 and 198 of the 1956 Constitution of Pakistan. Officially recognized in 1962 and again in 1973, the CII was a research-based Islamic center, which was set up to assist the government in the implementation of Islamic ideology in different areas of government. The responsibilities and role of the CII were defined in 1973 under Article 230 of the Constitution. Since the constitutional responsibility of the CII was to protect the Islamic character of the polity in Pakistan, its recommendations were to be given serious consideration by the government of the day.

In March 1963, the first interest-based transaction in Pakistan was referred to the CII. In 1969, the CII advised the Government of Pakistan (GoP) for the first time that borrowing on the basis of Riba should not be permitted and that the establishment of an interest-free economy should no longer be delayed. Later, in December 1969, the CII passed a resolution suggesting that interest was forbidden by Islamic law and that the government should constitute a committee consisting of Islamic jurists, legal experts and economists to help the CII to strengthen and support the plan to Islamize the national economy. In November 1977, a panel of 15 economists, bankers and financial experts were appointed (see Appendix A) to examine the technical aspects of restructuring the existing economy and finance sector along Islamic lines. As a result, the panel examined the practice and existing theory of Islamic banking and finance.

In February 1980, the panel submitted its findings to the CII. On the basis of these findings, the CII made some necessary changes in light of the shari'ah and of Islamic jurisprudence. Later in 1980, the CII submitted its report, known as "the 1980 CII Report", to the government. The CII Report of 1980 became the first official, written statement on an interest-free economy and financial system ever made in the Muslim world.

In 1983, President Muhammad Zia ul Haq requested Shaykh-ul-Islam Prof. Dr. Muhammad Tahir ul-Qadri, an eminent scholar; expert in Qur'anic exegesis, Hadith sciences and Islamic jurisprudence; writer of a biography of the Prophet (pbuh); and the founder of Minhaj-ul-Quran International, to develop a workable model for Islamic banking in the country while keeping in view the CII 1980 report and other developments in Islamic banking in various parts of the world. Consequently in 1984, a practical model for an Islamic banking system was presented to the President and to his cabinet by Shaykh-ul-Islam (Qadri, 1994).

In his presentation, Dr. Tahir ul-Qadri criticized the double standards shown by the GoP in allowing two systems of banking to operate at the same time, one system accepting interest and the other system refusing to take interest.

He listed the three main reasons for the failure of the Islamic banking system in Pakistan as follows:

1 Partial and half-hearted enforcement of the new system
2 Continuation of the former, discredited system along with new
3 Desire for a new economic system without paying attention to its conditions and requirements.

He suggested the elements of an Islamic banking system, its instruments, products and right terminology as follows:

a Structure of bank funds
b Structure of public deposits
c Modes of lending
d Benevolent loan
e Ordinary lending
f The multiple counter loan
g Modes of financing and various instruments of investment
h Islamic modes of financing
i Various instruments of investment
j Agricultural banking
k Trade banking
l Inland trade banking
m Foreign trade banking
n Cooperative bank
o Specialized financial institutions
p Monetary policy and central banking
q Reserve ratio
r Liquidity ratio
s Selective credit control
t Moral persuasion
u Bank rate control
v Government transactions in the national economy
w Practical steps for loan-free economy

18.5.1 Policy instruments for eliminating interest

The CII 1980 report, Shaykh-ul-Islam's Islamic banking model and other theoretical works explained the prohibition of interest in light of the Holy Qur'an because of its exploitative nature (The 1980 CII Report, p. 5) and provided both essential and optional strategic instruments for eliminating interest (Qadri, 1994). These documents all stated that charging interest on business and utilization advances was the underlying cause of numerous financial disasters in Pakistan, and, for this reason, charging interest should be abandoned.

These instruments were divided into three sets according to their capacity to build up the IBF model. They approved PLS instruments as an alternative to interest. Moreover, they endorsed leasing, venture selling, Bai Muajjal (Murabaha or deferred payment sale), hire purchase, normal rate of return, time multiple counter loans and special loan facilities as further alternatives to interest. However, they rejected the service charge and indexation systems, judging them to be unsuitable alternatives to interest (The 1980 CII Report, Chapter 1).

18.5.1.1 Primary and ideal instrument: the PLS system

Under the PLS system, rather than charging a fixed rate of interest on lending, the bank enters into an equity-sharing relationship with the customer and shares the risk and return of a joint venture.

18.5.2 Practical developments of Islamic banking in Pakistan

Figures 18.7–18.9 have been taken from the State Bank bulletin of June 30, 2017, which presents the practical development of Islamic banking in Pakistan.

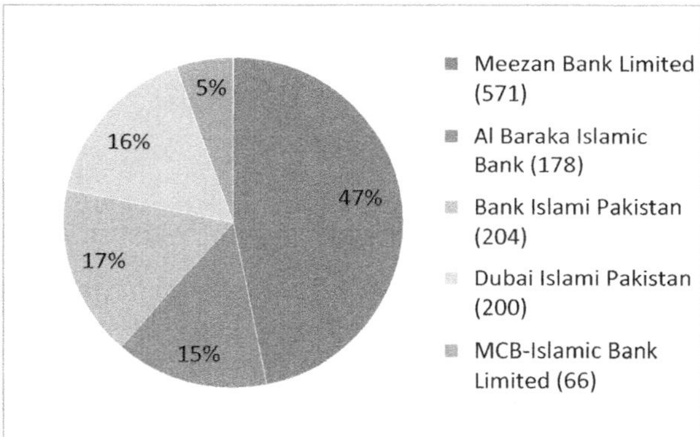

Figure 18.7 IBB network in Pakistan (June, 2017).
Source: State Bank of Pakistan.

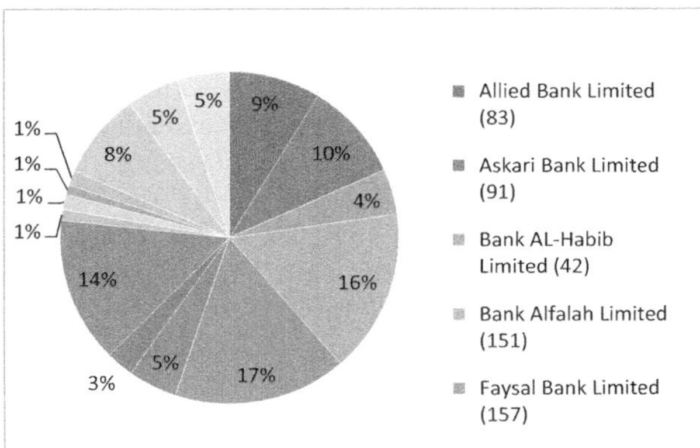

Figure 18.8 Islamic banking branches of conventional banks (June, 2017).
Source: State Bank of Pakistan.

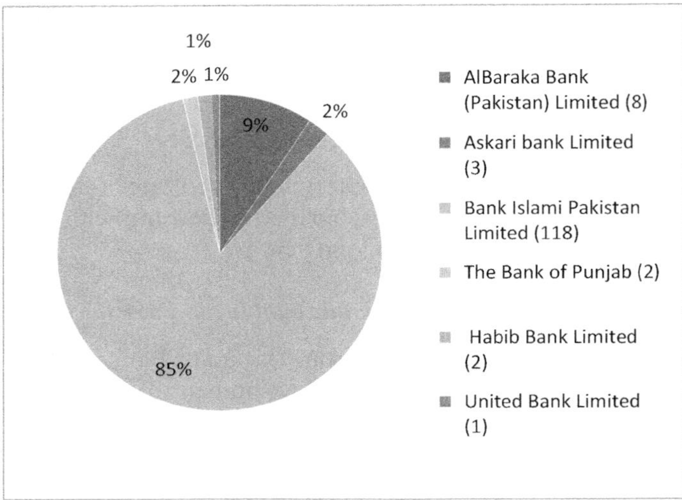

Figure 18.9 Subbranches of IBI's in Pakistan (June, 2017).
Source: State Bank of Pakistan.

18.6 The current state of Islamic banking in Pakistan

Between April and June, 2017, assets of the Islamic banking industry have seen a growth of PKR 150 billion and were recorded at PKR 2,035 billion compared with PKR 1,885 billion in the prior quarter. On the funding side, deposits of Islamic banking industry have grown by PKR 156 billion during the review quarter to reach PKR 1,720 billion compared with PKR 1,564 billion in the previous quarter. The market share of Islamic banking assets and deposits in the overall banking industry was recorded at 11.6% and 13.7%, respectively, by end of June 2017 (Tables 18.1–18.3).

Diminishing Musharaka remained as the leading method of financing followed by Murabaha and Musharaka (Table 18.4).

A review of the financing of each sector shows that the major portion of financing of the Islamic banking industry was extended to the production and the transmission of the energy and the textile sectors. This is in line with the overall trend of the banking industry (Table 18.5).

Current (non-remunerative) and saving deposits increased by PKR 74 billion and PKR 67 billion, respectively, while fixed deposits declined by PKR 14 billion during the review quarter (Table 18.6).

The capital base of the Islamic banking industry increased by 5.6% (PKR 7 billion) between April and June 2017, and reached PKR 134 billion compared to PKR 127 billion in the previous quarter (Table 18.7).

Table 18.1 Industry Progress and Market Share (June 30, 2017)

Particulars	*Industry Progress*			*YoY* Growth (%)*	*Share in Overall Banking Industry (%)*		
	Jun-16	*Mar-17*	*Jun-17*	*Jun-17*	*Jun-16*	*Mar-17*	*Jun-17*
Total assets (Rupees in billions)	1,745	1,885	2,035	16.6	11.4	11.7	11.6
Deposits (Rupees in billions)	1,461	1,564	1,720	17.8	13.2	13.2	13.7
Number of Islamic banking institutions	22	21	21	(4.5)	–	–	–
Number of Islamic branches[a]	2,146	2,317	2,320	8.1	–	–	–

Source: Data submitted by bank under quarterly reporting chart of account (RCOA); SBP (2017).

a Including subbranches.

* Year-over-Year (YoY).

Table 18.2 Branch Network of Islamic Banking Industry (June 30, 2017)

Province/Region	*Total Number*	*Share (%)*
Punjab	1,091	47.0
Sindh	699	30.1
Khyber Pakhtunkhwa	258	11.1
Baluchistan	99	4.3
Gilgit Baltistan	10	0.4
FATA	8	0.3
Federal Capital	119	5.1
AJK	36	1.6
Total	2,320	100

Source: SBP (2017).

Table 18.3 Financing Mix (% Share)

	Jun-16	*Mar-17*	*Jun-17*
Murabaha	20.1	16.4	17.0
Ijarah	7.2	6.4	6.8
Musharaka	12.9	16.3	17.9
Diminishing Musharaka	35.8	32.3	29.6
Salam	3.3	5.2	5.2
Istisna	7.3	8.9	7.2
Others	13.4	14.5	16.3
Total	100.0	100.0	100.0

Source: SBP (2017).

Table 18.4 Financing Concentration (% Share)

	Jun-16	*Mar-17*	*Jun-17*	*Industry*
Chemical and pharmaceuticals	6.5	6.1	5.4	4.1
Agribusiness	4.0	5.2	8.5	8.9
Textile	13.9	13.2	11.8	12.8
Cement	1.7	1.6	1.7	1.3
Sugar	2.8	4.7	4.1	3.9
Shoes and leather garments	0.6	0.5	0.4	0.4
Automobile and transportation equipment	1.4	1.2	0.9	1.5
Financial	0.6	0.6	1.1	3.1
Electronics and electrical appliances	1.1	1.2	1.2	1.2
Production and transmission of energy	14.9	15.4	14.2	14.6
Individual	13.2	11.7	11.7	8.9
Others	39.2	38.6	39.0	39.3
Total	100.0	100.0	100.0	100.0

Source: SBP (2017).

Table 18.5 Breakup of Deposits

	Rupees in Billion			*% Growth*	
	Jun-16	*Mar-17*	*Jun-17*	*YoY*	*QoQ*
Customers					
Fixed deposits	314	344	330	5.1	(4.1)
Saving deposits	567	616	683	20.4	10.9
Current accounts – remunerative	9	7	9	–	28.6
Current account – non-remunerative	460	507	581	26.3	14.6
Others	9	9	14	55.6	9.0
Subtotal	1,359	1,483	1,617	18.9	9.0
Financial Institutions					
Remunerative deposits	100	79	102	2.0	29.1
Non-remunerative deposits	2	2	1	(50.0)	(50.0)
Subtotal	102	81	103	0.9	27.2
Total	1,461	1,564	1,720	17.7	10.0

Source: SBP (2017).

Table 18.6 Capital Ratios (%)

	Jun-16	*Mar-17*	*Jun-17*	*Industry*
Capital to total assets	6.2	6.7	6.6	7.8
Capital (net non-performing assets) to total assets	6.1	6.3	6.1	7.2

Source: SBP (2017).

Table 18.7 Profitability and Earning

	Jun-16	*Mar-17*	*Jun-17*	*Industry*
Profit after tax (rupees in billions)	6.1	3.8	8.8	90.0
Return on assets	0.7	0.8	0.9	1.1
Return on equity	11.3	12.2	13.8	13.1
Operating expense to gross income	75.6	71.1	68.2	55.8

Source: SBP (2017).

18.7 Islamic capital market

Following financial liberalization, Islamic capital markets (ICMs) experienced economic growth. In Malaysia, ICM was launched in the 1980s, and it commenced its operation in Pakistan, Bahrain and other countries in the beginning of the 1990s. In the 1970s and 1980s, Structured Involvement of Islamic Finance in Financial Markets was set up by creating many institutes of takaful, Islamic financial institutes and investment corporations (Shah, 2015).

A slow but sure pickup in economic growth has been attributed to fresh trends in international capital markets and the reduction of global policy reservations since 2017. Moreover, the last year saw a surge in investors' taking risks, moderation in financial instability and stability of the stock market in hosts of jurisdictions in a positive international financial and liquidity environment.

Throughout 2017, ICMs experienced positive growth, particularly sizeable growth in *sukuk* driven by large sovereign issuances, an upturn in Islamic assets under management and strong performances by Islamic shares (IFSB, 2018).

18.7.1 ICM in Pakistan

The top regulator of capital markets in Pakistan is the Securities and Exchange Commission of Pakistan (SECP). Its functions include supervising and controlling the development of the capital market, the intermediaries operating in the capital market and the Self-Regulatory Organizations (SROs). The SROs comprise the Pakistan Mercantile Exchange Limited (PMEX), the National Clearing Company of Pakistan Limited (NCCPL), the Central Depository Company of Pakistan Limited (CDC) as well as the Pakistan Stock Exchange (PSX). The agents and intermediaries working in the capital market are underwriters, brokers and managers, share registrars, credit rating companies and security advisers. In Pakistan, *sukuk* issuance was launched in 2006 when Islamic banking in the country was still at adolescent stage.

In the period under evaluation for the advancement of the ICM, the ensuing big steps were taken:

- On August 31, 2016, tax neutrality for *sukuk* in relation to conventional instruments was effected through an amendment to the Tax Ordinance.
- Under the enabling provision given in the proposed Companies Bill, an all-inclusive shari'ah governance structure was drafted.
- SECP consultative forum on Islamic finance, which comprised of representatives from industry and financial sector, was established.
- All Shares Islamic Index was set up at PSX. The index represents corporations which meet particular shari'ah compliance criteria. Extra disclosure requirements for corporations listed on PSX have been embraced in the suggested Companies Bill with the intention of Shari'ah screening; this measure aims at inclusion or removal of a scrip from the index.
- In order to handle a range of industrial issues and challenges in Islamic banking and finance, SECP-SBP Joint forum on Islamic business is striving in an efficient and organized way. SBP-SECP, after evaluating the Commodity Murabaha Product forwarded by PMEX, suggested alteration so that it might sit comfortably with shari'ah directives.
- Through the Finance Act, 2016, a 2-percentage point tax refund for shari'ah-compliant listed corporations was introduced. Federal Board of Revenue (FBR) has announced the criteria for the tax refund. The tax refund for suitable listed companies, in addition to tax impartiality for *sukuk*, will speed up the development of ICM.
- Comprising eminent Muslim academics, an Independent Shari'ah Advisory Board (SAB) was established at SECP. This board offered proposals to the commission concerning issues associated with shari'ah (Economic Adviser's Wing, Finance Division, Government of Pakistan, 2017).

18.7.2 Shari'ah-compliant stock index

In 2008, KSE-Meezan Index (KMI-30) came to the fore so as to fulfill the rising demand for Islamic equity investments. This stock index, compatible with shari'ah, was formed for those of the faithful who are eager to align their financial activities with their creed and religious norms. On the one hand, KMI-30 index won and boosted investor trust. On the other hand, it conducted quality research in an attempt to measure the performance of shari'ah-compliant stocks.

At present, the Karachi Stock Exchange (KSE) has three key indices. They are KSE-30 index, KSE-All Shares index and KSE-100 index. KMI-30 index consists of 30 stocks that are compatible with shari'ah and is listed at KSE. It is rebalanced every six months, and, for index construction, "Free-float market capitalization" method is practiced: the world's prominent index providers (FTSE, S&P, MSCI, STOXX and SENSE) employ this

List of 30 Shari'ah-Compliant Stocks

No.	*Name*	*Symbol*
1.	Fauji Cement Ltd.	FCCL
2.	K-Electric Limited	KEL
3.	Pakistan Petroleum	PPL
4.	Hub Power Company	HUBC
5.	Engro Corporation	ENGRO
6.	Lucky Cement	LUCK
7.	National Refinery	NRL
8.	Sui Southern Gas Pakistan	SSGC
9.	Pakistan Oil Fields	POL
10.	Dawood Hercules Corporation	DAWH
11.	Sui Northern Gas Pakistan	SNGP
12.	Millat Tractors	MTL
13.	Engro Fertilizers	EFERT
14.	D.G Khan Cement	DGKC
15.	Treet Corporation Ltd	TREET
16.	Packages Ltd.	PKGS
17.	Nishat Mills	NML
18.	Maple Leaf Cement	MLCF
19.	Mari Gas Company	MARI
20.	Engro Polymer and Chemicals Ltd	EPCL
21.	GlaxoSmithKline Pakistan	GLAXO
22.	The Searle Company Ltd	SEARL
23.	Pak Elektron Ltd	PAEL
24.	Kot Addu Power Company Ltd	KAPCO
25.	Attock Petroleum Ltd	APL
26.	International Steels Ltd	ISL
27.	Attock Refinery Ltd	ATRL
28.	International Industries Ltd	INIL
29.	Oil and Gas Development	OGDC
30.	Hascol Petroleum Ltd	HASCOL

Source: Chen and Jebran (2017).

method. Each stock is capped at 12% on weights and the SAB of Meezan Bank regulates KMI-30 index.

18.7.3 Modaraba

In the growth and development of Islamic modes of financing at home, modarabas have played a significant role; their certificate holders have earned highest dividend percentage. The modarabas are offering diverse Islamic financial products and services in agreement with Islamic directives.

So that they might benefit SMEs and groups on low incomes, the modarabas were directed to make efforts to expand their outreach. Four modarabas opened first Islamic financing facility centers in Rawalpindi in order to offer inexpensive financing compatible with shari'ah injunctions. Deriving benefit from the Islamic financing facility centers, the people of the area buy motorcycles and other products.

18.7.3.1 Current developments for Modarabas

To overcome practical difficulties, currently the modaraba regulatory framework is reconsidered and re-examined in accordance with international practices. The resultant exercise will bring about operational flexibilities. The key reforms are as follows:

- Stipulating fresh limits concerning certificate holding of Modaraba Company and its linked parties in a modaraba so as to boost and increase equity participation by the people.
- Presentation of fresh ideas of fund-raising through issuance of Term Equity Certificates.
- Presentation of the idea of unlisted modarabas in order to assist recent entrants and facilitate the development of Islamic financial services industry.
- The suggested amendments, when they are sanctioned, would be effective in advancing modarabas as genuine Islamic financial institutions. Moreover, they would offer stimulus for the development of the sector (Economic survey Pakistan 2016–2017).

18.7.4 Sukuk

In 2017, global *sukuk* issuances saw a development of 22.8%. The full volume of yearly issuances reached USD 91.9 billion at the end of 2017, compared to USD 74.8 billion in 2016. This maintains the slow but sure recuperation of *sukuk* markets over the last two years in the wake of the economic downturn of 2015. At the end of 2017, the entire volume of unpaid *sukuk* stood at USD 399.92 billion – a 10% increase in volume of unpaid *sukuk* from 2016. Nevertheless, full issuances for 2017 stayed below the USD 131 billion mark. While the latest development trajectory points to a steady closing of this gap, it is the highest yearly volume of *sukuk* issuances so far.

In the Pakistani market, on the whole 107 *sukuk* valuing USD 10,472 million were issued in 2017. Of these, 19 are GoP Ijara *Sukuk*, whereas 88 have been issued by corporate or quasi-sovereign bodies; the *sukuk* issued are medium term. Although most of them are privately placed, some commercial *sukuk* have been recorded at the stock exchange (Figures 18.10–18.13).

This subsection examines the development trends of the *sukuk* market over the last year (Figure 18.14).

18.7.4.1 Sovereign sukuk

The complete sovereign issuances in 2017 comprised in the region of USD 4.8 billion (6.3%) of liquid assets raised by means of short-term *sukuk* (that is, less than one-year maturity), which is less than in preceding years (2016: 19.7%; USD 11.7 billion).

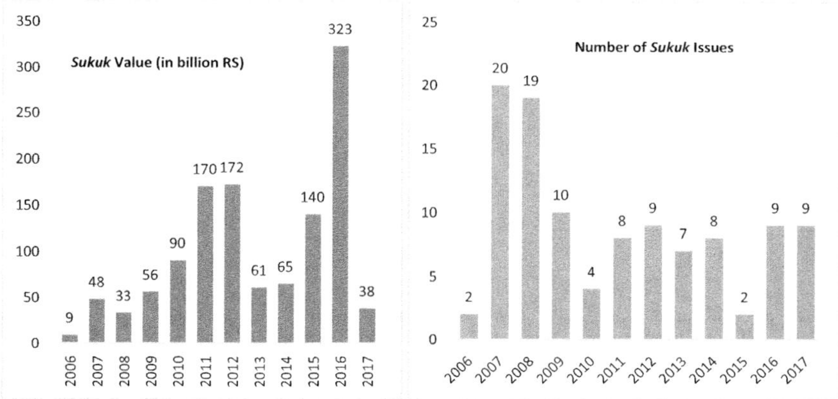

Figure 18.10 Year-wise domestic *sukuk* summary.
Source: State Bank of Pakistan (2018).

Year	Corporate	Sovereign	Quasi-Sovereign
2006	7.2	0.0	92.8
2007	55.5	0.0	44.5
2008	48.6	14.0	37.4
2009	43.3	29.0	27.7
2010	27.1	55.7	17.2
2011	15.9	72.7	11.4
2012	11.5	79.3	9.2
2013	10.7	78.5	10.8
2014	11.0	78.3	10.7
2015	9.2	79.3	11.5
2016	8.9	74.2	16.9
2017	10.5	73.1	16.4

Figure 18.11 Entity-wise and year-wise breakup of *sukuk* (cumulative as of end year in per cent).
Source: State Bank of Pakistan (2018).

Auction	Issue Date	Maturity Date	Amount of *Sukuk*
Pakistan first International *Sukuk*	Jan-05	Jan-10	US$ 600 million
Pakistan second International *Sukuk*	Nov-14	Nov-19	US$ 1,000 million
Pakistan third International *Sukuk*	Oct-16	Oct-21	US$ 1,000 million
Pakistan fourth International *Sukuk*	Nov-17	Nov-22	US$ 1,000 million

Figure 18.12 International *sukuk* issued by the GoP.
Source: State Bank of Pakistan (2018).

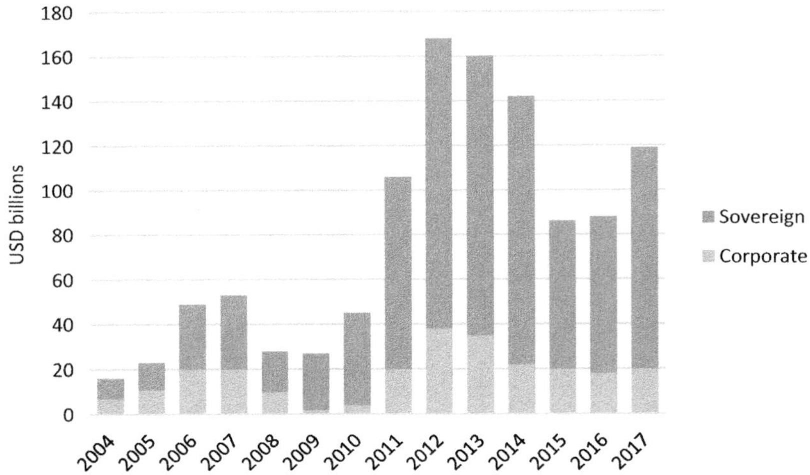

Figure 18.13 Sukuk issuance trend.
Source: IFSB (2018).

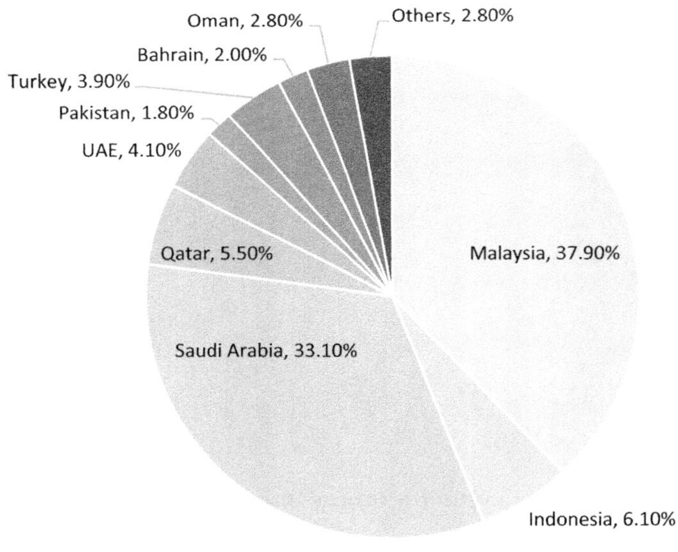

Figure 18.14 Ṣukuk issuances by jurisdiction and share (2017).
Source: IFSB (2018).

The GoP took advantage of the *sukuk* market through two *sukuk al-ijra*, increasing a total of around USD 1.7 billion which comprised of a 5-year US dollar-denominated tranche of USD 1 billion, advancing a profit rate of 5.63%, and a 3-year local currency issuance of roughly USD 677.2 million, advancing a profit rate of 5.24% (Figure 18.15).

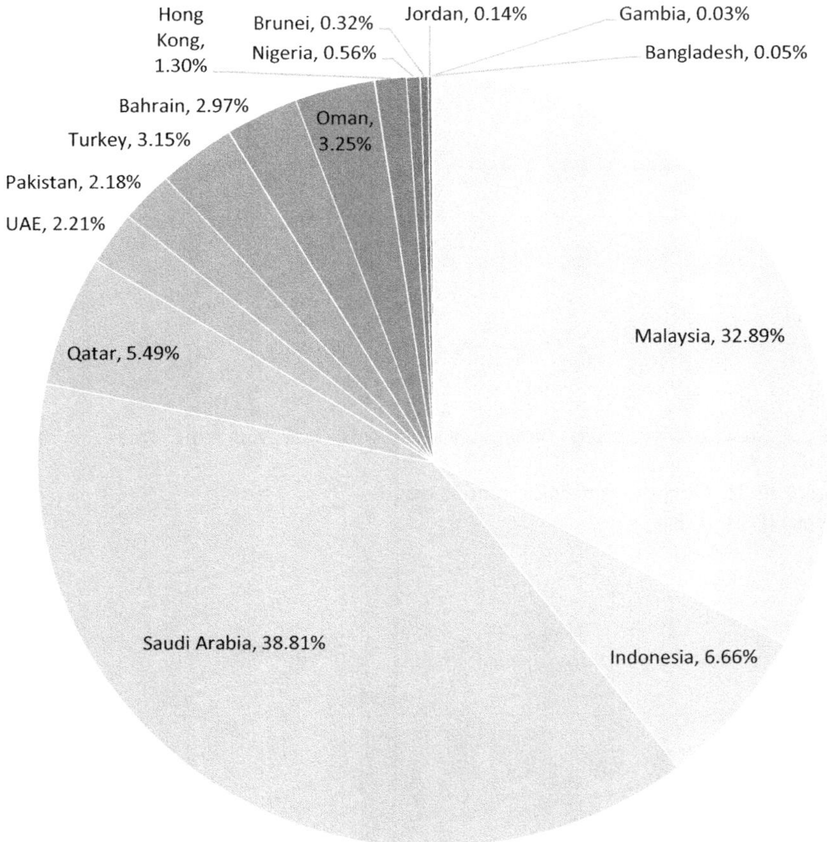

Figure 18.15 Sovereign *sukuk* issuance by jurisdiction (2017).

Particularly, the increase in sovereign issuances in the course of 2017 is basically by reason of an upsurge in the volume of sovereign issuances by four jurisdictions from the Gulf Cooperation Council (GCC) region: Bahrain, Oman, Saudi Arabia and Qatar. There was a conspicuous falloff in sovereign issuances from the UAE, Indonesia and Pakistan in comparison with the last year's issuances, and decrease, in terms of total volume, of issuances from Brunei, Malaysia, Jordan and Turkey.

18.7.4.2 Corporate sukuk

In 2017, business *sukuk* issuances, breaking the relentless sinking trend noted in business issuances from 2012, experienced a humble recovery. Issuances by corporates made a total of USD 15.75 billion in 2017; it signifies a 2.3% growth from the last year [2016: USD 15.4 billion; 2015: USD 20.7 billion] (Figures 18.16 and 18.17).

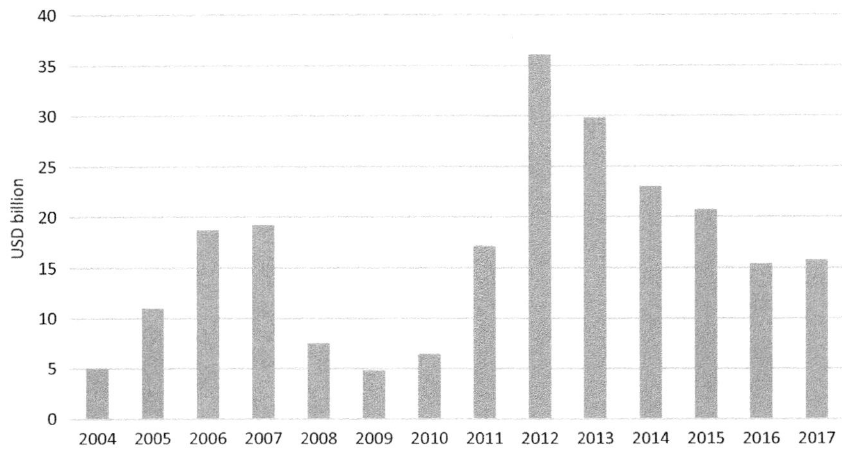

Figure 18.16 Corporate *sukuk* issuance trend.
Source: IFSB (2018).

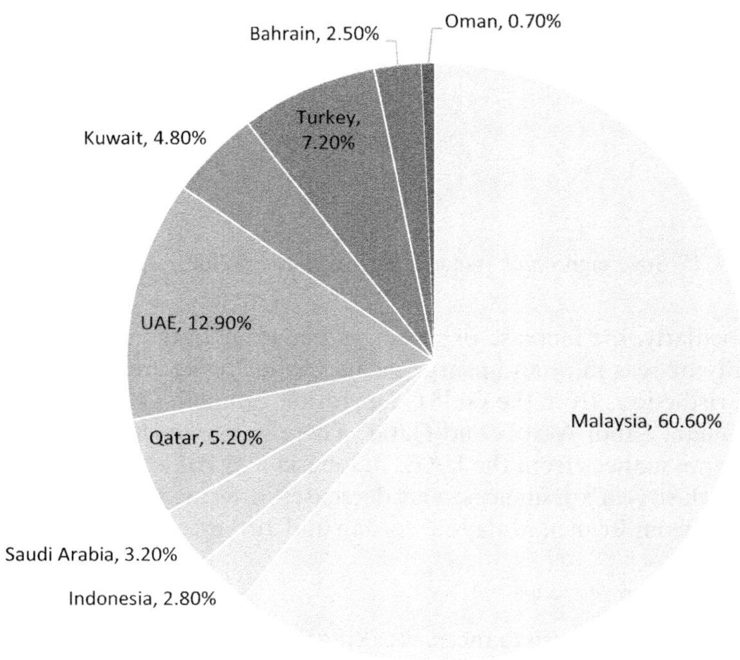

Figure 18.17 Corporate *sukuk* issuance by jurisdiction (2017).
Source: State Bank of Pakistan (2018).

The moderate general growth in corporate issuances was the outcome of increases in issuance by corporates from Oman, Malaysia, Kuwait and Indonesia, although the general volume of corporate issuances sank in a good number of jurisdictions. The reduced levels of corporate issuances from numerous jurisdictions are attributable to various factors such as high charges of issuance of *ṣukuk*, complicated legal structures, dearth of standardization of *ṣukuk* as well as suitable assets, along with dearth of monetary enticement and a level playing field in various jurisdictions for *ṣukuk* issuance compared to bonds.

18.7.5 Islamic funds assets by domicile

In the Islamic funds industry, 1,161 Islamic funds were holding approximately USD 66.7 billion of assets under management at the end of 2017 (2016: 1,167 Islamic funds, USD 56.1 billion AuM) (see Figure 18.18). Even though the number of Islamic funds plummeted somewhat, the total AuM rose by 18.8% – a conspicuous improvement from the constant decrease in total AuM noted from 2014. Out of the entire number of Islamic funds, 821 funds were ranked effective, holding approximately USD 61.6 billion AuM (2016: 826 active funds, USD 51.2 billion AuM). Even though the number of funds has dropped, the size of funds increased on the whole in 2017, with the typical AuM of all active funds standing at USD 79.8 million as at the end of 2017 (2016: USD 64.9 million). This is an encouraging development taking into consideration the need for Islamic funds to acquire greater economies of scale, a mighty challenge in this sector. The Islamic funds that have become dormant added up to 29%, or 341 funds, holding roughly USD 5.1

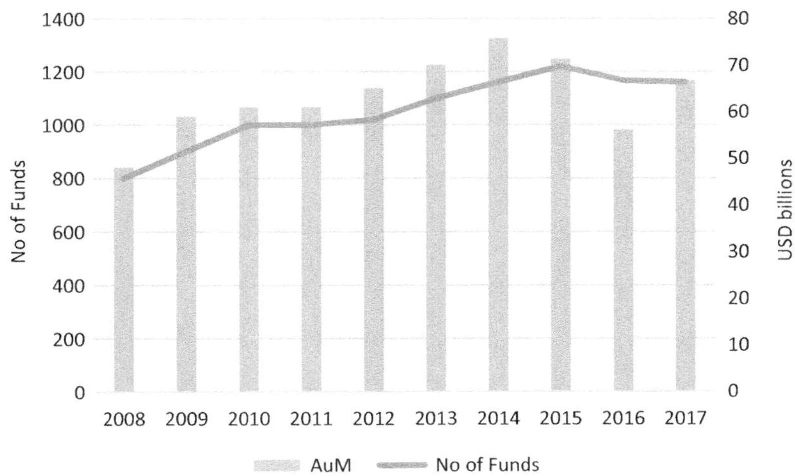

Figure 18.18 Growth in assets under management and number of Islamic funds.

billion AuM in total or an average of USD 15 million per fund; it implies that minor Islamic funds may be confronting challenges.

In 2017, the allocation of Islamic funds by domicile and share of total AuM across the top five jurisdictions was in keeping with 2016. Funds based in five jurisdictions constitute approximately 88% of the total Islamic funds' AuM in 2017 (2016: 85%; 2015: 87%). The reminder of 12% AuM, worth USD 8.4 billion, was distributed across 29 jurisdictions (2016: 85%, USD 8.2 billion across 32 jurisdictions). The number of jurisdictions in which Islamic funds were domiciled sank to 34 in 2017, compared to 37 in 2016. However, an overall growth occurred in total AuM to USD 66.7 billion (2016: USD 56.1 billion).

Shari'ah-compliant mutual funds have touched colossal development in Pakistan. The Share of Islamic Mutual Funds represented 38% of the total Mutual Fund industry as on January 31, 2017, and there were 37 modaraba corporations and 28 modarabas as on March 31, 2017. What is more, the aggregated equity of modarabas was Rs. 20,712.00 million, while the complete possessions of the modaraba sector stood at Rs. 41,473.00 million. Out of the 25 operational ones, 19 modarabas announced cash dividends. The complete possessions for Mutual Funds were recorded 2,391 million US dollars and 130 million US dollars for Islamic Pension Funds.

In 2017, out of the 34 jurisdictions that were domiciles for Islamic funds, 20 jurisdictions are non-OIC countries. The main domiciles for Islamic funds in this category were from Luxembourg, Ireland and the US (Figure 18.19).

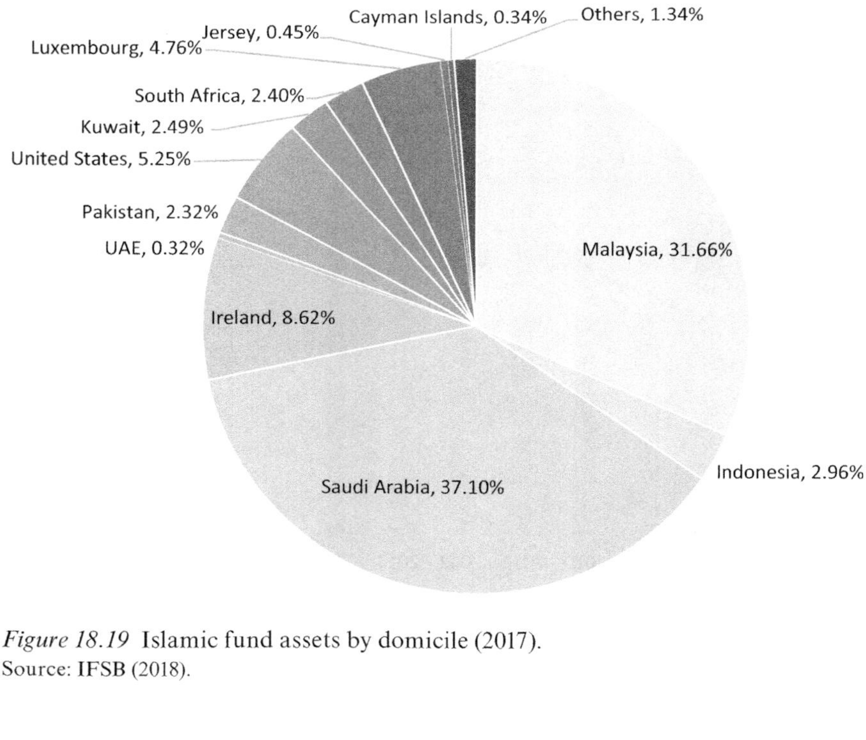

Figure 18.19 Islamic fund assets by domicile (2017).
Source: IFSB (2018).

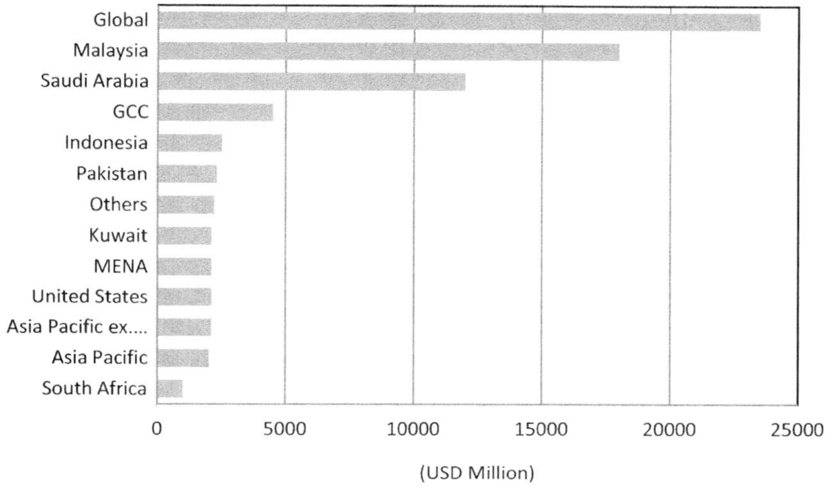

Figure 18.20 Islamic fund assets by geographical focus (2017).
Source: IFSB (2018).

In 2017, the three leading categories for geographical focus of investing Islamic funds stayed in the main unaffected from 2016, with funds that had an international investment focus remaining the chief category, making 35% of total AuM in 2017 or USD 23.2 billion in dollar terms (2016: 34%, USD 18.9 billion) (see Figure 18.20). The mounting worldwide focus of Islamic funds indicates the need for resources in order to attain greater portfolio diversification in view of the volatility of recent geopolitical and economic circumstances. Funds with a Malaysian focus were the second-largest class, which multiplied in 2017, accounting for 26% of total AuM or USD 17.4 billion in dollar terms, compared to 25% of total AuM or USD 14.2 billion, in 2016. The Saudi market, accounting for 19% of total AuM, represented the third-biggest focus [2016: 21%; 2015: 31%].

18.8 AAOIFI (Accounting and Auditing Organization for Islamic Financial Institution)

In 1991, Accounting and Auditing Organization for Islamic Financial Institution (AAOIFI) was established in Bahrain. It is an international not-for-profit organization mainly responsible for the growth and determination of standards for the global Islamic finance industry. Among its most outstanding accomplishments so far is the determination of 94 standards in the areas of Shari'ah, accounting, auditing, ethics and governance. In a number of countries, central banks and regulatory authorities implement the AAOIFI standards both on a compulsory basis and simply as a guideline.

From over 45 countries, AAOIFI is supported by numbers of official affiliates; consisting of central banks; and governing authorities, financial institutions, accounting and auditing firms and legal firms. Currently, the leading Islamic financial institutions of Pakistan are following its standards and have introduced a progressive degree of harmonization of international Islamic finance practices.[11]

18.9 Establishment of Islamic Microfinance Banks in Pakistan

With the growing popularity of this sector, it became necessary to recommend strategies for Islamic microfinance services in Pakistan. For the smooth introduction of microfinance products and services that were Shari'ah compliant, the following steps were taken.

Under the Microfinance Institutions (MFI) Ordinance of 2001, all sponsors eager to establish full-fledged Islamic microfinance banks (IMFB) were obliged to obtain licenses from SBP (SBP, 2005). This ordinance allowed the formation of four categories of microfinance banking in the country as follows:

1 National Microfinance Banks
2 Provincial Microfinance Banks
3 Regional Microfinance Banks
4 District Microfinance Banks

Under the MFIs Ordinance of 2001, the standards and conditions for obtaining a license for IMFB were made available through the official website of SBP.[12] Moreover, the following criteria were also determined for persons/entities applying for an IMFB license:

i All financial transactions of IMFB would take place in accordance with the principles of Shari'ah.
ii Each IMFB may be required to name a Shari'ah consultant who should meet the established criteria of Shari'ah advisors, which were issued in IBD Round 2 in 2007 and which were subject to regular amendment. The appointment of a Shari'ah consultant may require the endorsement of the SBP. Information about Shari'ah consultants should be submitted to the SBP on form SAP of the aforementioned circular.
iii The application should outline the modes of finance and the product structures that will be adopted to create assets and to give financial assistance to customers.
iv The applicant should also have the ability to guarantee that their microfinance banking business will run according to the principles of Shari'ah.

v All the deposits accepted by the microfinance banking should be acknowledged either on demand or on PLS basis.

Since 2001, many Islamic microfinance institutions have been established, which follow the guidelines provided by SBP. Examples of such institutions are Akhuwat[13] and Al-Mawakhat Islamic Microfinance[14] (AMIM).

18.10 Islamic finance education in Pakistan

Three centers of excellence in Islamic finance were established by SBP in renowned institutions[15] such as the Institute of Business Administration, Karachi (IBA); Lahore University of Management Sciences, Lahore (LUMS); and the Institute of Management Sciences (IMS), Peshawar (GIFR, 2017). Other independently established Islamic financial institutes have been set up in certain private sector universities of Pakistan such as the School of Islamic Economics, Business and Finance at Minhaj University Lahore. It is expected that these centers will increase the pool of skilled professionals by enhancing the number of certifications, degree programs and training programs related to Islamic banking and finance.[16]

Appendix A

Members of the Panel of Economists and Bankers Appointed by the Council of Islamic Ideology in November 1977

Chairman

Dr. Ehsan Rashid
Professor of Economics and Director Applied Economic Research Centre University of Karachi, Pakistan.

Memberseda

1 Dr. Rafiq Ahmed
Pro-Vice Chancellor, University of Punjab, Lahore, Pakistan
2 Sheikh Mahmood Ahmad
Lahore, Pakistan
3 Mr. Abdul Jabbar Khan
President Habib Bank Limited, Karachi, Pakistan
4 Dr. Nurul Islam Mian
Director, Institute of Economic Studies, University of Peshawar, Peshawar, Pakistan
5 Dr. Syed Nawab Haider Naqvi
Director, Pakistan Institute of Development Economics, Islamabad, Pakistan
6 Dr. Mian M Nazeer
Professor of Economics, University of Peshawar, Peshawar, Pakistan
7 Mr. D M Qureshi
Managing Director, Banker's Equity Limited, Karachi, Pakistan
8 Professor Shakrullah
Head of the Economics, Department Baluchistan University, Quetta, Pakistan
9 Dr. A H Siddiqi
Director of Studies, Administrative Staff College, Lahore, Pakistan
10 Mr. Khadim Hosain Siddiqui
Member of Pakistan Banking Council, Karachi, Pakistan
11 Mr. A K Sumar
Karachi, Pakistan

12 Mr. Abdu Wasay
Bank of Credit and Commerce International, Karachi, Pakistan
13 Dr. S M Hasan-uz-Zaman
Chief, Islamic Economics Division Research Department, State Bank of Pakistan, Karachi, Pakistan

Convenor

Dr. Ziauddin Ahmad
Deputy Governor, State Bank of Pakistan

Notes

1 Abu 'Ubayd, *Kitab al-Amwal*, p. 41, §82.
2 al-Suyuti, *Tarikh al-Khulafa'*, p. 110.
3 al-Sarakhsi, *al-Mabsut*, 18:22.
4 al-Ya'qubi, *al-Tarikh*, 2:155.
5 www.ciis.org.cn/english/2017-11/10/content_40064710.htm
6 www.dawn.com/news/1290523
7 www2.deloitte.com/content/dam/Deloitte/pk/Documents/risk/pak-china-eco-corridor-deloittepk-noexp.pdf
8 www.meezanbank.com/meezan-bank-awarded-as-the-best-islamic-bank-of-pakistan/
9 IBD Circular No. 03 of 2012, November 19, 2012.
10 http://www.sbp.org.pk/ibd/bulletin/2014/IBB-Dec-2014.pdf
11 http://aaoifi.com on October 19, (2017).
12 www.sbp.org.pk/about/micro/criteria.htm
13 www.akhuwat.org.pk/
14 http://almawakhat.org/
15 www.sbp.org.pk/press/2016/SBP-Best-CB-08-Jan-16.pdf
16 www.mul.edu.pk/education/106/SIEBF.html

References

Abdul Kadir, Dato' M. R. (2009). Islamic Banking & Finance at the Crossroads of Global Financial Crisis: The Way Forward, Kuala Lumpur.

Akhtar, S. (2007). Islamic banking: Past, present and future outlook. *Keynote Address by the Governor of the State Bank of Pakistan, at Dawn Asia Finance Conference, Karachi, 11.*

Ayub, M. (2007). *Understanding Islamic Finance*. Chichester, UK: John Wiley & sons Ltd.

Chapra, M. U. (2001). *The Future of Economics: An Islamic Perspective*. Jakarta: Shari'ah Economics and Banking Institute.

Chen, S., and Jebran, K. (2017). Examining Anomalies in Islamic Equity Market of Pakistan. *Journal of Sustainable Finance & Investment*, 7(3), 275–289.

CIFP-Part 1 Study Material. (2006). *Islamic Financial Institutions and Markets*. Kuala.

Ebrahim, M. S., and Joo, T. K. (2001). Islamic Banking in Brunei Darussalam. *International Journal of Social Economics*, 28(7), 314–337.

Economic Adviser's Wing, Finance Division, Government of Pakistan. (2017). *Pakistan Economic Survey 2016–2017* (Survey Report). Islamabad: Government of Pakistan, 462. Retrieved from www.finance.gov.pk

Erol, C., and El-Bdour, R. (1989). Attitude, Behavior and Patronage Factors of Bank Customers towards Islamic Banks. *International Journal of Bank Marketing*, 7(6), 31–37.

Global Islamic Finance Report, GIFR (2017), Edbiz Consulting, UK

Haron, S., and Yamirudeng, K. M. (2003). Islamic Banking in Thailand: Prospects and Challenges. *International Journal of Islamic Financial Services*, 5(2), 1–11.

Hamoud, S. H. (1985). *Islamic Banking*. London, UK: Arabian Information Ltd.

IFSB. (2018). Islamic Financial Services Industry Stability Report. Bank Negara Malaysia. Retrieved from www.ifsb.org/download.php?id=4811&lang=English&pg=/index.php

Joni, T. B. (2001), and Hadenan, T. (2006). *Untung Dalam Sistem Perbankan Islam*. Kuala Lumpur: University Malaya Press, 70.

Karim, A. A. (2001). *Ekonomi Islam Suatu Kajian Tempororer*. Jakarta: Gema Insani Press, Indonesian.

Karim-Abd al-Z. (1996). *Madkhal Li Dirasah al-Syari`ah al-Islamiyyah*. Beirut: Muassasah al-Risalah

Khan, M. M., and Bhatti, M. I. (2006). Why Interest-Free Banking and Finance Movement Failed in Pakistan, *Humanomics*, 22, 145–161. doi:10.1108/08288660610703320

Khan, M. M., and Bhatti, M. I. (2008). *Developments in Islamic Banking: The Case of Pakistan*. Basingstoke, UK: Palgrave MacMillan.

Lee, M. P., and Detta, I. J. (2007). *Islamic Banking & Finance Law*. Malaysia: Pearson.

Mohamad, M. T. (2013). The Historical Development of Modern Islamic Banking: A Study in South-East Asia Countries.

Qadri, Dr, Tahir ul. (1994). *Bila Sood Bankari aur Islami Maeeshiyat*. Pakistan: Minhaj-ul-Quran Publications.

Qadri, S. Q. (2008). Islamic Banking: An Introduction. *Business Law Today*, 17 (6), 59–60.

Rahardjo, D. (1998). The Question of Islamic Banking in Indonesia. In Ariff, M., (ed.). *Islamic Banking in Southeast Asia*. Singapore: Institute of Southeast Asian, 137–163.

Runde, D. (2015) Pakistan: The Next Colombia Success Story? Retrieved from www.forbes.com/sites/danielrunde/2015/08/03/pakistan-the-next-colombia success-story/#13d498b330da

SBP. (2005). Guidelines for Islamic Microfinance Business by Financial Institutions. Retrieved from www.sbp.org.pk/ibd/2007/Annex-c5.pdf

SBP. (2017). Islamic Banking Bulletin June 30, 2017, Retrieved from www.sbp.org.pk/ibd/bulletin/2017/Dec.pdf

SBP. (2018). The Role of Sukuk in Islamic Capital Markets. Presented at the 10th Meeting of

COMCEC Financial Cooperation Working Group Ankara, Turkey.

Shah, I. A. (2015). *Islamic Capital Markets*. Institute of Management Sciences (University of Arid Agriculture Rawalpindi, Pakistan). Retrieved from www.slideshare.net/IntazarAliShah/islamic-capital-markets-53048826

The Banking Companies Ordinance. (1962). Pakistan; from Zaidi, N. A. (1987). *Eliminating Interest from Banks in Pakistan*. Pakistan, Royal Book Company.

Vizcaino, B. (2016). *Pakistan Steps Up in Islamic Finance in Infrastructure Deals*. UK, Reuters.

Zahid, W. (2017). "Pakistan Predicted to Be World's Fastest-Growing Muslim Economy in 2017," *The Express Tribune*, Retrieved from https://tribune.com.pk/story/1290084/pakistan predicted-worlds-fastest-growing-muslim-economy-2017

19 Islamic safety nets for the poor

Pakistan's experience

Nasim Shah Shirazi

19.1 Introduction

Islamic finance (IF) plays a pivotal role in the development of the real economy. It helps and stimulates economic activities and entrepreneurship, addresses poverty and income inequality, ensures financial stability, and promotes comprehensive human development in complex societies of the 21st century. IF and Islamic economics (IE) recognize the significant role of the voluntary Islamic financial sectors which uplift poverty, and eliminate homelessness and hunger. Some of the tools being used to accomplish these targets include *sadaqat*, *zakat*, *Khairat*, and the development of the institution of *Bait-ul-Mal* and *qard-e-hasana*[1] (interest-free loans) in providing relief and assistance to the needy and the sparse population of the country. The voluntary sector can be used not only for poverty alleviation through simple transfers but also as a system of social protection and assistance.[2] These IE and IF tools target a broader group than the *zakat* recipients, but it can also be used to build social and public institutions in which private for-profit sector may not have incentives to develop but which are however needed for economic development and poverty alleviation of the communities in developing and the developed countries where Muslims are in minorities.

For example, obligation of *zakat* at the national *zakat* foundation (NZF) and *Qard Hassan* Australia (QHA) at the Islamic council of Victoria encourage charity directly that address poverty issues and provide mechanisms to bring people into mainstream economic activity, including their access to a formal financial sector. There are many studies in the literature showing that *zakat* has the potential to alleviate poverty from the country (see, for example, Shirazi, 2014). However, if the proceeds of the voluntary sector including *zakat* and *Waqf* are used in a more organized and planned manner (see example of QHA online transactions in Australia), it can enable the poor to not only meet their immediate consumption needs, but also develop their skills and provide them the capital to start up small businesses and become self-sustained, thus having a far more significant impact on economic development.

This chapter is a review and summary of author's previous work in this area. It overviews the incidence of poverty and income distribution, and analyzes the role of safety nets, including Islamic social protection programs in reducing poverty. The present chapter is structured as follows: Section 2 discusses the incidence of poverty and income inequality covering methodological background and history of the poverty in Pakistan. Section 3 presents an overview of safety nets programs in Pakistan. Section 4 focuses on the deficiency of the social protection programs in the country and seeks to explore why social safety nets did not bring a significant change in poverty reduction. The final section contains some concluding remarks.

19.2 Poverty and inequality in Pakistan[3]

19.2.1 Methodological background for poverty estimates

This section provides the methodological background of poverty estimates and the incidence of poverty in the country and across the regions of the state. The first step to measure the poverty ratios, a poverty line is needed. Poverty lines have been determined differently by different authors over time. Therefore, poverty estimates are not comparable across regions and over time. Arif and Farooq (2012) divided the time period between 1963 and 2008 into two broad groups. First, 1963–1992, for which poverty estimates are usually based on secondary or published grouped data, generally using the calorific norm of 2,550 calories per day per person. The second group, between 1992 and 2006, has been applying official poverty lines (based on 2,350 calories per adult per day) on micro-data (Household Income and Expenditure Surveys, HIES). During the early period, or until 1992, it was common to have different threshold levels for urban and rural areas, keeping in view the higher calorific requirements of the rural population for physical activities. In the late 1990s, a uniform threshold of 2,350 calories per adult per day was used for rural as well as urban poverty estimates. However, in general, poverty trends can be found despite the methodological differences.

19.2.2 Poverty in Pakistan

Although poverty is widespread in Pakistan, it is more prevalent in rural areas than in the urban ones. While there was an increase in the incidence of poverty during the 1960s, the trend was reversed from 1970 onwards. The changes occurring in the agrarian structure during the 1960s contributed to rural poverty. Some of the factors responsible for the decline in poverty from 1970 onwards and throughout the 1980s were overall economic growth and foreign remittances. The introduction of *zakat* and *ushr* also played its role in the 1980s.[4] However, poverty re-emerged and aggravated further during the 1990s and in the early 2000s.

The estimates of the incidence of poverty presented in the following Table 19.1 do not show unidirectional trends. The country has been experiencing increasing poverty levels during the 1990s, rising from 26.8% in 1992–1993 to 30.6% in 1998–1999. Rural poverty increased from 28.3% to 34.7%, while urban poverty declined from 24.4% to 20.9% during the same time. Rural poverty significantly contributed to the overall poverty levels of the country during the 1990s. A number of factors including a decrease in economic growth, political uncertainty, economic instability, and large fiscal and current account deficits were responsible for the increase in poverty during the 1990s. The incidence of poverty, which was gradually increasing in the 1990s, continued rising until it reached 34.5% in 2000–2001. Both rural and urban poverty rose to 39.3% and 22.7%, respectively. The incidence of overall poverty then dropped, reaching 22.3% in 2005–2006. During the same period, the drop in rural poverty was faster (12.3% points) than the reduction (9.6% points) in urban poverty. The possible contributing factors for the decline in poverty could be high economic growth combined with increasing public sector spending on education, health, and infrastructure. However, the country could not sustain the decline in poverty, and level of poverty started rising again 2007–2008 onward. Since the mid-2000s, the Pakistan economy has been facing a number of problems including declining economic growth, high food, and oil prices, and thus high inflation, power shortage, week governance, and above all, terrorism. Among others, these have been the main factors, which shattered the declining trend in poverty that the country observed during 2000–2001 to 2004–2005 and 2005–2006.

Table 19.1 Pakistan: Trends in Poverty (Headcount Ratios)

Year	*Urban*	*Rural*	*Overall*
1963–1964	44.53	38.94	40.24
1966–1967	40.96	45.62	44.50
1969–1970	38.76	49.11	46.53
1979	25.94	32.51	30.68
1984–1985	21.17	25.87	24.47
1987–1988	14.99	18.32	17.32
1990–1991	18.64	23.59	22.11
1992–1993	24.4	28.3	26.8
1996–1997	22.6	33.1	29.8
1998–1999	20.9	34.7	30.6
2000–2001	22.7	39.3	34.5
2004–2005	14.9	28.1	23.9
2005–2006	13.1	27.0	22.3

Source: Poverty estimates from 1963 to 1991 are reported from Amjad and Kemal (1997) and from 1992 onward are reported from Arif and Farooq (2011).

Malik and Whitney (2014) provide consistent estimates of money-metric poverty based on HIES data sets during 2001/2002–2010/2011. Consistent and realistic poverty estimates are essential for anti-poverty programs and their impact evaluation. The estimates of poverty from 1998–1999 to 2005–2006 are based on official poverty lines. The official poverty line was estimated in 2001–2002 based on HIES 1998–1999 data set, which has been adjusted for inflation in the subsequent years using the Consumer Price Index (CPI). The chapter finds following four problems in this methodology: (1) outdated sampling frames underlying the HIES, (2) a non-representative sample used initially for estimating the poverty line, (3) sensitivity of estimates to caloric threshold underlying the poverty lines, and (4) changes in the consumption basket due to price fluctuations not being adequately represented in the CPI and hence in the estimation. The food price increased much faster (39.5% points during 2006–2008), which is not sufficiently captured in the CPI. The prices subsequent to 2007 are based on Food Expenditure Survey that understates the weight of food category in overall consumption than HIES data sets.

19.2.3 Poverty updates

Malik and Whitney (2014) estimated the calories expenditure function from data for each of the available survey years. Poverty line expenditure consistent with maintaining a minimum intake of 2,350 Kcal per adult equivalent was estimated for each of the surveys. The Foster, Greer, and Thorbecke (1984) class of decomposable money-metric poverty estimates was computed for each of the years based on these poverty lines. In order to account for the provincial variation and variation across rural and urban sectors, the calories expenditure functions were estimated using the intercept and slope dummies. The consistent results are presented in Table 19.2. The results show a persistent increase in the headcount ratios over the years. The official estimates based on official poverty lines adjusted for inflation for the subsequent years are misleading. As it has already been mentioned above, poverty is widespread but is primarily a rural phenomenon. This is also evident from Table 19.2. The incidence of poverty is high in all the rural areas of the four provinces. In the year 2010–2011, the highest rate of poverty was found in Sindh-rural (48.5%) followed by Baluchistan-rural (40.8%), Punjab-rural (38.0%), and the lowest in KPK-rural (36.4%). However, the official figures show that the incidence of poverty decreased to 24.3% during 2015–2016.[5] The poverty estimates presented by Social Policy and Development Centre (SPDC) reveal that poverty increased to 38% in overall in 2015–2016 and 32% in the urban areas, while it was 41% in the rural years in the same period.

Table 19.2 Estimated Headcount (%) by HIES Year

Region	*2001–2002*	*2004–2005*	*2005–2006*	*2007–2008*	*2010–2011*	*2015–2016*[a]
Pakistan	30.1	30.6	34	33.1	35.6(38)	24.3(38)
Urban	22	20.7	24.1	25	27.7(32)	(32)
Rural	33.4	35.4	39.3	37.3	39.7(39)	(41)
Punjab – Urban	24.8	22.9	24.1	24.7	28.5	...
Punjab – Rural	32	33.4	33.8	33.3	38	...
Sindh – Urban	16.5	15.7	21.2	23.5	24.8	...
Sindh – Rural	38.7	40.1	53.4	48.7	48.5	
KPK – Urban	25.7	29	34.2	29.5	32.4	
KPK – Rural	32.5	36.7	39.7	34.8	36.4	
Baluchistan – Urban	22.8	20.7	43.9	38	39.3	
Baluchistan – Rural	32.1	34.9	54.6	53.7	40.8	

Source: Malik and Whitney (2014).

a Pakistan Economic Survey 2017–2018. The figures in parentheses under the year 2010–2011 and 2015–2016 are from http://spdc.org.pk/Data/Publication/PDF/RR-99.pdf.

19.2.4 Income inequality

Gini coefficient is commonly used for measuring income distribution. Figure 19.1 presents income distribution in the country over the last three decades. The graph shows a moderate income inequality in the country. The Gini index was 33.3% in 1987. Compared to 1987, income distribution improved slightly in the subsequent years, and Gini index reached to 28.7% in 1996. However, its trend reversed from 1996 onward, and Gini index increased to 33.1% in 1998. The decade starting from 2001 saw the income inequality in the range of about 30%–33%. However, Gini index was recorded 33.5% in 2015, which is higher than the previous years. On the other hand, it may be noted that the official estimates of poverty showed a declining trend during 2010–2011 to 2015–2016. This was due to the modest economic growth among other factors. During the same period, income inequality increased. A comparison between the estimates of poverty with Gini coefficients reveals that the country experienced a negative correlation between poverty reduction and income distribution. Economic growth reduced poverty but increased income disparity, thus implying that benefits of growth were more for the rich than for the poor.

Economic growth is a necessary but not a sufficient condition for the reduction of poverty. Whether growth is pro-poor[6] essentially depends on how the benefits of growth are distributed amongst the different income groups. Haq and Zia (2009) provided analysis of linkages between governance and pro-poor growth in Pakistan for the period 1996–2005. On the aspect of pro-poor growth, they demonstrated that the poor do not benefit

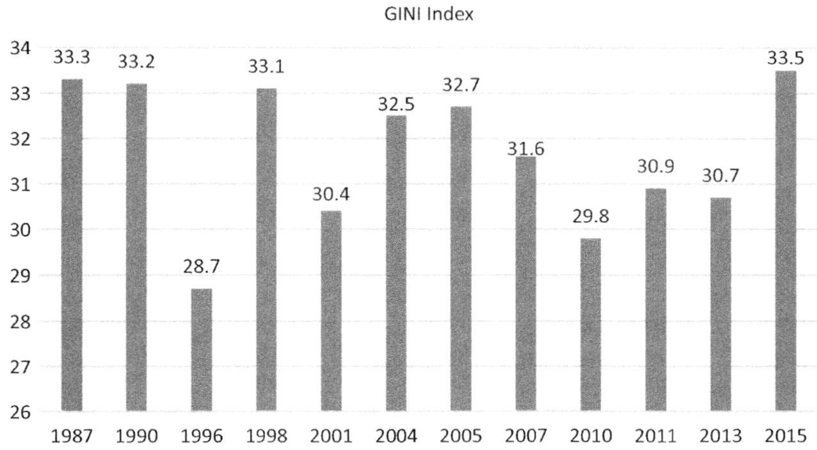

Figure 19.1 GINI index.
Source: https://knoema.com/atlas/Pakistan/topics/Poverty/Income-Inequality/GINI-index.

proportionately from economic growth. The income and expenditure share of the rich increased more than the income and spending share of the poor. Over time the share in income and expenditure for the bottom 20% of the population remained positive but decreased, while inflation for this lowest income group was high as compared to the highest income group.

19.3 Social safety nets

In order to protect the hardcore poor and the vulnerable, the country has started many social protection programs. These programs are considered essential for creating an environment in which the hardcore poor are protected from the social and political costs of economic and structural reforms. Some social protection programs have been implemented over the last three decades. While the Pakistan Poverty Alleviation Fund (PPAF) was initiated in 2000, the Benazir Income Support Program (BISP) was launched in 2008–2009.

Social protection or safety nets programs of Pakistan can be classified into two categories. The first category is meant for the employed labor force or those who have retired from the formal sector. This category does not cover the employees in informal areas or contract employees. The other one is much broader and includes those who are outside the labor market, the poor and the indigent. The first set of programs provides benefits in the event of contingencies like sickness, invalidity, maternity, old age, and work-related injury. These include the Provincial Employees' Social Security Scheme, the Employees' Old-Age Benefits Institution, the Government

Servants' Pension Fund, the Public Sector Benevolent Funds and Group Insurance, the Workers' Welfare Fund, and the Workers' Children's Education Ordinance. The second category includes schemes like the PPAF, BISP, the *zakat* and *sadaqat* program, the Pakistan *Bait-ul-Mal* (PBM) program, and *Qard al Hasan* microfinance. The following sections will highlight these vital safety nets including the Islamic social safety nets.

19.3.1 Pakistan Poverty Alleviation Fund

PPAF was established in 2000 as an apex body, with an aim to reach the poor communities through NGOs and Community-Based Organizations (CBOs). PPAF supports microcredit (major financier of microfinance market), water and infrastructure, drought mitigation, education, health, and emergency response interventions. PPAF disbursed Rs. 9.207 billion during July 2016–March 2017 to its Partner Organizations (POs) under its core interventions administered through various operational units. During the year, PPAF disbursed about Rs. 5,415 million for Microfinance Portfolio Management; paid Rs. 413 million for water and infrastructure projects; and provided Rs. 375 million for health and education projects, Rs. 522 million for institutional development and social mobilization, Rs. 213 million for Livelihood, Employment and Enterprise Development, and Rs. 2,269 million for Prime Minister's Interest-Free Loan.

PPAF has disbursed Rs. 178 billion since its establishment till June 2016. Its credit and enterprise development programs received 61% of the funds followed by project and relief activities, including Prime Minister Interest-Free Loan Scheme and *Waseela-e-Haq* program (14%). Human and institutional development (including social mobilization) /livelihood enhancement and protection received 13%, and community physical infrastructure received 9%, while health and education received 3%.[7]

19.3.2 Benazir Income Support Program

BISP was launched in 2008 to provide direct and speedy relief to the poor who have lost their purchasing power due to high inflation. BISP was started with an initial allocation of Rs. 34 billion (the US$425 million approximately) to cover 3.5 million families in the financial year 2008–2009. The program was initiated to provide a cash grant of Rs. 1,000 each month (Rs. 3,000 quarterly) to the families having an income of less than Rs. 6,000 per month. However, the quarterly cash grant has been gradually increased from Rs.3,000 per family to Rs. 3,600 in 2013–2014, Rs. 4,500 in 2014–2015, Rs.4,700 in 2015–2016, and Rs.4,834 in 2016–2017. Since its inception in 2008, BISP has multiplied. It is now the largest single cash transfer program in Pakistan's history. The BISP has been successful in reducing poverty by 7% point and increasing consumption expenditure of Rs. 187 as per Oxford Policy Management (Final Impact Evaluation Report, 2016).

The number of beneficiaries has increased from 1.7 million in FY 2009 to approximately 5.42 million at the end of March 2017. BISP's annual disbursement has risen from 16.0 billion in 2009 to Rs.115 billion in 2017. Since inception, BISP has transferred Rs.486 billion (21 April 2017) as cash transfers.

Initially, the targeting of the beneficiaries was the responsibility of politicians. A simple application form was designed and distributed among the Members of Parliament in equal number (8,000 to each member of the National Assembly and Senate and 1,000 to each member of the Provincial Assemblies) for the selection of the poor families. In order to avoid subjectivity in targeting the beneficiaries, the government stopped this practice in 2010–2011 and replaced it with an objective poverty scorecard approach.

The BISP has been supported by multilateral and bilateral institutions and donors including the World Bank, USAID, Asian Development Bank, and DFID. BISP has been providing cash grants to an increasing number of families. In addition to the cash grant, BISP includes graduation programs, emergency relief, and expenditures on conducting a nationwide poverty scorecard survey.

The graduation programs including *Waseela-e-Rozgar*, *Waseela-e-Haq*, *Waseela-e-Sehat*, and *Waseela-e-Taleem* have been started to transform the lives of the poor. *Waseela-e-Rozgar* was initiated by providing technical and vocational training to one member per beneficiary family to enable them to become the earning hand for the family. Such training is provided by both public and private sector training institutions. About 39,374 members are currently enrolled under this program, and 11,644 members have been trained so far.

Under *Waseela-e-Haq*, interest-free loans of Rs. 300,000 each were provided to select (by monthly computerized random draw) members for starting small businesses. Up till March 2013, Rs. 1.8 billion has been disbursed among 40,868 beneficiaries.

Waseela-e-Sehat is a group life insurance scheme of Rs. 100,000 for the bread earner of beneficiary families, which was launched in January 2011 in collaboration with State Life Insurance Corporation of Pakistan. During 2011–2013, about 7,000 death claims were processed. A comprehensive Health Insurance Scheme covering all members of BISP beneficiaries' families has been started in one district, Faisalabad, since April 2012. Other districts will be brought gradually under this scheme.

Waseela-e-Taleem supports the beneficiaries' children of ages between 5 and 12 years for their primary education. Under this scheme which targeted to enroll about 2.0 million children by December 2018, a monthly cash transfer of Rs. 250 per child (up to three children) will be provided subject to their compliance with the school admission requirement and an encouraging level of school attendance. Since the initiation of the field of operation of this program, over 1.3 million children have benefitted from about Rs. 2.9 billion disbursements as a stipend.

19.3.3 Zakat

The President of Pakistan, on 20 June 1980, promulgated the *zakat* and *ushr* Ordinance, 1980. The clauses of the Ordinance relating to *zakat* became effective from the same date, and the first deductions were made by the banks on 21 June 1980. The clauses relating to *ushr* were enforced with effect from 15th of March 1983. *Zakat* funds are utilized for the needy, indigent, poor, orphans, widows, handicapped, and disabled. The deserving people are provided assistance directly through the local *zakat* committees (LZC) or indirectly through the institutions.

Zakat is deducted compulsorily[8] once a year at the rate of 2.5% on specified assets.[9] The owners of all other assets[10] related to the Schedule 2 of the Ordinance on which *zakat* is payable under the Shari'ah are expected to pay *zakat* on self-assessment basis to the *zakat* fund or to other eligible beneficiaries (*mustahqueen*), e.g., the poor of their choice.

The amount of *zakat* deducted at the source, as described in Schedule 1 of the Ordinance, by the financial institutions is deposited in the central zakat fund. *Zakat* funds have been established at three levels, namely, the central level, the provincial level (in each province), and the local level (in each of the localities). The provincial *zakat* funds receive six monthly transfers from the central *zakat* fund, and similarly, the local *zakat* funds receive six monthly transfers from the provincial *zakat* funds. A minimal amount of voluntary *zakat*, atiyat (donations), and so on is also deposited with these funds.

The central *zakat* council has laid down guiding principles for the disbursement of *zakat* funds by the provincial *zakat* councils and the LZC. At the provincial level, the payment of *zakat* money from provincial *zakat* funds has been suggested in the following manner:

1 Transfer to LZC 60%
2 Transfer to institutions for eligible beneficiaries (*mustahiqueen*) 40%

The breakdown of the transfer to institutions is given below:

i Educational institutions 18%
ii *Dini Madaris* 8%
iii Health institutions 6%
iv Social welfare institutions 4%
v Others 4%

At the level of the LZC, the utilization of *zakat* funds has been suggested in the following way:

1 Subsistence grant to eligible beneficiaries (*mustahiqueen*). Not more than 45%
2 Permanent rehabilitation of eligible recipients (*mustahiqueen*). At least 45%
3 Administrative expenses. Not more than 10%

The *zakat* program covers a small number of beneficiaries compared to the number of poor in the country. The utilization of *zakat* has been minimal,and it remained between 0.04%and 0.06% of GDP during 2004–2008. The total collection was 0.05% of GDP to 0.08% of GDP during the same time, while it was about 0.3% during the 1980s. Compared to actual *zakat* collection by the official sources, its potential is much higher, which is estimated to be in between about 2% and 4% of the GDP (Shirazi and Amin, 2010).

The disbursement of *zakat* has remained uneven. The number of total beneficiaries barely reached 1.5 million in 2010–2011, while it has consistently hovered around 1 million. This is reported in Table 19.3. According to Household Integrated Economic Survey (HIES, 1990–1991), about 18% of the total households in the lowest income decile were benefited on an overall basis, 16.5% in urban, and 18.5% in the rural areas. Out of the total households in the second income decile, 3.6% overall, 3.7% in the urban, and 3.6% in the rural areas received *zakat* in the same year. The percentage of households in third through fifth income deciles, who received *zakat*, varied between 1.5% and 1.8% in overall Pakistan level. However, the total families that benefited in all the income deciles were 2.7% on the whole basis, 1.4% in the urban areas, and 3.2% in the rural areas of Pakistan in 1990–1991 (Shirazi, 1996). Issues and Policies Consultants (2004) reported that 2.7% of poor households received 40% of *zakat*, while 1.4% of non-poor households received 60% of *zakat* in 2001–2002, which clearly indicates possible misappropriation of *zakat* funds. The CPRSPD study (2007) reported 27% of the non-poor households as *zakat* recipients. The same study pointed out that 32% of *Guzara* allowance and 45% of rehabilitation grant went to non-poor. The contribution of *zakat* in poverty alleviation was just 0.5% in 1988 and 0.75% in 1990–1991 (Shirazi, 1996).

As mentioned above *zakat* deduction at source from specified assets was mandatory until March 1999 and became optional after that. This has negatively affected the collection of *zakat* by the government. Even before the decision of the Supreme Court of Pakistan, people used to withdraw their money before the date of deduction of the *zakat* by banks. Because of the 18th constitutional amendment, the institution of *zakat*, which was hitherto

Table 19.3 *Zakat* Utilized and Number of Beneficiaries

	2008–2009	*2009–2010*	*2010–2011*	*2011–2012*	*2012–2013*
Amount utilized (Rs. million)	2,877	2,874	9,909.753	3,125.975	3,951.667
No. of beneficiaries	1,085,378	1,289,050	1,542,283	1,040,960	–

Source: PRSP progress Report 2008/09–2010/2011 and PRSP progress Report 2011/2012. Figures for the year 2012/2013 are reported from the Economic Survey of Pakistan (2013).

Table 19.4 Disbursement of *Zakat*

S. No	*Provident/Other Areas*	*(Rs. Million)*
1	Punjab	4,038.687
2	Sindh	1,669.408
3	Khyber Pakhtunkhwa	973.059
4	Balochistan	359.792
5	ICT	186.230
6	Gilgit-Baltistan	98.414
7	FATA	245.320
Total		7,570.910

Source: Ministry of Religious Affairs and Inter-Faith Harmony.

centrally managed, devolved to the provinces. This has led to a change in the business rules that assigned the collection and distribution of *Zakat* to the Ministry of Religious Affairs and Inter-Faith Harmony at the federal level. Overall, it appears that the collection of *zakat* has not been paid due attention and consequently, an excellent institution that can potentially make a dent on poverty has been neglected.

As at the end of 2017 Fiscal year, a total of Rs. 7,570.910 million was distributed among the provinces and administrative areas. This is depicted in Table 19.4.

19.3.4 Pakistan **Bait-Ul-Mal**[11]

PBM was established in 1991 to provide financial assistance to the destitute, widows, orphans, invalids, infirm, and other needy persons irrespective of their gender, caste, and religion through its different projects and schemes. Under the Individual Financial Assistance (IFA) scheme an amount of Rs. 6,186.402 million was disbursed during the last four years to benefit 1,47,361 individuals including the poor, widows, destitute women, and orphans for their medical treatment, education, rehabilitation, and general assistance. PBM has established 30 orphanages across the country, where about 3,000 children have been registered. An amount of Rs. 261 million has been spent to provide them with food, medical treatment, and education. PBM is planning for an orphanage in every city. PBM provides wheelchairs to disabled in the country. PBM has established 157 vocational training centers for providing free training to widows, orphans, and poor girls in different skills. PBM has spent an amount of Rs. 478.54 million since its inception and trained about 60,000 female students.

*19.3.5 Interest-free loans (***Qarz Hasana***)*

Interest-free loans (*Qarz Hasana*) is another microfinance program that has been started by Akhuwat in 2001 to support and empower the needy families. The generosity and empathy of donors enabled Akhuwat to assist over

2.7 million low-income families in Pakistan through interest-free microfinance. Akhuwat has been expanding and now has 789 branches in Pakistan. Akhuwat has about PKRs 15.47 billion in outstanding loans as of 12 July 2018. Its total disbursement stands at about PKRs 65.35billion with a recovery rate of 99.67%.[12] The financing process at Akhuwat involves the establishment of a credit pool and making small loans (*Qard al Hasan*) to the poor from this pool. The pool itself is created through donations and the spirit of brotherhood. It is like a revolving fund from which is continuously depleted with disbursal of loans and replenished and enhanced with their recovery and new donations. In July 2018, the cumulative disbursement was PKR 65.35 billion.

In the initial years of operation, Akhuwat charged 5% of the loan amount to recover the actual cost, which was termed anadministrative fee. Further, small loans (amount less than PKR 4,000) were to be entirely cost-less as these were targeted at the ultra-poor with least affordability. The sustained growth in donations and the donations from the graduated borrowers enabled Akhuwat to provide interest-free loans at zero cost in 2010.

The core administrative tasks relating to loan management are carried out from the places of worship that result in substantial savings in administrative costs. Furthermore, the CEO and the top management and about one-third of Akhuwat staff work voluntarily without any remuneration. The organization has made minimal investments in office assets. It owns no vehicles. Its team sits on the floor as its clients do. It has found a way to do business with the poor keeping costs to a bare minimum. Consequently, its operational expenses fell to 5% in 2015.[13]

19.3.6 Peoples' Works Program-I and II

People Works Program (PWP)-I and II was started in 2008–2009 replacing the *Khushal* Pakistan Fund and the Village Electrification program. PWP-I and PWP-II provide small development schemes for electricity, gas, farm to market roads, telephone, education, health, and water supply to the rural poor. PWP-I and PWP-II were politically motivated development projects, which are implemented on recommendations of Parliamentarians as well as utilized discretionary funds at the wishes and whims of the Prime Minister of the country.

Rs. 4.3 billion and Rs. 33.6 billion were allocated for PWP-I and PWP-II, respectively, in 2011–2012. Rs. 2.2 billion and Rs. 30.6 billion have been spent on these two schemes sequentially up to the mid of the year 2012–2013. During Pakistan People Party's regime of five years, the government had spent about Rs. 150 billion to Rs. 170 billion on PWP-1 and PWP-11.[14]

19.3.7 Employees' Old Age Benefits Institution

Employees' Old Age Benefits Institution (EOBI) provides monetary benefits to the old age workers through different schemes including old age pension, invalidity pension, survivors' pension, and old age grants. An amount of Rs. 7,961.2 million has been spent during 9 months of the financial year 2011–2012. During July-December of the fiscal year 2012–2013, an amount of Rs. 6,603 million has been utilized for the benefits of 373,433 individuals.

A minimum monthly payment of pension is Rs. 5,250. However, it will rise to Rs. 10,920 depending on the wage of the insured person and the period of the insurance scheme. A lump sum, which is equivalent to one months' average salary, is paid as old age grant for every completed year of insurable employment. From 1 July 2016 to 31 March 2017, an amount of Rs. 17,921.7 million was disbursed to about 405,460 beneficiaries. As of June 2017, an additional Rs. 6,728.3 million was added to widen the net of recipients.

19.4 Reasons for low impact of social protection programs

Pakistan has witnessed a number of programs being started and implemented to reduce poverty. But the fact remains that poverty and income inequality persist. This is attributable to a number of factors. One may observe that different social safety net programs are managed by various agencies, and there is a distinct lack of coordination among them. This has led to duplication of efforts and identical recipients benefiting from different safety net programs while leaving others who may be more deserving unserved. It has been observed that when cash is transferred to the poor or they are given funds/assets for rehabilitation under rehabilitation scheme, it has resulted in misappropriation of funds. No proper records are maintained, nor there is any systematic follow-up. In the case of *zakat*, for instance, the selection of the poor/beneficiaries is supposed to be made by the LZC, but local power structures play havoc with the selection process. As Arif (2006) noted, 42% of *zakat*-recipient households in rural areas were selected on the recommendation of local councilors or other influential persons, including local landlords, religious leaders, or relatives of members of the LZC, while the rest were selected by the LZC. The system is characterized by a high degree of favoritism, nepotism, and lack of transparency. No lists of the beneficiaries are available for any third-party evaluation/screening. Many other deficiencies have also been highlighted by IMF (2010) in the context of Poverty Reduction Strategy Paper-II (PRSP-II).

Funding for specific safety net programmes has traditionally been insufficiently given programme objectives and target populations. As a result, safety net programmes are fragmented and often duplicative; have limited coverage and are poorly targeted with small benefit levels relative to household income and the poverty gap; payments are infrequent and irregular; administrative arrangements are inadequate; and Monitoring and Evaluation capacity is not up to the mark, which negatively affects programme efficiency and quality of service delivery. Consequently, these programmes have limited impact on poverty and vulnerability.

Arif and Farooq (2012) have identified some critical factors for failure to get tangible results. Policy gaps or poor implementation, weak institutions, poor governance, and deteriorating law and order situation, neglect of the social sector, power structures in rural areas and lack of effective targeting are significant factors responsible for affecting the economy and thus the levels of poverty. They are of the view that the Afghan crisis, since the late 1970s, has changed Pakistan's external and internal dynamics and has promoted extremism, drugs, and weapons in Pakistan. The recent U.S.-led war on terror in Afghanistan, since 2001, has significantly affected the internal and external scenario of Pakistan, by promoting regional instability and creating severe economic challenges for her.

However, there is a strong need for proper planning and management of the safety net programs. These should be well-integrated and transparent, remove duplication, pool the sources of funds, and provide benefits to the targeted poor. These institutions, especially BISP, PBM, and *zakat* need to be integrated and synergized for a significant quantitative change in the incidence of poverty.

19.5 Concluding remarks

The chapter highlights the incidence of poverty and provides an analysis of the safety nets program of the country. The official estimates show a decline in poverty,but the independent sources reveal that poverty has been increased in recent years. Income distribution is moderate but showing an increasing trend in recent years.

The safety net programs including Islamic social safety nets are providing support and financial assistance in cash and in kind. Despite the safety nets program, poverty still persists in the country. One may observe that different social safety net programs are managed by various agencies, and there is a lack of coordination among them. This has led to duplication of efforts and identical recipients benefiting from different safety net programs while leaving others who may be more deserving unserved. Moreover, the governance problem has also been observed in the distribution of cash funds. For the success of safety nets program, the coverage of the poor and the amount of the transfer should be enough to cover the poverty gap. However, this is not the case in Pakistan. Additionally, in Pakistan the targeting efficiency is low (0.20%), which means a beneficiary gets only Rs. 0.20 when Rs. 1.0 is transferred to fill the poverty gap. Consequently, these programmes have limited impact on poverty and vulnerability.

However, there is a strong need for proper planning and management of the safety net programs. These should be well-integrated and transparent, remove duplication, pool the sources of funds. and provide benefits to the targeted poor. These institutions, especially BISP, PBM, and *zakat*, need to be integrated and synergized for a significant quantitative change in the incidence of poverty.

Notes

1 For example, Akhuwat, Pakistan and *Qard Hassan* Australia (QHA),www.icv.org.au/icv-stories-nils/
2 NZF, Australia and the united kingdom nzf.org.au/ and NZF.org.uk
3 Part of the paper is based on my previous unpublished working paper No: 1435-17, IRTI, Jeddah, Saudi Arabia.
4 For detail refer to Shirazi (1994).
5 Unfortunately, consistent incidence of poverty are not available for the all the financial years.
6 Haq and Zia (2009) defined pro-poor growth as (1) a growth that is good for the poor; a reduction in the proportion of the poor in the population; (2) or growth that results in an increase in the income of the poor or (3) that associates with larger proportionate increases in income of the poor than the rest of the population.
7 PPAF, Directors' Report & Audited Financial Statements, June 2016.
8 As per the decision of Supreme Court of Pakistan on March 9, 1999 any person from all recognized fiqhs can claim *zakat* exemption from the compulsory deduction at source on filing the requisite affidavit. These people can pay their *zakat* of their own choice instead of paying to government. This is also one of the reasons that Central *Zakat* Fund is getting small collection compared to potential.
9 The *zakatable* assets which are mentioned in the first schedule of ordinance are: Savings Bank Accounts and similar Accounts; Notice Deposits Accounts, receipts and similar Accounts and Receipts; Fixed Deposit Accounts and Receipts and similar Accounts and Receipts, on which the return is receivable by the holder periodically or is received earlier than maturity or withdrawal; Savings/Deposit Certificates Accounts and Receipts and similar Certificates/Accounts/Receipts on which return is receivable and is received by the holder only on maturity or encashment; National Investment Trust Units (NIT);Investment Corporation of Pakistan Mutual Funds Certificates; Government Securities on which the return is receivable by the holder periodically; Securities including Shares and Debentures of Companies and Statutory Corporations on which return is paid; (Annuities; Life Insurance Policies; and Provident Fund Credit Balances).
10 Gold, silver and manufacturing thereof; Cash; Prize bonds; Current accounts and foreign currency accounts; Loans receivable, Securities including shares and debentures; Stock in trade of Commercial undertakings [(i) Industrial undertakings; (ii)Precious metals, stones and manufactures thereof; (iii) Fish and other catch/produce of sea]; Agricultural produce other than that liable to compulsory *ushr*; Animals fed free in pastures, and Wealth and financial assets other than those listed in schedule on which '*zakat*' is payable according to *shari'ah*.
11 All figures in this section is reported from Economic Survey of Pakistan 2013.
12 Extracted on 24th July, 2018 from www.akhuwat.org.pk/progress-report/
13 For further details see Obaidullah, Shirazi and Izhar (2014).
14 See www.thenews.com.pk/Todays-News-13-23379-Govt-to-change-name-of-Peoples-Works-Programme

References

Amjad, Rashid, and A. R. Kemal, (1997). Macroeconomic Policies and their Impact on Poverty Alleviation in Pakistan. *The Pakistan Development Review*, 36: 1, pp. 39–68.

Arif, G.M., (2006).Targeting Efficiency of Poverty Reduction Programs in Pakistan. Pakistan Resident Mission Working Paper Series 4. Islamabad: ADB.

Arif, G.M. and Shujaat Farooq (2011). Background Study for the MCPs Document for Pakistan on Poverty, Inequality, and Unemployment. Dhul-Qa'dah: Pakistan Institute of Development Economics and Islamic Development Bank, pp. 1–75.

Arif, G.M. and Shujaat Farooq, (2012).Poverty Reduction in Pakistan: Learning from the Experience of China, PIDE Monograph Series 2012:5, Pakistan Institute of Development Economics, Islamabad.

CPRSPD, (2007). A Social Protection Strategy to Reach the Poor and the Vulnerable. Islamabad: CPRSPD, Planning Commission.

Foster, James, Joel Greer, and Erik Thorbecke, (1984). A Case of Decomposable Poverty Measures. *Econometrica* 52:3, pp. 761–766.

The government of Pakistan, (2013, 2015–2016 and 2017–2018).Pakistan Economic Survey.

The government of Pakistan, PRSP Secretariat Finance Division, PRSP Progress Report 2008/2009–2010/2011 and PRSP Progress Report 2011/2012.

Haq, Rashidaand Uzma Zia, (2009). Does Governance Contribute to Pro-poor Growth? Evidence from Pakistan, PIDE Working Papers, 52.

International Monetary Fund, (2010). IMF Country Report No 10/183.

Issues and Policies Consultants, (2004).Pakistan: Review of Selected Social Safety Net Programs, Final Report. Lahore: Issues and Policies Consultants.

Malik, Sohail J. and Edward Whitney, (2014). Consistent Estimates of Money-metric Poverty based on the available HIES Datasets between 2001–2010. Pakistan Strategic Support Program (PSSP) Report, Second Annual Conference January 21–22, Islamabad.

Obaidullah, Mohammed, Nasim Shah Shirazi, S. Dadang and H. Izhar, (2014). Islamic Social Finance Report, Thomson Reuters.

Oxford Policy Management, (2016). Benazir Income Support Programme: Final Impact Evaluation Report.

Poverty Reduction Strategy Paper (PRSP-II), (2008). Ministry of Finance, Government of Pakistan, 2008.

Shirazi, Nasim Shah, (1994).An Analysis of Pakistan's Poverty Problem and Its Alleviation through Infaq. Ph.D. thesis, International Institute of Islamic Economics, International Islamic University, Islamabad, pp. 1–226.

Shirazi, Nasim Shah, (1996). System of *zakat* in Pakistan: An Appraisal. IIIE, International Islamic University, Islamabad.

Shirazi, Nasim Shah, (2006).Providing for the Resource Shortfall for Poverty Elimination through the Institution of *Zakat* in Low-Income Muslim Countries. IIUM. *Journal of Economics and Management*, 14: 1.

Shirazi, Nasim Shah, (2014). Integrating *Zakāt*and *Waqf* into the Poverty Reduction Strategy of the IDB Member Countries. *Islamic Economic Studies*, 22:1, pp. 79–108.

Shirazi, Nasim Shah and Md. Fouad Bin Amin, (2010). Prospects of Poverty Elimination through Potential *Zakat* Collection in OIC Member Countries: Reappraised. *Journal of Islamic Economics, Banking and Finance*, 6:3, pp. 55–74.

Concluding remarks on the growth of the IBF industry

Hussain Mohi-ud-Din Qadri and M. Ishaq Bhatti

This chapter makes concluding remarks on the contribution of this volume to the wider literature on Islamic economics and finance. The edited volume is a collection of selected papers on the theme of Muslim economies in Islamic Finance. They are chosen from the WIEFC – 2018 conference, held on 3rd and 4th January, 2018 at MUL in collaboration with IRTI and La Trobe University. The book begins with a preface written by Rodney Wilson of Durham University, followed by an introductory note of editors and an inspirational paper by Shaykh-ul-Islam Muhammad Tahir-ul-Qadri on the standardisation of Islamic financial contracts using *Taqlid al-Madh'hab* techniques to build bridges between various schools of thoughts. Moreover, the book provides a fascinating contribution which critiques the different approaches to the translation of the verses dealing with economic matters in the Qur'an is a part of the present work. The present volume contains a total of 19 chapters covering a wide range of topics including Islamic bonds (*sukuk*), Islamic insurance (*takaful*), *Zakat* distribution, concept of IBOR, *riba*, Islamic commercial and social finance, and the resolution of disputes in Islamic finance through arbitration. As the book contains the papers presented at an IBF conference in Pakistan, it includes more papers based on Pakistani experiences and lessons learnt from Pakistan are applied to the economy of other Islamic countries including Malaysia, Indonesia, Saudi Arabia and Iran. The three last chapters on the country's experience are complementary, with one focusing on social finance and the other on *shari'ah* compliance financing in Pakistan, and the last on Islamic Safety Nets for the Poor: Pakistan's Experience.

Overall, the work expands the boundaries of research in Islamic banking and finance. The conference organisers, sponsors, referees, contributors, research associates and publisher are to be congratulated for bringing together this edited volume.

Index

Note: **Bold** page numbers refer to tables; *italic* page numbers refer to figures and page numbers followed by "n" denote endnotes.